ARCHAEOLOGICAL LABORATORY METHODS

AN INTRODUCTION

MARK Q. SUTTON
BROOKE S. ARKUSH

with contributions by

Joan S. Schneider
Robert M. Yohe II

KENDALL/HUNT PUBLISHING COMPANY
4050 Westmark Drive   P.O. Box 1840   Dubuque, Iowa   52004-1840

CONTENTS

LIST OF FIGURES

LIST OF TABLES

PREFACE

Archaeological Laboratory Methods: An Introduction is intended primarily for college and university students who are beginning to analyze archaeological materials. It is limited to the basic methods, but there are many techniques and analyses that require specialized technical training and sophisticated equipment well beyond an introductory level course. We fully realize that there is no single, "standard" method for conducting analyses of prehistoric and historical material culture, and do not intend this text to constitute a "cookbook" approach to laboratory methods. Furthermore, it is not meant to discourage innovative and imaginative analytic approaches at the undergraduate, graduate, or even professional level. Because it is impossible to provide coverage of every analytic method employed by archaeologists, we have focused on common, widely used laboratory techniques that will allow students to analyze and report on a variety of archaeological materials.

The text is meant to provide instructors with an organized format for teaching basic archaeological laboratory methods. Individuals are encouraged to elaborate upon various methods described herein and to introduce different techniques, specific research questions, problems, and analytic goals.

The book has developed from our own experiences of teaching introductory laboratory methods courses without the benefit of any available text. After several years of compiling "readers" from disparate sources, sending our students to the library to obtain references on specific techniques, and continually reiterating ourselves on basic analytic methods, we decided to write a simple handbook to use in our classes. As the project progressed, it took on a life of its own; it became larger, more detailed and complex, and covered more and more subjects. The end-product is the first edition of this text; as complete and detailed as we could make it while still maintaining its introductory nature. We feel that this text is an important learning and teaching resource because it:

- Provides instructors with a framework for teaching an introductory course in laboratory methods;

- Provides a comprehensive primary text for students taking a class in laboratory methods;

- Serves as a comprehensive supplemental text for those students in classes that contain a limited laboratory component;

- Serves as a comprehensive supplemental text for those students in classes that do not contain a laboratory component (e.g., Introduction to Archaeology);

- Provides students with introductory sections on how various artifacts were produced;

- Provides a reference source to professional archaeologists in academic, governmental, or private fields;

- Contains a wide variety of references that can be consulted for different and/or more complex analyses than those presented here;

- Contains examples of figures, tables, and maps specifically developed for archaeological reports;

- Contains sections on specialized studies of archaeological materials and approaches to interpreting results; and

- Contains an outline example of an excavation report.

The book is biased toward prehistoric material culture of western North America, but the concepts and techniques it contains are applicable to many New World archaeological assemblages. The goal of the book is to provide students with a basic structure upon which they can build their own description and analyses of archaeological materials.

ACKNOWLEDGEMENTS

We are grateful to a number of individuals who provided materials, comments, and suggestions on draft versions of this book, including Lynn Cozzens, Linda B. Eaton, J. Jeffrey Flenniken, Jill Gardner, Mike Glassow, Ken Gobalet, Tom Green, Patti Jeppson, Melinda Leach, Robert E. Parr, Seetha N. Reddy, Fred Schneider, Kristen D. Sobolik, and James C. Woods.

Bob Yohe extends his thanks to Sara Pedde for her illustrations. Joan Schneider is indebted to Jennie Adams and Lee Fratt for their input on her chapter. Clark Taylor produced the photographs of the ceramic and perishable artifacts. The staff at Kendall/Hunt, particularly Marc Sabol, Deborah L. Kucia, and Stacy Elliott were most helpful in the production of the book. Jill Gardner provided considerable, and much needed, editorial help.

Each of the authors were students of E. N. Anderson, Sylvia M. Broadbent, R. E. Taylor, and Philip J. Wilke, who were instrumental in our growth as anthropologists. We are especially grateful to Phil Wilke for exposing us to his insightful and original way of studying the past. Many interpretations regarding the use and significance of prehistoric materials presented herein are Phil's, and we acknowledge his indirect contribution to the content of this book.

Chapter 1

INTRODUCTION

An archaeological project typically includes at least four phases: (1) research design and planning; (2) fieldwork; (3) laboratory work; and (4) reporting the results. Here we focus on the laboratory component of archaeological work, probably the most time-consuming aspect of a project. An archaeological laboratory is much more than a place where things are sorted, cleaned, and given numbers; it is where the picture of the excavation is pieced together, where conclusions are formed from the data, where other scholars come to conduct research, where comparative collections are kept and used, and where plans for future fieldwork are made based on the results of past work. The maintenance of a functional laboratory is an integral aspect of what archaeologists do.

Before we detail methods in archaeological laboratory work, it seems appropriate to ask: What is archaeology? Why do we do it? What kinds of things can we hope to learn from doing it? Why should we bother?

ANTHROPOLOGY

Archaeology is a subfield of anthropology, the study of human beings. Anthropology includes the study of human biology, language, prehistory, religion, social structure, economics, evolution—anything that applies to humans. Thus, anthropology is a very broad field and is holistic in its approach to the study of humans. Everything humans do or think about is of interest to anthropologists. As one might suspect, this has resulted in the division of the field into many subfields and in the specialization of many anthropologists. The traditional division of anthropology is into four basic subdisciplines: cultural, physical (or biological), linguistics, and archaeology. There are many specialized areas of interest within these four basic subdivisions; areas that connect the basic four and are in a continual state of change.

CULTURAL ANTHROPOLOGY

Cultural anthropology (sometimes called social anthropology) is the study of existing (or recent) peoples and cultures. Sociology is a similar field, however, cultural anthropologists generally work with groups that are not industrialized, while sociologists typically work with groups that are industrialized. While there are major differences in approach, methods, scale, and purpose of the two fields, the distinction often is blurred, with considerable overlap. Cultural anthropologists strive to learn everything they can about a culture, such as kinship systems, marriage customs, the economy, political organization, etc. Cultural anthropologists can ask people questions and can observe behavior. They can sometimes participate in (and so can better record) community activities. Cultural anthropologists can learn a great deal about a particular group at a particular point in time. Archaeologists often use the information gathered from living cultures to try to explain past human behavior from the remains of those cultures.

INTRODUCTION

PHYSICAL OR BIOLOGICAL ANTHROPOLOGY

Physical anthropologists study human biology through the study of their physical attributes, evolution, and the behavior of other primates (humans are primates) for clues to human behavior. Biological variation may include stature, blood type, adaptations to cold or altitude, and many other things (including some behavior). Archaeologists are very interested in past human biology, since the details of the biology of a population can suggest relationships with other populations (intermarriage, migration, etc.), changes in past environments, and changes in subsistence (e.g., hunter-gatherers as opposed to agriculturalists).

Physical anthropologists specializing in the study of the "first" humans often are called *paleoanthropologists*. These researchers deal with fossil materials and are interested in the biological and cultural origins of humans. Their work combines archaeology, biology, geology, and paleontology.

LINGUISTICS

Linguists study human language, including the historical relationships between languages, common "ancestors" of languages and language groups, syntax, meaning, cognition, and other aspects of communication. Much can be learned about a culture by examining its language. Archaeologists are interested in linguistics, especially historical linguistics, since certain aspects of language (and so cultures) can be traced back in time.

ARCHAEOLOGY

Archaeologists study past cultures, rather than living ones (although there is overlap). Archaeologists want to know everything about a past culture that a cultural anthropologist wants to know about a living one. The big difference is in the available data: a cultural anthropologist can participate in activities, observe people, and question them about what they do and why. An archaeologist can look only at traces of human activities and infer from those traces the "what, why, how, and when." The link between cultural anthropology and archaeology is the assumption that present human behavior can serve as an analogue to understanding past human behavior.

Archaeology presents a great challenge to its practitioners. Although archaeological evidence often seems meager, four million years of human history are available to study. We must take the philosophical position that the past is knowable; otherwise, we will not inquire or learn. Archaeologists must press the frontiers.

Cultural anthropology and archaeology have similar goals; archaeology has a disadvantage in that the material remains of past human behavior are limited, partly by the lack of preservation of some items, and partly because of the way the material is obtained. This results in an incomplete picture of a past culture. Cultural anthropologists, on the other hand, can get a full and rich record of a group, its material culture, language, marriage patterns, political structure, and other aspects of the culture. Cultural anthropology, however, for all the richness of the available data, cannot detect long-term cultural change. Archaeology can document change over long periods of time, can identify broad trends, and can examine transitions, such as the change from a hunting and gathering to an agricultural way of life.

BASIC LABORATORY METHODS IN ARCHAEOLOGY

There are two broad categories of archaeology: prehistoric and historical. *Prehistoric archaeology* deals with materials that date prior to written history within the region under consideration. *Historical archaeology* deals with materials dated after the presence of written records in an area. History begins at different times at different places. To further confound this issue, written languages were imposed upon many societies, literate and preliterate, by outside groups, resulting in written records that can be very biased. In North America, prehistoric archaeology is defined as being concerned with native cultures, while historical archaeology is concerned with nonindigenous (i.e., Euroamerican) cultures.

This definition is inadequate since many native groups passed through a period where they continued to practice some traditional pursuits but were heavily influenced by Euroamericans; much Euroamerican material culture (tools, foods, etc.) was incorporated into their own. This transition period is often called the *Proto-historic* or *Historic* period of aboriginal culture, not to be confused with historical archaeology.

Terms and definitions always vary, and the terms prehistoric and historical archaeology are no exception. For example, the Maya had writing but Mayan archaeology is not considered historical. The use of the term "Pre-Columbian" to refer to the archaeology before A.D. 1492 and "Columbian" to refer to that after A.D. 1492 solves this problem. In the Old World, historical archaeology could date to anytime after the introduction of writing, 8,000 years ago in some places! Prehistoric archaeology refers to anything older than historic, up to four million years old.

WHY DO ARCHAEOLOGY?

There are many reasons why we do archaeology, some esoteric and some practical. Humans are a very curious primate; what has happened in the past holds a great fascination to many of us. Learning from the mistakes of the past is a commonly held theme. We are tied to the past through religion, nationalism, family, land, etc., and an understanding of the past benefits us all. Some of the reasons we do archaeology are listed below.

1. In Western science (there are other sciences) knowledge is sought for its own sake. As scientists, anytime we can learn something, we feel that we have made a contribution. What is learned may not have apparent immediate practical value, but it may be the missing piece to a different puzzle. Pure research is valued not only for what is learned, but for what others can do with the new information to gain further knowledge.

2. The diversity of human behavior is truly immense and very difficult to predict. Anything we can learn about past human behavior can help us to understand present and even perhaps future behavior. Increasing the breadth of human understanding and identity are important goals in archaeology.

3. All peoples believe that they are superior to other peoples, a phenomenon known as *ethnocentrism*. Throughout human history, cultures have used this belief as justification for the subjugation and destruction of other peoples and cultures. For example, when Europeans encountered the remains of ancient civilizations, the remains were attributed to ancient European peoples rather than to the indigenous groups of the region. Ethnocentrism led to the belief that native groups were too

inferior to have created them. Archaeologists have, over the years, investigated ancient ruins and cultures and established that native cultures were quite sophisticated and were able to develop complex civilizations. The Great Zimbabwe, an ancient city in East Africa, is an excellent example.

4. Many cultures have lost some or much of their identity. Rediscovering the past of a group (understanding Native American prehistory for the benefit of Native Americans) can serve both for outsiders to gain a greater understanding of the group and for the group to better understand itself. Both results are quite beneficial.

5. Like biological diversity, cultural diversity is important to the survival of the species. If we were all the same, either biologically or culturally, life would be very boring and highly precarious. Diversity is strength; to discover and archive cultural diversity is an important goal of archaeology.

6. Westerners often arrogantly assume that ''primitive'' (i.e., nonindustralized) peoples, past and present, have little to offer ''modern'' industrialized societies. It is not understood that many cultures have (and had) a far more extensive knowledge of the natural world than do industrialized societies, who tend to be isolated from, and ignorant of, nature. The same is true of traditional philosophy, art, and science. As western civilization expands, more and more traditional knowledge is lost. Archaeology can recover and document past knowledge and practices, as well as facilitate application of that knowledge to present needs.

7. Archaeology studies past interactions of culture and environment. Archaeologists expend considerable effort learning about prehistoric environments. This information can be used in planning for future events, such as 100-year floods and long-term environmental change.

8. It is often believed that humans have a particular response to certain conditions, but there is no reason to expect that all people have responded the same way in the past. By understanding the responses of past peoples to various conditions, we can better anticipate and plan our own responses.

9. Most species that have ever lived are extinct. In addition, all of the domesticated plants and animals upon which we are so reliant were modified from species that lived in the past. One goal of Archaeology is to discover and archive the biological diversity of the past. For example, an understanding of the genetic origin and diversity of corn (a critical plant to our culture), plus the preservation of that diversity, could prevent its elimination by some disease or other disaster.

10. Archaeology has major commercial value. Archaeology provides much raw material for movies, and archaeologists are often depicted in films and on television. In addition, archaeology and anthropology are widely used in advertising. Without archaeologists to discover the past, industry could not use it.

11. The study and interpretation of archaeology are critical to many countries that are economically dependent on tourism. A number of these countries (Egypt, Greece, Mexico, Peru) focus their tourist industries on their cultural heritage and archaeological resources to attract visitors. The same is true in some parts of the United States (e.g., Arizona, Colorado, Pennsylvania, South Dakota, Virginia).

12.   Lastly, archaeology is fun!   It can be romantic, exciting, fun to talk about, and the discoveries can be thrilling.   It is an excellent profession and avocation.   There is so much more to learn.

THE ARCHAEOLOGICAL RECORD

The archaeological record consists of all things, known or yet to be discovered, that pertain to the past.   This includes all sites, artifacts, ecofacts, features, and all associations between them.   Some archaeologists define the archaeological record as only those things that are so far known, but that definition is rejected herein because our lack of knowledge about something does not mean it does not exist.

ARTIFACTS

The basic "unit" of archaeological analysis is the *artifact*.   An artifact is a portable object (clothing, tool, ritual object, etc.) made, modified, or used by humans.   An artifact must retain and show *evidence* of having been made or used.   Such evidence can take the form of manufacturing scars (such as flake scars on stone tools) or use wear (such as flattening of a stone through grinding or battering at the end of a hammerstone).   Some artifacts consist of a single part (e.g., a modern nail file) and are called *simple* tools; others are made of multiple parts (e.g., a modern knife with a metal blade and a wooden handle) and are called *composite* tools.

Some artifacts are not necessarily tools.   A ceramic vessel is an example of an obviously manufactured item made for a particular purpose, such as storage or cooking.   Although not usually thought of as a tool, it is definitely an artifact.

This presents a problem.   We look for things that show evidence of having been used.   However, if you use a stone to pound in a tent stake during your next backpacking trip, it is a tool by definition, but 10,000 years from now an archaeologist would probably never recognize it as such.   Many such "ephemeral" tools must be present in the archaeological record, but are rarely recognized or recovered by archaeologists.   Thus, we miss an entire class of technology; casual tools that were only used once or twice.

Most materials recovered from archaeological contexts are broken and fragmentary.   People do not generally discard useful items; thus, most of the artifacts recovered from a site were discarded at the end of their useful life span and do not represent the actual form of the tools when they were first made.   To be sure, some perfectly good (functional) artifacts are lost or may have been intentionally hidden by their owners in antiquity and never retrieved, only to be recovered later by archaeologists.   For the most part, though, we deal with broken and used-up material (trash).

Looking at an artifact at the end of its life cycle presents a problem to the archaeologist.   If a complete arrow point is lost and later found by archaeologists, we would classify it as "Type X."   If an identical arrow point was broken and resharpened, it may look quite different and be classified as "Type Y."   Archaeologists could view these as two completely different types of arrow points without realizing that the second is just a reworked version of the first.

INTRODUCTION

We often assume that we have a fairly good idea of how artifacts were used in the past. However, we have trouble recognizing intended uses of even recent artifacts from our own culture. For example, the hold of the *Bertrand* (a cargo ship that sank in the Missouri River just after the Civil War and was excavated in the early 1970s; see Switzer 1974) contained numerous examples of goods (destined for general stores throughout the West) that had never been seen by historical archaeologists and whose function was (and still is) unclear. We do not even fully understand our own fairly recent technology: how can we say that we understand the technology of a past culture largely unrelated to ours?

ECOFACTS

Another common constituent of archaeological sites is *ecofacts*. Ecofacts are unmodified (and so are not artifacts) biological (plant or animal) remains resulting (mostly) from human activity. Many of the bones from a site would commonly be interpreted as food refuse and not the remains of tools (if a bone had been made into a needle then it would be an artifact). Plant remains, such as seeds, charcoal, pollen, also fall into a this category. For example, corn cobs found in a site are not artifacts but represent human activity. Thus, ecofacts are not artifacts but are still remains that resulted from human activity, and can tell us a great deal about such activity.

Ecofacts might also be noncultural in origin. Plant pollen from a site could provide information regarding the local environment at the time the site was occupied. The kinds of rodent bones or insect remains in a site could provide clues to the local environment as well.

HUMAN REMAINS

Human remains in sites can be present for various reasons and can take various forms. Isolated human teeth, such as baby teeth or those subjected to infection or injury, are lost during life. Such remains do not indicate that people actually are interred (buried) in a site. If people are interred in a site, the remains can occur either as cremations or inhumations, and may be in primary or secondary contexts.

Cremation is the practice of disposing of the dead by burning the remains. Much, but not all, of the bone is destroyed in the fire. Cremated remains may still contain considerable information regarding the age, sex, stature, and health of the individual, information important to understanding the past. *Inhumation* is the disposal of the dead by burial. Inhumations tend to be more intact than cremations (depending on soil chemistry) and more information can be obtained from them. Some human remains are neither buried nor cremated, but placed in the open, such as in the scaffold burials of the Plains Indians or bodies (now mummified) placed in crevices or caves.

Both cremations and inhumations can be in either a *primary* or *secondary* context. Primary context means that the remains are in their original position while secondary context means that they have been moved from their original location. Most inhumations are primary, although sometimes persons are placed somewhere until the flesh has decayed and then the bones are buried elsewhere. Many cremations are secondary, as the remains were buried in a spot away from the original cremation fire. In other regions, elaborate burials and mummification rituals have been documented in the archaeological record.

THE "OTHER" CATEGORY

Some materials recovered from archaeological sites do not neatly fit into any particular category and often are classified as "other." An example of this would be a *manuport*, something clearly brought into the site by humans but not modified in any way, such as an unusual stone from a distant source. Its presence in the site is culturally related, but the item is not an artifact in the usual sense. Another example is the burned rock that was part of an oven or hearth (often called fire-affected rock [FAR] or fire-cracked rock [FCR]); they are not tools but are the result of human activity.

GEOFACTS

Natural forces sometime shape a stone so that it appears to have been modified by humans. Such items might fool even an expert into believing they were artifacts, even though they were "manufactured" by natural processes. Such items are often called *geofacts*. One must exercise caution in the interpretation of such items.

ASSEMBLAGES

An *assemblage* is ALL of the material collected from a site. We speak of the "flaked stone assemblage from Site X" or the "faunal assemblage from Site Y," but these actually are subassemblages, portions of the entire assemblage from a site. It is easy to confuse these terms.

FEATURES

Features are discrete occurrences within a site or locus that represent an event and that cannot be removed without destroying (or disturbing) their overall integrity and relationships. They may represent actual constructions (structures, hearths, posts, etc.) or they may be things such as the grinding surface of a stone in a bedrock outcrop or a burial. Features are different from artifacts in that they are not tools and they are not portable.

MIDDEN (SITE DEPOSIT)

Many sites contain culturally modified soil comprised of the discarded material remains from the people living at the site; this soil is called *midden*. A midden is literally a decomposed garbage pile; a place where broken tools, used-up artifacts, shell, plant materials, bones, grease, charcoal and ash from fires, general household trash, etc., were thrown. In prehistoric sites, people often lived directly on such middens. Deposits accumulated as people continued to live on them. Middens can contain house foundations, burials, hearths, and other remains from everyday life. In historical sites, trash often was removed and deposited elsewhere (still the practice in our culture; we use garbage collection and landfills [giant middens!]).

Midden soils often are discolored and chemically altered by the materials within them. Many prehistoric middens are dark-colored from the charcoal and ash from fires, and greasy from the decomposed animal fat in the soil. However, these materials leach out of the soil over time and an "old" midden may look just like the surrounding soil. One often can tell from the soil color where midden *is* but in the absence of soil discoloration, one cannot determine the absence of midden. Soil chemistry testing can sometimes be used to distinguish middens. Since some plants have a soil preference, a clue to the existence of a midden might be the plant distributions in an area.

ARCHAEOLOGICAL SITES

One of the basic concepts in archaeology is the *site*. A site can be defined as any geographic place where there is evidence of past human activity. Typically, archaeologists define sites by the physical presence of artifacts and features, but a site could be defined based on other evidence, such as photographs or historical accounts. This is intentionally a broad definition; archaeologists are interested in past human behavior, so we are interested in anything that can tell us something about what people did and how they behaved in the past. Realistically, though, the definition of site must be more limited because, technically, everything humans do leaves some trace, even if it occurred just a few minutes ago.

There must be some *detectable evidence* of human activity present to define a site. For example, if someone walked through mud 5,000 years ago, leaving footprints, that location would be a site (at the instant it was created). If a subsequent storm washed those footprints away, the evidence of the existence of the site (the footprints) would cease to exist and the event would go unrecognized in the archaeological record. For a site to be discovered, we must be able to recognize the evidence of human activity. We sometimes miss sites because we do not recognize them in the field.

By definition, a site must have geographic boundaries (it already has time boundaries, even if we do not recognize them). It cannot go on forever; even Los Angeles has boundaries to its physical remains, a place where the houses and freeways end. Often boundaries are drawn almost arbitrarily by an archaeologist. Material remains (i.e., the artifacts and features that archaeologists use to define sites) are distributed over an area (both vertically and horizontally), but they tend to be concentrated in some areas and be thinly distributed in others. At some point, remains are no longer present and the site boundary has been reached. At some other geographic point, other remains are present and the boundary of a different site starts. (Some archaeologists have a different view and consider everything to be part of the pattern of human habitation and/or use and so see beyond the "site" concept. While this is actually true, most archaeologists deal with geographically limited sites and consider site interrelationships as part of settlement pattern studies.) In the analytical sense, where sites ARE NOT is as important as where sites ARE. If we want to understand human land use and environmental adaptation, we must know where people did not go.

Where we draw lines between sites is sometimes of considerable concern. If a scatter of material remains exposed on the surface is continuous over a large area (which may not match the subsurface extent of the site), we may define the location as a single large site. If the remains are clustered, and actually separated, we may define them as several smaller sites. In a modern farming community, for example, Farm "A" exists and occupies five acres for a house, barns, machine shops, and other buildings. Farm "B" contains similar facilities and is located one-half mile away. The two farms are connected by roads, wires, and pipes. Fields are present between the two farms and the whole complex could be viewed as a single site. More likely though, they would be considered as two separate sites, since they are discrete concentrations of artifacts and features, separated by mostly vacant (even though used for farming) space. The discrete localities within a city would be viewed differently, however, since they would tend to be closer to each other; all localities within the city would be considered part of a single, large site.

In a large site there often are areas that seem separate from each other while still contained within the site. Each such area within a site is called a *locus* (plural loci). A locus is a place that the archaeologist decides to set apart from the rest of the site for some reason. At our hypothetical Farm "A," we could define a barn locus and a house locus, separated by a yard which contains few actual physical remains, but still within the "farm" site. Loci designations may be based on function (e.g., a stone workshop locus and a plant processing locus within a village) or on temporal and/or ethnic considerations. At an old mining town in Nevada, for example, there may be the main locus where Euroamericans lived and a nearby historical aboriginal locus where Indians lived at the same time.

If a small scatter of nine stone flakes is found, is it a site? What activity might it represent? Is it important for archaeologists to know about it? There are no easy answers to these questions. The locality might represent a place where a hunter stopped to resharpen an arrow point, or to make a new one, or to butcher a small animal. If it can be determined that the scatter of flakes represents a cultural event, then archaeologists want to know about it because it illustrates a portion of the total activities of a people. If the nine flakes were deposited there by a small stream, then it does not represent a place where human activity occurred but a secondary deposition of artifacts from a site located elsewhere. Deciphering the situation is a challenge.

TYPIFYING SITES

Archaeologists usually classify sites into types. Two basic considerations regarding site type may be considered: geography and function. The geography of a site considers its situation (e.g., in a cave, on a terrace, on a hill, next to a lake). The function of a site is concerned with what activities took place there.

Site Geography

Open Sites. Open sites are those that are geographically located (on land) such that they are exposed to the elements, not protected from the weather. Most archaeological sites would be classified as "open." Since they are exposed to the elements, open sites rarely contain perishable materials (artifacts made of fiber, hide, wood, etc., that ordinarily decompose; see below). As a result, the artifact assemblage of an open site likely would be limited to those materials that preserve fairly well, primarily stone and bone.

Caves and Rockshelters. Some sites are located in natural shelters, such as caves and rockshelters. A "cave" can be defined as an opening in a rock face or cliff that is deeper than it is wide. A rockshelter is a shallow rock overhang at a cliff, or a place where large boulders have formed a shelter; a small cave might also be called a rockshelter. Sometimes water does not reach the soil of the cave or shelter; in such a case the site deposit may be "dry." A dry cave or rockshelter may well contain perishable artifacts preserved in the dry environment. Such situations are rare and the artifacts from such sites provide a glimpse of material culture not commonly studied.

Other. Some sites do not fit neatly into these two geographic categories, e.g., sites located underwater or underground. Underwater sites could be shipwrecks or terrestrial sites drowned by a rise in sea level (or ground subsidence). Another such example would be a purposefully built underground facility, such as a tomb in Egypt, China, or Peru.

Site Function

Site function is determined from the activity or activities inferred to have taken place at a site. Some sites may have served multiple and/or complex functions while others may have had single and/or simple functions. Site function can change over time, as the environment changes, or as a new group enters an area. The function of a site is not always apparent from a brief inspection. While the function of some sites is relatively easy to identify, identifying site function can often be quite difficult. A site may also be identified as an "X" function site based on what is believed to be the *primary* function of the site, even though other functions may be evident (e.g., a habitation site may have evidence of food processing but it is still called a habitation site).

Every site is part of a larger system of settlements and site functions: the *settlement pattern*. There are sites where people lived, other sites where they gathered and/or processed food, sites where religious ceremonies took place, trails over which travel occurred, places where trade was conducted, and sites with many other functions. To understand a culture, it is necessary to comprehend the entire settlement system, the pattern of sites related to geography, natural environment, and other cultures. Understanding one site is just the first step.

Habitation Sites. Habitation sites are places where people lived and had their residences for some period of time longer than just a few days. Places where a large number of people lived for a long period of time (although not necessarily all year) are called villages. Villages generally contain a wide variety of artifact types that reflect domestic activities related to habitation, the full range of material culture of that group. Structures, cemeteries, and a fairly substantial midden are common criteria for calling a site a village.

A site that may "look" like a village but lacks the full range of material remains might be a long-term camp; a place where a group of people camped for a relatively long time or a place where the entire group camped, but not long enough to invest in substantial structures or a formal cemetery. In our culture, we have a primary residence where we live all year (our village) but we may spend the summer in a vacation home (our long-term camp).

A smaller habitation site could be a short-term camp; a place where just a few people camped for a short period of time. One would expect that only a few of the activities represented at a village would be present at a short-term camp. It may well be that the small camp was located in an area where specialized activities took place, such as gathering certain plants or hunting certain animals.

Processing Sites. Processing sites are places where people processed foods and other materials, usually on bedrock metates and/or mortars. These activities can take place at a habitation site, and if that were the case, processing would be only one function of that larger site. There are many sites where processing seems to have been the only activity (or at least the primary one). Sites where processing was the only function tend to be small. If a great deal of processing activity had occurred at a site, there would probably have been a number of people there for extended periods and an associated camp would likely be present.

Agricultural Sites. Agriculture was practiced across much of North America for the last several thousand years, and there are many sites associated with that activity. These would include cleared or raised fields, artificial fields made with check dams, specialized habitation and storage structures (field houses), irrigation facilities (canals and furrows), specialized artifacts (hoes), and perhaps associated ceremonial sites.

Hunting Blinds/Trap Complexes. Prehistoric people hunted, trapped, killed, and butchered animals as part of their subsistence systems. Many animals were caught using nets, pits, corrals, drive lines, fish weirs, and other devices. To the trained eye, such sites can sometimes be discovered in the landscape. The large bison drive/kill/butchering sites on the Plains (e.g., the Olsen-Chubbuck site, Wheat 1972) are good examples. Hunting blinds may be small, isolated rock walls situated along game trails (or former game trails) but may contain few artifacts. Drive lines may consist of burned-off posts barely visible in the ground or extensive rock walls and/or lines of cairns (piles of rocks). Kill/butchering sites and small camps could be expected in the vicinity of blinds and traps.

Animal Kill/Butchering Sites. Animals were sometimes trapped, killed, and butchered at the same site. However, places where animals were killed may or may not be the place where they were butchered, cooked, and/or eaten. A deer shot in the forest might be dragged elsewhere (perhaps even taken to the village) for butchering; we may find the bones of the deer at some location but never find the kill site. Sometimes animals were butchered at a special site away from other sites. One would expect to find a specific set of artifacts (arrow points, knives, etc.) and the remains of specific parts of the animals at such sites.

Quarries, Prospects, and Lithic Scatters. People procured and processed stone for the manufacture of tools. A *quarry* is a place where stone was removed from a larger source (e.g., a mine) to subsequently manufacture tools. However, not all toolstone was quarried; sometimes cobbles were obtained and used to make tools. A *prospect* is a site where stone was tested for suitability; where the stone may or may not have been used. A *lithic scatter* is a common class of sites where tools were made or repaired. Lithic scatters are often associated with quarries and prospects. Most archaeologists associate quarries and lithic scatters with the manufacture of flaked stone tools, but the same types of sites are also associated with the manufacture of ground stone tools.

Storage Sites. Items were often stored and/or hidden in the landscape. Such localities are called storage or cache sites (a storage pit or cache within a habitation site would be a feature). Such sites might contain ceramic or basketry vessels, storage facilities (e.g., rock- or fiber-lined pits, standing granaries), or other features used to store materials (e.g., nets, stone) and/or resources (e.g., seeds). Some caches may not have been placed in a formal container but may have just been stashed for future use or to hide them.

Ceremonial Sites. A long-standing joke in archaeology is that if the function of a specific site or artifact is unknown, it must have been "ceremonial" or "ritual." In fact, ceremonial sites are present, even if we lack the necessary knowledge to properly identify them (such knowledge may still persist in the traditional knowledge of Native Americans). Sites of ceremonial or ritual significance include places where power was sought (e.g., the Vision Quest of the Plains), places where offerings were made (e.g., shrines), or locations where initiations were conducted. In some cases, ceremonial locales may have no archaeological visibility—that is, a sacred place may not be an archaeological site (as defined above)—but may be a very important spot. In other cases, ceremonial locations may be highly visible, such as medieval cathedrals, kivas in the Southwest, and temple mounds in central North America.

Rock Art Sites. There are at least three types of rock art: pictographs, designs painted on rock surfaces; petroglyphs, designs pecked onto rock surfaces; and geoglyphs, designs placed on the surface of the earth by lining up rocks or by scraping designs into the soil. Such sites may or may not be associated with other sites. There is considerable argument regarding the function of such sites.

Cemeteries. A cemetery is a place where a number of people were interred (either as inhumations or cremations). Such places often are associated with large habitation sites, although they may not be located in direct association with such a site. A cemetery located away from a habitation site, where no midden or artifacts are visible may be difficult to detect. Other cemeteries might be very visible, as they are in our culture. In some parts of North America, burials were made in mounds.

Aboriginal Trails. People moved about in the landscape and often traveled the same path or trail. Such trails sometimes are still visible as shallow linear depressions across the surface of the ground and can even be traced from site to site. Many trails have been utilized by others later in time (many modern roads now follow old trails) and many have been destroyed. Nonetheless, aboriginal trails still exist in many areas and may be identified by a thin scattering of artifacts in a linear route or by blaze marks still visible on standing trees.

Other. A number of other site types exist, including rock alignments (earthen art) and bow trees (where wood was removed for the manufacture of bows).

HISTORICAL SITES

Historical sites are extremely varied in types; many of these types remain in use in our culture (e.g., towns, roads, railroads, farms, ports, cities). Thus, historical sites are often more "recognizable" in the archaeological record. Although some site types defined for prehistoric sites are applicable to historical sites (e.g., habitation, ceremonial, and food procurement), many other functional types may be assigned to historical sites, as we recognize and understand them better.

ISOLATES

Sometimes archaeologists encounter single artifacts, or a very small number of artifacts, that are not associated geographically with a larger site. While the presence of even a single artifact is evidence of human activity (although not necessarily at the place where the artifact was found), many archaeologists prefer to record these occurrences as *isolates* (sometimes called "Isolated Archaeological Occurrences") and not as sites. Whether an isolated artifact or feature, or group of artifacts or features, is defined as a site depends on who is defining the terms. Some agencies consider fewer than 10 artifacts within a 25-square-meter area to be an isolate and not a site. Such a definition presupposes that the archaeologist has counted the number of artifacts precisely, that there are no buried artifacts, and that the area (25 square meters) has been precisely defined. Features, even single isolated ones, are generally considered to be sites.

CONTEXT AND PROVENIENCE

Archaeologists deal with a variety of objects and places, as well as their relationships. It is this relationship, or *context*, that provides much of the information that archaeologists seek. In order to understand an object beyond its immediate morphology (physical attributes), it is necessary to understand its context. The context of objects and features requires careful recordation; this is why archaeologists spend so much time and effort digging carefully. In most instances, the objects themselves are rather durable; they can be excavated intact by rough and crude methods, like a backhoe. While a scoop of dirt from a backhoe contains all of the objects that would have been recovered by more careful excavation, the exact location, or *provenience*, of the artifacts is destroyed, and with it, valuable information.

For example, if you were told that an inhumation of an adult, an inhumation of an infant, a grinding stone, an arrow point, and a house were found in a site, what would you know? You would know little more than people lived and (probably) died at the site. If, however, you know that the two skeletons were found together (you now know their context!), then what additional knowledge would you have? You could postulate that part of a family unit had died and were buried together.

If you knew that the grinding stone was found buried with the bodies, you could postulate that a female-related artifact was buried with the two people, perhaps indicating that the adult was a female (we would want more evidence of this than merely the presence of a grinding stone). If you discovered that the arrow point was embedded in one of the ribs of the adult, you would have evidence of a violent death. If you knew that the arrow point was found at the other end of the site and was not associated with the burials, then you would have no evidence of a violent death. What if we did not know where the arrow point came from or whether the bodies were found buried within the house or outside of it, or whether the house was burned, or if there were other grave goods . . . ?

The more information we have about the relationships between things in an archaeological site, the more we can say about them. The presence or absence of things tells us little; it is the context of the material that creates archaeological knowledge. Archaeological excavation destroys part of a site. In order to study the materials excavated from a site, it is important to keep careful records of everything we do. Others should be able to reconstruct a site and the relationships of the recovered materials from the excavation records.

A note on private collecting of artifacts. The context of artifacts is one of the critical pieces of information needed to understand prehistory. People who collect artifacts as a hobby destroy most of the information contained in an artifact because its context is lost. It is analogous to removing the evidence from the crime scene and then expecting the police to solve the crime. Many collectors are unaware of the destruction they cause, but some do know and do it anyway: this knowledge is the difference between ignorance and vandalism.

INTRODUCTION

SITE FORMATION PROCESSES

Much can be learned about a site and its occupants by gaining an understanding of how the site was formed (see the comprehensive book on this subject by Schiffer 1987). For example, a tell in the Near East is a high mound of soil (midden) formed from the debris of a series of towns that had been built over and over on the same spot. Tells are formed by the gradual (or sometimes sudden, as with earthquakes or war) disintegration of the mud-brick and stone blocks that made up the buildings. Once every few generations, buildings had to be leveled and rebuilt. Over thousands of years, a very large amount of cultural debris accumulates.

A site along a river might have a very deep cultural deposit. One would tend to think that since the deposit is deep, it is old. However, if the river flooded regularly, soils could rapidly accumulate in a relatively short period of time. Flood episodes may result in the segregation of individual habitation events; flood deposits can be recognized and are of great value in interpreting sites. It is critical for archaeologists to understand the origin and structure of the sites they study.

TAPHONOMY

Taphonomy is the study of what happens to something after it enters the archaeological record. The study of taphonomic processes includes how something decomposes or preserves, how it is affected by plants and/or animals, how it gets moved around, etc. Taphonomy is related to site formation processes (discussed above).

PRESERVATION

Not all things preserve in forms that are recognizable to an archaeologist. As an object gets older, preservation becomes less likely. Most organic remains decay rapidly and so will be ''lost'' (by that we mean unrecognized) in the archaeological record. Of the material remains that are lost and discarded at a site, most do not preserve well and so are never recovered by an archaeologist. Degree of preservation depends on a variety of factors, including temperature, moisture, and soil chemistry. Generally, the only items preserved in a site are those that are durable, such as stones and bones.

Stones and Bones

The great majority of the artifact assemblage from most sites will consist of stone tools and debris, plus some materials of bone, shell, and ceramic. What is preserved represents an unknown, but probably small, percentage of the total material culture of a group. Thus, our understanding of that group is limited. This situation is improving as we learn to recognize and recover more materials.

Perishables

Organic materials that are usually subject to rapid decomposition can preserve under certain circumstances and are called *perishables*. Circumstances of preservation are those of consistent/constant extremes: always very cold, very hot, very wet, very dry, and/or charred by fire. Some ecofacts might be considered to be in this category, such as charred seeds in a midden. However, the term perishable usually is reserved to refer to preserved artifacts such as plant fiber sandals, basketry, clothing, rope and cordage, and mats. For example, in dry conditions (''dry caves'' or ''dry deposits'') overall preservation is excellent; baskets and textiles are protected from moisture, animal remains may become mummified, and wooden items may preserve. Sometimes, material is intentionally protected (e.g., in Egyptian tombs) and at other times preservation is accidental, such as some of the mummified burials in the deserts of Egypt, Peru, and Chile (only the rich could afford formal mummification). Perishables are also found in other extreme conditions, such as the mummies of the Arctic or wooden ships preserved in very cold water.

SITE DISTURBANCE

Virtually all sites have been disturbed in some manner, either by natural or human forces. Perhaps the most common natural site disturbance is *bioturbation*, the alteration of the site by nonhuman biological agents. Burrowing rodents are particularly bothersome in this respect, as they dig in sites and move around significant quantities of soil and artifacts. Rodents cannot move features, but they can damage them. Ground-dwelling insects, such as ants, also impact sites. Roots from plants can damage a deposit and result in natural seeds and charcoal (if they burn) entering the cultural deposit. Natural erosional processes can damage and destroy sites by the action of both wind and water. Volcanic and tectonic activity also can damage or destroy (or sometimes preserve) sites.

Human disturbance also is a serious problem. People accidentally damage sites through recreational activities (e.g., motorcycle riding), by building on them, or by altering the landscape (e.g., a river channel) so that sites are impacted. Purposeful vandalism is a significant source of site destruction.

REFERENCES

Schiffer, Michael B.
    1987   Formation Processes of the Archaeological Record. Albuquerque: University of New Mexico Press.

Switzer, Ronald R.
    1974   The Bertrand Bottles. Publications in Archaeology 12. Washington: National Park Service.

Wheat, Joe Ben
    1972   The Olsen-Chubbuck Site: A Paleo-Indian Bison Kill. Society for American Archaeology Memoirs No. 26.

Chapter 2

THE ARCHAEOLOGICAL PROJECT

Prior to starting the laboratory work necessary to complete an archaeological project, it is essential to know about the nature of the project; its goals, the research design, field methods used, personnel who worked on the project, and other information. If the person who conducted the fieldwork is also conducting the laboratory work, then this information is already known. If you are doing the laboratory work for a project conducted by someone else, it is necessary to fully understand the project. If possible, talk to the project and/or field director; familiarize yourself with any documentation available, such as the field notes, maps, and written proposals.

RESEARCH DESIGN

What was the research design for the project; what questions did the project seek to answer? What were its goals? Different research designs will result in different materials coming into the laboratory for analysis, and such materials may even be organized in different ways. If the goal of a particular project was to obtain a sample of grinding stones, for example, other tools may have been present but not collected. The laboratory worker would receive only grinding stones to analyze and thus would have a biased sample of the assemblage from the site.

It may be that many soil samples were taken from a site. The type of processing and analysis of these soils would depend on the kinds of information desired from each of the samples. The analytical goals would determine the type of processing used; there may be different goals for different samples.

INVENTORY (SURVEY)

Inventory (often called survey) is the process of looking for, and providing a preliminary assessment of, archaeological sites. In the process of conducting inventories, sites will be located and some artifacts may be collected. Such artifacts may only be those that caught the eye of the surveyor and may not at all represent the full range of artifacts present at a site, thus resulting in a biased artifact sample.

EXCAVATIONS

Excavations involve digging into a site and collecting the materials from that excavation. Excavations are conducted at sites for two basic reasons: (1) *small-scale excavations*, often called *test excavations*, are conducted to determine the presence, nature, extent, content, age, structure, and research potential of a site; and (2) *large-scale excavations*, sometimes called data recovery or mitigation, are designed to recover information useful to answer specific questions generated in the research design.

Excavations usually are conducted in discrete areas called units or pits. A unit is the hole made by the excavation and forms part of the provenience (coupled with ''levels''; see below) of the materials within it. The size and shape of excavation units vary depending on the research design and field methods.

An excavation unit, called Unit X, Test Unit X, Trench X, or some other appropriate label, is usually dug in *levels*. Levels are specific layers of soil removed during excavation and processed for cultural materials. Levels might be arbitrary (e.g., 10 cm. at a time) or might follow distinct soil layers (stratigraphic levels). When possible, stratigraphic levels are used since it may better relate to the way the soil was deposited in prehistory and prevent mixing the deposits from different times. Arbitrary levels are used if no obvious stratigraphy is visible. In addition, the use of arbitrary levels insures a consistent volume of soil from level to level, making comparisons of recovered materials easier.

Materials removed from an excavation unit usually are processed through steel mesh screen so that the soil falls through and the cultural items larger than the mesh size stay in the screen to be picked out and saved by the screener. Thus, the provenience of an artifact might be the "30 to 40-cm. level of Unit 10." Sometimes the soil from the unit is processed through the screen dry and sometimes water is used. This latter technique is called "wet" or "water" screening and, in effect, cleans the materials in the screen, making artifacts and ecofacts much more visible. Thus, the recovery of cultural materials should improve when wet screening is used.

Sometimes artifacts are found in the excavation unit during the digging before it is screened. In such cases, the items are called *in situ* (this is a Latin phrase meaning "found in place" and is always italicized or underlined). An *in situ* item has a precise provenience; the exact measurements of its location in the unit (rather than only a level-specific location). *In situ* items should be recorded and bagged separately from the screened constituents.

Other samples are often taken in the field, including soil samples for chemical, geological, pollen, phytolith, radiocarbon, protein, and other analyses. Each is processed and examined in special ways.

Small-Scale (Test) Excavations

The purpose of testing an archaeological site is to determine the general contents of a site, its size, and its structure (sometimes testing is needed just to determine whether an area is a site or not). Test excavations may be quite limited; a single unit in a site may be sufficient to determine whether midden is present, and if so, how deep it is. Testing may be accomplished by any of a variety of means, or a combination of methods. Excavation units may dug, backhoe trenching might be used, small shovel test pits ("STPs") might be excavated, or an auger might be employed to "drill" small units.

Large-Scale Excavations

Large-scale excavations employ many of the same methods as testing; however, where only one or two units may be used to test a site, 30 or more might be used on a major excavation. The purpose of a large-scale excavation is to recover important information as defined in the research design. Most sites where large-scale excavations are undertaken have been previously tested. People working in the laboratory on a large-scale excavation project should read the testing report to familiarize themselves with the site.

BASIC LABORATORY METHODS IN ARCHAEOLOGY

FIELD METHODS

It is important for the laboratory worker to understand how the material to be analyzed was obtained. If screening was not used in the excavation, it may be that only larger materials would have been found and collected. If 1/4-in. mesh screen was used, the bones of larger animals would dominate the faunal assemblage and someone analyzing that collection would assume that only large animals were obtained and eaten. The use of a smaller screen size (e.g., 1/8-in.) would result in the recovery of many more bones, including those of smaller species. Thus, the use of larger mesh screens would likely create an erroneous interpretation of the diet of the occupants of that particular site. The same would hold true for small artifacts, such as beads, flakes, projectile points, and fragments of other items as well. Additionally, if the soil was wet screened, visiblity would have been better and the recovery greater.

WHAT COMES IN FROM THE FIELD

Materials from the field will be in marked bags (paper and/or plastic), and temporarily stored in larger containers such as boxes or buckets. These bags should be secured in the field so that they do not tear, fall over and spill, or get lost before they get to the laboratory. Trying to determine which bag a loose flake came from is virtually impossible.

FIELD PROVENIENCE: SITES, UNITS, LEVELS, AND *IN SITU*

Almost all materials processed in a laboratory will be from sites; few will be isolates. Materials get collected in a variety of ways—from the surface, from actual surface collection units, and from excavation units. Each of these is a different analytical unit and must be considered separately. Much of the material is grouped by a general provenience, say the 20 to 30-cm. level of Test Unit 2. In this case, the precise location of individual items is not recorded, just the general location (level) of the material within Test Unit 2. This material is considered separately from any other level of any other unit. All *in situ* items should be in their own bags and should be cataloged separately.

BAGS

Each collection unit (surface, excavation, level, stratum) will have its own field bag or bags containing the materials recovered and saved from that unit. Within each bag may be other, smaller containers (bags and/or vials) that hold the various items from the unit and level. These smaller containers may include materials that were sorted in the field according to artifact class, *in situ* items, or other samples. The provenience for the contents of the bag is listed on the outside (see Fig. 1). DO NOT MIX UP THE MATERIALS FROM DIFFERENT BAGS! While it may seem that there is considerable repetitive information on the bags and notes, it is much better to be redundant than to lose contextual information. If more than one bag from a level is present, the bags should be labeled "1 of 2," "1 of 3," etc. Make sure you find each bag before you proceed with any laboratory analysis.

NOTES AND RECORDS

Included in the documentation from any site will be both general field notes, level notes (Fig. 2), maps of the site in general (showing the location of units and features), and maps of each of the collection

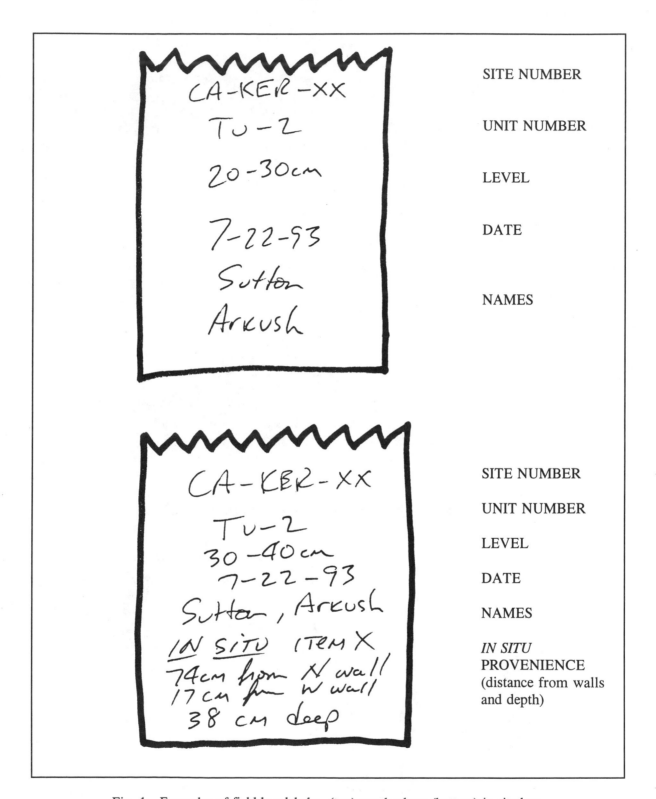

Fig. 1. Examples of field bag labels: (top) regular bag; (bottom) *in situ* bag.

ARCHAEOLOGICAL FIELD NOTES
Unit Level Record

Site _CA-Ker-XX_   Unit _TU-2_   Level _30-40 cm_
Excavators _Sutton, Arcush_   Screen Size _1/8_
Unit Orientation _N/S_   Excavation Method _trowel_

DESCRIPTION OF MIDDEN

Soil Type _Sandy loam_
Color _Med Brown_   Consistency _Soft_
Ease of Excavation _easy_   Disturbances _some rodents_
Features _none_

MATERIALS RECOVERED

Debitage (quantities and material) _≃ 100 chalcedony flakes, a few rhyolite flakes_

Faunal Remains (quantities, general ID) _some large mammal (burned) and lots of small mammal, no fish or shell_

Formed Artifacts (list and draw; use reverse side of form if necessary)

— one mano _in situ_ (item X on map)

(sketch) |5cm|

— 1 small chalcedony core

Comments _Some charcoal and burned rocks in unit, we may be near a hearth or some other feature._

Recorder _Sutton_   Date _7-22-93_

Fig. 2. Example of a level record sheet (level notes).

units (Fig. 3). Level notes and maps may be in any of various styles and contain information regarding the locations of features, *in situ* items, disturbances, errors in excavation, and a brief review of what was found in each level or unit. Information on the content of a unit can be very useful in the event a mistake was made in the field; perhaps an error can be corrected by comparing the materials in the bag to the notes. The availability of the field records is an indispensable aid in the cataloging process.

FIELD BIAS

The only materials delivered to the laboratory are those that were saved in the field; many items from the units are not saved and so are never seen by the laboratory people. We assume that the field people made correct decisions about what to keep and what not to keep, but the truth is that artifacts and ecofacts are invariably discarded accidentally in the field, resulting in a biased sample. Field workers are taught to keep any questionable material; it can always be discarded later. In some cases, the field crew may have purposefully saved nonartifactual materials for cataloging and analysis (such as stones from a hearth feature). If apparent noncultural material is in the field bags, it is important that the laboratory worker look through the field notes and/or ask if it should be saved; perhaps someone had a reason to save it.

Field bias may also occur as a part of the planned research design. If only certain kinds of data were being sought, other data may have been intentionally discarded. This is one reason why it is important to understand the research design and field methods prior to any analysis of the collection.

BORROWING COLLECTIONS FROM OTHER INSTITUTIONS

Collections from other institutions will vary in condition: supporting documentation may or may not be available; the artifacts might not be cataloged; artifacts might be mixed up with other material. It is important to obtain all the available records of any collection. Make sure there is an inventory of what was borrowed so that an accounting can be maintained.

Store the borrowed collection in a secure place. When you are finished with the material, it must be returned to the lender/owner/curator. It is essential that the material returned matches the material borrowed and that you obtain a receipt for its return.

Some collections lack records and/or provenience. There may be no field notes or maps, and in some cases, the location of the site itself may be lacking. If you decide to continue your analysis regardless of the condition of the collection, do the best you can with the available information. Keep in mind, however, that it is possible that the lack of records and/or provenience is such that working with the collection is not worth the effort.

REPORTING THE RESULTS

It is the ethical and scientific obligation of all researchers to report their data and interpretations. Failure to do this is a very serious ethical offense. A report on an archaeological excavation/collection should follow a general format (Appendix 1 presents a general format recommended by the California State Office of Historic Preservation).

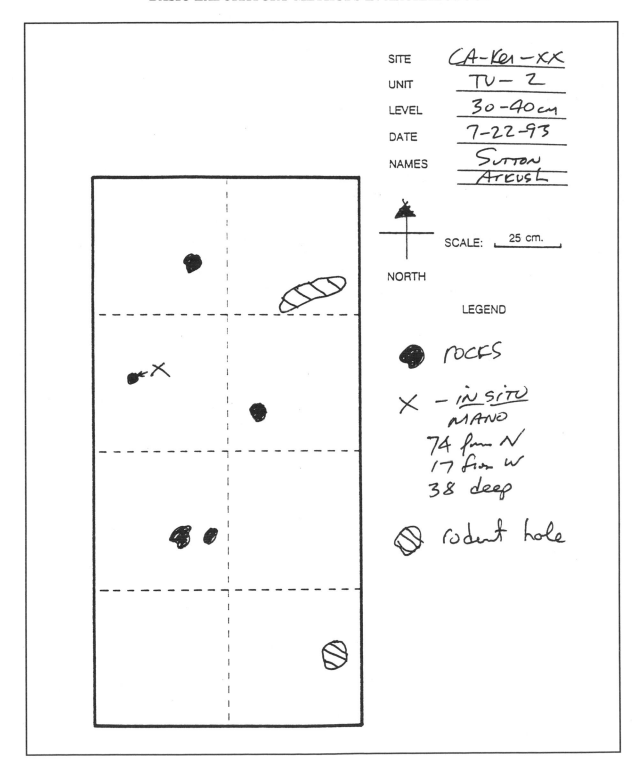

Fig. 3. Example of a level map (part of the level notes).

THE ARCHAEOLOGICAL PROJECT

The results of your various analyses should be presented in an organized fashion so that the knowledge that you have acquired can be communicated to others, both scientists and laypersons. This means that:

1. all terms used should be defined;
2. the writing is clear and concise; and
3. figures should enhance or replace written descriptions.

All repetitive information, such as catalog numbers, provenience, and metric measurements should be presented in tabular form, especially when the collection is large. As a general rule, do not repeat information in the text that is available in the tables.

Include descriptions of the methods you have used for the various analyses. There are no perfect ways to analyze or look at collections, but always explain what was done, why it was done, and what conclusions were reached. All interpretations should be presented as such, and not as factual data. All references that are cited in the text must be listed in a reference section at the end of the text.

TABLES

Tables present data in lists that are easy for the reader to follow. Anytime you have more than three items in the same category (such as three projectile points), their provenience and attributes (measurements, weight, style, completeness, etc.) should be presented in a table. Three items or less can be described in the text. Examples of both ways of reporting are included in Appendix 1.

FIGURES

Figures enhance a report, present nonmetric data (e.g., shape), and make the report more meaningful to the reader. At the very least, two maps as well as drawings of significant artifacts should be included in any report.

Maps

At least two maps (see Chapter 14) are necessary. First, a map of the location of the site in your region is needed. A general location is adequate and advisable so that vandals cannot use the map to locate the site (a qualified archaeologist can obtain the specific location if necessary). Second, a map of the site itself is needed, showing the location of features, units, the datum, and natural features (e.g., streams and cliffs). You may also need maps of individual features. Always include a north arrow and bar scale so that the image can be enlarged and/or reduced without losing the information on size. Alternatively, the size can be stated in the figure caption, but the former presentation is preferred. Consult the United State Geological Survey convention for map symbols.

Artifact Illustrations

Artifact figures may be drawn using pen and ink (see Chapter 14), or photographs may be used. When drawing an artifact, it is usually presented in both a plan view (view from above) and in a cross-sectional view (view of the shape if the artifact was split longitudinally). In this way, both the overall shape and size of the artifact can be seen, as well as any nonmetric details. Other views may be used for specific purposes. With drawings and photographs, a metric bar scale should be included. Use figure captions that tell the reader what you are illustrating and why. Not all artifacts need to be illustrated, but representative examples of major types should be included. This subject is considered in greater detail in Chapter 14.

Photographs

Photographs can be very useful (see Chapter 14). However, very few publishers will use color photographs because they are very expensive to reproduce; black-and-white glossy prints are much less expensive and are the standard for most archaeological reports. The publisher should be provided with prints close to the actual size needed in the publication.

THE ARCHAEOLOGICAL CATALOG

The purpose of an archaeological catalog is to identify, classify, and record the attributes of all materials recovered from an archaeological project. A paper (and/or electronic) record of the materials is thus created with information about each of the items recovered from the site encoded into it. The catalog is the permanent record of the recovered artifacts, ecofacts, and other constituents and is an essential part of any project analysis. The catalog should contain as much information as possible. In theory, one should be able to write the site report using only the catalog, without having to examine the artifacts again (this is never actually the case, but it should be).

ACCESSION, LOT, AND CATALOG NUMBERS

Each artifact, ecofact, or geofact (or grouping thereof, depending on the category) from a site is assigned an individual, unique number. This number is the code that indicates where the information on the particular item is located in the catalog. Thus, it is vital that no two items have the same number; each catalog number must be unique.

A catalog number actually consists of at least two, and sometimes more, sets of numbers. The first number is the accession number, a code for an assortment of information. The accession number may identify the site the collection is from, the year of excavation, the place of storage, a reference to a particular report, and/or other information. For example, the California State Department of Parks and Recreation uses an accession number that has encoded into it the site, year, and contract of an excavation (e.g., P-1068 indicates the collection from a Parks project [the P] at site CA-MER-295 in 1993). The meaning of the ''P'' may be obvious to people familiar with the California system, but few would have any clue as to what the ''1068'' meant.

The University of California, Riverside, uses a slightly more obtuse linear accession number system. When a new collection is obtained, the next number in the accession log is used. Thus, ''108'' is the accession number for the collection from site CA-RIV-1179. The next site collection would be ''109'' and the next ''110.'' The problem with this system is that it is in code and the reader must know the code to use them. If you saw the catalog number ''108-178,'' you would have no idea what it meant, or from what site (or even what state) the item was from. Accession number 108 might be used by dozens of different schools or museums. Perhaps the addition of an institution code would help; ''UCR-108-178'' is more decipherable.

Some people use lot numbers that code the general location of the item within the site. For example, lot ''S'' may mean surface and lot ''1'' may refer to Unit 1. An item could be cataloged with the number ''108-1-024,'' meaning it was from site/project 108 (the accession number), lot 1 (the unit number), and catalog number 024. The entire code would then mean that this was item 24 from Unit 1, at Site X (whatever accession number 108 meant). While this system can quickly convey useful information, it is still a code and the reader must know the code. In our experience in creating and using catalogs, we have found the use of a lot number confusing and do not recommend it.

Some laboratories use an even more complex system consisting of a five-part numbering system. For example, an artifact may have the number 93-89-15-3-1. The "93" is the year of acquisition; the "89" is the accession number (the 89th collection from the year 1993); the "15" is the Field Serial Number (FSN) (i.e., a unit and/or level, the equivalent of a lot number); the "3" is the Laboratory Serial Number (LSN), a code for the material/functional class of the item (ceramics, lithics, bone, etc.); and the "1" is the Analytical Serial Number (ASN) that identifies the specific type of artifact. Thus, "93-89-15-3-1" would designate the 89th collection from 1993, Unit 15, projectile point, Dalton type. This system is quite an elaborate code and does not appear to allow for the separate number of two Dalton points from the same unit. The absence of a unique number for each artifact could confuse the results of special analytical tests.

We prefer a more direct system: using the state-assigned site trinomial designation as the accession number. While this is somewhat more cumbersome when trying to write numbers on small artifacts (we suggest that this never be done anyway, see below), trinomials are recognized throughout the United States and probably would never be confused. For example, instead of the UCR number "108-178" (see above) we would have used "CA-RIV-1179-178" (California, Riverside County, Site Number 1179, Catalog Number 178). The actual catalog number is usually the final number in the series (although some would consider an entire sequence [accession, catalog, etc.] to constitute the "catalog number"). This is the number that distinguishes an item from all others. The accession number designates the site; the lot number designates the general location in the site; and the catalog number designates the item.

RECORDATION

When material is cataloged, each item is assigned a catalog number (including accession and, if used, lot numbers). Many archaeologists will write the number directly on the surface of the artifact if it is large enough. However, since the advent of increasingly sophisticated methods of retrieving data from the surface of artifacts (e.g., protein residue and DNA analyses; see Chapter 13), we do not recommend this method. We prefer that the catalog number be recorded on a sheet of paper and placed in a plastic bag with the item (this is not a perfect method either). The information from that item (type, provenience, material, measurements, weight, etc.) is recorded in the catalog. The catalog may take any of several forms: (1) sheets of paper upon which the information for all the material recovered from a site is written; (2) an individual paper card for each item; and/or (3) a computer record of the information (that can be printed out, since you always want a hard copy of your catalog).

PAPER CATALOGS AND RECORDS

Paper (hard copy) catalogs may be in a variety of styles. One is a form upon which the information for a number of items can be recorded. Using such a form, all of the material from Level X of Unit Y would be cataloged on the same sheet(s) of paper in order to keep all the information together. The next unit and level would be recorded on a new catalog sheet. Examples of various catalog sheets are shown in Figures 4 and 5. An example of a catalog card, where each item gets a separate card, is shown in Figure 6.

CATALOG SHEET

SITE CA-SBR-XXX (The Pretend Site)   EXCAVATED BY Sutton and Arkush
UNIT TU-1   CATALOGED BY Sutton
LEVEL 0-10 cm.   CATALOG DATE 7-22-93
EXCAVATION DATE 6-22-93

Cat. No.	Description	Material	Quantity	Measurements	Comments
001	mano	granite	1	183 x 117 x 17 mm., 1,283.9 g.	unburned, ground on both sides
002	triangular projectile point	obsidian	1	14 x 5 x 1 mm., 2.1 g.	tip is missing
003	flakes	chert	67	54.3 g.	--
004	bone	bonc	15	6.7 g.	some burned
005	ETC.				
006					
007					
008					
009					
010					
011					
012					
013					
014					
015					
016					

Fig. 4. Example of a catalog sheet (adapted from the onc uscd by Antelope Valley College; note that accession and lot numbers are not used and that only one level is on the page [sec top of form]).

ARCHAEOLOGICAL CATALOG

Acc. No. **XXX** Site No. **CA-SBR-XX** Site Name **The Pretend Site** Project Name/Date **The Pretend Project/6-22-93**

Collector **Sutton and Arkush** Cataloger **Sutton** Date Cataloged **7-22-93**

Catalog No.	Quantity	Description	Provenience	Remarks
XXX-1-001	1	granite mano (183 x 117 x 17 mm., 1,283.9 g.)	TU-1, 0-10 cm.	unburned, ground on both sides
XXX-1-002	1	obsidian triangular projectile point (14 x 5 x 1 mm., 2.1 g.)	"	tip is missing
XXX-1-003	67	chert flakes (54.3 g.)	"	--
XXX-1-004	15	animal bone (6.7 g.)	"	some burned
XXX-1-005	1	granite metate fragment (89 x 65 x 22 mm., 189.3 g.)	TU-1, 10-20 cm.	unburned
ETC.				

Fig. 5. Example of a catalog sheet (adapted from the one used by UC Riverside; note the use of accession and lot numbers and that more than one level is on the same page).

30

Cat. No.	Acc. No.	Field No.	Date Coll.	Date Acc.	
Collector			Donor		No. Pieces
Description					
Location					
Material and Techniques					
Archaeological Context/Associations					
Attributions of dates, culture, and use					
Published					Photo ☐
References					

Fig. 6. Example of a catalog card (adapted from the type formerly used by the Hearst Museum, UC Berkeley).

COMPUTER CATALOGS AND RECORDS

Instead of hand-writing catalog data onto a sheet of paper, the catalog can initially be entered onto a computer using a program that contains a "catalog form" and coded entries. One popular cataloging program is *Lab Assistant* (or *Archaeomation*). This program operates from MS DOS and was written in dBASE so that all of the functions possible in dBASE can be carried out within the program. When using a computer, scales and calipers can be hardwired into the machine, making initial data entry easier and virtually error-free.

A computerized catalog can facilitate your analyses. You may even want to computerize an older paper catalog to make analysis easier. Your computer catalog program should have the capability to be read into a program that can be used to manipulate the collection data (e.g., sorting by artifact type and/or material) and making statistical computations (e.g., SPSS). If your disk "crashes," all data will be lost, so always keep a hard copy of the printout.

There are now computer scanners that have the capability to scan artifacts into a computer (but be aware that they consume a large amount of memory space). Scanners can provide an "instant" picture of the artifact, depicting its two-dimensional attributes (length, width, shape), but not the attributes of the third dimension (thickness), or nonmetric attributes (where it was ground, pecked, flaked, painted, etc.). These attributes must be measured or described and entered manually into the catalog. Scanners *augment* traditional catalog records, they cannot yet replace them.

STORAGE OF RECORDS

All records—field and laboratory, paper, magnetic, photographic, or other—must be stored properly. This means paying careful attention to details such as acid content of paper, type of film, environment of storage facilities, and accessibility to the records for future research. A detailed guide to these issues was presented by Kenworthy et al. (1985).

ARTIFACT TREATMENT

Always be careful when handling archaeological materials. Two major problems should be considered: damage and contamination. While many of the materials recovered from an archaeological site are relatively durable, even stone can be damaged. Many artifacts may be very fragile and require great care when handling. Washing can damage materials by removing soil that serves to support weak parts of an item (this is often true in bone and perishables). Some damage may have occurred in the process of excavation, transport in the field bags, and/or during sorting (called bag wear). Damage of this type may be mistaken for use wear (e.g., small flakes removed from the edge of a flaked stone tool; see discussion of use wear in Chapter 4).

Contamination is the other major concern. Ancient proteins, for example, may survive on artifacts. Handling such items may introduce new human proteins that could bias any tests for such proteins. This is to be avoided. Wearing white cotton laboratory gloves or latex examination gloves when handling artifacts helps reduce the possibility of contamination. Never handle organic materials that may be used for radiocarbon dating (particularly charcoal). The carbon in the oils on your hand will contaminate the sample. Radiocarbon laboratories usually are able to adequately "clean" samples of accidental contamination, but conservative and careful treatment in both field and laboratory settings reduces the risk of contamination.

BASIC LABORATORY METHODS IN ARCHAEOLOGY

PROCESSING THE MATERIAL

When you begin to process your materials, first make sure you have all the materials from a specific level in one place (for example, there might be more than one bag from one level). We suggest that all the material from a unit be cataloged in order; that is, do the 0 to 10-cm. level first, then the 10 to 20-cm. level, etc. While catalog order is not critical in terms of the catalog number (remember that each artifact has a unique number and so cannot be confused with another), it does make the catalog better organized and using it more convenient.

EQUIPMENT

Certain tools and supplies are needed to catalog an archaeological collection. It is very handy to have trays (e.g., cafeteria trays) on which to place the contents of the level bag(s) while sorting and classifying the material. A lighted magnifier and small tools, such as tweezers, are useful for sorting through small objects on the tray. After sorting and cataloging, you will need labels and/or tags (for the catalog numbers) and plastic bags and/or vials in which to place the material. When the cataloging is complete, the cataloged materials should be placed in properly labeled boxes for storage (a heavy-duty cardboard file box is perfect). The completed catalog forms should be kept in order in a three-ring binder (or in a file box if catalog cards are used). Always use pencil on paper records; the forms are often updated and corrected, and pencil marks are much easier to erase and correct than ink. Also, records written in pencil preserve better than those written in ink.

A gram scale is used to weigh the specimens. This scale should have a capacity of at least several thousand grams (anything larger can be weighed on a medical scale in pounds and converted to grams; 459.53 grams equals one pound). A triple-beam balance scale (Fig. 7, top) is commonly used and has a capacity of about 3,500 grams (with the add-on weights). This scale is usually accurate to 0.1 gram. Electronic scales (Fig. 7, bottom) are becoming more common and are easier to use (they also can connect to a computer for direct data entry). Some electronic scales are accurate to 0.001 grams.

Calipers (Fig. 8) are used to measure specimens. This instrument should measure in the metric system; centimeters and millimeters. A good calipers will have the capability of taking both outside and inside measurements. For large specimens, a large bow calipers may be quite useful. A metric tape measure may be used on very large objects if necessary. As with the scales, electronic calipers (Fig. 8, bottom) are more precise, easier to use, and can be plugged into a computer for direct data entry.

INITIAL SORTING AND CLEANING

When you have all of the field bags organized and your equipment and supplies present, you are ready to begin cataloging. First, WASH YOUR HANDS so that any contamination can be kept to a minimum (see special analyses discussion in Chapter 13); some laboratories advocate wearing gloves. Remove the materials from the field bag(s) and place them on the sorting tray. Organize the materials on the tray into categories; bone in one place, formed tools in another, flakes in another, etc. You may not be able to identify some of the material on the tray; the screeners in the field are instructed to save all materials they think might be cultural. The cataloger must make decisions about what to keep and what to call an item. Seek advice from your instructor/laboratory director when making such decisions.

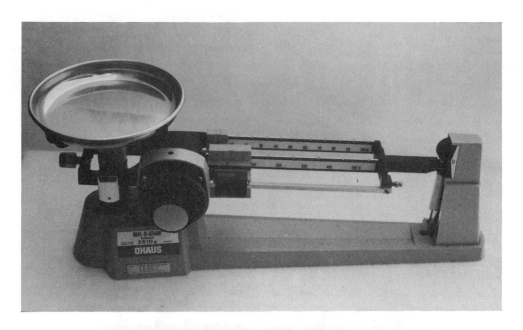

Fig. 7. Scales: (top) triple-beam balance scale; (bottom) electronic scale (no scale).

Items may be cataloged as "unknown." It is best to handle the artifacts as little as possible. This will reduce the possibility of damaging specimens and lessen the chances of contamination.

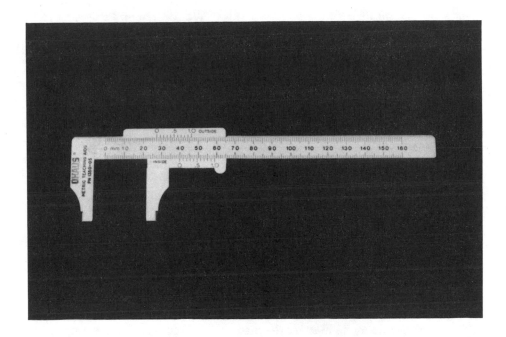

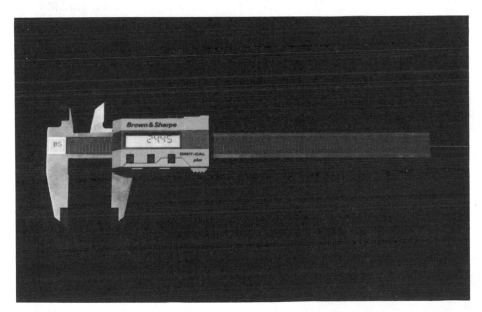

Fig. 8. Examples of calipers: (top) standard sliding calipers; (bottom) electronic calipers (no scale).

Many laboratories wash the materials from the field bags prior to sorting and cataloging. Although this does make it easier to identify specimens and allows greater precision in recording weight (since soil adhering to items is removed), washing artifacts may result in a **loss of information**. It has recently been discovered that organic residues can survive on objects for thousands of years. By washing artifacts, critical information on their function may be lost. We recommend that you **DO NOT WASH YOUR MATERIALS!** Gently brush away the excess soil from your specimens, being careful about anything that may be adhering to the surface (e.g., a burned seed). Do not scrape out and discard the soil from a container-like artifact (e.g., a bowl or ceramic vessel); preserved materials may be present in that soil and it should be saved for analysis. Perishable materials (e.g., basketry, textiles, plant parts) should only be cleaned when absolutely necessary and with the greatest of care.

If you insist on washing the materials, be gentle and do not use detergent. Make sure that all items from one level are kept together and are not mixed with other specimens; keep the level bag with the material as it dries.

CLASSIFICATION

As materials are sorted, the process of *classification* (deciding what items go into which categories) begins. It is critical to recognize that many of the categories we use are constructs of *our* minds; categories that may or may not have anything to do with the way in which past peoples categorized the same items. Bias in classification is always present.

In spite of the bias problem, we classify the materials we recover, as it is a necessary prerequisite for analysis. To reduce bias, it is generally best to classify things by morphology rather than by function. For example, if you have a flaked stone tool with a used edge, you might be tempted to classify it as a "scraper." However, the term "scraper" is a functional rather than a descriptive term. The artifact may be a unifacial (worked on one face) tool, but you do not know (at the time of cataloging) whether it was used to scrape things.

As discussed in Chapter 1, we generally classify things into a number of broad classes or categories: artifacts, ecofacts, human remains, etc. These classes are further broken down into types based on a variety of criteria. Each of these classes are discussed in detail in the following chapters and are briefly outlined here.

Artifacts

Artifacts (items made or used by people) come in a great variety of forms, but there are several basic categories into which artifacts are classified, including ground stone, flaked stone, ceramics, perishables, and historical. *Flaked stone* artifacts (see Chapter 4) are produced by the removal of flakes (or chips, commonly referred to as debitage) from the stone to create a sharp surface. Projectile points, bifaces, unifaces, and cores are common flaked stone artifact types. *Ground stone* artifacts (see Chapter 5) are those that have been modified or produced by grinding or pounding stone on stone, as in the processing seeds or other materials. Manos, metates, mortars, and pestles are common ground stone artifacts. *Ceramics* (see Chapter 6) are clay (often fired) artifacts, usually vessels. *Perishables* (see Chapter 8) are artifacts made from organic materials that ordinarily would decay but for some reason were preserved. Such artifacts include basketry, cordage, and leather. *Historical* artifacts (in North America, see Chapter 9) are those produced by non-Native (e.g., Euroamerican) cultures.

Ecofacts

Ecofacts are divided into two major categories: animal (*faunal remains*, see Chapter 10) and plant (*floral remains*, see Chapter 11). If such remains are modified (e.g., a bone sharpened into an awl or plant fibers woven into cordage) they are artifacts. Ecofacts are those unmodified remains, such as food residue, resulting from cultural activities. However, some ecofacts are unassociated with cultural activities but may be useful for environmental reconstruction.

Human Remains

Human remains (see Chapter 12) are the biological remains of humans, primarily skeletal, but including preserved tissues such as mummies. Most definitions specify that such remains are the result of death and interment (either burial or cremation) and not of loss during life (e.g., baby teeth). It is not really clear whether preserved human blood or other proteins, or fossilized (containing no organic elements) human materials, constitute "human remains."

Other

Materials that do not easily fit into the categories discussed above (or any other category) can be placed into a category called "other," or perhaps "unknown." Do not hesitate to admit that you do not know what something is; label it as unknown, attempt to identify it later (perhaps with the help of a specialist), and then change the description in the catalog. Odd materials, even if not modified, may be important. For instance, people will sometime carry "pretty" rocks or other things to their homes for a variety of reasons (such imported, unmodified items are called *manuports*). Be sure to consider this as a possibility.

"ROUGH" CATALOGING

In the process of cataloging any collection, some materials may be easily identified and classified. Many times, however, final classification must await more sophisticated sorting and analysis, often conducted by a specialist after the initial cataloging process is complete. A projectile point may be recognized as such by the cataloger but the specific type may be unknown to that person. The catalog would read "projectile point." At some later time, a point specialist may identify the specimen as a "Clovis" type. This new information can then be added to the catalog description. Until all of the analysis of a collection is complete, the catalog should be considered "rough" or "draft." The final catalog is produced at the end of the analysis and adds greatly to the production of the report.

STORAGE OF THE COLLECTION

Once the collection has been cataloged and analyzed, it must be stored (long-term storage is often called *curation*, see Kenworthy et al. [1985]). Curation is a major problem in most institutions due to a lack of adequate and/or properly controlled space. Collections must be stored in strong containers. Sturdy cardboard file boxes may be used. The Arkansas Archaeological Survey recently began using 10-gallon Rubbermaid boxes; this is a good idea as they are quite sturdy. Remember to label the outside of the boxes with adequate information about what is in them.

Packing materials that will not adhere to the artifacts (cotton may stick to some artifacts but polyfelt liner generally will not) or chemically interact with them (use acid-free paper) should be selected. The use of bubble-wrap materials may be quite useful in some instances. Proper environmental control for curation includes regulation of temperature, humidity, and light (incandescent lights can cause fading of designs).

Various types of damage can occur during storage. Insects and rodents directly damage bone and perishables and indirectly damage other materials by destroying containers or labels, resulting in a loss of information. Pest control in the storage area is imperative. Flooding, fire, and theft are other concerns. Materials should be kept from direct contact with the floor, adequate fire detection and suppression devices should be present, and the storage area should be secure and locked. Duplicate copies of all paper and computer records (e.g., the catalog) should be kept in a separate location. Food should not be in the vicinity of collections.

ACCESS

Archaeological collections should always be accessible to other researchers. As new analytical techniques and approaches are developed, and as fewer and fewer sites are available to excavate, stored collections will become increasingly important as a source of new data. The collections, along with the associated records, must be well organized and easily accessible.

REFERENCE

Kenworthy, Mary Anne, Eleanor M. King, Mary Elizabeth Ruwell, and Trudy Van Houten
    1985   Preserving Field Records: Archival Techniques for Archaeologists and Anthropologists. Philadelphia: University of Pennsylvania, the University Museum.

Chapter 4

ANALYSIS OF FLAKED STONE ARTIFACTS

Robert M. Yohe II
Archaeological Survey of Idaho

DEFINITION

Flaked stone artifacts are those cultural items created from stone by the removal of flakes rather than by grinding or polishing (as we will see in Chapter 5, some "ground stone" artifacts also are flaked during the early stages of manufacture). Typically, the materials used for the production of flaked stone tools are vitreous or fine-grained silicates, such as chert, obsidian, quartzite, or even modern glass or ceramics. The most common artifacts associated with the majority of prehistoric archaeological sites are either flaked stone tools or the production detritus left from their manufacture, in part due to the enduring nature of stone.

Before we consider the analysis of flaked stone artifacts, it is important to be familiar with the basic physics of toolstone and the process of tool production.

FUNDAMENTAL FLAKED STONE MECHANICS

The breaking of stone in a predictable fashion is only possible due to the physical structure of certain types of stone. The types of stones most often used for "knapping" by prehistoric peoples are largely comprised of silica and have a crystalline matrix. These types of rocks behave like glass when met with a directed force and are said to fracture *conchoidally*. A conchoidal fracture represents a portion of what is known to physicists as a *Hertzian Cone of Force* (Fig. 9). In other words, when glass is struck with a directed force that is focused on a small surface area, the resulting breakage will be cone-like in shape. A perfect example of such a phenomenon is what happens to a pane of window glass when it is hit by a BB. The energy of the projectile impact radiates through the structure of the glass in the form of a cone. Many rocks with a high silica content, like glass, will produce cones when struck. The flake that is removed by such a strike is actually a portion of a Hertzian cone.

FLAKED STONE RAW MATERIALS

Two common forms of raw material that are most like glass in terms of their physical behavior are quartz crystal and obsidian. Other materials, containing varying degrees of other minerals, also produce Hertzian cones, but due to the nonsilica components and variations in the crystalline lattice, a cone may be more difficult to produce. The terms "microcrystalline" or "cryptocrystalline" are often used by archaeologists (as well as mineralogists) to describe highly siliceous sedimentary rocks such as chert, flint, chalcedony, opal, or jasper. Other rocks, such as quartz, quartzite, fine-grained basalt, and rhyolite have been widely used as a source of toolstone by humans over the broad span of prehistory.

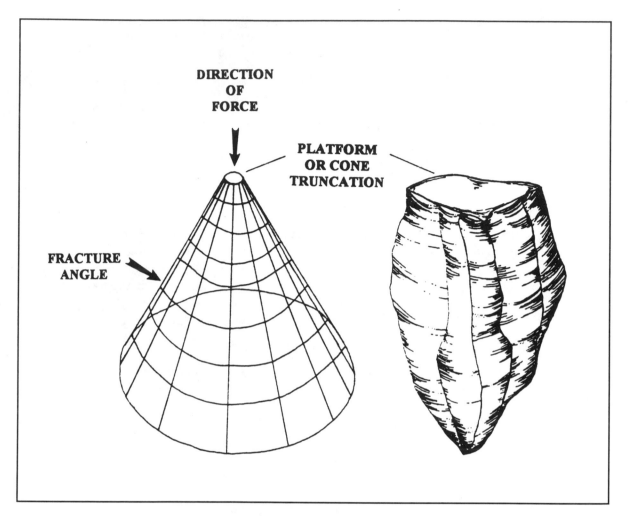

DIRECTION OF FORCE

PLATFORM OR CONE TRUNCATION

FRACTURE ANGLE

Fig. 9. The Hertzian Cone of Force and the Hertzian components of a flake (redrawn from Crabtree [1982]).

Recognizing certain lithic (from *lithos*, Greek for stone) materials frequently can be challenging to the beginning student. It is useful to take at least an introductory course in physical geology or have access to a keyed study collection of common rocks and minerals. Texts or other books with colored photographs of rocks and minerals with physical descriptions (such as the *National Audubon Society Guide to Rocks and Minerals*, for example) may also be helpful in making raw material identifications.

HEAT TREATMENT

Many microcrystalline or cryptocrystalline stones do not fracture in neat or predictable ways during stone tool production and are difficult to work in their natural form (obsidian is a notable exception). However, certain lithic raw material can be "heat-treated" so that its flaking characteristics are vastly improved. To do this, the stone is literally cooked beneath a hearth or in an earthen oven for a specified amount of time. One popular theory (Flenniken and Garrison 1975) concerning the physical changes that occur during heat treatment is that heat causes the moisture within the stone to turn to steam, expand, and microfracture the lattice of the stone. Force (e.g., percussion or pressure) applied to the stone will then follow the microfractures creating a smooth and more predictable break. The freshly broken surface of heat-treated stone often takes on a waxy or glossy appearance, whereas raw stone is dull-looking.

Overheating of toolstone leaves characteristic patterns that are observable in flaked stone assemblages containing cryptocrystalline materials. Occasionally, small portions of the stone may spontaneously "pop off" due to rapid heating or excessive temperature, creating many small flake scars on the surface. This is called *pot lidding* and is characteristic of the stone being heated to a high temperature too rapidly (though not necessarily from heat-treatment). *Crazing* is another result of excessive temperature exposure and is characterized by numerous small fractures, often in a cross-hatched pattern, observable on the surface of the stone.

THE PRODUCTION OF STONE TOOLS

In addition to the mechanics of flaked stone, it is important that the archaeologist have a familiarity with the fundamental principles of stone tool production prior to beginning any form of analysis. The common term for producing stone tools is "flintknapping," which is also the term used to describe the experimental replication of stone tools by archaeologists. The goal of the flintknapper, today as in the past, is the *production* of an artifact from a mass of stone through *reduction*. Flaked stone tools are often made from flakes; the stone from which the flakes are removed is known as a *core*. Cores can be bifacial, unidirectional, or multidirectional (see discussion of cores, below), and may themselves be used as tools at some point in their use life. A roughly shaped flake or piece of raw material is sometimes referred to as a *blank*. A *preform* constitutes the early stage of the production of an artifact, the result of shaping a blank toward a final product.

There are two major methods used in reduction: *percussion* and *pressure*. Percussion involves the use of a *hammer* of antler, wood, or stone. If the hammer is held in the hand and used to strike the stone directly, it is called *direct percussion* (or *free-hand percussion*). Another form of percussion, known most commonly from Old World stone technologies, is called *indirect percussion* (see Fig. 10). Indirect percussion involves the use of a bone, wood, or antler punch that is struck with a stone, wood, or antler hammer (or billet). A less common form of percussion is known as *bipolar reduction*. This type of percussion involves the placement of raw material (usually small rounded or oval cobbles) on an anvil stone and striking it from the top. Pressure flaking (see Fig. 10) is usually reserved for the completion of bifacial tools (such as projectile points), although some pressure blade technologies are known (a *blade* is a specialized type of flake that is long and narrow with nearly parallel margins, very small blades are called *microblades*).

Hammers may be made from a variety of materials, including stone and antler. Stone comes in varying degrees of hardness (1 to 10 on the Mohs stone hardness scale, diamond being 10). The raw lithic material will have a hardness as will the hammer. If the hammer is antler, it will be softer than most raw material stone; if the hammer is stone, it may or may not be softer than the raw material stone. If the hammer is softer, then a *soft-hammer* technique is being used; if it is harder, it is called *hard-hammer* technique. The type of hammer used is dictated by the types of raw materials available and what may work better for a particular type of stone (for example, antler billets work particularly well for

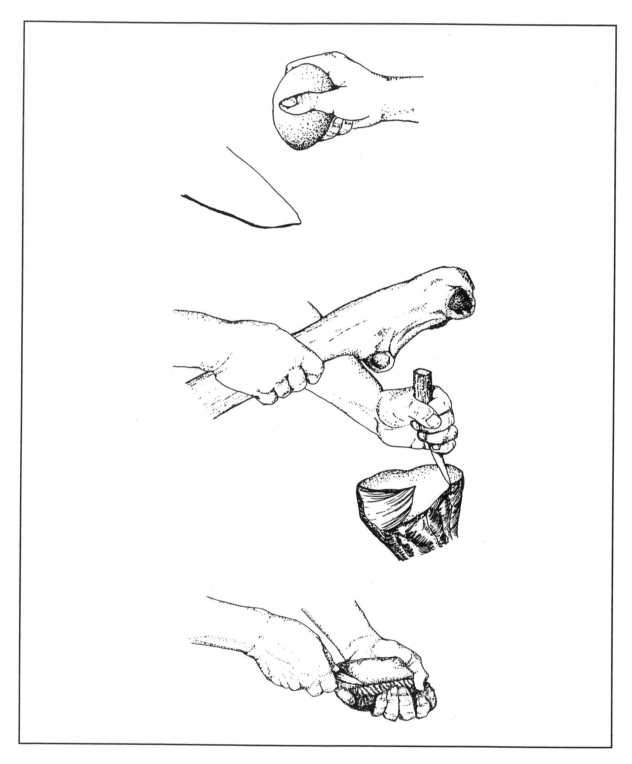

Fig. 10. Direct (top) and indirect (center) percussion. Pressure flaking, done with a protective palm pad, can be seen in the bottom illustration.

thinning bifaces of certain fine-grained basalts). Some lithic analysts suggest that each technique can result in specific flake attributes of the striking platform that can be observed in the debitage (see below).

Production of flaked stone artifacts is the result of a **reduction sequence** (Fig. 11). The sequence begins with the acquisition of the appropriate toolstone and ultimately results in a finished tool. As you will see as you read through this chapter, it is important to analyze all the flaked stone materials that are recovered archaeologically, not just the finished projectile points, knives, and other tools.

It is critical to recognize that flaked stone tool production is a *process* in which raw material is transformed into the desired implement. *The original production of a completed tool is not necessarily the end of the tool's use-life*. The tool may break, be reworked, break again, and be reworked again into a tool with a different function before finally entering the archaeological record as discarded material. Sometimes this process involves several phases of a long *use-life continuum*. As seen in Figure 11, a piece of raw material becomes a bifacial core that is used as a source of material for smaller stone tools. When it becomes so small that it can no longer produce flakes for tools, it becomes a preform for a knife or projectile point. This knife or projectile point may become broken in use, then reworked into a smaller projectile point, or perhaps a drill. When an item that may have started out as a core enters the archaeological record, it may be far removed from its original function and could have been used for numerous tasks during its use-life.

ANATOMY OF A FLAKE

Since most flaked stone artifacts are made from flakes, it is important for the student to have an understanding of the basic attributes of a flake. A typical flake is shown in Figure 12. It consists of a **platform** (where the core was struck by the hammer), a **bulb of percussion** (on percussion flakes), an **eraillure scar**, and **compression rings**. Flakes have dorsal (top) and ventral (bottom) aspects (Fig. 12). The dorsal aspect of a flake is important to consider in debitage analysis because it often bears clues to production/reduction stages. If the dorsal aspect bears evidence of **cortex** (the outer rind of cobbles or other raw material), then the flake represents an early stage of reduction (flake removal). When reference is made to cortex (all cortex, some cortex, etc.), it is only the dorsal aspect being considered.

Stone waste flakes comprise the bulk of many archaeological assemblages in pre-agricultural sites. Most of these are production detritus resulting from stone tool manufacturing, or what archaeologists call **debitage**. The analysis of these artifacts can supply insight into production intensity, the stage in the reduction sequence(s) represented at a site, and sometimes even the types of stone tools that were being produced (even if the stone tools themselves are absent from the site). This type of analysis will be described in more detail below.

FLAKED STONE TOOLS

The classification of flaked stone is the first step in the analysis of this important artifact grouping. Flaked stone tools (as opposed to debitage, considered separately) can be divided into any number of categories (as all things can); archaeologists prefer a descriptive rather than a functional system, since function is usually assumed, often on little evidence. Flaked stone tools are generally divided into the following categories: bifaces (including most projectile points), unifaces, cores, and flake

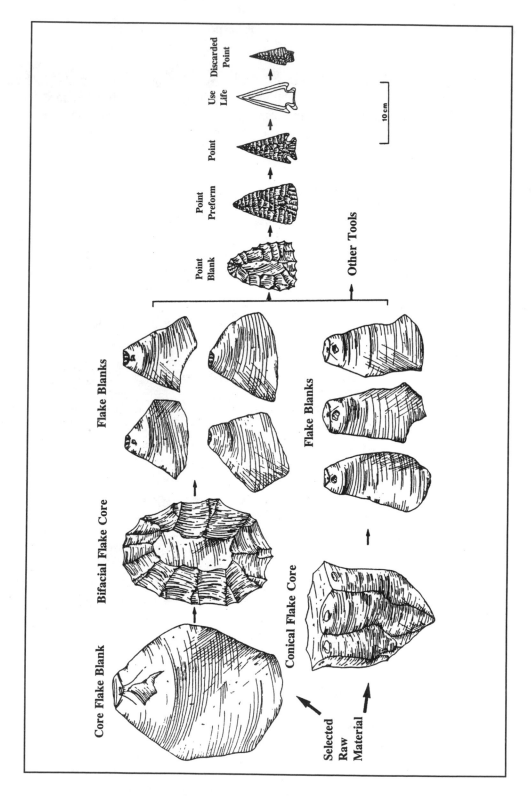

Fig. 11. A core reduction/tool production sequence and use-life continuum (courtesy of J. J. Flenniken).

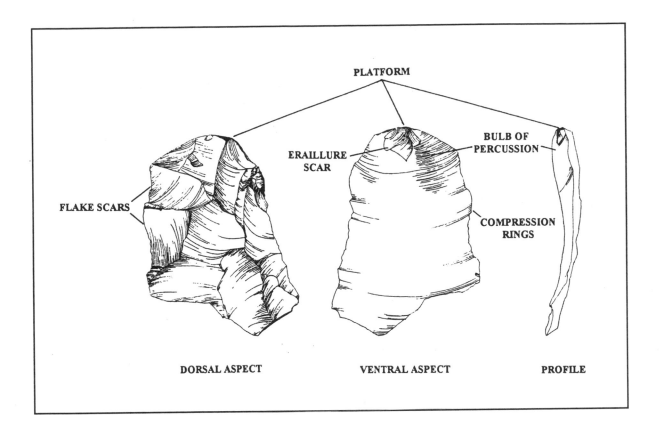

Fig. 12. A typical flake with attributes shown

tools. Two exceptions to the descriptive "rule" are projectile points and cores (both functional categories). These exceptions are justified since these two artifact classes are well-known. Each of these categories of stone tools and tool production by-products is discussed below, beginning with a discussion of bifaces.

BIFACES

A biface is defined as any lithic material flaked on two sides or surfaces. Most classic stone tools, from small arrow points to large hand axes, fall into this category. Cores (see below) usually do not fall into the biface category, although some bifaces were used as cores.

Projectile Points

Often refereed to by the layperson as "arrowheads," projectile points are perhaps the most commonly recognized North American artifact. Most points are flaked on both sides and so fall into the category of biface (however, there may be unifacial projectile points).

The term projectile point is used as a generic classification, since in the field it may not be easy for the archaeologist to differentiate between arrow points and dart points. The bow and arrow is a recent technology in the New World, having appeared south of the Arctic only within the last 2,000 years. In the Old World, the bow and arrow may date as far back as 15,000 years. Prior to this, the *atlatl* (''spear thrower'') was the common weapon launching system for *darts*, which had the appearance of large arrows. The atlatl first appeared in Europe approximately 20,000 years ago. Dart points are generally larger than arrow points and are often used as a general indicator of time at archaeological sites. *Thrusting spears* were used throughout the human occupation of both the New and Old worlds. Spear points are often larger than dart points and are generally lanceolate in form. Typical representatives of these projectile points are presented in Figure 13.

Different regions of North America have variations in the series (within which are types) of projectile points found in archaeological sites. The separation of projectile points into specific groupings based on similarity in shape, size, and weight is known as *typological segregation*. For instance, projectile point series for the Great Basin of western North America include Desert (including the Cottonwood Triangular, Desert Side-notched types), Rose Spring, Elko, and Pinto. Common projectile point typological references for North America include Heizer and Hester (1978), Thomas (1981), and Justice (1987). As noted above, projectile point types can be used in some regions as *general* temporal indicators.

It is important to bear in mind that you should not try to *force* a projectile point into a typological category if it does not clearly fit into any known type within your research area. It is better to be cautious and call such specimens ''unclassified'' than to make a questionable series or type assignment. Another issue to consider is whether unnotched points (especially ovate or triangular specimens) are finished or unfinished specimens. If such specimens appear crude or unfinished in any way, you may want to call them projectile point preforms.

In addition to determining whether your projectile points fit within an existing regional typology, metric attributes are important to record to be able to classify the specimens. Artifact measurement is discussed in greater detail below.

Bifaces as Tools

It is generally an accepted practice today to classify all other bifacially flaked stone artifacts as bifaces rather than with the function-specific terms such as ''scrapers'' or ''knives.'' Function can be difficult to assign to such artifacts without corroborating evidence such as haft (handle) elements (for knives), use-wear, or residues. Exceptions would include items such as drills (Fig. 14), which have ethnographic equivalents, or finely pressure-flaked bifaces that appear to be finished products that could be knives. The danger here, however, is that what look like knives may have also served as lance/spear points. In the absence of special studies (i.e., edge wear, immunological residue analysis) or other clear means of determining function, it is easier to assume that many bifacial tools may have served a variety of functions.

Bifaces as Cores and Preforms

Only recently has the notion that bifaces in North America were oftentimes used as a source of material for tool flakes (Kelly 1988; Wilke and Flenniken 1988) become widely accepted. The biface makes an efficacious core that is easy to transport (unlike large, blocky polyhedral or unifacial cores).

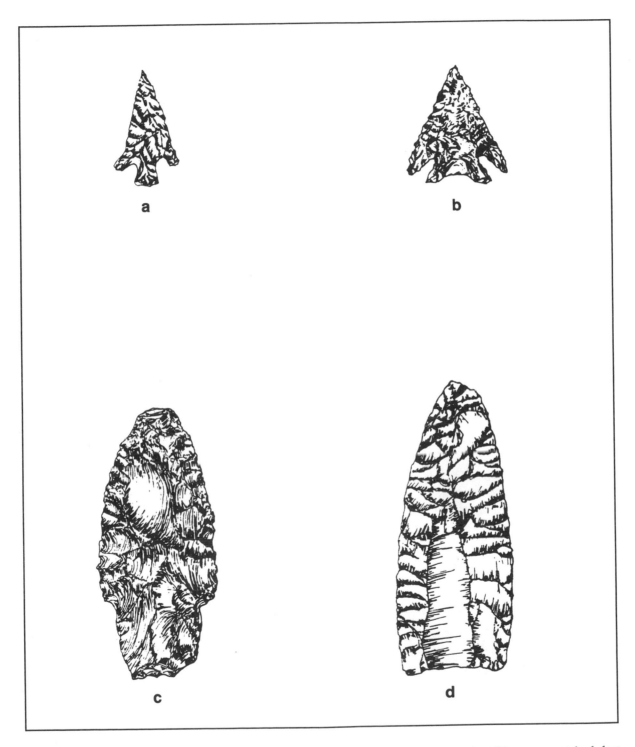

Fig. 13. Typical North American projectile points: (a) corner-notched arrow point; (b) corner-notched dart point; (c) early Archaic stemmed (dart/spear/knifc?) point; (d) Paleoindian "fluted" (Clovis) thrusting spear point.

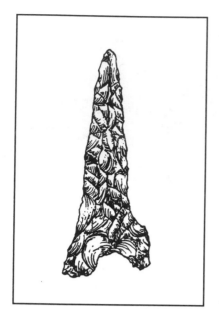

Since it is a source of numerous flakes, a biface also maximizes the amount of cutting edge (in terms of flake tools) the core can produce. The difficulty in categorizing bifaces as cores specifically is that once the core was exhausted, it was probably used as a preform for a pressure flaked tool, or perhaps an item suitable for trade purposes.

Biface Classification

Since it is likely that most biface specimens represent a point in a continuum rather than an end product (especially fragmentary specimens), it may be more useful to classify bifaces as to stage of production/reduction. *Early-stage* bifaces (Fig. 15a) have sinuous edges (called *margins*) and simple surface topography (simple referring to a limited number of flake scars). *Late-stage* bifaces (Fig. 15b) have straight margins and complex surface topography (numerous, patterned flake scars). For a useful discussion of biface staging, refer to Callahan (1979).

Fig. 14. An example of a drill (no scale).

UNIFACES

Unifaces are stone artifacts that are worked only on one side and are generally made on flakes. Unifaces are often called "scrapers" and have ethnographic equivalents in the form of hide scrapers throughout North America and elsewhere. Figure 16 shows an example of a unifacial tool.

As noted above, some scholars have categorized what could be unidirectional cores (see below) from the American Southwest as pulping tools or "scraper planes" (presumed to have been used to process yucca fiber and other plant products). Which is it? When faced with this conundrum, you should not be concerned as long as you are consistent and present all the data about the artifact in your report, including clear illustrations. If future scientists disagree with your assessment (and someone always will), they at least will have the data to properly evaluate your findings.

CORES

Cores are the lithic mass from which flakes are removed. They can be bifacial, as we have seen, or they can be uni- or multidirectional. Examples of cores can be seen in Figure 17. *Unidirectional cores* have flakes removed from one direction, while *multidirectional cores* have flakes removed from two or more directions.

As with bifacial cores, uni- and multidirectional cores may be only a step in one use-life continuum. Figure 18 illustrates how a core, for example, can become a tool (hammerstone) then become a core again later in its use-life. *Core tools* are often made from discarded cores and often appear to have been used as hammers, choppers, or scraping tools (Fig. 19). Sometimes there is indisputable evidence of the use of an expended core as a tool, such as battering or polished edges. Unfortunately, this

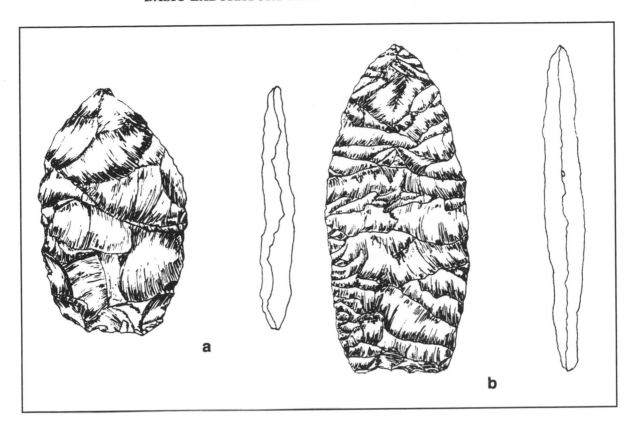

Fig. 15. Examples of early (a) and late (b) stage bifaces (note margin and surface topography, no scale).

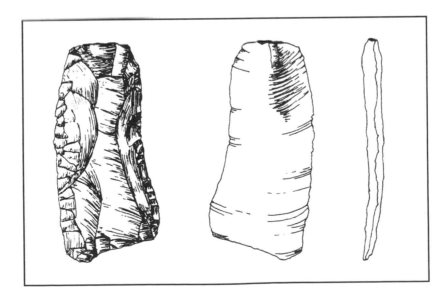

Fig. 16. A unifacial flake tool (no scale). In addition to remnant detachment scars on the dorsal surface, two edges have been worked, but only on one side.

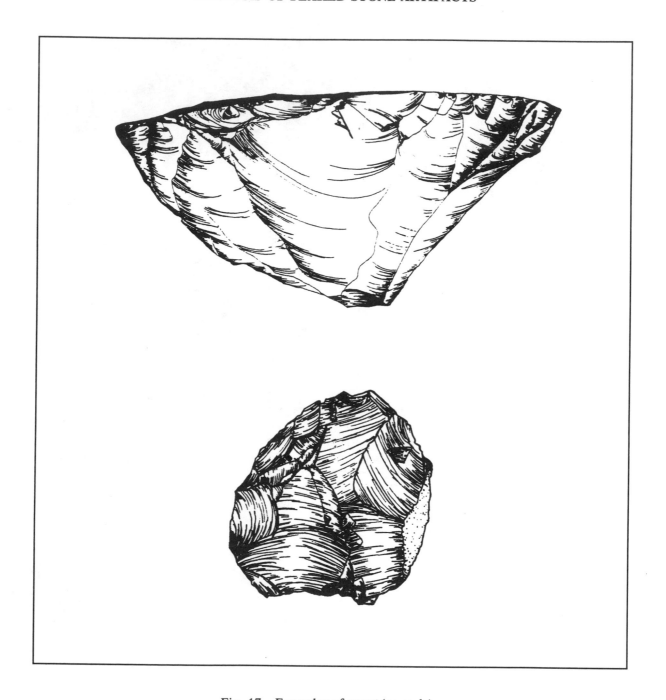

Fig. 17. Examples of cores (no scale).

distinction is not always clear-cut. The most perplexing example is that of the ''scraper plane'' commonly described as a scraper by some (and would make it fall under the heading uniface rather than core) and simply a unidirectional core by others. For purposes of this text, it is best to opt for the more parsimonious of the two positions and describe such specimens as cores. As with bifaces, maximum dimensions and weight should be metrically recorded in tabular form.

50

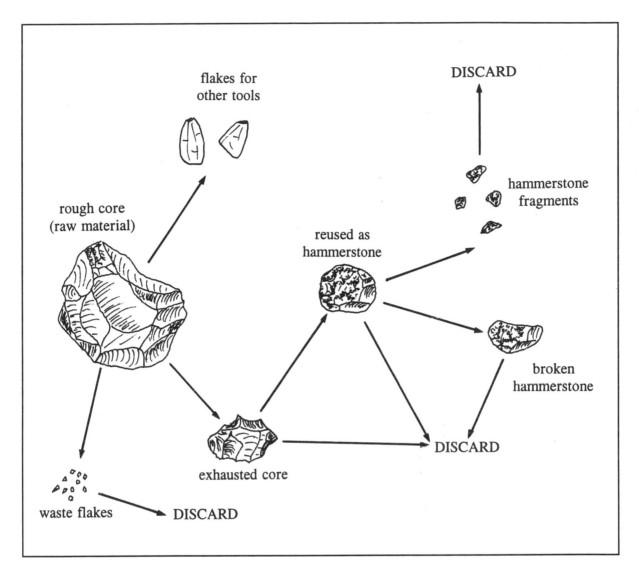

Fig. 18.   The hypothetical use-life continuum of a core. The initial core produces numerous flakes that will be used to manufacture tools; once no further flakes can be removed, it may be discarded or reused as a hammerstone. If the hammerstone breaks in a way to create a workable platform, then the hammerstone fragment could be used as a unidirectional core for microblades. This scenario is based on the interpretation of flaked stone artifacts from the Las Montañas site in southern San Diego County, California.

FLAKE TOOLS

Stone flakes hold the sharpest edges known in the natural world. A freshly produced flake off a core has an edge that is, in many instances, only a single molecule in thickness. Therefore, it is not surprising that flakes with worn or microflaked edges are common in archaeological flaked stone assemblages. Flakes make great cutting and butchering tools in themselves, but not all wear on the edge

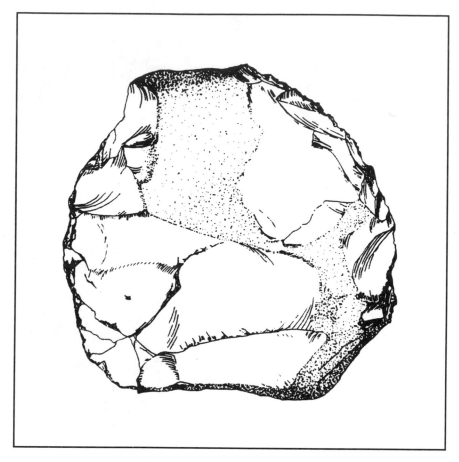

Fig. 19. Example of a chopper/core tool (no scale).

of a flake is necessarily the result of such activities. During cataloguing, the edges of flakes should always be examined for evidence of modification. When such evidence is found, the most parsimonious classification would be *edge-modified flake* rather than "flake with use wear," since there is always the possibility that some other process (e.g., prehistoric or modern trampling) may have produced the modification in question. It is also important to observe whether the edge modification looks recent; sometimes excavation, screening, or even transportation from the site (so called "bag wear") can result in spurious "use" wear on flake edges. However, any edge-modified flakes should be catalogued separately so that they can be examined microscopically and selected as possible candidates for residue and/or edge-wear analysis during flaked stone studies (described below).

WHAT ABOUT HAMMERSTONES?

Hammerstones themselves are generally not flaked stone tools, but they are used in the production of such and are common artifacts in sites where stone tool manufacturing activities have taken place. Although hammerstones have been fashioned from multidirectional cores (see above), they are often fist-sized cobbles with evidence of multiple impacts or unusual wear on one or more ends (see Fig. 20). Their presence or absence in a site may provide important information about stoneworking activities.

52

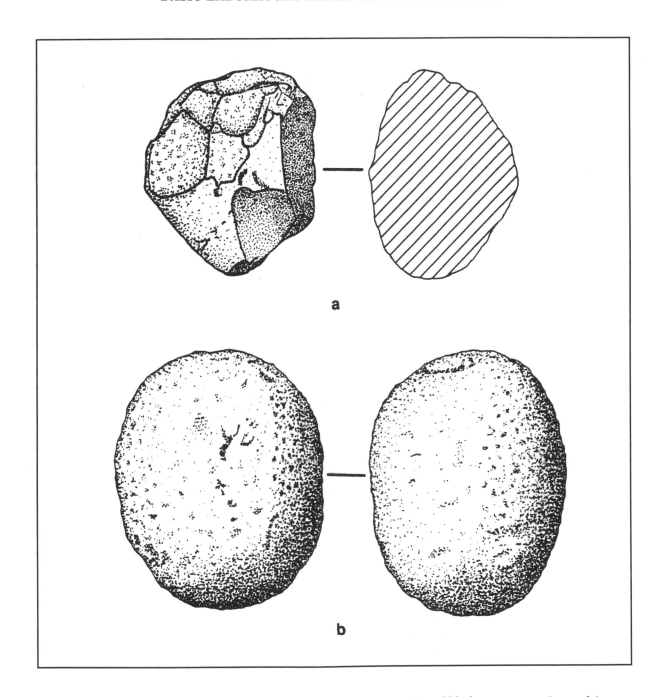

Fig. 20. Examples of hammerstones: (a) core hammerstone; (b) cobble hammerstone (no scale).

MEASUREMENT OF FLAKED STONE ARTIFACTS

Accurate measurements of artifacts is an important part of the data presentation of an archaeological report. This information may be employed in the typological classification of projectile points (e.g., Thomas 1981). It can also be used in the statistical analysis of attributes that can assist in the identification of intra- and intersite patterning of stone tool types. In other words, by looking at the measurement data, archaeologists can compare artifacts that are found within a site or between numerous sites in a region. With this information, archaeologists (today and in the future) can address issues such as chronology (e.g., can certain flaked stone artifacts, such as projectile points, be used as time markers?), diffusion, and even technological change through time.

Flaked stone artifacts generally have a distal and proximal aspect. The distal end is that area toward the tip (or working end), and the proximal region that portion of the artifact that includes the base (the butt or handle area). When referring to artifact fragments, they are described as being proximal, distal, or midsection. Many bifacial and unifacial artifacts and simple flake tools are measured using "standard" dimensions (length, width, thickness). Each measurement should be taken three times. Incomplete specimens should be noted as such. All flaked stone artifacts should be weighed to the nearest tenth of a gram.

Typically, projectile points have a greater number of measurable attributes than most flaked stone artifacts. These include maximum length, maximum width, base width (if different from maximum width), neck width (the measurement between the most distal points in the notch) and maximum thickness. An example of these measurements on a projectile point are shown in Figure 21. An example of typical projectile point data as it would be reported in an archaeological report can be seen in Table 1.

DEBITAGE ANALYSIS

Debitage (a French word for "waste") consists of the flakes, shatter, and other debris from the manufacture or maintenance of flaked stone tools. Until recently, debitage was not considered to be particularly significant to our understanding of human behavior and in some instances was not collected at all during archaeological excavations. The analysis of debitage has, however, taken on a new, important role in flaked stone studies, in large part due to replicative or experimental flintknapping. By identifying flakes to particular technological categories, it is possible to gain valuable insights into site-specific reduction/production strategies. The study of flakes adds an additional dimension to the traditional flaked stone analysis.

TECHNOLOGICAL ANALYSIS

The technological analysis of flakes involves the categorization by technological attributes (type of platform, presence/absence of cortex, evidence of bipolar reduction, biface-thinning flakes, etc.). This type of analysis is very specialized and still in its infancy. Archaeologists are becoming increasingly aware of the importance of studying lithic flakes and most are engaging in at least some level of debitage analysis.

Debitage Types

Separating debitage into various technological types is a relatively new practice and various investigators have differing approaches based on experimental flake assemblages (Sullivan and Rozen 1985; Amick and Mauldin 1989; Ingbar et al. 1989; Prentiss and Romanski 1989; Rozen and Sullivan 1989; Flenniken et al. 1990; Patterson 1990; Yohe 1992). Most investigators agree that there are several

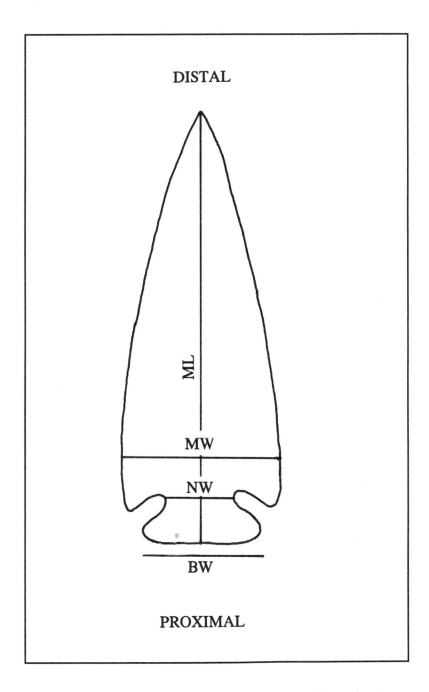

Fig. 21.   Typical attributes of a projectile point: ML = maximum
length; MW = maximum width; BW = base width; NW =
neck width (if present).

types of flakes that have specific attributes that allow them to be technologically segregated.   These
include *primary* (or *cortical*) flakes (flakes with the dorsal aspect completely covered by cortex),
secondary (or *partially cortical*) flakes (flakes possessing some cortex on their dorsal aspect), and *tertiary*

Table 1
PROVENIENCE AND ATTRIBUTES[a] OF PROJECTILE POINTS, CA-SBR-288

Cat. No.	Provenience	Material	Length	Width	Thickness	Weight	Fig.
PINTO SERIES							
487	TU-7, 40-50 cm.	rhyolite	24.9[b]	25.3	7.5	4.2[b]	12a
930	TU-9, 10-20 cm.	chalcedony	35.8	17.0	6.7	3.6	12b
HUMBOLDT SERIES							
820	TU-8, 110-120 cm.	rhyolite	43.2[b]	17.2	5.2	5.3[b]	12c
ELKO SERIES							
363	TU-6, 10-20 cm.	chalcedony	16.0[b]	19.2	5.0	1.5[b]	12d
1955	TU-7, 10-20 cm.	rhyolite	27.9	25.4	5.2	4.3	12e
1605	TU-10, 100-110 cm.	rhyolite	30.1[b]	30.0	7.2	5.6[b]	12f
1623	TU-10, 110-120 cm.	chert	29.0[b]	23.8	7.1	5.8[b]	12g
ROSE SPRING SERIES							
1186	TU-10, 10-20 cm.	chalcedony	41.0	10.5	4.9	1.7	12h
EASTGATE SERIES							
1583	TU-10, 90-100 cm.	chert	30.0	16.8	3.0	1.1	12i
DESERT SERIES (Desert Side-notched)							
1868	surface	chalcedony	14.0[b]	6.9[b]	2.5	0.1[b]	13a
309	TU-5, 30-40 cm.	chalcedony	19.2[b]	17.5	4.0	1.4[b]	13b
446	TU-7, 20-30 cm.	obsidian	17.0[b]	13.3[b]	3.0	0.4[b]	13c
963	TU-9, 20-30 cm.	chalcedony	25.0	9.9	2.8	0.5	13d
1057	TU-9, 70-80 cm.	jasper	18.5[b]	9.4[b]	4.0	0.7[b]	13e
1159	TU-10, 0-10 cm.	chalcedony	10.0[b]	10.0[b]	2.4	0.3[b]	13f
1205	TU-10, 10-20 cm.	chert	21.2	15.1	4.0	0.7	13g
1368	TU-10, 30-40 cm.	chert	20.7[b]	12.8	3.1	0.6[b]	13h
1409	TU-10, 30-40 cm.	rhyolite	20.2	14.5[b]	2.1	0.5[b]	13i
1410	TU-10, 30-40 cm.	chert	17.0	10.9	2.5	0.3	13j
1446	TU-10, 40-50 cm.	rhyolite	19.7	10.5[b]	2.7	0.4[b]	13k
1957	TU-10A, 40-50 cm.	rhyolite	17.1	17.0	2.9	0.5	13l
DESERT SERIES (Cottonwood Triangular)							
505	TU-7, 50-60 cm.	jasper	16.0[b]	14.0	3.8	0.8[b]	14a
524	TU-7, 60-70 cm.	rhyolite	36.0	20.2	6.0	3.2	14b
705	TU-8, 20-30 cm.	chert	20.9	16.0	3.9	0.9	14c
1314	TU-10, 20-30 cm.	chalcedony	25.5	6.7[b]	2.0	0.3[b]	14d
1624	TU-10, 110-120 cm.	chert	12.6[b]	12.1	3.1	0.4[b]	14e
1802	TU-10A, 60-70 cm.	chalcedony	17.9[b]	17.8	3.2	0.8[b]	14f

[a] metric attributes in millimeters and grams
[b] incomplete measurement

(*interior* or *noncortical*) flakes (those having no cortex), all of which are illustrated in Figure 22. In the study of a collection of debitage from an archaeological site, a comparatively high incidence of primary flakes (usually > 25%, based on experimental data) and broken early-stage bifaces would be indicative of quarrying activity involving early-stage raw material reduction. Conversely, if the site contains few

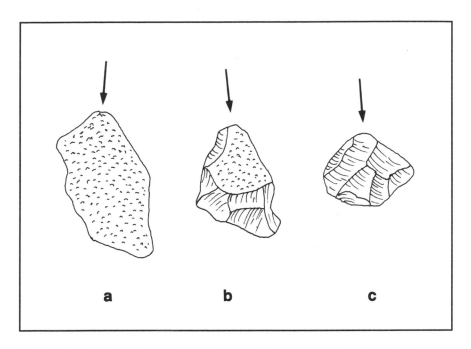

Fig. 22.   Examples of flake types (stippling denotes cortex): (a) primary or
cortical (all cortex on the dorsal aspect); (b) secondary (some cortex
on the dorsal aspect); (c) tertiary (no cortex on the dorsal aspect).
Arrow indicates direction of force (no scale).

or no primary flakes but numerous late-stage bifaces and projectile points, this would suggest the other
end of the continuum, that raw materials had been reduced elsewhere (a quarrying area) and were brought
to the site in pieces that had been worked only slightly (in most instances to reduce weight if the raw
material occurs in large pieces).

Another debitage type usually agreed upon by flaked stone analysts is the *biface thinning flake*.
Biface thinning flakes are usually curved in cross section longitudinally from the platform to the
termination, since they have been removed from a curved surface (Fig. 23). They also typically possess
either single or multifaceted platforms.   *Single-facet platforms* are those with a single plane of
detachment (Fig. 24a) while *multifaceted platforms* are the detached margins of bifaces or some
multidirectional cores, so their morphology is more complex (Fig. 24b) than single-facet platforms.
Single-facet platforms can also be indicative of simple flakes removed from a unidirectional core. *Early-*
versus *late-stage* biface thinning flakes can be differentiated by the complexity of the surface topography
(number of remanent flake scars) on the dorsal aspect of the flake and the flake curvature. The utility
of identifying, separating, and quantifying biface thinning flakes by early and late stages is that it may
help, along with sorting by presence/absence of cortex, to define the level of lithic reduction activity
occurring at a particular archaeological site.

A type of nonflake debitage is called *shatter*. Shatter is a term used to define all angular waste
resulting from stone toolmaking activities that is not otherwise diagnostic. Other flake types that have
been proposed include platform preparation flakes, notching flakes (such as the notches found in certain

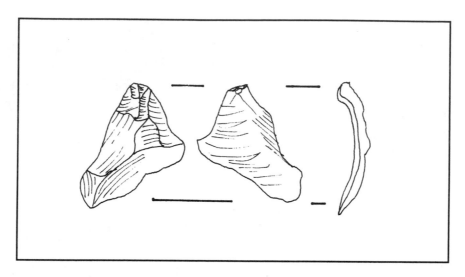

Fig. 23. A typical biface thinning flake (no scale).

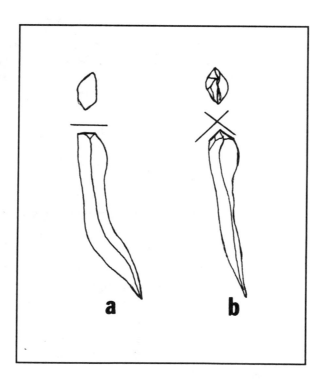

Fig. 24. Superior views and profiles of two flakes showing the two major platform types: (a) single-facet platform; (b) multifaceted platform. Multi-faceted platforms, characteristic of later stage biface thinning, are frequently comprised of a portion of the detached biface margin.

projectile points), and pressure flakes, to name a few. At present, these distinctions are qualitative and will require a full descriptive treatise before they receive general use. An example of a debitage analysis/classification form is presented as Figure 25.

DEBITAGE ANALYSIS FORM

SITE_____   UNIT_____   LEVEL_____

MATERIAL_____   CAT. NO._____

Flake Type	Classification			Totals	Weight (g.)	Comments
	Primary (all cortex)	Secondary (some cortex)	Tertiary (no cortex)			
complete, early-stage biface thinning						
fragment, early-stage biface thinning						
complete, late-stage biface thinning						
fragment, late-stage biface thinning						
complete, pressure						
fragment, pressure						
shatter						
nonbiface reduction						
bipolar						
other						

Fig. 25. Example of a debitage classification form.

Up to this point, the discussion has focused on the specific analysis of each individual flake. The analysis of the technological attributes of individual flakes may be too expensive or time-consuming in some instances, and specialized skills often beyond the experience of the beginning student are required. A type of debitage analysis that is employed by many archaeologists today is known as *aggregate* or *mass analysis*. The shift in focus in this form of analysis is from the attributes on individual flakes to recording fewer technological attributes of a larger sample of debitage. The main advantage of this approach is that larger samples can be analyzed and still provide some technological interpretation.

Mass analysis is a type of aggregate analysis that groups flakes by size using nested screens of various meshes (see Ahler 1989). For example, a sample of debitage is size graded using standard sieve sizes (1", 1/2", 1/4", 1/8", etc.). The weight and number of these flakes are recorded, as well as the number of cortical (primary and secondary) flakes. These data can be used to compare ratios of weight to number of flakes per group, as well as the relative number of cortical flakes per size class. However, at this point in the development of debitage analysis, the linkage between some of the patterns observed in mass analysis and the tool manufacturing processes they represent are not clearly established. Like individual flake analysis, the variables recorded are dependent on experimental data for behavioral interpretation. Archaeologists conducting such studies will need to continue to develop a data bank assembled from a wide range of experimental studies before such analyses can reach their full interpretive potential.

REPORTING THE RESULTS

Once the particular types of flakes have been sorted out from the debitage analysis, it is then necessary to tabulate the results. Depending on the size of the site and the sample (a 20,000-flake sample from a site may be both time and cost prohibitive), only a portion of the site (i.e., excavation units from the interior of a rock shelter surrounding a feature) or a sample (flakes from selected units) might be selected for a full-scale analysis. Once your analytical universe is defined, the flakes should be sorted by material type (i.e., obsidian, chert, basalt), then by technological type within each category of raw material. The vertical aggregation unit should always be the excavation level (whether it be natural or arbitrary).

General maximum size of each flake should also be noted. For example, if the flakes from one level are, on average, 10 cm. larger than the flakes of the same material in the levels below and above it, there may be a drastic change in raw material or core size that is important to record. As described above, flakes can be rapidly size-graded with the use of rested sieves of various sizes, or, if a small sample size is being analyzed, the maximum dimension of complete flakes can be measured with sliding calipers. You may wish to produce a tally sheet with columns for the flake types and attributes (see Fig. 25) to simplify the process and make it easier to input your flake information into a data base program for analytical manipulation.

The presentation of the data should be in tabular form, similar to the example seen in Table 2. In this example, only one flake attribute variable, presence/absence of cortex, is considered. If one is using multiple variables (as would be the case if you used a form like the one presented in Fig. 25), you may wish to express these data in separate tables (i.e., ratio of biface thinning flakes to "other" flakes), or express the information graphically as illustrated in Figure 26. Several data can be displayed more clearly in graphs such as this one. As shown in Figure 26, change in the maximum length of both early and late stage biface thinning flakes by depth (hence time) is readily apparent.

Interpretation will depend on patterning; usually it is presumed to be vertical but it may also apply horizontally in some features (microsampling around a fire hearth, for example). Gross changes in both material types and/or technological types of flakes through time may be indicative of changes in stone

Table 2
SITE-WIDE VERTICAL DISTRIBUTION OF CRYPTOCRYSTALLINE
FLAKE TYPES, CA-SBR-6580

Depth (cm.)	Primary	Secondary	Interior	Totals
0-10	--	1	10	11
10-20	--	--	23	23
20-30	2	3	27	32
30-40	3	1	25	29
40-50	--	1	23	24
50-60	--	--	22	22
60-70	--	1	13	14
70-80	--	1	8	9
80-90	--	--	12	12
90-100	--	--	5	5
100-110	1	--	1	2
110-120	--	--	2	2
120-130	--	--	2	2
130-140	--	--	1	1
140-150	--	--	--	--
150-160	--	--	1	1
160-170	--	--	--	--
170-180	--	--	1	1
TOTALS	6	8	176	190

tool production activities or even site function. Remember, it is important to compare these data with the other data sets from any archaeological site, such as numbers and/or types of flaked stone tools, presence or absence of particular artifacts (ground stone, ornamental) or features (fire hearths, house pits), as well as the types and numbers of floral and faunal remains. This will give you a framework within which to develop your interpretation of the data as presented in the example below.

An Example

An example of this holistic approach to site interpretation using debitage analysis in conjunction with other site data is presented in the following scenario. Stratum A at the hypothetical Wingnut Site (dating 4,000 to 2,000 B.P.) contains a large number of cortical flakes of chert, the majority having single-facet platforms, a few early-stage biface fragments, numerous large flake tools, no projectile points, a large number of milling implements, and few faunal remains. Stratum B (dating from 2,000

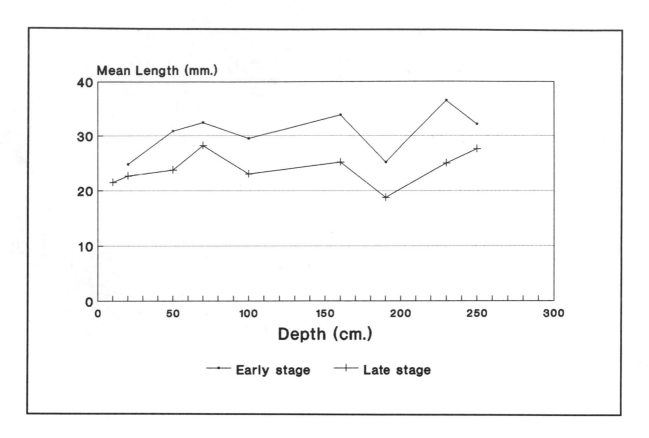

Fig. 26. An example of a graphic presentation of debitage analysis data. Changes in early- and late-stage biface thinning flake size through time is readily apparent when the data are plotted on a simple line graph. Also shown are the mean values of experimentally produced flakes following an hypothesized reduction strategy for this site (from Yohe [1992]).

to 500 B.P.) contains no cortical flakes, numerous small projectile points and late-stage bifaces, debitage of small size, no milling implements, and thousands of faunal remains, which are mostly deer. The change in flaked stone usage corresponds to change in site function; the earlier occupation of the site (Stratum A) seems to have involved a focus on plant food resources and the importation of chert cobbles to be made into rough flake tools for use along with the milling equipment for plant processing. With a complete absence of plant processing equipment, the later occupation apparently focused on deer hunting, with flaked stone activities involving only late stage knife and projectile point production. Stone materials were brought in as shaped blanks or preforms, requiring only final shaping into hunting implements. As we can see from this simplistic hypothetical example, the information from the flaked stone studies and the analysis of other site materials reinforce each other.

SPECIAL STUDIES

Two possible areas of potential utility regarding the discrimination of artifact function should be considered by the archaeologist during the laboratory analysis of flaked stone: (1) use-wear analysis and (2) protein residue analysis (Newman and Julig 1989). There is a vast body of literature dealing with the first of these, including a good summary of the more recent developments in Yerkes and Kardulias (1993). Numerous investigators have experimentally used replicated stone tools for a variety of tasks (cutting meat, vegetal matter, bone, etc.) and have analyzed the edge wear resulting from these tasks for the purpose of consistently identifying a particular wear pattern with a specific processing activity. The experts are divided as to how useful this type of analysis is for discriminating artifact function. For purposes of general descriptive analysis, however, low power magnification (10X to 30X) observation of flaked stone artifacts for edge damage, striae (series of parallel lines), and polish is appropriate for most novice investigators with access to a binocular dissecting microscope. A review of references on use wear studies may be found in Yerkes and Kardulias (1993) or at the end of this chapter.

Immunological analysis is a new avenue of research that may lead towards a better understanding of tool function (although there is considerable debate regarding its validity, see Chapter 13). All plants and animals produce immunoproteins that are found in their bodily fluids. These proteins apparently become attached to stone implements during killing (projectile points) and processing (knives, scrapers, hammerstones). Because of their robusticity and affinity for silica, these proteins have been demonstrated to survive thousands of years in the soil. These proteins can be removed and analyzed using a method called cross-over immunoelectrophoresis (CIEP) to identify the *general* taxonomic group (family level of classification) of plants or animals to which the proteins belong. This type of analysis is in its infancy, and only a few laboratories in North America specialize in CIEP analysis of proteins.

FLAKED STONE ANALYSIS AND CULTURAL PROCESS: EXPERIMENTAL STUDIES

A brief description of how to differentiate the basic types of stone tools and the waste materials resulting from their production was presented above. The importance of using the flaked stone data in concert with other archaeological information from a site in order to arrive at a clearer interpretation of cultural process through time is critical. However, as discussed above, much of this understanding is a result of experimental studies that have only recently become a part of flaked stone analysis. The production of stone tools experimentally by "flintknapper" archaeologists gives us an idea of what to expect in the archaeological record. Examining the detritus resulting from attempts at replicating specific technologies has led to a more complete functional understanding of the various levels of human activities flaked stone assemblages may represent. There is still much to be learned from such studies, and as more archaeologists begin to use this avenue of research, a greater number of ways to approach flaked stone analysis will emerge.

REFERENCES

Ahler, Stanley A.
   1989   Mass Analysis of Flaking Debris: Studying the Forest Rather Than the Trees. In: Alternative Approaches to Lithic Analysis, D. O. Henry and G. H. Odell, eds., pp. 85-118. Washington, D. C.: Archaeological Papers of the American Anthropological Association Number 1.

Amick, Daniel S., and Raymond P. Mauldin
   1989   Comment on Sullivan and Rozen's "Debitage Analysis and Archaeological Interpretation." American Antiquity 54(1):166-168.

Callahan, E.
1979   The Basics of Biface Knapping in the Eastern Fluted Point Tradition: A Manual for Flintknappers and Lithic Analysts. Archaeology of Eastern North America 9(1):1-180.

Flenniken, J. Jeffrey, and E. G. Garrison
1975   Thermally Altered Novaculite and Stone Tool Manufacturing Techniques. Journal of Field Archaeology 2:125-132.

Flenniken, J. Jeffrey, Terry Ozbun, and J. A. Markos
1990   Archaeological Testing and Evaluation of the Sycan Marsh Site, 35LK2336. Report on file at Fremont National Forest, Oregon.

Heizer, Robert F., and Thomas R. Hester
1978   Great Basin Projectile Points: Forms and Chronology. Socorro: Ballena Press Publications in Archaeology, Ethnology and History 10.

Ingbar, E. E., M. L. Larson, and B. A. Bradley
1989   A Non-Typological Approach to Debitage Analysis. In: Experiments in Lithic Technology, D. S. Amick and R. P. Mauldin, eds., pp. 117-136. Oxford: BAR International Series 528.

Justice, N. D.
1987   Stone Age Spear and Arrow Points of the Midcontinental and Eastern United States: A Modern Survey and Reference. Bloomington: Indiana University Press.

Kelly, Robert L.
1988   The Three Sides of a Biface. American Antiquity 53(4):717-734.

Newman, Margaret E., and P. Julig
1989   The Identification of Protein Residues on Lithic Artifacts from a Stratified Boreal Forest Site. Canadian Journal of Archaeology 13:119-132.

Patterson, Leland W.
1990   Characteristics of Bifacial-Reduction Flake Size Distribution. American Antiquity 53(3):550-558.

Prentiss, W. C., and E. J. Romanski
1989   Experimental Evaluation of Sullivan and Rozen's Debitage Typology. In: Experiments in Lithic Technology, Daniel S. Amick and Raymond P. Mauldin, eds., pp. 89-100. Oxford: BAR International Series 528.

Rozen, Kenneth C., and Alan P. Sullivan, III
1989   On the Nature of Lithic Reduction and Lithic Analysis. American Antiquity 54(1):179-184.

Sullivan, Alan P., III, and Kenneth C. Rozen
    1985   Debitage Analysis and Archaeological Interpretation. American Antiquity 50(4):755-779.

Thomas, David H.
    1981   How to Classify the Projectile Points from Monitor Valley, Nevada. Journal of California and Great Basin Anthropology 3(1):7-43.

Wilke, Philip J., and J. Jeffrey Flenniken
    1988   Experimental Reduction of a Bifacial Core. Paper presented at the Great Basin Anthropological Conference, Park City, Utah.

Yerkes, R. W., and P. N. Kardulias
    1993   Recent Developments in the Analysis of Lithic Artifacts. Journal of Archaeological Research 1(2):89-120.

Yohe, Robert M., II
    1992   A Reevaluation of Western Great Basin Cultural Chronology and Evidence for the Timing of the Introduction of the Bow and Arrow to Eastern California Based on New Excavations at the Rose Spring Site (CA-INY-327). Ph.D. dissertation, University of California, Riverside.

ADDITIONAL READING

Below are some references for those interested in pursuing flaked stone analysis further.

Anderson, P. C.
    1980   A Testimony of Prehistoric Tasks: Diagnostic Residues on Stone Tool Working Edges. World Archaeology 12:181-194.

Bamforth, Douglas B.
    1988   Investigating Microwear Polishes with Blind Tests: The Institute Results in Context. Journal of Archaeological Science 15:11-23.

Bloomer, William W.
    1991   Reduction Assemblage Models in the Interpretation of Lithic Technology at the Tosawihi Quarries, North-Central Nevada. Journal of California and Great Basin Anthropology 13(2):204-216.

Cotterell, B., and J. Kamminga
    1979   The Mechanics of Flaking. In: Lithic Use-Wear Analysis, Brian Hayden, ed., pp. 97-112. New York: Academic Press.

Crabtree, Don E.
    1967   Notes on Experiments in Flintknapping 4: Tools Used to Make Flaked Stone Artifacts. Tebiwa 10(1):60-71.

1982   An Introduction to Flintworking. Occasional Papers of the Idaho Museum of Natural History No. 28.

Domanski, Marian, and John A. Webb
1992   Effect of Heat Treatment on Siliceous Rocks Used in Prehistoric Lithic Technology. Journal of Field Archaeology 19:601-614.

Flenniken, J. Jeffrey
1981   Replicative Systems Analysis: A Model Applied to Vein Quartz Artifacts from the Hoko River Site. Washington State University Laboratory of Anthropology Reports of Investigations No. 59.

1984   The Past, Present, and Future of Flintknapping: An Anthropological Perspective. Annual Review of Anthropology 13:187-203.

1991   The Diamond Lil Site: Projectile Point Fragments as Indicators of Site Function. Journal of California and Great Basin Anthropology 13(2):180-193.

Flenniken, J. Jeffrey, and Anan Raymond
1986   Morphological Projectile Point Typology: Replication, Experimentation, and Technological Analysis. American Antiquity 51(3):603-614.

Henry, D. O., and George H. Odell (eds.)
1989   Alternative Approaches to Lithic Analysis. Archaeological Papers of the American Anthropological Association No. 1.

Holmes, D.
1990   Review of Alternative Approaches to Lithic Analysis. Antiquity 64:429-431.

Hurcombe, L. M.
1993   Use Wear Analysis and Obsidian: Theory, Experiments, and Results. Sheffield Archaeological Monographs 4.

Juel Jensen, H.
1988   Functional Analysis of Prehistoric Flint Tools by High-Powered Microscopy: A Review of Western European Research. Journal of World Prehistory 2(1):53-88.

Newcomer, M. H., and L. H. Keeley
1979   Testing a Method of Microwear Analysis with Experimental Flint Tools. In: Lithic Use-Wear Analysis, Bryan Hayden, ed., pp. 195-205. New York: Academic Press.

Nielsen, Axel E.
1991   Trampling the Archaeological Record: An Experimental Study. American Antiquity 56(3):483-503.

Ozbun, Terry
    1991   Boulders to Bifaces: Initial Reduction of Obsidian at Newberry Crater, Oregon. Journal of California and Great Basin Anthropology 13(2):147-159.

Plew, Mark G., and James C. Woods
    1985   Observation of Edge Damage and Technological Effects on Pressure-Flaked Stone Tools. In: Stone Tool Analysis: Essays in Honor of Don G. Crabtree, Mark G. Plew, James C. Woods, and Max G. Pavesic, eds., pp. 221-227. Albuquerque: University of New Mexico Press.

Plew, Mark G., James C. Woods, and Max G. Pavesic (eds.)
    1985   Stone Tool Analysis: Essays in Honor of Don E. Crabtree. Albuquerque: University of New Mexico Press.

Scott, Sara A.
    1991   Problems with the Use of Flake Size in Inferring Stages of Lithic Reduction. Journal of California and Great Basin Anthropology 13(2):172-179.

Sheets, Payson
    1975   Behavioral Analysis and the Structure of a Prehistoric Industry. Current Anthropology 16:369-378.

Titmus, Gene L., and James C. Woods
    1986   An Experimental Study of Projectile Point Fracture Patterns. Journal of California and Great Basin Anthropology 8(1):37-49.

Vaughn, P.
    1985   Use-Wear Analysis of Flaked Stone Tools. Tucson: University of Arizona Press.

Wilke, Philip J., and Adella B. Schroth
    1989   Lithic Raw Material Prospects in the Mojave Desert, California. Journal of California and Great Basin Anthropology 11(2):146-174.

Young, D., and Douglas B. Bamforth
    1990   On the Macroscopic Identification of Used Flakes. American Antiquity 55(2):403-409.

Chapter 5

ANALYSIS OF GROUND STONE ARTIFACTS

Joan S. Schneider
University of California, Riverside

DEFINITION

Traditionally, archaeologists have divided stone tools and other objects into two classes: *flaked stone* and *ground stone*. The term "ground stone" has been used in the past to identify stone tools or objects that do not easily fit into the "flaked stone" tool category. This dichotomy is unfortunate. First, it has artificially divided tools and other objects into two classes based on the way they were thought to be made, not the way they were used. Second, the division is invalid because "flaked stone" tools that were used for piercing, cutting, and scraping, such as projectile points, knives, woodworking, and skinworking tools, although often made by removing flakes from a larger piece of stone, were also made by grinding stone into sharp points or edges. In addition, "ground stone" tools that were *used* for grinding and crushing foods (or other materials or objects) that were eventually ground to a smooth surface, were often manufactured in the same way as "flaked stone" tools; they were initially shaped by removing flakes from a larger piece of stone.

Although the term "ground stone" is technically incorrect, it has been used in most, if not all, of the archaeological literature to date and, by convention, is used here. Ground stone artifacts fall into two basic categories: (1) tools that were used to process (grind, smash, crush, smooth, scrape) resources (plant, animal, mineral) and thus became ground and/or polished through *use*; and (2) objects that were ground or polished to produce a smooth finish, as one stage of *manufacture*. Both categories share a common characteristic; a *specific wear pattern* that develops through friction of stone upon stone, or stone upon other substances such as hides, shell, clays, plant fibers, etc.

Examples of artifacts that are ground through *use* are milling implements (milling stones [metates], handstones [manos], pestles, mortars; see below), pottery anvils, abrading tools for working shell, bone, wood, and stone, hideworking tools, and tools used in fiber processing. Examples of objects that are polished in *manufacture* include stone palettes, stone pipes, stone beads and pendants, effigy figures, discoidals and stone balls, arrowshaft straighteners, axes, and hoes. In general, the ground surfaces that resulted from *use* were probably not desirable because the abrasive qualities of the working surfaces were lost, while surfaces that were ground and smoothed in *manufacture* were highly desirable for aesthetic and functional reasons.

In this chapter, the emphasis is on the classification and analysis of ground stone processing tools known as milling implements, one of the most common types of tools found in archaeological sites and the type of tool that you will most often be called upon to describe and interpret during routine archaeological analysis. Please remember that most tools (irrespective of archaeological classification) were used to perform a variety of tasks. This is especially true of milling implements; often they were multipurpose tools.

A NOTE ON PRESERVATION

It often is assumed that stone tools preserve intact in the archaeological record. However, such tools and their surfaces are subject to decomposition and erosion, although it is true that such processes usually act relatively slowly on ground stone tools. Over time, the surfaces of ground stone tools will erode, removing the "ground" surface and making identification as a ground stone artifact very difficult.

Burning greatly accelerates this process. Burning causes the matrix of the stone to break down rapidly and the surface erodes in short order. The identification of burned ground stone tools is sometimes based on general shape (rather than the presence of a ground surface), context, and judgment (experience).

IDENTIFICATION OF GROUND STONE SURFACES

Most rocks are relatively rough-surfaced due to their crystalline nature; there are peaks and troughs on the surface. As the rock surfaces are acted upon by natural forces, such as wind or water, both the peaks and troughs may become smoothed. Human-caused mechanical action and friction of rock-against-rock also smooths rock surfaces. In the case of rock-against-rock, the rough peaks become smoothed and the crystals within the rock become faceted (sheared off), leaving the troughs rough. This is the major characteristic of ground stone used to process hard seeds and other substances where there is a great deal of rock-against-rock contact: surfaces having smoothed or faceted peaks with troughs that are not smoothed (Fig. 27). When other types of substances are processed (e.g., hides, wood, dried meat, plant fibers), this characteristic is not as easy to identify. Sometimes it is very difficult to distinguish surfaces that have become ground or polished by natural forces (e.g., wind and water) from those that have become ground or polished by human action. Careful observation, consideration of the context in which the possible artifact was found, and a few easy techniques can help distinguish the artifact from naturally smoothed rock. In the long run, a "sense" for identification can be developed through experience.

VISUAL IDENTIFICATION

You may be called upon to identify stone artifacts with ground surfaces in the field or in the laboratory. Several helpful hints can help you with this identification.

Look at the artifact. Are there differences in the smoothness of the surface on certain parts of the rock? If a rock is equally smooth on all surfaces, it is unlikely to be a handstone (mano) or a milling stone (metate) used for grinding; the smoothness was probably caused by natural forces.

When the smooth surface of a rock is held up to a strong light at eye level, does this surface glint and shine? This characteristic is due to the shearing or faceting of the crystal faces within the rock, evidence that the smoothing is a result of human action. When viewed with a low-power magnifying

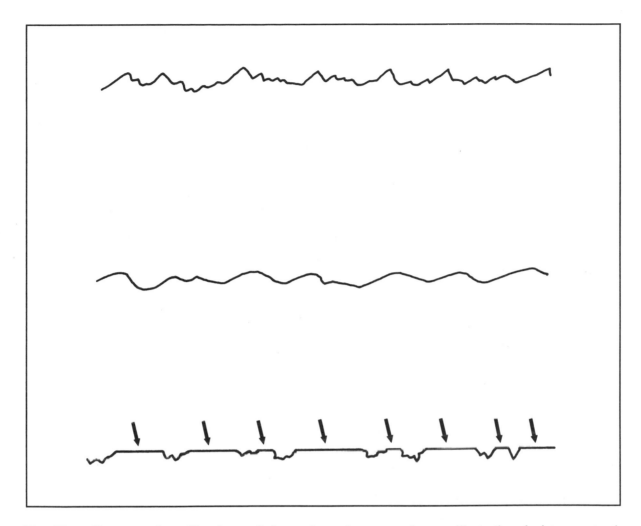

Fig. 27.   Exaggerated profile views of the surface of stones: the top illustration depicts a natural, unweathered surface (note the rough nature of the surface); the middle illustration shows a natural, but waterworn surface (note that all surfaces are smooth); the lower illustration shows a ground surface (note that the tops of the "peaks" are sheared off and flattened [see arrows] while the "valleys" retain their natural surfaces).

glass (e.g., 10X), is the smoothness limited to the rock peaks (the higher portions of the surface), the troughs (lower portions) remaining unsmoothed? This is a characteristic of stone surfaces that are ground by human action.

Do you see a distinct transition between the smooth surface and the rest of the rock, a transition that might even be described as an "edge"? This is a strong indication that you are looking at a ground stone artifact.

Does the rock appear to have a shape that is not natural? In many cases, rocks were purposefully shaped, but often a naturally occurring stone was used without modification.

TACTILE IDENTIFICATION

Sometimes your sense of touch can help you identify ground surfaces. Run your fingertips lightly over the surfaces of a suspected ground stone artifact. Is there a different "feel" on some surfaces when compared to the rest of the rock? Does the surface feel as smooth as satin? This may be an indication that this surface has been achieved by the human mechanical action of rock-upon-rock, especially when ultrasmoothness is combined with one or more of the characteristics described above.

TYPES OF GROUND STONE ARTIFACTS

Milling implements are the most common ground stone artifacts recovered from archaeological sites. They are common because they were used for everyday household chores. Other types of ground stone artifacts were used for special purposes, such as personal adornment, ceremonial occasions, and in the manufacture of other items such as arrowshafts, shell beads and ornaments, and pottery. Still other ground stone artifacts were used for weapons and agricultural tools. We do not know the functions of some ground stone artifacts.

GROUND STONE ARTIFACTS GROUND THROUGH USE

The Mill (Milling Unit)

A mill (milling unit) is always composed of two parts: a moveable stone and a stationary stone. Here, we are considering only stone tools. The student should recognize, however, that there are many cultures where wood and other substances were used for milling tools. For example, the Yuman groups along the Lower Colorado River used wooden mortars; African groups commonly used (and still use) wooden pestles and grinding slabs; among Australian aborigine peoples, grass seeds were (and are) sometimes ground on wooden grinding boards.

In New World cultures (and early Old World cultures), the moveable stone is held in one or both hands and moved upon the stationary stone; it may be called a handstone or a pestle. The stationary stone is a platform of some type; it may be called a milling stone, grinding platform, metate, quern, grinding stone, grinding slick, mortar, bowl, or a variety of other names. It may be flat, concave, or bowl-shaped; it may be readily portable, or too big or heavy to carry around, or may be part of the landscape (as bedrock "slicks" and mortars; see below). Here, two basic types of milling units are considered: (1) the *handstone* and *milling stone*; and (2) the *mortar* (or bowl) and *pestle*.

In Old World cultures, intensive grain milling led to the development of more sophisticated mills, such as the hopper mill, the Pompeii-style mill, and the rotary millstone that was human- or animal-powered. In spite of their sophistication, they still retained the basic two-part milling system and used a moveable stone against a stationary stone platform (see Bennett and Elton [1898] and Curwen [1927] for more information).

Handstones (Manos). A handstone is held in one or both hands and is moved upon the milling stone in a circular, back-and-forth, chopping, or rocking motion. Handstones may be any one of a variety of shapes and sizes and may have one or multiple working surfaces (see Fig. 28 for examples).

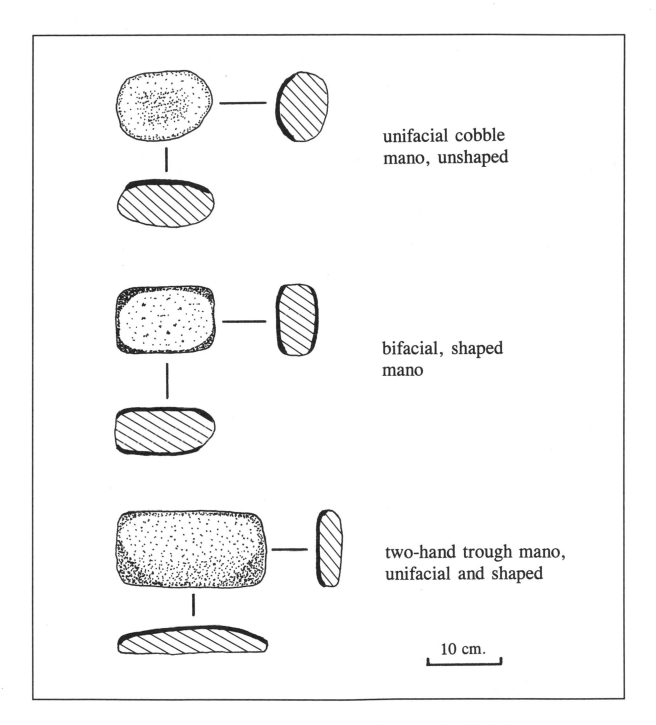

unifacial cobble
mano, unshaped

bifacial, shaped
mano

two-hand trough mano,
unifacial and shaped

10 cm.

Fig. 28. Examples of manos (working surface shown by thick line).

Handstones are often categorized in different ways as a means of grouping them. The "Description and Analysis" section of this chapter presents a handstone typology based loosely on a typology developed by Adams (1991) that considers the number and position of the grinding surfaces on

73

each artifact (Fig. 29). This typology is presented as an example of one way of categorizing handstones, but it is not the only way. Students may follow this typology in their laboratory work, but should be aware that other typologies can be developed that might better suit the questions being asked and the collection being analyzed.

Milling Stones (Metates). Milling stones are the stationary stones upon which some substance is processed and against which the handstone is moved. Milling stones may be portable or nonportable, although some "portable" specimens would be difficult to move because of their size and/or weight. Nonportable milling stones, often found on bedrock outcrops and boulders, are referred to as "bedrock milling features," or "slicks." These features are seldom dealt with in the laboratory, but the same identification and analytical procedures used on portable specimens are applicable.

Milling stones may have one or more flat, slightly concave, basined, or troughed working surfaces, or a combination of any of these (see Fig. 30). The thickness of milling stones limit the possible types of grinding surfaces: a relatively thin milling stone (a slab type) could have a flat or slightly concave grinding surface; a thicker milling stone could exhibit any type of grinding surface.

Pestles. Pestles are cylindrical or subcylindrical stones of varying length, usually showing wear at one or both ends, and generally are used within a mortar to crush, pound, or grind materials (see Fig. 31). Pestles are often shaped in manufacture, but it is not uncommon for appropriately shaped stones to be used as pestles without any type of modification. The latter artifacts may have been used in a "casual" manner with no effort made to select a cylindrical stone; a stone with an end that would fulfill the demands of the task at hand was simply picked up and used. Such artifacts may be very difficult to recognize.

Mortars or Bowls. A mortar is a rock (although there are wooden mortars and bowls) with a manufactured concavity (usually approximately circular) of varying depth and diameter within which materials are pounded, crushed, or ground. The concavity is usually bowl-shaped or cylindrical so as to accommodate a pestle. Mortars are more easily recognizable when their depths exceed their diameters. Mortars may be portable or formed within bedrock outcrops. Like bedrock milling features ("slicks"), bedrock mortars are seldom considered in the laboratory, but are subject to the same identification and analytical procedures as the portable types.

Portable mortars are of two basic forms: "bowl-like" mortars and *hopper mortars*. Bowl-like mortars were manufactured from cobbles and boulders; they have exterior and interior stone walls (Fig. 32). A hopper mortar (Fig. 33) is usually a flat stone with a slight central concavity to which a bottomless basket was attached with some type of mastic material (e.g., asphaltum); the sides of the basket acted as the walls of the mortar. Hopper mortars are much lighter and more portable than bowl-like mortars, but probably required repairs more often because of the limited durability of the basket fibers as compared with stone. The stone base of a hopper mortar can be identified by the circular configuration of the residue of the mastic that was used to attach the basket to the stone.

Other Tools

Experimental archaeology and ethnographic descriptions have suggested that some handstones were used for other purposes besides grinding and pulverizing, and that these also develop ground and

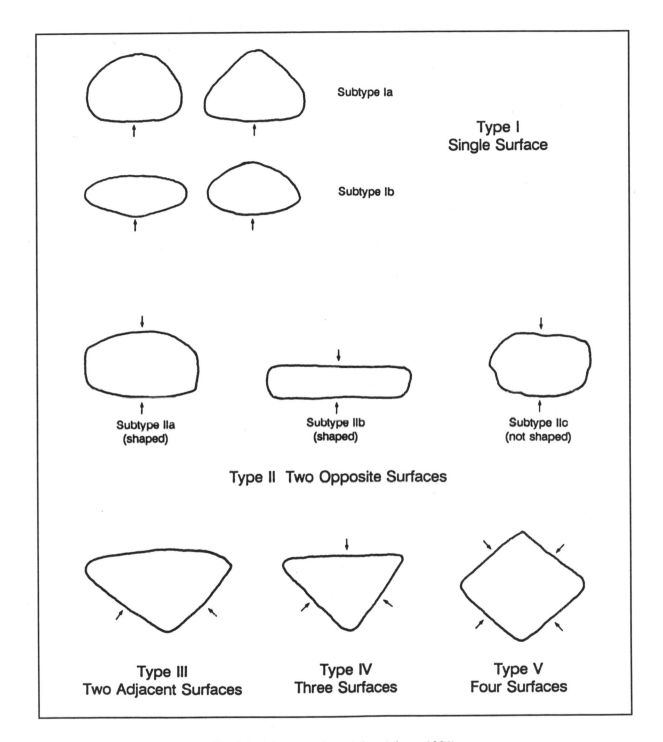

Fig. 29. Mano typology (after Adams 1991).

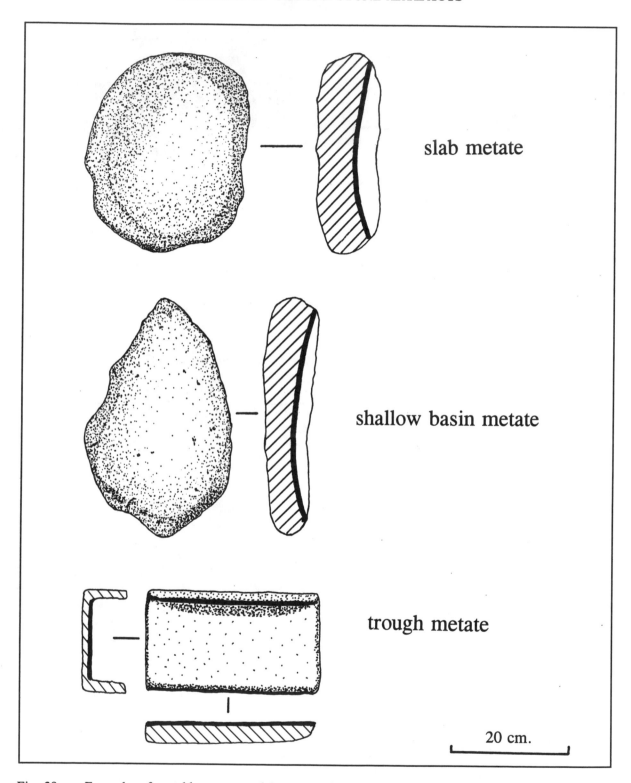

slab metate

shallow basin metate

trough metate

20 cm.

Fig. 30.   Examples of portable metates: slab metate, shallow basin metate, and deep basin (trough) metate (working surfaces shown by thick line).

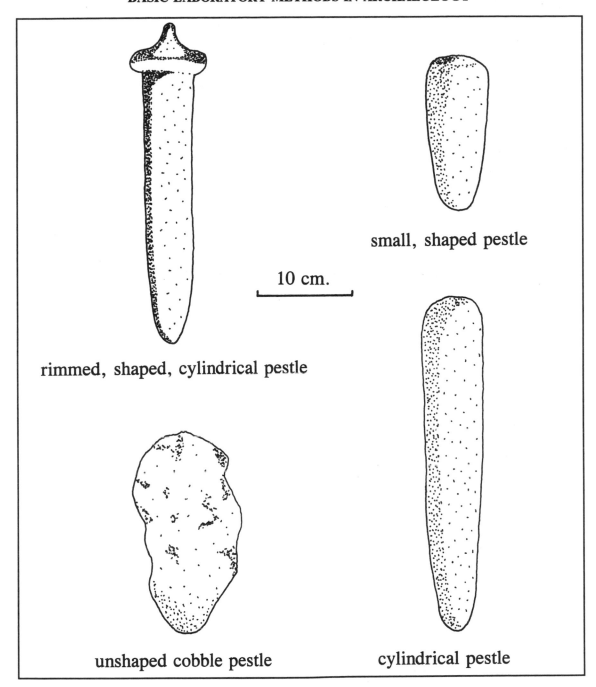

Fig. 31. Examples of pestles.

polished surfaces through use. Among these are hideworking tools (Adams 1988, 1993a), pottery anvils, and smoothing stones used on a variety of substances.

Abrading tools used to smooth shell, bone, wood, and stone also develop smooth surfaces with wear. When the abrasiveness was lost through wear, these tools may have been discarded or recycled.

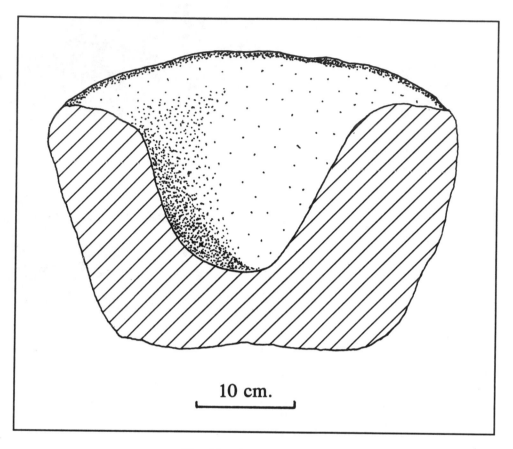

Fig. 32. A stone mortar.

GROUND STONE ARTIFACTS GROUND IN MANUFACTURE

Utensils

A number of tools used for storage, serving, cooking, agriculture, and heavy chopping or cutting were ground as part of their manufacture. These tools are not as common in the archaeological record as are milling implements.

Bowls. Bowls are utensils used to store and mix things, rather than to grind or otherwise process them. Although these tools have a shape similar to mortars, they generally have walls that are thinner and are less bulky overall (Fig. 34). It is sometimes difficult to distinguish a bowl from a well-worn mortar.

Hoes, Axes, Hammers, and Mauls. Artifacts such as hoes, axes, hammers, and mauls (see Fig. 35) were more common in agricultural societies. Hoes were presumably used for turning soil. Axes, hammers, and mauls (actually grooved hammers) are assumed to have been used for heavy-duty tasks such as chopping, pounding, and rock excavation.

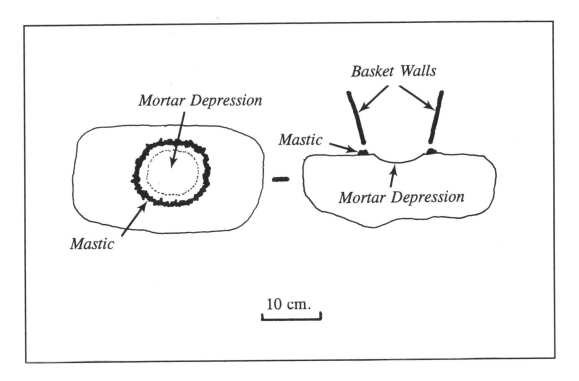

Fig. 33. A hopper mortar, note mastic.

Arrowshaft Straighteners. Arrowshaft straighteners (Fig. 36) are tools used to straighten and smooth wood and/or reed arrowshafts. In use, these tools were probably first heated in a fire, after which the arrowshafts were straightened and smoothed by running them back and forth within the carved and polished groove of the tool. Arrowshaft straighteners were often finely ground and polished and sometimes elaborately decorated.

Palettes. Palettes are small, flat utensils that are characteristic artifacts of some agricultural societies. They were probably used to grind pigments, perhaps in ceremonial contexts. They are shaped and polished, and often have elaborately carved decorations (Fig. 36).

Cooking Slabs. Cooking slabs are large, thin, flat stones that may or may not be ground to smoothness. They were used, especially in Southwestern and other cultures, much the same way as a modern griddle. These utensils probably have not been recognized at many archaeological sites.

Tabular Knives. Tabular knives take advantage of the natural tabular configuration of certain geological outcrops (often schists). They are often thought to represent agave-processing tools.

Ornaments and Ritual Objects

Items of personal and household adornment and objects used in ceremonial contexts were often ground and polished for aesthetic and functional reasons.

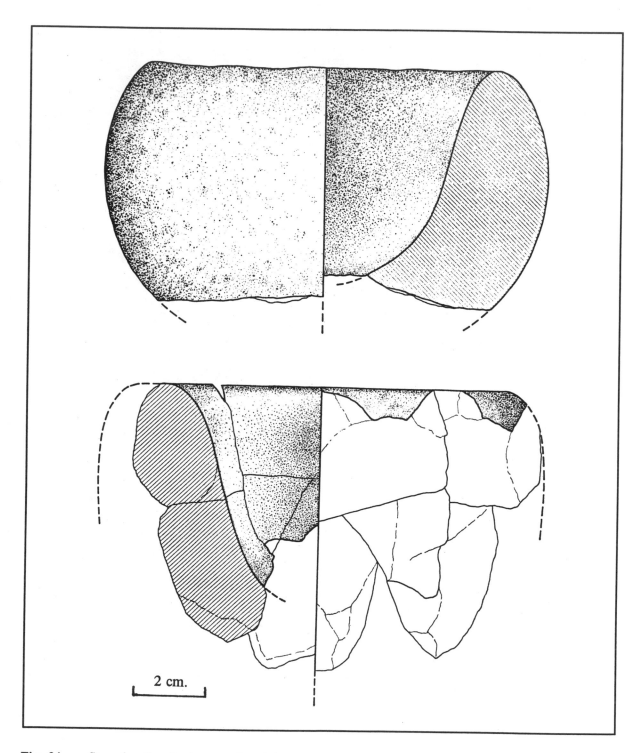

2 cm.

Fig. 34.   Stone bowls: (top) mortar/bowl from Tahquitz Canyon (CA-RIV-45), left is exterior; (bottom) partly reconstructed mortar/bowl from Tahquitz Canyon (CA-RIV-45). Courtesy of Cultural Systems Research, Inc.

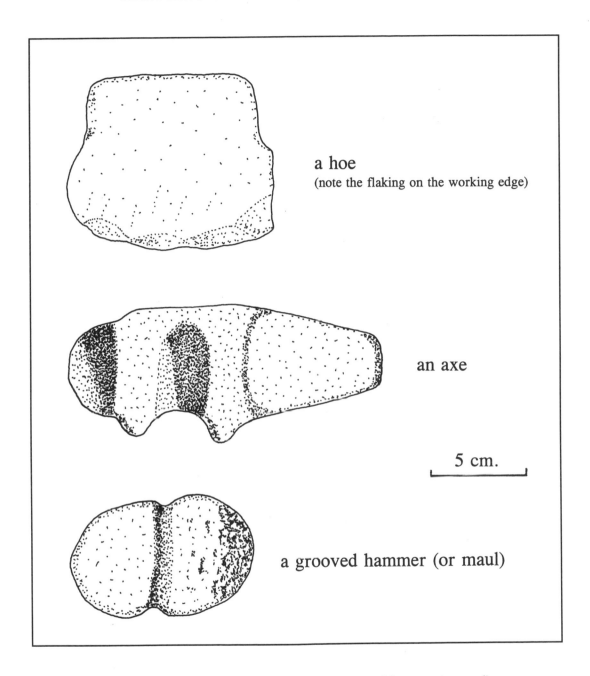

a hoe
(note the flaking on the working edge)

an axe

5 cm.

a grooved hammer (or maul)

Fig. 35. Examples of a hoe, an axe, and a grooved hammer (or maul).

Stone Beads and Ornaments. Stone beads and pendants (e.g., Fig. 37) were carved or flaked to shape, then ground and polished to finished form. Perforations were drilled so that they could be attached to or suspended from clothing or cordage. Such artifacts are relatively well-represented in large archaeological assemblages throughout North America. Types range from the reel-shaped slate gorgets of the Early (Adena) and Middle Woodland (Hopewell) periods in the Northeast to the diverse array of stone ornaments from various prehistoric and ethnographic native California cultures.

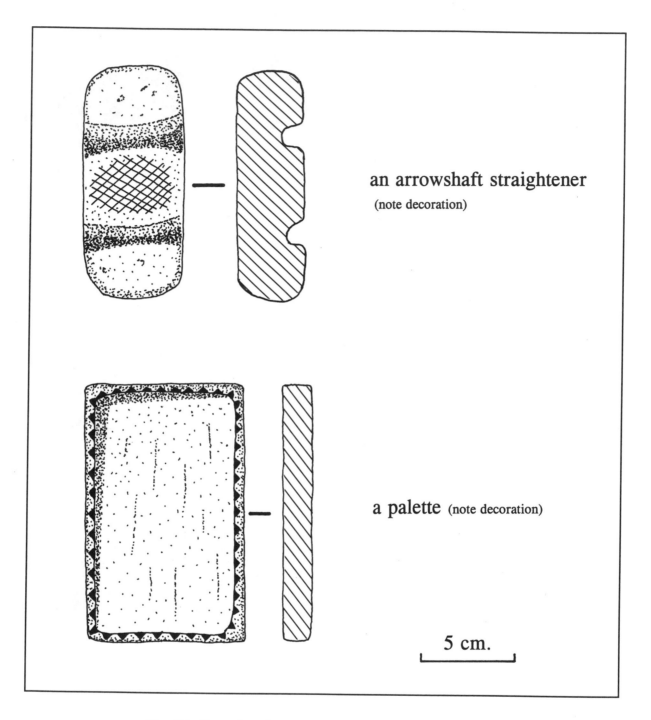

an arrowshaft straightener
(note decoration)

a palette (note decoration)

5 cm.

Fig. 36. Examples of an arrowshaft straightener and a palette.

The basic forms of stone ornaments essentially are the same as those of shell, and fall into one of two major classes, depending upon the way in which they were perforated and presumably worn. A "bead" form indicates that the specimen is either disk- or cylinder-shaped and has been drilled

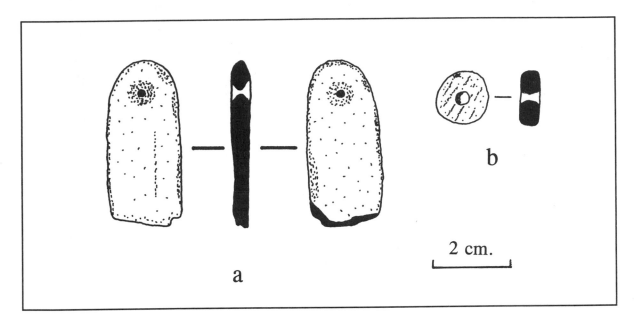

Fig. 37. Examples of stone ornaments: (a) pendant; (b) bead.

longitudinally, whereas a stone "pendant" exhibits a globular, ovate, rectangular, or square shape and usually has been uniconically or biconically drilled at one end. The former shape suggests that when worn for personal adornment, these specimens were strung edge-to-edge or face-to-face; the latter shape implies that the objects were suspended from the body (presumably most often from the neck) with a cord.

Some native North American groups specialized in making one or two types of stone ornaments, such as the turquoise pendants produced by the Anasazi (Cordell 1979) and Hohokam (Haury 1976). Other groups, most notably those in California, crafted stone ornaments from a wide variety of materials—alabaster, diorite, magnesite, obsidian, quartz crystals, schist, serpentine, and steatite (Orchard 1929; Heizer 1949). Magnesite cylinders and steatite disk beads occur in late prehistoric, protohistoric, and early historical archaeological contexts in various parts of California, and were used both as currency and to affirm one's social status. Steatite disks also were traded eastward across the Sierra Nevada into the western Great Basin.

The Southeastern Pomo of the lower Clear Lake region of northern California held a monopoly on the two magnesite quarries that apparently served all of central California with material for cylinder beads (Heizer and Treganza 1944:334). The Eastern Miwok commonly traded two yards of clamshell money for a one-inch-long magnesite cylinder from the Pomo quarries (Kelly 1978:418). Several of the 13 major steatite quarries scattered across California include those on Santa Catalina Island, located off the southern California coast, and along the western base of the Sierra Nevada (Heizer and Treganza 1944:306-308). The former were exploited by both the Chumash and Gabrielino, and the latter were mined primarily by various Yokuts groups.

ANALYSIS OF GROUND STONE ARTIFACTS

Perhaps the most conspicuous nonutilitarian stone artifacts recovered from sites in the Sacramento and San Joaquin valleys of California are the highly polished plummet- and phallic-shaped charmstones (Fig. 38): Many specimens exhibit a biconically drilled hole at one end, suggesting that the objects were suspended in some fashion. Their purpose is unknown, but many specimens have been found in association with human burials, and probably had some sort of ceremonial/magical function. The stones evidently were carefully guarded against damage, as they typically exhibit little or no battering, chipping, or signs of wear (Wallace 1978:32-33).

Stone Pipes. Pipes for smoking tobacco (or perhaps other substances) were sometimes made of stone (others were ceramic). Pipes tend to be relatively small and either cylindrical (Fig. 39a) or cone-shaped (Fig. 39b), while others (e.g., calumets, Fig. 39c) are larger. All have a central longitudinally drilled channel. Pipes were ground and polished on the exterior and interior. Although complete specimens are easy to recognize, fragments are more difficult to identify. A very small, finely ground surface may be the only clue that a fragment is part of a stone pipe. Residues of tobacco or other substances may be retained within the central channel of a pipe. A collection of papers on smoking pipes from eastern North America was compiled by Hayes (1992).

Stone Figurines. Stone was sometimes used to make figurines or effigy figures. These were ground and polished to shape. While it is easy to recognize complete figurines, small fragments are much more difficult to identify.

Stone Disks, Rings, and Balls. Stone disks, rings, and balls made of stone were shaped by flaking and/or pecking and were sometimes ground. A number of functions has been hypothesized, including digging stick weights, net sinkers, gaming pieces, and other recreational items.

Unidentified Ground Stone

Small fragments with ground surfaces are commonly recovered from archaeological sites. Sometimes the fragments are too small to determine what type of artifact the fragment represents. In this case, the fragment would be classified as "unidentified."

DESCRIPTION AND ANALYSIS

A preliminary description of ground stone artifacts (as well as all other archaeological materials) is generally carried out as part of cataloging (see Chapter 3) in order to describe the collection, to help other investigators identify individual artifacts, and to correct errors of misplacement or record keeping. Each artifact should be described as fully as possible using certain measurements and a specific vocabulary. While cataloging ground stone, the information recorded should include the catalog number assigned to the artifact, its provenience, measurements, the material from which it was made, whether it had been burned, and whether it is complete or fragmentary. Further detailed description may be carried out later, as part of the analysis of the collection.

The types of analyses used for ground stone artifacts, as well as any group of artifacts or any archaeological collection, are based on the questions the investigator wishes to ask. This point is often overlooked when beginning students are intent on following their instructor's directions during laboratory analysis classes. What you want to know (i.e., your research design, see Chapter 2) determines the types

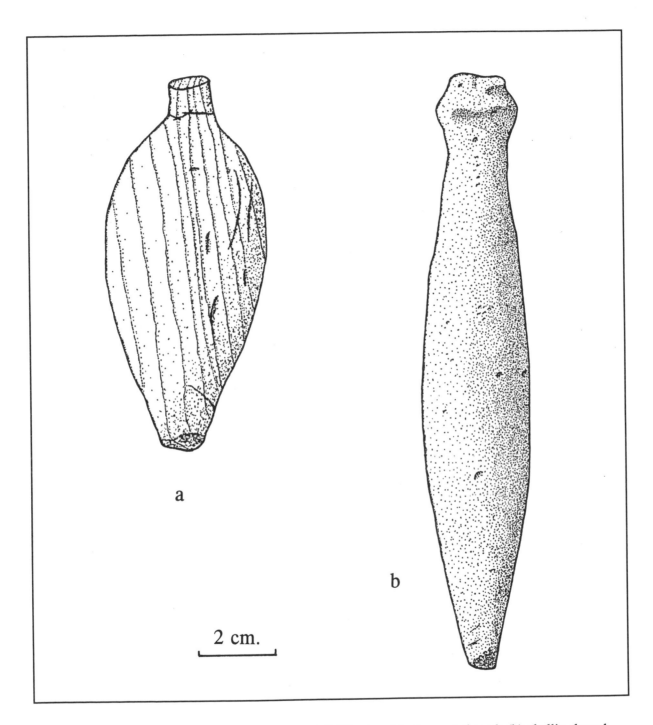

Fig. 38. Examples of charmstones from central California: (a) plummet-shaped; (b) phallic-shaped.

of analyses used. For example: do you want to know the size and shape of certain tools? how the tools were used? if the characteristics changed over time? If so, ask yourself why you want this information. This is important to think about *ahead of time*.

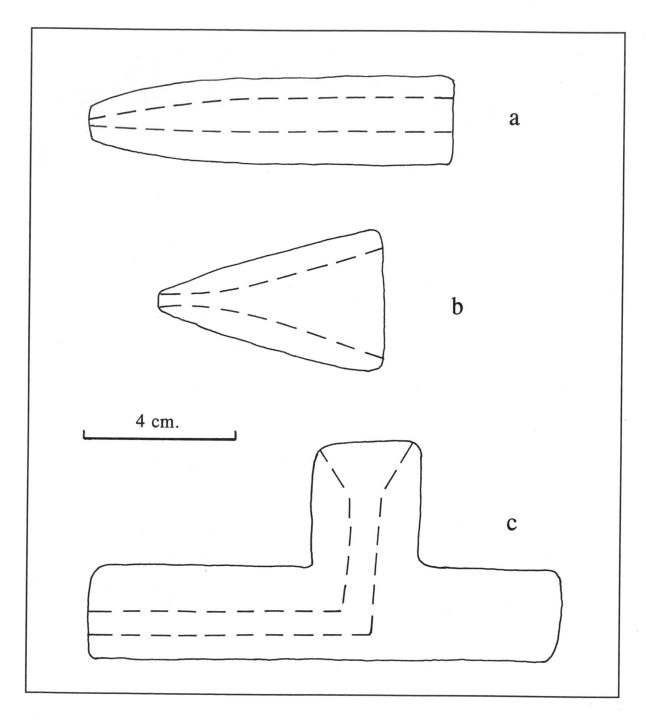

Fig. 39. Examples of stone pipes: (a) cylindrical; (b) cone-shaped; (c) calumet.

After cataloging and analysis is complete, it is important to accurately and fully report your methods, results, and interpretations. The content and format of a report are discussed in Chapter 3 and a sample outline report is provided in Appendix 1.

HOW TO DESCRIBE GROUND STONE ARTIFACTS

The first obligation of the investigator (you) is to describe artifacts fully, so that others will be able to determine what the artifacts look like without actually seeing them. You can describe the artifacts individually, or you can describe general types of artifacts and determine how many artifacts in your collection fall into each type; this is called a typology.

The following example of a typology for handstones was useful in the description and analysis of a large collection from a Millingstone Horizon site in the San Bernardino Mountains, California (Sutton et al. 1993). The typology was loosely based on previous work by Adams (1991), who was interested in the number and position of grinding surfaces on handstones and their relationships to intensification of grinding in Southwestern cultures (Fig. 29).

Handstone - Type I. Type I has a single milling surface and may be referred to as a "unifacial" handstone. Subtype Ia is oval-to-subtriangular in cross section, has one primary convex milling surface and two other secondary surfaces that are either very minimally ground or may be hand polished or polished by another type of wear. Almost all Type I handstones show battering on both ends and some display battering on margins of the other surfaces. It is likely that these tools were used as grinding tools and as pestles (pulverizing and/or crushing). This subtype is formed from a natural stream cobble and is not shaped. Subtype Ib is elliptical-to-oval in cross section, has one milling surface and an opposite surface that is polished (probably by wear). It is not shaped.

Handstone - Type II. Type II has two milling surfaces, one opposite of the other, and may be referred to as a "bifacial" handstone. Subtype IIa has two convex oval milling surfaces and has been shaped, by pecking, from a cobble. Subtype IIb has two flat oval milling surfaces, and has been shaped, by pecking, from a cobble. It has an extremely regular form and often exhibits a slight central, pecked concavity on one or both milling surfaces. Subtype IIc has two milling surfaces that may be either flattened or convex, or a combination of both. It is not shaped.

It should be noted that Subtype IIa may develop into Subtype IIb, but this is uncertain. The development of pronounced "shoulders" (i.e., prominent corners at the transition from the working face to the margin), a characteristic of Subtype IIb, may result from the progression from a convex surface to a flat surface.

Handstone - Type III. Type III is also bifacial but has two adjacent milling surfaces rather than opposite milling surfaces.

Handstone - Types IV and V. These types exhibit three or more milling surfaces. These are formed on natural cobbles and are not shaped.

ANALYSIS OF GROUND STONE ARTIFACTS

Organizing the Collection

On a suitable working surface, spread out the collection of ground stone you are analyzing. Make sure that you keep track of the provenience for each artifact. Group the artifacts into types. This is not always easy, especially when you are dealing with small fragments. Put aside small fragments that you cannot identify until you are more familiar with the collection. You may be able to identify some of them later; some of them you may have to classify as "unknown" or "unidentified." Once you have grouped the collection, e.g., handstones, milling stones, pestles, mortars/bowls, and others, you can proceed to describe each artifact and take measurements.

Verbal Description

In words that are clearly understandable, describe each artifact. Use words such as flat, concave, convex, rounded, rough, smooth, oval, square, rectangular, triangular, plan view, cross section, round, irregular, or other words you think appropriate. Describe the artifact overall; look at it from all sides and at a variety of angles. Describe it as fully as you can. With experience, you will become expert and work out your own routine. Ask yourself, "If I were describing this to someone who could not see it, how would I proceed? Using my description, could someone identify this particular artifact in a collection?"

Taking Metric Measurements

All measurements are taken using the metric system. You will need a metric tape measure and a metric caliper. Traditionally, the greatest measurements are recorded, but this does not mean that additional measurements cannot be taken. Use your judgment. Calipers are used for measuring smaller artifacts; tape measures are generally used for larger items. The following measurements are usually taken: greatest length, greatest width, and greatest thickness of the entire artifact; length, width, depth (if any) of each grinding surface. Each of these measurements should be recorded for every artifact in tabular form, with each artifact identified by its catalog number.

Measuring Curvatures

There are at least two ways to measure the curvature of a working surface (i.e., the extent of the concavity or the convexity) on milling tools. The first method uses a straightedge and a metric measuring tape (Fig. 40). Establish a horizontal baseline with the straightedge and use the metric tape or ruler to measure the greatest extent of the concavity (depth) or convexity (height). Using this method, one could say, for example, that the concavity of the working surface of a milling stone is 3 cm. deep or that the convexity of the working surface of a handstone is 0.5 cm. at its greatest point. This method usually assumes that the curvature slopes gradually and symmetrically from the greatest point of convexity or concavity to the edge of the working surface.

A second and more exact and reliable way to describe curvature is by using special tools designed to do just that. One such tool is called a *flexible rule* (Fig. 41a) and is available at most art supply stores. The other (and better) tool is called a *copy cat* (Fig. 41b) and is available at most hardware stores. Both tools actually reproduce the curvature you want to describe so that you can draw the curvature on a piece of paper. You may then either make your measurements from the horizontal

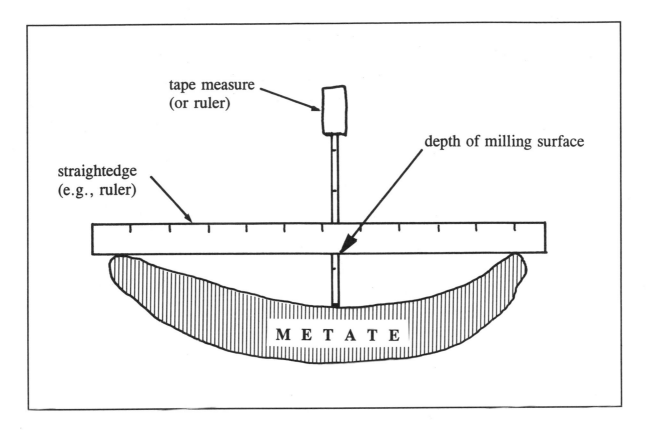

Fig. 40.   One way to measure the concave curvature of a milling stone, using a straightedge ruler and a metric measuring tape.

(as described in the first method) or you can simply present the replication of the curved surface as your description.

The flexible rule and the copy cat are also very useful tools in reconstructing the shape and size of a whole milling implement from a fragment (see below). This technique is dependent upon assumptions of symmetry in tool design.

HOW TO ANALYZE GROUND STONE ARTIFACTS

As stated above, the type of analysis is determined by the questions you want answered as part of your research design. The questions may be as simple as "what kind of tools are represented?" or as complex as you wish, depending on the particular focus of the research questions that have been posed. One might ask if the collection can tell us something about what foods were processed and how; or if milling tools were used intensively or occasionally; or if the ground stone artifact was made of local material or material imported from a distance; or if the style of milling implements changed over time. The answers to these questions (and others) would be important to the interpretation of the archaeological site where they were recovered. Some basic types of analyses of milling implements are described below.

Fig. 41. Ways of measuring curvature with two different tools: (upper) a flexible rule; (lower) a copy cat.

Reconstructing the Shape of a Tool from Fragments

It is common for milling implements in archaeological collections to be in the form of fragments. Some of the fragments may fit together; more commonly, you will be dealing with fragmentary specimens of many different tools. It can be fun and challenging to reassemble more complete artifacts from several fragments. It is also possible to reconstruct the size and shape of a complete tool from a single, reasonably sized, fragment. The purpose of reconstruction is to get a better idea of how many tools or other objects are represented in the collection, and what a tool looked like so that an assessment of how it was used can be made.

In order to determine what fragments may fit together, first look at the thickness of all fragments for each tool type; group the fragments into similar thicknesses. Next, look at the type of stone. (Or, you may want to look at the type of stone first, and then the thickness.) When you think you have good matches for stone type and thickness, the fun starts. Being careful to control the catalog numbers of all the pieces, try to fit the broken surfaces together; it is like working a jigsaw puzzle, only your success will be somewhat limited. It is very rare to find and fit together all pieces of a tool. When two fragments match, you will be able to feel it in the way the fragments fit together. You can glue the fragments together with Duco Cement (although this is not recommended as it may contaminate the piece and limit future chemical analyses). Be sure, however, that the match is a good one and that the catalog numbers remain visible on each fragment (the numbers may have to be written on the stone itself if the artifact is removed from its bag).

To reconstruct the original size and/or shape of a tool or of the grinding surface from a fragmentary specimen, you will need to use a copy cat or flexible rule (see above). The fragmentary specimen needs to retain enough of a surface to make a ''pattern'' for reconstruction (half or nearly half of a tool is preferable). First, reproduce the outline or curvature with the copy cat or flexible rule. Draw this outline on paper. Then, flip the copy cat or flexible rule over, so that a mirror image of the shape or the curvature makes up the rest of the tool that is missing. This method rests on the assumption that milling implements are symmetrical in shape (not always true).

The diameters of pestles and mortars can be reconstructed from only a small curved fragment by using the copy cat or the flexible rule. This type of reconstruction is based on the assumption of symmetry; that the artifacts are basically circular in diameter (this is not always the case). Establish the curvature of the existing surface using the copy cat or the flexible rule. Draw the curve on a piece of paper; the diameter can be determined by fitting that curve to the curvature on a standard diameter-measurement template (see Fig. 41).

Determining How Tools Were Used

Direct evidence of the way milling implements were used is not always easy to find. One clue the archaeologist looks for is certain marks on the working surface(s). These marks are called ''striations'' (scratch marks on the surface of the stone) that are the result of sharp edges being rubbed on the opposing part of the milling unit during use. The alignment of these striations (if they are present) can tell you, for example, whether the tool was used in a back-and-forth motion or a sideways motion in relation to its longer axis. If there are striations that do not seem to line up in the same direction, it may mean that the milling implement was used with a circular motion, or in a number of different ways. Sometimes short chopping motions can be detected when they leave small gouges in the working surface. A surface that has been polished by use, but not ground, may be an indication that a relatively soft substance was worked on the surface. High polish on ground surfaces is an indication that the surface was used very intensely and/or that the substance processed had an oily content (Adams 1993b).

In all cases, one of the best ways to look for these types of use-marks is in a moderately darkened room, using low intensity light (a flashlight also works well). Have your light source at a low angle to the surface you wish to examine (almost as if you were looking at a land surface at sunset). This creates shadows of even the smallest scratches and gouges. Note if the marks are parallel to each other and where they appear on the working surface. These can be clues to the way the tool was used.

Note if there are any pits or depressions in the working surface. Although these are often visible in ordinary light, sometimes they are only visible in low-angle light. A small central depression may mean that the milling implement was used as a platform to crack open nuts, to split open pebbles, or to crush hard chunks of clay. When there are small pits evenly distributed over a highly polished working surface, you might suspect that a milling implement was purposefully hit with a hammerstone so that tiny divots would be removed in order to recreate a rough surface, and thus improve the abrasiveness of the grinding tool.

Look for signs of battering or crushing at the ends and margins of milling implements, especially handstones and pestles (see Fig. 28). These signs can tell you if the tool was used for hammering and crushing in addition to grinding. The combination of hammering and grinding is very common, because larger chunks often had to be reduced and hard outer shells had to be removed before grinding could take place.

Sometimes the shape of the tool itself can tell you something about how it was used. For example, a very long or large handstone most likely would be used with a two-handed grasp; hence, the grinding motion would probably be back-and-forth. A milling stone with a circular basin or circular grinding surface would most likely be the result of using a handstone in a circular motion. A milling stone with a trough (a flat or nearly flat surface with raised edges on either side), such as those commonly found in the Southwest, would represent a back-and-forth movement with a handstone that gradually wore down the central working surface, leaving the edges raised on opposite margins. The handstone used for this kind of work would show ground edges at the ends, in addition to ground working surfaces; the ground ends result from the ends of the handstone rubbing against the edges of the trough.

Determining How The Artifacts Were Made

Many milling implements and other objects with ground surfaces (e.g., stone balls, discoidals, axes, and mauls) were made in a manner very similar to the way bifaces and other flaked stone tools were made; they were first flaked to shape, then refined by pecking and ground either by use or in manufacture. However, sometimes a natural shape was used with little or no modification. The best way to ascertain if a milling implement or other object was shaped is to determine whether it looks like a naturally occurring form (see above section on determining if a rock is a ground stone artifact). Look for very flat surfaces that might be the result of purposefully splitting a boulder or a cobble in half. Look for flake scars (see Chapter 4 on the analysis of flaked stone), especially around the edges and on the nonworking surfaces. Flake scars may be present as the result of flaking the artifact to shape. Look for flake scars and pecking marks on the sides of pestles and mortars. Almost all pestles that are not simply natural cobbles and all mortars (and axes, discoidals, and balls) are most certainly first shaped by flaking and then further refined by pecking.

Note whether the rock type from which the ground stone artifact was made is available near the archaeological site where it was found (visit the site, if you can; look at geological sources of information, such as geological maps). Stone that is not locally available probably had to be carried for some distance; often special care is taken in manufacture if the material is nonlocal.

Look for pecking marks (tiny pits) that are evenly distributed on polished surfaces. This usually means that the surface has become too smooth to be an efficient working surface and the aboriginal worker probably attempted to renovate the surface by restoring abrasiveness; the polish was removed by light hammering (or pecking) with another stone (see above section on examination under low-angle light). Archaeologists often refer to this process as "resharpening."

Determining What Was Processed With The Ground Stone Tools

Many archaeologists assume that milling implements were used to process plants; the milling stone/handstone (metate/mano) complex is commonly assumed to reflect hard seed processing, while the mortar/pestle complex is assumed to have been used for processing nuts (e.g., acorns). These simplistic assumptions are no longer supported by the data; milling tools were used to process a wide variety of materials, including plant and animal parts, and minerals (Schneider 1993a). Do not assume that plants were the only materials processed with milling tools.

It is difficult to determine exactly what materials were processed with milling tools, at least at the usual level of laboratory description and analysis. Occasionally, visible particles of a processed substance may remain in pits or fissures in the grinding surface, but this is very unusual, except in cases where pigment (e.g., red ocher) was ground with milling implements. In this case, because the processed material is nonorganic, it might remain in fissures or pits in the rock and be visible with low-level magnification, or sometimes even without magnification. Most organic substances would not survive in the archaeological record and therefore would not be visible to the naked eye or under ordinary magnification. It is good analytic practice, however, to look at the pits and fissures on the working surfaces with 10X to 40X magnification to see if there is any indication of residues present.

New, sophisticated analyses can identify protein residues, starches, lipids, cellulose, pollens, phytoliths, and probably other particles and residues left on stone surfaces. These analytical tests are still in the experimental stage, and are highly technical, often expensive, and beyond the scope of student analyses (but see Chapter 13).

Use-wear experiments are sometimes carried out in an attempt to determine what was processed and how it was processed. These types of experiments replicate aboriginal behaviors; different seeds, for example, are ground with modern replicas of aboriginal milling tools. The wear, striations, and other significant features on the modern tools are compared with the same features on the archaeological specimens. The same type of replication experiments have been carried out with agricultural tools, such as hoes, sickles, and axes.

The best way to make a knowledgeable guess about what was processed on milling implements at a site is to know as much as possible about the site environment at the time the site was occupied; to look at clues for use-wear (see above); to find out if any organic remains (e.g., seeds, pollens, nuts, bones) were found in hearths and soil samples from the site; and to consider the entire archaeological assemblage in an attempt to determine what might have gone on at the site and at what season of the year.

Another way to interpret the use of milling implements and other ground stone artifacts, especially for late period sites that can be identified as being within the territories of ethnographically known groups, is to examine the ethnographic data for analogies.

Analyzing Other Types of Ground Stone Artifacts

Many of the same techniques described above for milling implements are also used for other types of ground stone artifacts. For example, an examination of the surface of a stone pipe could provide clues to the way it was made. Analysis of residues within the channel of the pipe could provide information on the substance (e.g., tobacco) that was burned in the pipe. Wear patterns on pendants and/or stone beads can indicate whether the specimens were strung on a necklace or sewn to clothing.

INTERPRETATION

Many analyses of ground stone tools have made functional inferences from morphological attributes (size and shape). Classifying milling stones as "flat," "basined," or "troughed," and handstones as "oval" or "rectangular," does not necessarily mean that the morphological differences reflect functional differences. Archaeological morphology is often related more to longevity of use than to function (Kraybill 1977:487). For example, a "basined" milling stone may be functionally identical to a flat slab milling stone, but may have been used longer or may have been made of a different type of rock. A similar explanation might be in order for the difference between a "shallow basin" and a "deep basin" milling stone. Ground stone tools were also frequently recycled and were incorporated into rock clusters, hearths, storage features, and architectural features.

The notion that items within a ground stone collection can be assigned to sex-specific tasks (e.g., milling stones being "female" tools or projectile points being "male" tools) remains uncertain. Some investigators (e.g., Gero 1991) have recently argued for such assignments, thereby gaining more insight into male-female social, political, and economic interactions.

Various other aspects of ground stone tools that have not often been considered until recently include the acquisition of raw materials for the tools, the manner in which the tools were produced, and whether tools were transported and/or traded. A wide range of variation probably existed on the continuum between expedient gathering of local materials and the quarrying of special stone at certain locations. The same variability probably existed in the effort that went into preparing tools for use (Schneider 1993b).

The Use of Ethnographic Analogy in Interpretation

Ethnographic analogy (using written descriptions of certain cultural behaviors to interpret archaeological materials) is very commonly used by archaeologists to make interpretations of archaeological materials, and is *often misused*. Different cultural groups, in different ecological situations, use different materials in different ways. Always think of the cultural, geographical, and chronological context of your collection. Look at the ethnographic literature most closely related to the cultural groups in the specific area where the milling implements were recovered. Using comparisons from different areas of the world may be interesting and may present possibilities, but the applications to the collection you are analyzing may be invalid. In general, the further you get from the site, both geographically and chronologically, the less valid will be your use of ethnographic analogy.

REFERENCES

Adams, Jenny L.
    1988   Use-Wear Analysis on Manos and Hide-Processing Stones. Journal of Field Archaeology 15(3):307-315.

    1991   The Mechanics of Manos and Metates and Grinding Intensification. Paper presented at the annual meetings of the Society for American Archaeology, New Orleans.

    1993a   Toward Understanding the Technological Development of Manos and Metates. Kiva 58(3):331-344.

    1993b   Mechanisms of Wear on Ground Stone Surfaces. Pacific Coast Archaeological Quarterly 29(4):61-74.

Bennett, Richard, and John Elton
    1898   The History of Corn Milling. New York: Burt Franklin.

Cordell, Linda S.
    1979   Prehistory: Eastern Anasazi. In: Handbook of North American Indians, Vol. 9, Southwest, Alfonzo Ortiz, ed., pp. 131-151. Washington: Smithsonian Institution.

Curwen, E. C.
    1927   Prehistoric Agriculture in Britain. Antiquity 1:261-289.

Gero, Joan M.
    1991   Genderlithics: Women's Roles in Stone Tool Production. In: Engendering Archaeology: Women and Prehistory, Joan M. Gero and Margaret W. Conkey, eds., pp. 163-193. Oxford: Basil Blackwell, Ltd.

Haury, Emil W.
    1976   The Hohokam, Desert Farmers and Craftsmen: Excavations at Snaketown, 1964-1965. Tucson: University of Arizona Press.

Hayes, Charles F., III (ed.)
    1992   Proceedings of the 1989 Smoking Pipe Conference: Selected Papers. Rochester Museum & Science Center, Research Records No. 22.

Heizer, Robert F.
1949   The Archaeology of Central California, I: The Early Horizon. University of California Anthropological Records 12(1).

Heizer, Robert F., and Adan E. Treganza
1944   Mines and Quarries of the Indians of California. Journal of Mines and Geology 40(3):291-359. (Reprinted by Ballena Press, Ramona, California, 1972.)

Kelly, Isabel T.
1978   Coast Miwok. In: Handbook of North American Indians, Vol. 8, California, Robert F. Heizer, ed., pp. 414-425. Washington: Smithsonian Institution.

Kraybill, Nancy
1977   Pre-agricultural Tools for the Preparation of Foods in the Old World. In: Origins of Agriculture, C. Reed, ed., pp. 485-521. The Hague: Mouton.

Orchard, William C.
1929   Beads and Beadwork of the American Indians: A Study Based on Specimens in the Museum of the American Indian, Heye Foundation. Contributions from the Museum of the American Indian, Heye Foundation 11.

Schneider, Joan S.
1993a   Milling Implements: Biases and Problems in Their Use as Indicators of Prehistoric Behavior and Paleoenvironment. Pacific Coast Archaeological Society Quarterly 29(4):5-21.

1993b   Aboriginal Milling-Implement Quarries in Eastern California and Western Arizona: A Behavioral Perspective. Ph.D. dissertation, University of California, Riverside.

Sutton, Mark Q., Joan S. Schneider, and Robert M. Yohe II
1993   The Siphon Site (CA-SBR-6580): A Millingstone Horizon Site in the Summit Valley, California. San Bernardino County Museum Association Quarterly 40(3).

Wallace, William J.
1978   Post-Pleistocene Archeology, 9000 to 2000 B.C. In: Handbook of North American Indians, Vol. 8, California, Robert F. Heizer, ed., pp. 25-36. Washington: Smithsonian Institution.

ADDITIONAL READING

The following list of references is highly selective and is not to be considered exhaustive.

Classic Ground Stone Analyses

Aikens, C. Melvin
1970   Hogup Cave. University of Utah Anthropological Papers No. 93.

Haury, Emil W.
    1950   The Stratigraphy and Archaeology of Ventana Cave. Tucson: University of Arizona
            Press.

Jennings, Jesse D.
    1957   Danger Cave. Memoirs of the Society for American Archaeology No. 14.

Riddell, F. A.
    1960   The Archaeology of the Karlo Site (LAS-7), California. University of California Survey
            Reports No. 53.

Riddell, F. A., and W. Pritchard
    1971   Archaeology of the Rainbow Point Site (4-Plu-594), Bucks Lake, Plumas County,
            California. University of Oregon Anthropological Papers 1:59-102.

Sayles, E. B.
    1937   Stone Implements and Bowls. In: Excavations at Snaketown: Material Culture, by H.
            S. Gladwin, E. W. Haury, E. B. Sayles, and N. Gladwin., pp. 101-134. Gila Pueblo
            Medallion Papers No. 25.

Woodbury, Richard
    1954   Prehistoric Stone Implements of Northeastern Arizona. Papers of the Peabody Museum
            of American Archaeology and Ethnology, Vol. 34.

Recent Milling Implement Analyses

Adams, Jenny L.
    1975   Stone Implements. Miscellaneous Ground Stone. Miscellaneous Stone Artifacts and
            Natural Objects. In: Stone Artifacts from Walpi, pp. 1-220. Walpi Archaeological
            Project Phase II, Vol. 4, Part I. Flagstaff: Museum of Northern Arizona.

Clark, John E.
    1988   The Lithics of La Libertad, Chiapas, Mexico: An Economic Perspective. Brigham
            Young University, Papers of the New World Archaeological Foundation No. 52.

Fratt, Lee
    1991   Ground Stone. In: Homol'ovi II: Archaeology of an Ancestral Hopi Village, Arizona,
            E. C. Adams and K. A. Hays, eds., pp. 57-74. University of Arizona Anthropological
            Papers No. 55.

Regional Syntheses

Fratt, Lee
    1992   Ground Stone in Arizona. In: Making and Using Stone Artifacts: Lithic Studies in
            Arizona, by M. C. Slaughter, L. Fratt, K. Anderson, and R. V. N. Ahlstrom, pp. 16-25,
            84-105. Tucson: Arizona State Parks, State Historic Preservation Office.

Mikkelsen, Pat
> 1985   A Study of Millingtool Form and Function Applied to the North Coast Ranges, California. Master's thesis, California State University, Sonoma.

Typology

Wright, Katherine
> 1993   A Classification System for Ground Stone Tools from the Prehistoric Levant. Paleorient 18(2):53-81.

Use-Wear Studies

Adams, Jenny L.
> 1989   Methods for Improving Ground Stone Artifact Analysis: Experiments in Mano Wear Patterns. In: Experiments in Lithic Technology, D. S. Amick and R. P. Mauldin, eds., pp. 259-276. Oxford: BAR International Series No. 528.

Bartlett, Katherine
> 1933   Pueblo Milling Stones of the Flagstaff Region and Their Relation to Others in the Southwest. A Study in Progressive Efficiency. Flagstaff: Museum of Northern Arizona Bulletin No. 3.

Semenov, S. A.
> 1964   Prehistoric Technology. London: Cory, Adams, and Mackay.

Manufacture

Hayden, Brian
> 1987   Lithic Studies Among the Contemporary Highland Maya. Tucson: University of Arizona Press.

Huckell, Bruce B.
> 1986   A Ground Stone Implement Quarry on the Lower Colorado River, Northwestern Arizona. Phoenix: U. S. Bureau of Land Management Cultural Resource Series No. 3.

Schneider, Joan S.
> 1996   Quarrying and Production of Milling Implements at Antelope Hill, Arizona. Journal of Field Archaeology 23(1) (in press).

Treganza, Adan E., and Leonard L. Valdivia
> 1955   The Manufacture of Pecked and Ground Stone Artifacts: A Controlled Study. Berkeley: Reports of the University of California Archaeological Survey No. 32:34-36.

Wright, M. Elizabeth
> 1988   Bee Hive Quern Manufacture in the South-East Pennines. Scottish Archaeological Review 5:65-77.

Latest Trends

Fratt, Lee, and Jenny L. Adams (eds.)
  1993   New Trends in Ground Stone Research: It's Not the Same Old Grind. Kiva 58(3):313-428. (Issue devoted to ground stone symposium presented at the 1991 meetings of the Society for American Archaeology.)

Pritchard-Parker, Mari A. (ed.)
  1993   Ground Stone Analysis. Pacific Coast Archaeological Society Quarterly 29(4):1-74.

Wright, Katherine I.
  1994   Groundstone Tools and Hunter-Gatherer Subsistence in Southwest Asia: Implications for the Transition to Farming. American Antiquity 59(2):238-263.

Yohe, Robert M. II, Margaret M. Newman, and Joan S. Schneider
  1991   Immunological Identification of Small Mammal Proteins on Aboriginal Milling Equipment. American Antiquity 56(4):659-666.

ANALYSIS OF ABORIGINAL CERAMICS

DEFINITION

As used by most New World archaeologists, the term "aboriginal ceramics" commonly refers to both utilitarian and nonutilitarian prehistoric or protohistoric objects composed of clay and other organic and inorganic materials fired at relatively high temperatures (typically between 600 and 1000 degrees C.). Clay consists mainly of fine particles of hydrous aluminum silicates and irons, alkalies, and alkaline earths, and is plastic when moist but becomes hard when dried or fired. Prehistoric peoples who were familiar with the unique qualities of clay soon realized that they could fashion a variety of containers and other objects from it, and the numerous shapes, styles, and forms exhibited by clay artifacts have provided the foundations for thousands of archaeological analyses.

Along with flaked and ground stone artifacts, ceramic artifacts are among the most durable objects found in the archaeological record, and remain intact in a variety of depositional environments. Throughout the world, and especially in North America, ceramic technology is a relatively recent innovation and, as such, is an important dating tool for the archaeologist because most types are known to be associated with specific time periods. Hence, the analysis of an assemblage of ceramic vessel fragments (potsherds) can provide important information concerning site chronology as well as technology and prehistoric trade patterns.

In a very general sense, the development of pottery is associated with early horticulture/agriculture and increased sedentism, although numerous hunter-gatherer groups made and used pottery. The world's oldest known ceramic containers were produced between 10,000 and 12,000 years ago by the Jomon fisher-foragers of ancient Japan. Although many prehistoric cultures were heavily reliant upon ceramics for cooking and storage, various sedentary groups such as those of North America's Northwest Coast and northern California did not produce pottery, but instead relied upon a wide array of woven baskets for containers.

The oldest known ceramic objects in the world consist of 30,000-year-old baked clay human figurines from Upper Paleolithic sites in Czechoslovakia. Some contain crushed mammoth bone for temper, which helped to reduce shrinkage and cracking during firing. These specimens indicate that by Upper Paleolithic times, three important principles of clay were recognized: (1) moist clay can be shaped and formed, and will retain that form when dried; (2) fire and/or heat hardens clay; and (3) adding different materials to clay can improve its natural properties and utility (Rice 1987:8).

In the Near East, the earliest ceramic vessels found to date were manufactured in Anatolia (Turkey) between 8,500 and 8,000 B.C. In the New World, pottery was developed independently in several different places between about 3,000 and 2,500 B.C. New World pottery apparently was first produced in South America along the coast of Ecuador. Soon thereafter, it was made in coastal Colombia, Pacific coastal Mexico, and the southeastern United States.

ABORIGINAL CERAMICS

The earliest North American pottery seems to have been manufactured in the Savannah River region of Georgia around 2,500 B.C. Vessels were tempered with plant fiber such as Spanish moss, were of a soft paste, and somewhat fragile. A simple, undecorated thick-walled bowl was the dominant form. Ceramic technology then apparently spread from Georgia to the western and northern portions of the Eastern Woodlands, and by 1,000 B.C., sturdier wares decorated with incised lines and punctations were relatively common throughout the southern United States.

In both the Old and New World, the first pottery was crafted by hand. Most early vessels were constructed by either pinching and drawing (modeling) a mass of clay into the shape of a vessel or joining together a series of clay coils to form a container. Between 3,500 and 2,500 B.C., various cultures of the Near and Far East first used the potter's wheel to produce pottery. This innovation had the advantage of speed and standardization, and was used to mass produce thousands of similar vessels. In the Americas, fired clay vessels continued to be made either by modeling, coiling, or molding until Europeans introduced the potter's wheel in the sixteenth century.

RAW MATERIALS

Clays are the products of the breakdown and decomposition of silicate rocks that contain a high percentage of alumina, such as micas and feldspars. They are sedimentary deposits that, in geological terms, are relatively recent accumulations of the products of weathering and disintegration of much older rocks. The depositional history of clays is the most common basis for classifying them, and by this criterion, clays are either primary (residual) or secondary (transported or sedimentary) (Rice 1987:36; Orton et al. 1993:114).

PRIMARY CLAYS

Primary (or residual) clays are those deposits found within the same general location as the parent rock from which they originated. Through the processes of surface weathering, primary clays develop from various types of rock, such as granite, basalt, diorite, and tuff. Residual clays often contain coarse, unaltered, angular fragments of the parent source because the alteration and decomposition of that rock is incomplete (Rice 1987:37). These minerals usually include quartz, feldspar, mica, and pyrite, which often serve as the temper for ceramic objects made from primary clays. Because of their low organic content, residual clays are mostly coarse and of low plasticity.

SECONDARY CLAYS

Secondary clays typically are recovered from contexts far removed from the parent source, having been transported by various forces such as wind and water. Transported clays are more common than residual clays, and because of sorting and redeposition, usually are more homogeneous and finer in texture (Rice 1987:37). Sedimentary clays can be further categorized by different processes of deposition and transport. Therefore, one can refer to marine clays, lacustrine clays, eolian clays, glacial clays, etc.

COLOR

Raw clays acquire most of their color from two classes of impurities: organic matter and iron compounds. Clays that are more or less free of impurities typically are white in color. Organic constituents result in clays that are gray to black, depending upon the amount and condition of the organic materials (Shepard 1980:16). Oxides (e.g., hematite) and hydroxides (e.g., limonite) contain highly oxidized iron, and produce red, brown, buff, and yellow clays, whereas compounds in which the iron is not completely oxidized (such as magnetite and pyrite) produce gray clays. It is critical to note that the color of fired clay is not always indicative of its original raw color. This is because organic matter often hides the coloring effect of iron compounds, and subsequently is converted to a gas during firing. When a clay that is black because of a high organic content is completely oxidized in firing, it will change to any number of colors, from a cream to red-brown color or to white, depending on its composition (Shepard 1980:16).

Although there is no simple relationship between the color of raw and fired clay, there are some basic color change patterns that one can apply to ceramic assemblages in order to obtain information about the clay's original color. Generally speaking, white pottery derives from white, neutral gray, or black clays; buff pottery derives from cream, yellow, neutral gray, black, or brown clays; red and brown ceramics result from yellow, red, brown, gray, or black clays; and dark gray and black ceramics result from all colors of clay that were incompletely oxidized during firing (Shepard 1980:Table 1).

MANUFACTURING METHODS

Although some native potters were able to use local clays in their natural state without modification, most had to either add or remove materials to make their clays suitable for use. Organic debris, large mineral fragments, and pebbles often had to be removed from residual clays during early processing associated with ceramic *paste* production, and most sedimentary clays (many of which are fine-grained and therefore required minimal processing for paste production) had to be augmented with temper in order to produce an adequate ceramic *fabric*. [Most ceramic analysts (e.g., Bennett 1974:31) use the term "paste" to refer to the clay substance of the pottery excluding temper/filler additives, and the term "fabric" to refer to the body of processed clay and temper additives.] The consistency of the clay was critical, and usually involved several steps, such as drying, crushing, grinding, winnowing or sieving, and adding water to the mass to produce a paste that was even in texture (Rice 1987:118).

TEMPER

The addition of either organic or nonorganic agents, called *temper* (also referred to as *filler* or *nonplastic* material), often was necessary to reduce shrinkage and cracking of the clay during firing. Identification and characterization of temper is important to archaeologists because these materials usually are culturally distinctive, and associated with discrete temporal periods and regions. In North America, the more commonly known prehistoric tempers include sand and moss, as well as crushed rock, shell, and potsherds. As noted above, many residual clays are self-tempering, and prehistoric potters who used these clays simply removed the medium- to large-sized rocks and minerals from the clay and retained the naturally occurring small mineral fragments as temper.

VESSEL CONSTRUCTION

After the clay had attained the proper consistency, it was carefully kneaded to remove air bubbles and to make it as plastic as possible, allowing the potter to mold it more easily. New World native potters commonly employed three methods in making ceramic containers: *modeling*, *coiling*, and *molding*.

Modeling

Some potters, such as the Arikara and Mandan of the northern Plains, hand-worked a mass of clay into a rough approximation of the vessel through punching, pinching, and/or drawing, and then finished it by using the paddle-and-anvil technique (see below). Others used modeling to form the lower portion of a ceramic container and finished it using the coiling technique (see below).

Coiling

Coiling involved building the vessel from the base up with long coils or wedges of clay that were shaped and joined together. Basal portions of many coiled vessels were first molded or impressed on a basket, and rope-shaped coils were then added to complete the upper portion. The junctions of the coils usually were obliterated by subsequent finishing treatments that produced smooth vessel walls of a uniform thickness, although the corrugated coiled wares of the Anasazi were left as originally applied and indented for exterior decoration (see Figs. 42 and 43).

Molding

The molding technique consisted of pressing a flat, circular mass of clay paste into a concave mold, or placing it over the top of a convex mold. Molding techniques were commonly used in both Mesoamerica and South America to produce large numbers of vessels of a uniform shape and size, as well as figurines, fishing net weights, and spindle whorls. Sometimes two or three molds were used to make different parts of the same vessel.

FINISHING TECHNIQUES

Finishing served a variety of purposes, the first of which was to remove irregularities such as finger depressions and weld marks produced by forming and shaping the vessel. As surface irregularities were obliterated, surface contours were evened, and texture generally was improved (Shepard 1980:65). Final stages of construction involved either beating or scraping the vessel walls in order to thin them. These two finishing techniques essentially completed the manufacturing process. Thinning was then followed by smoothing and texturing, which completed the surfaces.

The most common kind of beating is known as the *paddle-and-anvil* technique (Fewkes 1941), in which a flat object such as a wood paddle was used to strike the exterior surface as a convex stone or clay anvil was held against the corresponding interior surface. The paddle-and-anvil technique of thinning usually is associated with finishing coil-built vessels, and leaves a series of distinct rounded impressions on the vessel interior (Fig. 44). It is well-represented in the ceramic technology of the Hohokam in the American Southwest, and of various native cultures in the eastern Woodlands and interior southern California.

Scraping was used to finish vessels shaped by coiling, molding, or pinching, and commonly occurred before the piece had completely dried, either while the clay was still wet or at a soft "leather-

Fig. 42. Body and base (upper row) and banded neck (lower row) sherds of six Anasazi corrugated jars from southeastern Utah representing several different types within the Mesa Verde Gray Ware series.

hard'' stage (Rice 1987:137). Most interior surfaces of vessel sherds thinned by scraping exhibit parallel striations left by an uneven or serrated tool such as a shell, stone flake, or potsherd (Fig. 45). Scraping was quite common among native groups of the Intermountain West, and is evident in sherds recovered from sites throughout the Great Basin and Colorado Plateau. The final construction stage associated with mold-made pottery usually consisted of trimming away excess clay and imperfections from the vessel when it was leather-hard.

After a ceramic vessel had attained its final shape, the surfaces often were finished by one of several techniques, most of which were variants of either texturing or smoothing. Smoothing created a finer and more regular surface, and usually was accomplished with a soft object such as a piece of cloth or leather, or the potter's hand before the piece was completely dry. Burnishing and polishing were two smoothing techniques associated with unglazed aboriginal ceramics that produced a luster on the unfired vessel and resulted in a fine finish.

Burnishing involved rubbing a surface back and forth with a smooth, hard object such as a stream pebble, bone, or horn. Through burnishing, the fine clay particles of the paste were compacted and

Fig. 43.   Rim and neck sherds of four Mesa Verde Gray Ware jars from southeastern Utah. The upper left specimen consists of five Mesa Verde Corrugated sherds that have been glued together, and exhibits alternating unobliterated, indented and unindented construction coils.   The upper right specimen consists of 10 Mancos Gray sherds that have been glued together and exhibits unobliterated, unindented construction coils.

reoriented, producing a lustrous finish as well as numerous easily recognizable, narrow, parallel facets on the surface of the vessel (Rice 1987:138; Orton et al. 1993:126). A polished finish was produced by carefully rubbing an unfired, leather-hard clay surface with a soft tool.   This technique produced a uniform luster without the distinct parallel facets associated with burnishing. In many parts of the New World, brushing was used to smooth the surface of an unfired vessel, and involved wiping or brushing the vessel surface with a textured but soft material, such as a handful of grass or hair. Vessel exteriors that exhibit either random or patterned brushing were brushed when the clay was still wet and plastic.

Fig. 44. Interior of a Promontory Gray Ware sherd from northern Utah showing dimpling associated with use of an anvil.

DECORATIVE TECHNIQUES

Surface Manipulation

Sometimes vessels were roughened, textured, or patterned, especially if they were to serve a utilitarian role. Textured surfaces also resulted from a particular construction technique, such as the corrugated and neck-banded wares of the Colorado Plateau and the plant fiber, cord-impressed wares of the Eastern Woodlands. Many decorative treatments such as impressing, incising, carving, stamping, and punctation involved displacing or penetrating the surface in order to create uniform designs.

Numerous techniques were employed to decorate a vessel by adding materials to or over the surface. For the most part, this process involved joining formed clay elements to the piece and applying slips and/or paints (see below). Decorative techniques based on joining included attaching small appliqués or modeled or molded elements and adding decorative inlays (Rice 1987:148). Appliqué refers to the

Fig. 45. Interior of an Anasazi black-on-white sherd that has been thinned by scraping.

application of small, shaped pieces of clay to the vessel surface, such as the coffee bean-sized clay pellets applied to jar necks by certain Fremont groups of Utah and eastern Nevada.

Coloring

Many aboriginal ceramic traditions of South and Central America and the American Southwest produced colored pottery through the use of slips and paints. A slip is a fine coating of clay and water applied over all or most of the surface of a vessel before firing to produce a smooth surface. Slips are usually a different color than the paste of a vessel, and can easily be identified by viewing the cross section of a sherd. The cross section of a slipped sherd usually exhibits a distinctly colored core, such as brown or gray, indicating the color of the paste, and is bordered by a thin band of the slip which may contrast markedly with the core color. If the slip color is the same as that of the paste, it may be difficult to verify its presence without the aid of a hand lens or microscope to reveal textural differences. In many cases, a slip functioned as the sole color addition and the vessel was left unpainted. White and other light-colored slips typically functioned as smooth, clean surfaces for subsequent painted decoration (Rice 1987:150).

Painting ceramic artifacts involved application of an organic or mineral pigment either before or after firing the vessel. Most prehistoric ceramic paints consisted of a mixture of pigments, fine clay, water, and a binder such as plant and animal oils. Most painted ceramics exhibit a slip, but some do not. Many unslipped, painted wares predate the slipped, painted wares of a given region, such as the early Lino Black-on-Gray ware of the Anasazi (Plog 1979:114), which consists of black pigments applied to gray bodies, or the early Estrella Red-on-Gray ware of the Hohokam (Gumerman and Haury 1979:78-79), which exhibits red painted designs over a gray ceramic body.

Vessels that have been painted with one color are sometimes referred to as monochrome, those with two colors may be described as bichrome, and those with three or more colors as polychrome. Use of organic paint can result in a black or gray color, and typically was used by Western Anasazi groups to produce beautifully designed black-on-white pottery (Fig. 46). Organic paints often consist of plant extracts, such as the black paint used by various Anasazi groups that was produced by boiling the young, tender growth of the Rocky Mountain bee plant. Some prehistoric groups undoubtedly applied organic paints to vessels after they were fired in order to avoid losing the design as a result of the organic pigment burning out during firing. However, many Puebloan groups of the Southwest applied carbon-based paints to their vessels before firing them, and by using adsorptive clays, proper slips, dense paints, and short firing time, produced pots with uniform, satiny black designs (Shepard 1980:33-34).

Inorganic pigments consist mostly of iron oxide minerals, such as hematite and limonite mixed with water and an organic binder. Depending on particle size and crystalline state, iron oxides exhibit a wide variety of colors after being dehydrated by firing (Shepard 1980:38). Hematite, for example, ranges from red to black, whereas limonite varies from yellow to red. Mineral paints made from manganese ores typically yielded a black or blackish brown color on oxidized pottery in the Pueblo (Fig. 46) and Maya areas (Shepard 1980:40).

DRYING AND FIRING

The final stages of ceramic production consist of drying and firing. Most modern native potters (and presumably those in antiquity as well) allow their formed vessels to dry for a period of several days, although some may use a drying time of several weeks. Drying time is largely determined by vessel thickness, paste content, and local weather or climatic conditions. It seems likely that wherever possible, most prehistoric New World potters relied upon sun-drying, while those in cool or wet climates/seasons allowed their vessels to dry indoors, perhaps near an open fire.

In general ceramic practice, there are three distinct phases associated with firing: (1) the dehydration period—when water is driven off at low heat to avoid rapid formation of steam and subsequent breakage; (2) the oxidation period—when carbonaceous matter is burned out from the clay; and (3) the vitrification period—when the pottery constituents begin to soften and fuse together (Shepard 1980:81). In order to avoid breakage from thermal shock during early firing, many prehistoric potters may have maintained a slow heat at the start of the firing process. Temperatures associated with New World native firing techniques were not sufficient to result in true vitrification (which is completed at about 1,200 degrees C.). However, because the composition of some clays may have lowered the temperature range required for vitrification considerably, and because fluxing impurities are common in the low grades of clay used by aboriginal potters, some groups produced ceramics that were at an incipient stage of vitrification (which begins between 800 and 900 degrees C.) (Shepard 1980:83).

Fig. 46.   Examples of Mesa Verde White Ware and Kayenta White Ware sherds recovered from several Anasazi sites in southeastern Utah.   Designs on the upper three specimens are of organic paint, while those on the lower four specimens are of mineral paint.

Aboriginal pottery was fired by two basic techniques: kiln and nonkiln. Although kilns were widely used throughout the Old World in prehistoric times (Orton et al. 1993:130), they were relatively uncommon among New World native groups and were mostly restricted to highland and gulf coastal Mexico (Payne 1982). Firing without kilns is called the open firing, bonfire, or clamping method, where the pots and the fuel were in immediate contact and were arranged in a stack on the ground or in a shallow pit. Nonkiln firings were always short and generally achieved relatively low temperatures. Open firing of pottery usually involved preparing a bed of slow burning fuel on the ground or in a pit, placing the pottery over the fuel, and placing more fuel and/or a layer of waste sherds around and on top of the pottery. Beginning with the lower layer, the fuel was then ignited, additional fuel was added, and after a short while, the fuel burned itself out and the firing was over (Rice 1987:153).

The type of fuel used to fire aboriginal pottery varied from area to area, and included wood, bark, brush, branches, coal, corncobs or cornstalks, and bison manure. There are various problems associated with open firing, including pots marked by smoke fireclouds, and cracked, dented, or overfired/underfired vessels resulting from rapid temperature rise. If a clear, uniform (oxidized) color was desired, it was necessary to protect the pottery from direct contact with the fuel. Most prehistoric potters who used open firing probably accomplished this by arranging large sherds around the pottery or between pottery and pieces of fuel (Shepard 1980:76). Such protection was not necessary for the pottery to attain a dark (reduced) color, or to be well-oxidized at the completion of firing. Temperatures attained by open firings usually ranged between 600 and 850 degrees C., although temperatures of 900 degrees C. or higher have been recorded historically among traditional native potters of the American Southwest through the use of a thermoelectric pyrometer (Colton 1951; Shepard 1980:83-84).

The firing atmosphere refers to the presence of gases, especially oxygen, while the clay is heated and cooled. An *oxidizing atmosphere* is characterized by an abundance of free oxygen which combines with elements (such as iron) in the paste and yields clear colors (e.g., yellows, buffs, or reds) of the ceramic body. A good draft affords an excess of oxygen over that required to burn the fuel and results in an oxidizing atmosphere in which carbonaceous matter in the paste or soot on the vessel surface will burn out. After the removal of carbon, the iron oxides in the paste will be brought to their highest stages of oxidation, resulting in the production of clear, uniform surface colors (Shepard 1980:216). Fuels that burn slowly and intensely, and which produce smokeless flames (such as juniper wood and coal), are ideal for producing an oxidizing firing atmosphere.

A *reducing atmosphere* is caused by insufficient oxygen for complete combustion of the fuel and insufficient draft resulting in the presence of reducing gases such as hydrogen, carbon, or carbon monoxide that prevent vessels from obtaining other sources of oxygen (Shepard 1980:216; Rice 1987:81). When this occurs, organic materials in the paste will remain unburned and iron oxides will be reduced to a lower state, producing dark colors such as grays (as opposed to reds). When there is insufficient draft, fuel will oftentimes produce smoke containing colloidal carbon, which will cause sooting or smudging of the pottery (Shepard 1980:216).

Many prehistoric ceramic sherds that display clear finishes also exhibit dark cores; this resulted from an oxidizing atmosphere that was not hot enough to burn away all of the organic constituents of the paste. In open firing, the atmosphere continually changes during different stages of combustion and with shifting draft and air currents. When wood first burns, volatile components are driven off and reducing gases are present; with poor draft and too much fuel, these gases will be excessive, resulting in a reducing atmosphere. However, the temperature range in such situations is usually low and the reducing gases may have little permanent effect upon the vessel surface. When the wood burns to charcoal, the fire is smokeless, and with adequate temperature and draft, an oxidizing atmosphere prevails. Unevenness in pottery colors reflects the fluctuations in firing atmosphere that result from shifting air currents, and the differential presence of gases and flames around the vessels (Shepard 1980:217).

CLASSIFICATION

Classification of a ceramic assemblage is the first critical step of ceramic analysis, and usually involves identification of wares and types that already have been established within the general region. Historically, most archaeologists have focused on ceramic typology in order to determine the general temporal associations of prehistoric sites, but more recent studies have used typological variation to study aspects of interregional and intraregional trade, population movements, and social organization. Most

ABORIGINAL CERAMICS

New World aboriginal ceramic traditions produced *terra-cotta wares*, which are defined as ceramics fired to a range sufficient enough for sintering of clay particles to begin. Sintering is when the edges of the particles soften and adhere to one another; this process begins at about 350 degrees C. and is completed by 700 degrees C. Terra-cottas are relatively coarse, porous (nonvitreous) wares fired at relatively low temperatures, usually 900 degrees C. or less. *Earthenwares* are fired at temperatures high enough for vitrification to begin, when the clay particles fuse together as glass (Hamer 1975). As mentioned above, this process starts between 800 and 900 degrees C.

All sciences use classification to impose order upon sets of data by creating groups whose members are very similar while the groups themselves may be very dissimilar. The principle is that the similarity of entities within groups does not occur randomly but reflects something inherently significant in their nature. Classifications of archaeological ceramics establish groups based upon common features of materials, techniques, and styles that are thought to be culturally significant. Most archaeological typologies are devised classifications created by the analyst, and are quite different from folk classifications which are based upon native categories. Therefore, our scientific classifications probably do not reflect the ways in which prehistoric peoples thought of and classified their products, because we are applying a completely alien set of values to the material remains of an extinct cultural tradition very different from our own. Nevertheless, classification schemes within archaeology are critical because they allow us to communicate through shared terminology and nomenclature, as well as furnishing a system for describing and naming the objects that we study.

CERAMIC WARES

When analyzing an assemblage of ceramic artifacts, first determine the number of wares present. This may vary, depending upon which culture area the assemblage comes from and the temporal span of site occupation. A ceramic *ware* can be defined as a class of pottery whose members share similar technology, paste, and surface treatment. Wares may be composed of a series of *types* or *styles* (or *varieties*) that refer to surface color, surface treatment, and vessel function. A *series* is a group of pottery types within a single ware that are known to follow one another in time. The most elementary classification of wares concerns identification of plain wares, textured/patterned wares, and painted wares.

Plain Wares

Native North American plain wares usually were made from black, brown, red, yellow, or gray clays, and have been assigned names based upon regional and/or technological affiliations and paste color. Hence, if one were to recover brown, paddle-and-anvil-thinned, quartz and/or feldspar-tempered potsherds from a prehistoric site in interior southern California, they probably would be classified as Tizon Brown Ware. Such a classification is an example of archaeologists assigning their materials to the established typology of a particular area. One should never rely solely upon surface color to classify unpainted pottery (especially sherds within a highly fragmentary assemblage) because various factors such as clouding during firing and sooting during use alter the original surface color. Always view freshly broken cross sections of sherds when classifying them, because soil-staining and sooting tend to obscure the true color of the fabric. A single plain ware may contain two or more types based on differences in manufacturing techniques, spatial distributions, and/or temporal affiliations. For example, the Lino Gray Style of Northern Anasazi Gray Ware consists of three types based on differences in temper and geographic association (Lucius and Breternitz 1992:9).

112

Textured Wares

Textured or patterned wares are unslipped and unpainted, but exhibit surfaces that have been decorated through carving, incising, impressions (e.g., fingernail, cordage), stamping, punctation, or corrugation. Plains Woodland pottery is well known for its relatively simple surface decoration, whereas both Hopewellian (Fig. 47) and Mississippian ceramics bear intricately carved and stamped designs. A single textured ware often consists of several styles based upon differences in exterior surface treatment and rim form. Each style typically dates to a discrete time period, but contains different types that are particular to a certain region, such as the Tusayan Corrugated Style of Northern Anasazi Gray Ware, which dates to ca. A.D. 900 to 1000 and consists of six types associated with at least four different regions (Lucius and Breternitz 1992:12).

Painted Wares

Painted wares derive their names from the colors of their slips and not the color of their pastes. Therefore, red wares, white wares, and orange wares all denote slip colors. Most slipped vessels exhibit designs painted in contrasting colors, such as the impressive black-on-white ceramic vessels produced by the Anasazi (Fig. 46) and Mogollon. Within a given painted ceramic ware, types and styles may be distinguished by a variety of factors, including different design elements, tempering agents, paint types, and regional affiliations. A good example of the complexity of painted ceramic typologies is the seven different types of black-on-white pottery (Chapin, Piedra, White Mesa, Cortez, Mancos, McElmo, and Mesa Verde) within the Mesa Verde White Ware series. Each type represents a distinctive decorative group of ceramics with consistent material combinations and manufacturing techniques that are affiliated with the Mesa Verde ceramic manufacturing region.

CERAMIC TYPES

Archaeologists traditionally have used the spatial and temporal information provided by ceramics to develop typologies, which are formal summaries of the technological and stylistic combinations required for the identification of ceramics into type categories. Lucius and Breternitz (1992:4) defined ceramic type as "a class of ceramics known to have been manufactured in a geographical region during a restricted time interval." In the American Southwest, the conventions for naming ceramic types (as well as series and wares) were established by researchers such as Kidder (1927), Gladwin and Gladwin (1930), and Colton and Hargrave (1937), and required the use of a geographical name followed by a descriptive term, such as Estrella Red-on-Gray, Mancos Gray, and Tusayan Black-on-White. The Southwestern ceramic classification system is a time/space typology, and numerous ceramic attributes have been used to establish different types thought to have temporal and spatial significance (Hargrave 1974).

As noted by Griset (1986a), some of these typologies are problematic because subsequent researchers have added new types or styles to an original typology based upon the requirements of project-specific research questions or problems. The new types within the modified typology may largely be determined by spatially restricted attributes that are not culturally significant. This causes confusion for archaeologists who try to classify ceramics that they have recovered from sites in the same region, but are unable to replicate the revised typology because various specimens do not exhibit the exact

113

Fig. 47. Incised Hopewell jar sherd and pipe fragment from Boone County, Missouri.

compositional attributes of the new types, even though the two collections are virtually identical with respect to manufacturing, surface treatment, and design element attributes. Hargrave (1974) believed that types should be used as technological indicators as opposed to cultural indicators, and restricted to consistent and distinct criteria, such as form, firing atmosphere, paste, decoration, etc.

A great deal of discussion has centered upon ceramic typology, especially the imposed artificial, nature of archaeologically derived types, the application of different classificatory criteria to the same wares and types of certain regions, and the lack of consistency in the use of ceramic terminology (the terms ''ware'' and ''type'' mean different things to different archaeologists). The typing of pottery is artificial in that its primary function in archaeology is to outline relative chronologies, a purpose that is totally unrelated to its conditions of native production and use. Virtually any ceramic feature that changes

114

through time has been used by archaeologists as a criterion of classification, regardless of its meaning (or lack thereof) to the aboriginal makers and users of that pottery (Shepard 1980:307). In the eastern Great Basin for example, five of the six types of Fremont Gray Ware pottery are distinguished primarily by regional differences in temper, which reflect different environmental resources (as opposed to different cultural traditions). This is simply the result of archaeologists using devised classifications to study aspects of prehistoric material culture.

Lyneis (1988) discussed the problems associated with the lack of a suitable taxonomic structure for the plain paddle-and-anvil-thinned ceramics of southern California, especially that of Tizon Brown Ware. As defined above, a ceramic ware refers to a grouping of pottery types that are similar in technology and manufacturing methods but which has minimal temporal or spatial association. When first formally defined by Dobyns and Euler (1958), Tizon Brown Ware was restricted to western Arizona, but since then, the term has been applied to most granitic-tempered, paddle-and-anvil-thinned brown pottery of the upland Colorado Desert, Mojave Desert, and Peninsular Ranges of southern California, and northern Baja California (Lyneis 1988:146-147). Application of the term "Tizon Brown Ware" to much of the pottery from the above areas is appropriate, because ceramic technology diffused westward from the Patayan regions of western Arizona sometime after about A.D. 600 or 700, and granitic-tempered, paddle-and-anvil pottery was produced throughout much of southern California by about A.D. 1300. However, a series of regionally and temporally specific types has never been devised for Tizon Brown Ware. As a result, many archaeologists in southern California use the term "Tizon Brown Ware" as if it were a type (with spatial and temporal meaning), which it is not.

An excellent example of the confusion that can arise from application of different criteria for defining types within the same ware by different researchers are the different typologies and chronologies for Lower Colorado Buff Ware of the Lowland Patayan tradition (Waters 1982). Malcolm Rogers, who pioneered the study of Patayan prehistory, devised the first typology and chronology for Lower Colorado Buff Ware based on differences in surface treatment, vessel form, and rim form (Rogers 1945). In the early 1950s, Schroeder (1952) developed a very different typology for Lower Colorado Buff Ware based primarily on temper differences, but used Rogers' type names. This caused a great deal of confusion in the Lower Patayan region over the next 10 to 20 years, and subsequent researchers have questioned the validity of many of Schroeder's types, whereas the Rogers typology has been supported by subsequent research (Waters 1982:279-280). The above situation resulted from a lack of communication (especially on Schroeder's part), as he either failed to examine or misinterpreted Rogers' 1945 paper and associated fieldnotes, and did not consult Rogers. Virtually every archaeologist who has analyzed a ceramic assemblage from the Colorado Desert has had to come to grips with the competing typologies for the region; and both Waters (1982) and Griset (1986b) have written interesting discussions on the topic.

Just as classificatory confusion can arise from different typologies within one ceramic ware, it also can result from different wares within the same region exhibiting similar attributes. A case in point comes from the northeastern Great Basin, where plain wares produced by Fremont groups (Great Salt Lake Gray Ware) from about A.D. 400 to 1400 and Shoshone groups (Shoshonean Ware) from about A.D. 1400 to 1850 both contain similar raw materials, and both were formed by coiling, thinned by scraping, and fired in a poorly controlled atmosphere. Dean and Heath (1990) pointed out that the current typological attributes applied to these wares preclude the easy classification of potsherds from northern Utah and southern Idaho as either Great Salt Lake or Shoshonean. This problem will not be solved until rigorous sets of objective typological criteria (if they exist) are developed for each ware and are applied systematically by local archaeologists.

When classifying ceramics, it is essential to have access to a relatively large comparative collection of all ceramic wares, types, and styles that occur within the region from which the assemblage has been recovered. This will allow the student to classify her/his assemblage through direct comparisons with specimens that have been properly identified and incorporated into the regional ceramic typology.

NONVESSEL CERAMIC ARTIFACTS

Various ceramic artifacts other than vessels, such as figurines, pipes (see Fig. 47), ornaments, rattles, and spindle whorls may be represented in a site assemblage. Such specimens comprise a distinct ceramic category, and should be considered separately from ceramic vessels. Information concerning the classification and analyses of nonvessel ceramics usually is presented under one or more distinct subheadings following those associated with ceramic vessels (e.g., pots, jars, bowls, cups, canteens, and plates).

BASIC ANALYSIS

The process of basic ceramic analysis involves three major areas: form and function analysis, technological analysis, and stylistic analysis. Upon separating an assemblage into respective wares and types and cataloging them accordingly, the student should begin the painstaking task of refitting all conjoinable sherds. Many soluble glues composed mostly of cellulose nitrate or polyvinyl acetate are well-suited for refitting sherds, which is an important early stage of form analysis because it helps to define the different shapes and sizes of vessels represented in the collection. A small sand box can be used to support sherds that have been glued together while the glue dries and hardens.

FORM AND FUNCTION ANALYSIS

Vessel Form

Major vessel forms produced by New World natives include bowls, jars, scoops, plates/trays, ladles, cups/mugs, and pitchers (see Figure 48 for some examples; each region has a different classification, check local references). Form analysis is based on careful classification of clusters of different vessel shapes, which are best represented by rim and shoulder sherds. To a large extent, aspects of vessel form are determined by the intended function of a vessel. It usually is safe to assume that, for the most part, bowls were commonly used for serving and eating, and jars were used primarily for cooking and storage. However, not every vessel was used only for its originally intended purpose, and many undoubtedly served different functions after they fulfilled their original role.

Original vessel forms can be reconstructed from such sherds by projecting measurements of vessel mouth diameter and height. Calculation of original mouth (or orifice) diameter is relatively straightforward, and is most easily achieved by fitting the curve of a rim sherd to a standard diameter-measurement template (Fig. 49). After using rim sherds (and perhaps body sherds that conjoin with rims) to determine the various vessel forms and mouth diameters represented in the collection, one can produce a figure illustrating rim sherd profiles along with their corresponding metric and form attributes (Fig. 50).

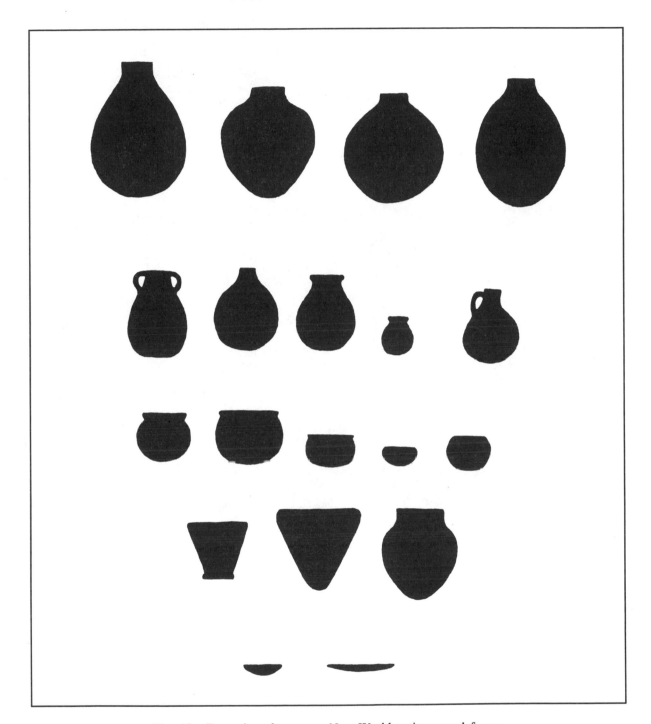

Fig. 48. Examples of common New World native vessel forms.

The base form or diameter cannot be determined unless the vessel fragment includes part of the base. Both Shepard (1980:224-255) and Rice (1987:215-226) presented comprehensive discussions of methods for determining and illustrating the forms of ceramic vessels. Senior and Birnie (1995) developed a

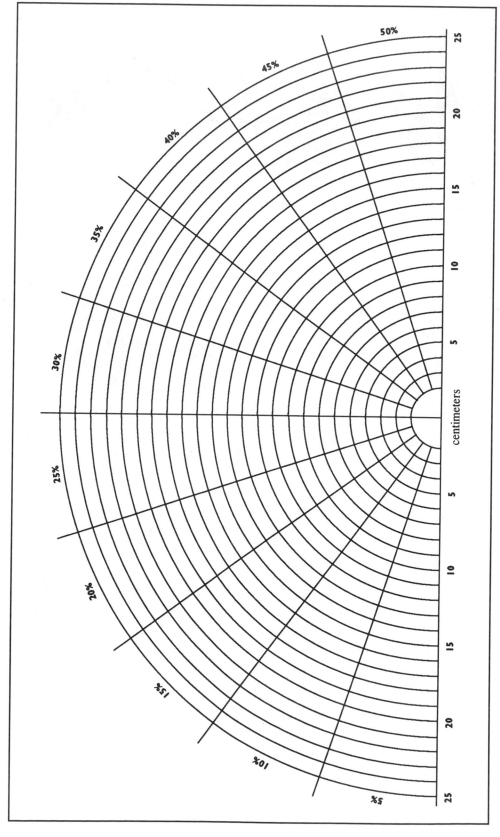

Fig. 49. A rim diameter-measurement template, which determines rim sherd radius and estimates the percentage of the total vessel rim circumference present.

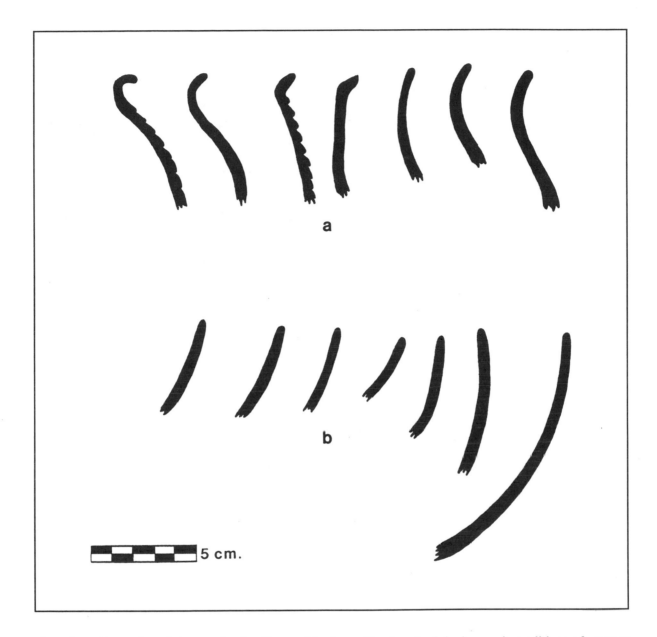

Fig. 50.   Examples of rim, neck, shoulder, and body profiles for aboriginal ceramic traditions of western
North America: (a) jars; (b) bowls.

computer program by which vessel volume may be determined from carefully prepared vessel profiles, constructed from relatively small portions of a vessel.

Another important aspect of form analysis includes determination of the range of wall thicknesses for each ceramic type represented in the assemblage. This can be accomplished by using a pair of metric bow calipers and reporting the thinnest and thickest sherds in millimeters. A tabulation of the type and vertical distribution of all recovered sherds also should be presented in the technical report, including

119

sherd totals and percentages by type (see Table 3). Some sherds may exhibit uniconically or biconically drilled repair holes, indicating that a vessel had cracked during its use and someone had attempted to mend the break (Fig. 51). Many native peoples often accomplished this by drilling a hole on each side of the crack, applying some sort of mastic to the crack faces, and binding the crack by stringing a thin strand of plant fiber cordage or sinew through the holes and tying it together. The presence of repair holes in a ceramic assemblage should always be noted, as should sherds with worn edges and those used for other specific functions, such as lids, beads/pendants, and scraping/smoothing implements.

Table 3
TYPE AND DISTRIBUTION OF CERAMICS RECOVERED FROM CA-RIV-1179,
LA QUINTA, RIVERSIDE COUNTY, CALIFORNIA
(adapted from Sutton 1988:Table 14)

Type	Depth (cm.)									Totals	%
	0-10	10-20	20-30	30-40	40-50	50-60	60-70	70-80	80-90		
Tizon Brown	4	160	144	98	32	13	10	--	2	463	36.4
Salton Buff	1	272	73	82	40	3	5	1	--	477	37.5
Colorado Buff	1	42	14	8	2	--	1	--	--	68	5.3
unclassified Buff	--	208	28	20	8	--	--	--	--	264	20.8
Totals	6	682	259	208	82	16	16	1	2	1,272	100.0

Vessel Function

Archaeologists oftentimes rely upon ethnographic analogies to assign specific functions to different vessel forms, an approach that assumes that the shape of a vessel directly reflects its function or functions. In areas where native peoples continued to produce pottery after contact with Euroamericans, and whose ceramic traditions are reasonably well-documented, this approach is relatively safe. However, there are numerous pitfalls associated with the direct historic approach, and many intangibles affect the function of prehistoric ceramics. Other indirect means of determining vessel function include the archaeological contexts in which they were uncovered and residues they may contain. Because many prehistoric vessels were used for a variety of purposes, their archaeological context simply reflects their final resting place (and perhaps their final function) and does not provide information concerning the entire use-life of a given vessel (Rice 1987:232-233).

Identification of the ancient contents of a ceramic vessel can provide important information regarding vessel function. Such evidence traditionally has been obtained from cooking pots where charring has preserved portions of the original contents, but now this approach is also being applied to storage vessels as well. As noted by Rice (1987:233), residue identification techniques are especially appropriate for unglazed vessels (which comprise the bulk of New World aboriginal ceramics), because their porous interior surfaces are likely to contain residues deposited during use. Animal fats and vegetable oils are the most common materials collected for ceramic residue studies, and specific organic contents can be identified by infrared absorption, mass spectrography, and gas chromatography. Each of these techniques identify certain fatty acids, lipids, cholesterol, triglycerides, and other organic components (Rice 1987:233). Analyses of plant pollen and phytoliths obtained from residue scrapings also has proven useful in identifying the contents of prehistoric vessels (e.g., Tuohy 1990).

Fig. 51. Example of a uniconically drilled repair hole in an Anasazi Gray Ware body sherd.

TECHNOLOGICAL ANALYSIS

Technological analyses of pottery focus mostly on description of the core and how vessels were constructed, finished, and fired. Core description revolves around analyzing the color and texture of the paste, identification of the temper, and perhaps identification of the clay source through various physicochemical methods. Technological analyses and characterization should begin with simple methods of observation rather than with the more complex and costly ones.

Describing the Ceramic Core

Preliminary sorting of sherds by paste color and texture of the ceramic core can be accomplished by breaking fresh cross sections of sherds with a pair of needle-nosed pliers and examining them under a low-power (10X to 20X) hand lens (Bennett 1974:31). Documentation of paste colors of ceramic cores (as well as those of the surfaces) can be accomplished in one of two ways, depending upon the level of precision required: (1) by their common English names (e.g., red, brown, tan); or (2) by using a standard (e.g., Munsell) soil color chart. For a thorough discussion of the application of Munsell colors to ceramics, the interested reader should refer to Orton et al. (1993:136-138).

121

Identification of paste colors provides information concerning ancient processing and firing techniques, as well as raw material content (Bennett 1974:24). For example, a clay that has fired to a red color indicates that it contains iron and probably was fired in an oxidizing atmosphere, whereas a clay that has fired to a uniform dark gray probably has a relatively high carbon content and was fired in a reducing atmosphere or was smudged during firing. Sherds that exhibit clear surfaces and dark cores most likely were incompletely oxidized in firing (Fig. 52).

As used here, *paste texture* refers to the appearance of the ceramic paste as determined by clay particle size, and not the size of temper additives. It is critical to use standardized terms and definitions for describing paste texture, and Wentworth's (1922) grade scale for classifying sediments (Table 4) has been used by archaeologists for describing the textures of both ceramic pastes and tempers. Most paste textures will range from silty to coarse, although a few will fall within the very coarse range.

Table 4
WENTWORTH'S SEDIMENT SIZE CLASSIFICATION

Name	Size (diameter in mm.)
pebble	64 - 4
granule	4 - 2
very coarse	2 - 1
coarse	1 - 1 1/2
medium	1/2 - 1/4
fine	1/4 - 1/8
very fine	1/8 - 1/16
silt	1/16 - 1/256

After grouping sherds according to different temper types (i.e., stone, sherd, shell, plant fiber), basic identification of specific temper materials usually can be accomplished by examining a representative sample of sherd cross sections under low power (15X to 45X) magnification. For example, if the entire assemblage has been tempered with mineral filler, it is possible to identify individual minerals such as quartz, feldspar, mica, hornblende, and olivine by comparing temper materials with mineral specimens collected from the same region as the sherds. Wentworth's sediment scale can then be used to classify the different sizes of mineral temper. An alternative scale for classifying temper size is the one devised by Powers (1953).

Describing Surface Condition and Treatment

After documenting the surface colors of sherds in your assemblage, you should determine the surface condition of specimens (without magnification) with regard to four main kinds of surface "damage," most of which result from the use of certain raw materials and construction and finishing techniques. This consists of inspecting the assemblage for the presence of: (1) wear, abrasion, and/or erosion; (2) crazing (a situation in which differential shrinkage causes the surface of the vessel to crack while the remainder of the vessel wall remains undamaged—crazing occurs on both slipped and unslipped [often burnished] surfaces); (3) pitting (caused by differential swelling or shrinking of the temper particles

122

and the clay body of the vessel); and (4) flaking (a frequent sequel to crazing) (Bennett 1974:34-38).

Methods of vessel construction and finishing also should be determined for all specimens. This includes determining how vessels were built (by modeling, coiling, or molding) and noting the presence of finishing techniques such as beating, scraping, wiping, burnishing and polishing.

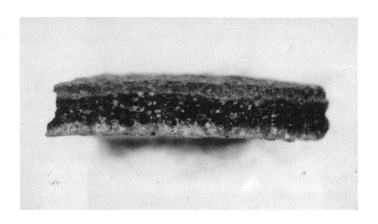

Determining Hardness

Hardness is one criterion by which the durability of pottery is determined, and, generally speaking, the hardness of a given clay increases with the temperature of firing. However, it is important to note that hardness

Fig. 52. Cross section of a Shoshonean Brown Ware body sherd exhibiting a black core and reddish-brown surfaces, indicating that it was fired in an incompletely oxidizing atmosphere.

is affected not only by firing temperature, but also by impurities that make the clay more fusible (Shepard 1980:114). Therefore, sherds may differ markedly in hardness, with softer specimens having been fired at a significantly higher temperature than harder ones, which have been made from a low-fusing, dense-firing clay. Scratching the surface with a fingernail or penknife, or tapping sherds against a hard surface is adequate for rough sorting sherds by hardness, but the most common hardness testing procedure used by archaeologists is the Mohs mineral hardness scale (Rice 1987:355-357). This scale uses a series of minerals of increasing hardness, ranked from 1 to 10, with talc being the softest and diamond the hardest. The Mohs test measures ''scratch hardness,'' the ease with which minerals will produce a scratch when drawn across the surface of a specimen. The Mohs test is conducted under a binocular microscope, starting with minerals at the harder end of the scale and moving toward softer minerals (Rice 1987:356). If a mineral is harder than the test sherd, it will produce a visible indentation on the sherd. If the test sherd is harder than a given mineral, it will abrade the mineral, which leaves a streak of crushed mineral on the sherd's surface. Most nonkiln-fired New World pottery ranges between 3 and 5 on Mohs scale, but hardness values as low as 2 and as high as 7 also have been documented.

Determining Firing Atmosphere

The major causes of pottery color are the composition of clay and the atmosphere, temperature, and duration of firing. Secondary modifications of color result from postfiring conditions such as deposition of carbon from cooking over fires, deposition of residues such as salts during storage, deposition of substances from the soil after discard, and reheating after discard (Shepard 1980:103). Students must be able to recognize the presence of secondary modifications and discount them when describing ceramic color. When color is studied in relation to clay composition and firing method, information may be obtained concerning ancient firing techniques—whether a vessel was fired in a reducing or oxidizing environment, or whether it was intentionally smudged at some point during the firing process.

ABORIGINAL CERAMICS

Colton (1939) was among the first archaeologists to note the effects of firing atmosphere on ceramic colors, and this brief publication heavily influenced pottery classification in the Southwest. Experienced archaeologists often can determine the firing atmosphere of a sherd simply by examining its color. Clear creams, oranges, yellows, and reds typically indicate fully oxidized clays, but determining the original firing atmosphere of whitish, brown, and gray ceramics is more problematic because they can result from different firing techniques. The original firing condition of any sherd can be determined by refiring it in an electric kiln equipped with a thermoelectric pyrometer in an oxidizing atmosphere. The objective here is to heat the specimen sufficiently to combust the vast majority of organic materials that may be present and allow the colors from any iron to develop fully. Refiring specimens for 30 minutes at temperatures of between 800 and 850 degrees C. usually is sufficient for most terra-cottas and earthenwares (Rice 1987:344). If there is no change in the color of the paste upon refiring, then the final stage of ancient firing occurred in an oxidizing atmosphere. Alternatively, if the paste turns to a clear color upon refiring, this indicates that the ceramic object was incompletely oxidized, reduced, or perhaps even smudged. Shepard (1980:220) indicated that a short firing at about 500 degrees C. may be sufficient to clear a sherd sample that originally was smudged.

Mineralogical Characterization

Detailed compositional analysis of both temper and paste can be accomplished by sending a representative sample of sherds to a specialist for viewing under a petrographic microscope in either thin section or powder form. Petrographic thin-sectioning requires removal of a portion of a sample sherd (usually a few millimeters thick and several centimeters long) which is prepared for viewing by being mounted on a glass microscope slide, ground to a thickness of approximately 0.03 mm., and then covered with a thin glass slip (Rice 1987:373; Orton et al. 1993:140). The slide is then viewed under a microscope with a polarized light source and a rotating stage, which allows for accurate identification of the sherd's mineral content. Determining the mineral composition of a ceramic sherd can provide important information about the origin of the clay or filler, which in turn can be used to discern the presence of trade wares in an assemblage.

As noted by Shepard (1980:157), the thin section has many advantages over a powdered sample because it shows the texture of the paste, the proportions of inclusions, the size and shape of grains, the relationship and proportions of different constituents, the texture and mineral components of rocks, and the structure and texture of the clay. Thin sections can be used for quantitative, as well as qualitative, studies, and have been important components of technological ceramic studies throughout North America. For a recent example of petrographic analysis of Southwestern ceramics, the reader should consult Hill (1994), who analyzed a Kayenta Anasazi ceramic assemblage recovered from Black Mesa in northeastern Arizona.

X-ray diffraction is another method of characterizing minerals and other crystalline materials within a ceramic fabric. Each mineral has a unique lattice distance which is part of its crystalline structure, and when X-rays are directed at a mineral-containing sample, they are diffracted at distinct angles which form a pattern for that mineral. Therefore, each mineral has a unique X-ray diffraction signature, and this technique can be used to determine the mineral composition of ceramic pastes and tempers. X-ray diffraction analysis recently has been used in the eastern Great Basin to document temper differences in Fremont and Promontory ceramics (Hendricks et al. 1990).

BASIC LABORATORY METHODS IN ARCHAEOLOGY

Chemical Characterization

Determining the chemical composition of archaeological ceramics has become increasingly popular during the last 25 years, mostly because instrumentation advances have increased the accuracy and speed of these techniques (Rice 1987:389-390). Chemical characterization studies yield important data concerning the type and amount of trace elements present in ceramics, and when combined with data from mineralogical studies, can provide information concerning production areas and the presence of trade wares containing exotic paste constituents. Chemical techniques recently applied to ceramic assemblages by archaeologists include X-ray fluorescence (Ballie and Stern 1984), atomic absorption spectroscopy (Tubb et al. 1980), and neutron activation analysis (De Atley et al. 1982; Harbottle 1982; Hurd et al. 1990).

As with most mineral analytic methods, chemical characterization studies usually require damage to the specimen by removing a sample for analysis, and in some instances, chemical analyses can be relatively expensive (on the order of several hundred dollars per sample). X-ray fluorescence analysis is nondestructive, and can analyze sherds and even small vessels without removing samples from them. Alternatively, neutron activation analysis is a destructive analytic technique that requires a crushed ceramic sample, but can be more accurate than X-ray fluorescence in producing a trace element profile of a core.

STYLISTIC ANALYSIS

Stylistic analysis emphasizes the presence of decorative elements within a ceramic assemblage. This approach is an important and powerful analytic tool because it documents the decorative styles and traditions of prehistoric potters, which are assumed to be culturally conditioned and therefore reflective of the social system behind the pots being studied. Stylistic studies of ceramics allow archaeologists to identify decorative trends within ceramic traditions and document change in those decorative techniques and motifs through time. Ceramic decoration can vary from a plain ware olla with simple thumbnail incisions along its lip to a complex polychrome bowl with human or animal figures.

One of the more traditional approaches to analysis of pottery styles focuses on identifying certain elements, motifs, configurations, and decorative layouts, and grouping vessels or sherds into classes or types based upon the presence or absence of certain stylistic features (Rice 1987:249). These design categories are then used to reconstruct local and regional site sequences by documenting gradual stylistic change through time from controlled stratigraphic contexts. The spatial distributions of design styles also provide information concerning social organization, trade, and diffusion.

Another method of stylistic analysis is that of design element analysis, in which one isolates individual elements of pottery design and attempts to explain their spatial occurrence in terms of the social behavior of the makers and users of that pottery (Rice 1987:252). A well-known early application of design element analysis to prehistoric social organization was conducted by Hill (1970) to infer the presence of matrilocal residence groups at Broken K Pueblo in eastern Arizona. Other researchers, such as Plog (1978), have argued that the spatial distribution of design patterns described by Hill could have resulted from chronological or functional factors. Another criticism of this approach concerns whether styles mostly reflect social relationships or whether they are equally influenced by other factors such as ecological conditions or ideological systems. The use of ceramic design element analysis to reconstruct aspects of ancient social organization also has been criticized on methodological grounds, questioning whether design elements are sensitive to the kinds of interactions being proposed and what sampling and statistical procedures are appropriate (Rice 1987:257).

Other popular approaches to the study of pottery design and style are pattern or symmetry analysis and design structure analysis. The first approach uses a standard set of terms for describing the property of symmetry with respect to the spatial position of geometrical figures and their movement across a line or around a point axis (Rice 1987:260). The second approach views design structure as the cognitive system that underlies a certain style and through which the style is produced by artists (Rice 1987:264).

Stylistic analysis of ceramics, especially those of sophisticated ceramic traditions, can be quite complex and tend to be plagued by both methodological and interpretive problems. These difficulties arise from the fact that the relationships between stylistic attributes of pottery decoration and prehistoric sociopolitical and/or ideological systems are poorly understood, and subject to a great deal of bias on the part of individual researchers according to their particular theoretical backgrounds.

DATING OF CERAMICS

A variety of methods are used to date ceramics: *relative* techniques (e.g., cross-dating, seriation, and stratigraphic association) that can tell you which is older than which; and *absolute* techniques (e.g., radiocarbon, archaeomagnetism, and thermoluminescence) that can give you an actual age. Each of these techniques has long been used by archaeologists to determine the ages of pottery, and are discussed in some detail in Chapter 13.

EXPERIMENTAL STUDIES

There is much to be said for the explanatory and comparative powers afforded by experimental replication of the styles and techniques of aboriginal ceramics. In order for such studies to be valid, vessels should be made by experienced potters using native materials and methods. A thermoelectric pyrometer can be used to document a series of firing temperatures for different pots, and subsequent use of these vessels for different types of cooking (e.g., simmering versus boiling) can determine how well they withstand thermal shock. Controlled experiments also have been conducted to assess the effects of different tempers (Skibo et al. 1989) and wall thicknesses (L. Cozzens, personal communication 1994) upon vessel durability. Experimental possibilities associated with the replication and use of native-style ceramics are many, and most studies date within the last twenty years or so (e.g., Holstein 1973; Skibo and Schiffer 1987). Figure 53 shows replicas of Shoshonean Brown Ware and Fremont Great Salt Lake Gray Ware open mouth jars just after production. Each will be used to cook different foods in different ways to assess their cooking efficiency. Ceramic experimentation is an exciting area of archaeological analysis that is growing in popularity and has tremendous potential to inform us about the past.

CONCLUDING REMARKS

One must always remember that the ultimate objective of a systematic analysis of archaeological ceramics is to improve our understanding of prehistoric human behavior. Therefore, the primary goal

Fig. 53.   Replicas of a flower pot-shaped Shoshonean Brown Ware jar and a globular Fremont Gray Ware jar. Both vessels consist of the same reddish-brown residual clay and quartz sand temper collected from central Utah. They were built by coiling, thinned by scraping, and then open-fired. The Shoshonean-type pot was fired in an oxidizing atmosphere, while the Fremont-style pot was fired in a reducing atmosphere. Vessels courtesy of Lynn Cozzens.

of such an exercise is to explain the role of ceramics within an extinct cultural system—a lifeway that has been partially (and oftentimes inaccurately) reconstructed from imperfectly preserved material remains. Ceramic assemblages are end-products of complex behavioral processes that reflect culturally defined standards, individual styles, diffusion of foreign manufacturing and decorating techniques, and trade of finished artifacts. As such, they provide archaeologists with unique opportunities to document prehistoric human interactions at a variety of levels. By clearly stating your research questions and problems, and carefully describing and analyzing your assemblage, it will be possible to arrive at meaningful interpretations regarding the complex behaviors that are associated with a collection of potsherds recovered from an archaeological site.

ABORIGINAL CERAMICS

REFERENCES

Ballie, P. J., and W. B. Stern
1984   Non-Destructive Surface Analysis of Roman Terra Sigillata: A Possible Tool in Provenance Studies? Archaeometry 26(1):62-68.

Bennett, M. Ann
1974   Basic Ceramic Analysis. Portales: Eastern New Mexico Contributions in Anthropology 6(1).

Colton, Harold S.
1939   The Reducing Atmosphere and Oxidizing Atmosphere in Prehistoric Southwestern Ceramics. American Antiquity 4(3):224-231.

1951   Hopi Pottery Firing Temperatures. Plateau 24:73-76.

Colton, Harold S., and Lyndon L. Hargrave
1937   Handbook of Northern Arizona Pottery Wares. Flagstaff: Museum of Northern Arizona Bulletin No. 11.

Dean, Patricia, and Kathleen M. Heath
1990   Form and Function: Understanding Gray Pottery in the Northeastern Great Basin. In: Hunter-Gatherer Pottery from the Far West, Joanne M. Mack, ed., pp. 19-28. Nevada State Museum Anthropological Papers No. 23.

De Atley, Suzanne P., M. James Blackman, and Jacqueline S. Olin
1982   Comparison of Data Obtained by Neutron Activation and Electron Microprobe Analyses of Ceramics. In: Archaeological Ceramics, Jacqueline S. Olin and A. D. Franklin, eds., pp. 79-88. Washington: Smithsonian Institution.

Dobyns, Henry F., and Robert C. Euler
1958   Tizon Brown Ware: A Descriptive Revision. In: Pottery Types of the Southwest: Wares 14, 15, 16, 17 and 18: Revised Descriptions, Alameda Brown Ware, Tizon Brown Ware, Lower Colorado Buff Ware, Prescott Gray Ware, San Francisco Mountain Gray Ware, H. S. Colton, ed. Museum of Northern Arizona Ceramic Series No. 3D. Flagstaff.

Fewkes, V. J.
1941   The Function of the Paddle and Anvil in Pottery Making. American Antiquity 7(2):162-164.

Gladwin, Winifred, and Harold S. Gladwin
1930   Some Southwestern Pottery Types: Series I. Gila Pueblo. Medallion Papers No. 6. Globe, AZ: The Medallion.

128

Griset, Suzanne
    1986a Notes on Ceramic Analysis. In: Pottery of the Great Basin and Adjacent Areas, S. Griset, ed., pp. 119-124. University of Utah Anthropological Papers No. 111.

    1986b Ceramic Artifacts. In: Excavations at Indian Hill Rockshelter, Anza-Borrego Desert State Park, California, 1984-1985, P. J. Wilke, M. McDonald, and L. A. Payen, eds., pp. 80-100. University of California, Riverside, Archaeological Research Unit Report No. 772.

Gumerman, George J., and Emil W. Haury
    1979 Prehistory: Hohokam. In: Handbook of North American Indians, Vol. 9, Southwest, Alfonso Ortiz, ed., pp. 75-90. Washington: Smithsonian Institution.

Hamer, Frank
    1975 The Potter's Dictionary of Materials and Techniques. London: Pitman.

Harbottle, Garman
    1982 Provenience Studies Using Neutron Activation Analysis: The Role of Standardization. In: Archaeological Ceramics, Jacqueline S. Olin and A. D. Franklin, eds., pp. 67-77. Washington: Smithsonian Institution.

Hargrave, Lyndon L.
    1974 Type Determinants in Southwestern Ceramics and Some of Their Implications. Plateau 46(3):76-95.

Hendricks, Joseph, Donald W. Forsyth, and Chun Jung
    1990 X-Ray Diffraction Analysis of Some Formative and Late Prehistoric Pottery from Utah. In: Hunter-Gatherer Pottery from the Far West, Joanne M. Mack, ed., pp. 30-51. Nevada State Museum Anthropological Papers No. 23.

Hill, David V.
    1994 Technological Analysis: Making and Using Ceramics on Black Mesa. In: Function and Technology of Anasazi Ceramics from Black Mesa, Arizona, M. F. Smith, Jr., ed., pp. 23-54. Southern Illinois University at Carbondale Center for Archaeological Investigations, Occasional Paper No. 15.

Hill, James N.
    1970 Broken K Pueblo: Prehistoric Social Organization in the American Southwest. University of Arizona Anthropological Papers No. 18.

Holstein, H. O.
    1973 Replication of Late Woodland Ceramics from Western Pennsylvania. Pennsylvania Archaeologist 43(3-4):75-85.

Hurd, Gary S., George E. Miller, and Henry C. Koerper
    1990   An Application of Neutron Activation Analysis to the Study of Prehistoric Californian Ceramics. In: Hunter-Gatherer Pottery from the Far West, Joanne M. Mack, ed., pp. 202-220. Nevada State Museum Anthropological Papers No. 23.

Kidder, Alfred V.
    1927   Southwestern Archaeological Conference. Science 66(1716):489-491.

Lucius, William A., and David A. Breternitz
    1992   Northern Anasazi Ceramic Styles: A Field Guide for Identification. Phoenix: Center for Indigenous Studies in the Americas Publications in Anthropology No. 1.

Lyneis, Margaret M.
    1988   Tizon Brown Ware and the Problems Raised by Paddle-and-Anvil Pottery in the Mojave Desert. Journal of California and Great Basin Anthropology 10(2):146-155.

Orton, Clive, Paul Tyers, and Alan Vince
    1993   Pottery in Archaeology. Cambridge: Cambridge University Press.

Payne, William O.
    1982   Kilns and Ceramic Technology of Ancient Mesoamerica. In: Archaeological Ceramics, Jacqueline S. Olin and A. D. Franklin, eds., pp. 189-192. Washington: Smithsonian Institution.

Plog, Fred
    1979   Prehistory: Western Anasazi. In: Handbook of North American Indians, Vol. 9, Southwest, Alfonso Ortiz, ed., pp. 108-130. Washington: Smithsonian Institution.

Plog, Stephen E.
    1978   Social Interaction and Stylistic Similarity: A Reanalysis. In: Advances in Archaeological Method and Theory No. 1, Michael B. Schiffer, ed., pp. 143-182. New York: Academic Press.

Powers, M. C.
    1953   A New Roundness Scale for Sedimentary Particles. Journal of Sedimentary Petrology 23:117-119.

Rogers, Malcolm J.
    1945   An Outline of Yuman Prehistory. Southwestern Journal of Anthropology 1(2):167-198.

Schroeder, Albert H.
    1952   A Brief Survey of the Lower Colorado River from Davis Dam to the International Border. The Bureau of Reclamation, Reproduction Unit, Region Three, Boulder City, Arizona.

Senior, Louise M., and Dunbar P. Birnie, III
1995 Accurately Estimating Vessel Volume from Profile Illustrations. American Antiquity 60(2):319-334.

Shepard, Anna O.
1980 Ceramics for the Archaeologist (11th edition). Washington: Carnegie Institution of Washington. (Reprinted: Braun-Brumfield, Inc., Ann Arbor, 1985.)

Skibo, James M., and Michael B. Schiffer
1987 The Effects of Water on Processes of Ceramic Abrasion. Journal of Archaeological Science 14(1):83-96.

Skibo, James M., Michael B. Schiffer, and Kenneth C. Reid
1989 Organic Tempered Pottery: An Experimental Study. American Antiquity 54(1):122-146.

Sutton, Mark Q.
1988 Material Culture from CA-RIV-1179. In: Archaeological Investigations at La Quinta, Salton Basin, Southeastern California, Mark Q. Sutton and Philip J. Wilke. eds., pp. 53-69. Salinas, CA: Coyote Press Archives of California Prehistory No. 20.

Taylor, R. E.
1987 Radiocarbon Dating: An Archaeological Perspective. Orlando: Academic Press, Inc.

Tubb, A., A. J. Parker, and G. Nickless
1980 The Analysis of Romano-British Pottery by Atomic Absorption Spectrophotometry. Archaeometry 22(2):153-171.

Tuohy, Donald R.
1990 Second Thoughts on Shoshoni Pots from Nevada and Elsewhere. In: Hunter-Gatherer Pottery from the Far West, Joanne M. Mack, ed., pp. 83-105. Nevada State Museum Anthropological Papers No. 23.

Waters, Michael R.
1982 The Lowland Patayan Ceramic Tradition. In: Hohokam and Patayan: Prehistory of Southwestern Arizona, Randall H. McGuire and Michael B. Schiffer, eds., pp. 275-297. New York: Academic Press.

Wentworth, C. K.
1922 A Scale of Grade and Class Terms for Clastic Sediments. Journal of Geology 30:377-392.

Chapter 7

ANALYSIS OF SHELL AND BONE ARTIFACTS

DEFINITION

Although somewhat less robust than stone or ceramics, artifacts (as well as ecofacts) of shell and bone are frequently recovered from sites. Shell artifacts generally are either beads or ornaments (stone beads and ornaments were discussed in Chapter 5), while many bone artifacts are utilitarian. Each category is discussed below.

SHELL ARTIFACTS

Most artifacts of shell are ornamental (nonutilitarian): beads, pendants, sequins or appliqués, or other ornaments. However, some shell artifacts, such as fishhooks and bowls, were used for utilitarian purposes (burials or cremations were sometimes placed in shell bowls). Perhaps the majority of shell artifacts were made from marine (ocean) rather than freshwater shell; marine shell is generally thicker, more robust, and easier to manufacture into artifacts.

BEADS AND ORNAMENTS

One of the more interesting and often enigmatic aspects of aboriginal material culture in North America concerns the recovery of shell beads and ornaments from archaeological contexts. Most of these artifacts served a nonutilitarian role, and loomed large in the body adornment practices of native groups, either for personal decoration or ceremonial costumes (sometimes indicating wealth and/or status). Aboriginal beads and ornaments were made from a variety of materials—marine and freshwater shell, pearl, copper, rock, crystal, and bone. After identifying the materials from which they were made, beads and ornaments can be further classified by their shape (disk, cylinder, tube, globular, and pendant), size (diameter and thickness), edge configuration (rounded or squared), and placement and type of perforation (King 1978:58).

Shell artifacts identified as "beads" exhibit central perforations, are relatively small in size, and often are assumed to have been strung together and worn in necklace or bracelet fashion. However, numerous ethnographic and early historical accounts of native cultures clearly indicate that many so-called "beads" actually were used as pendants, sewn on garments as sequins or appliqués, attached to baskets, etc. Therefore, it is important for the student to remember that not all small, centrally perforated, ornamental items functioned as beads as we traditionally view them.

Among the earliest and most thorough treatments of Native American beads and beadwork is that of Orchard (1929). Although much of the volume concerns historical glass beads and beadwork, it also contains valuable information on prehistoric beads of shell, pearl, bone, and stone, as well as manufacturing techniques used to produce them. As such, it is an important basic reference, and should be included in any paper concerning analysis of aboriginal beads and ornaments.

ARTIFACTS OF SHELL AND BONE

Beads and ornaments of shell, either of marine or freshwater origin, are widely distributed in prehistoric and protohistoric archaeological contexts in North America; marine shell artifacts dominate bead and ornament assemblages in coastal regions and adjacent interior areas. The vast majority of shell artifacts served mostly as ornaments and money, such as in the California culture area (Gifford 1947:2). An exception was the production of utilitarian items such as shell fishhooks, gouges, and containers. A collection of papers on shell beads from the eastern United States was presented by Hayes (1989) and a study of sourcing *Busycon* (a marine shell) artifacts in the eastern U. S. was presented by Claassen and Sigmann (1993).

Throughout much of the Far West, various styles of shell beads are associated with distinct time periods, and are used by archaeologists to assign relative dates to sites and components. Bennyhoff and Heizer (1958) first proposed refined dating schemes for a wide variety of *Olivella*, *Haliotis*, *Dentalium*, and clamshell beads and ornaments manufactured in California and traded into the Great Basin. Bennyhoff and Hughes (1987) then expanded and revised this work for the western Great Basin. Figure 54 depicts some of the shell beads and ornaments found in California and the Great Basin.

Two general categories of shell beads were widely used in California. Some served as currency, and could be used by anyone, regardless of their social status, to obtain commodities. Others were indicators of status, available only to those who had obtained or inherited positions of rank (King 1978:61). Both categories were composed of beads that differed in value according to the amount of labor associated with their manufacture. Along with disk, cupped, and lipped beads made from the callus or columella of the *Olivella* shell, disk and tube beads made from several clams, such as *Mytilus*, *Saxidomus*, *Tivela*, and *Tresus*, comprised the most common shell "money" beads used in California. Slender drilled tubes of clamshell up to 3.5 inches long were highly prized as money among the Coastal Chumash, and were sometimes worn by both sexes in the pierced nasal septum (Grant 1978:516).

The collumellae of univalves larger than *Olivella* were fashioned into pendants or longitudinally drilled tubes that were highly valued (King 1978:59-60). Disk beads made from the walls of shells and cylinder beads were not considered as "money" beads in California, but rather as "decorative" beads (King 1978:60). Figure 55 is an illustration of an *Olivella* shell, showing landmarks and loci of manufacture for various classes of beads.

Various types of shell beads and pendants produced in California have been traded eastward into the Great Basin for millennia, and became more valuable as the distance from their source of manufacture increased. The earliest known occurrence of California shell beads in the Great Basin has been documented at Leonard Rockshelter in western Nevada, where a string of 52 spire-ground *Olivella biplicata* beads dating from about 5,100 B.C. was recovered (Heizer 1951). Additional California *Olivella* shell beads have been found in slightly younger contexts at Danger Cave and Hogup Cave in Utah (Hughes and Bennyhoff 1986:251).

Southwestern groups, such as the Anasazi and Hohokam, also obtained whole shells and finished shell ornaments through trade with California groups, as well as through collecting trips to the Gulf of California. Some of the more impressive shell artifacts made by prehistoric Southwestern artisans are the Hohokam bracelets fashioned from *Glycymeris* clamshells. The interior of the shell was broken out and the edges were ground (Gumerman and Haury 1979). Both shell artifacts and whole shells from the Pacific Coast entered the Columbia Plateau, Great Basin, and Southwest along specific trade routes that

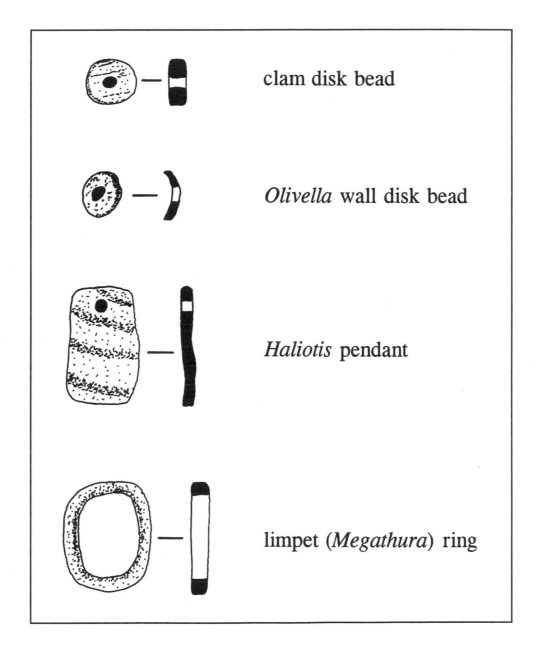

clam disk bead

Olivella wall disk bead

Haliotis pendant

limpet (*Megathura*) ring

Fig. 54.   Some shell beads and ornaments from California and the Great Basin (relative scale).

followed the Columbia, Snake, Humboldt, and Colorado rivers, and that crossed the Sierra Nevada and the Mojave Desert.

In western North America, shells most commonly used as ornaments and currency were *Dentalium, Haliotis, Olivella*, and clam (Gifford 1947:2; Suttles 1990:28-29). Most of the purple and white cylindrical "wampum" shell beads used to make the well-known belts and strings associated with

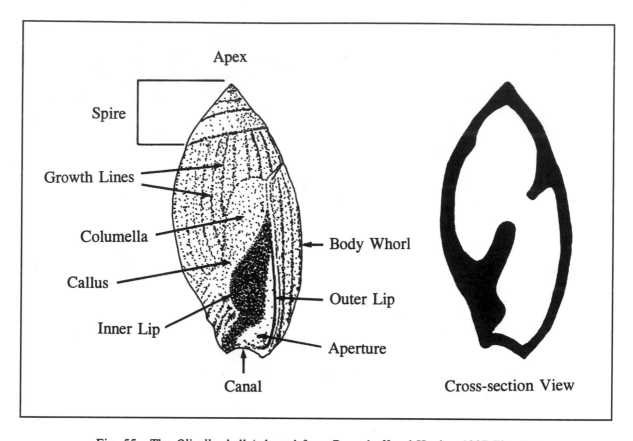

Fig. 55. The *Olivella* shell (adapted from Bennyhoff and Hughes 1987:Fig. 1).

the League of the Iroquois were quahog clamshell (*Venus mercenaria*), and date to the Historic Period, with most specimens associated with seventeenth and eighteenth century Iroquois sites (Orchard 1929; Tooker 1978:422). In the Southeast, marine shells were traded over vast distances during Mississippian times, with engraved conch shells being one of the more common forms (Fagan 1991:393).

Clamshell beads Were produced by first breaking the shells into small pieces with a hammerstone, after which the fragments were roughly shaped, drilled (either with bow- or pump-drills or hand-held flaked stone drills), and strung. The rough bead blanks were then rubbed with a wet hand back and forth on a flat stone slab to grind them into smooth and uniform beads (cf. Orchard 1929:26; Grant 1978:526).

Wherever shell artifacts functioned as currency, people used formal measurements to determine their value. In northwest California, Hupa, Chilula, and Whilkut men measured *Dentalium* shell money against a series of tattoo marks on the middle of their left forearm (Wallace 1978:168).

CLASSIFICATION AND ANALYSIS

The first step in studying a shell artifact assemblage is identification of the genera (and perhaps species) from which the beads and/or ornaments are made. This can be accomplished through consultation with appropriate specialists, such as marine biologists, as well as published field guides

136

concerning the region under study. For example, one of the most popular field guides for Pacific coast shells is that of Morris (1966). Morris (1973) also authored what is arguably the most thorough field guide for Atlantic and Gulf coast shells.

Once the genera and species of the specimens have been determined, the next task involves assigning your artifacts to the appropriate classes and types that have been established for the area or region from which the artifact assemblage has been recovered. An excellent early typology for California shell artifacts was produced by Gifford (1947), which contains excellent illustrations and is still used by archaeologists today. The *Olivella* shell bead typology for California and the Great Basin has recently been improved by Bennyhoff and Hughes (1987), incorporating newly analyzed, temporally significant types. The Bennyhoff and Hughes (1987) monograph also contains excellent line drawings and maps.

Formal laboratory analysis of shell beads and ornaments should include a thorough description of the specimens, emphasizing size (diameter, length, width, thickness [usually reported in millimeter units for smaller specimens, and in centimeter units for larger ones]), perforation type (conical, biconical, etc.), weight (in grams), species (if possible), place of origin (if known; some species have a restricted range), and temporal significance (if previously documented). The student also can include a discussion of other archaeological occurrences and illustrations of the same shell artifact class or type under examination.

The physical attributes of the shell artifacts should be presented in tabular format. Table 5 provides an example of how other archaeologists have done this in a clear and concise fashion. A representative sample of the assemblage (or if it is small, perhaps the entire assemblage) should be illustrated with either black and white photographs or ink line drawings. Good illustrations are a critical aspect of any archaeological report, as they provide the reader with important visual information concerning the materials being discussed.

BONE ARTIFACTS

Many artifacts were made from bone, including utilitarian and nonutilitarian implements. Bone preserves relatively well in many archaeological sites (there are important exceptions), so there are frequent opportunities to recover such artifacts.

Complete bone tools are relatively easy to identify. However, the identification of fragments is much more difficult and each piece of bone must be carefully examined before it is placed with the ecofactual faunal material (see Lyman 1994:338-352). One key to identifying modified bone is to detect *unnatural* shapes on the bone (this requires some understanding of bone anatomy and morphology). Another key is to identify manufacturing marks (e.g., scratches, grooves, polish) on the surfaces of bone.

Many bones used for tools were "long bones" that have marrow cavities. The absence of a marrow cavity in what appears to be a complete bone midsection is unnatural and so is a prime criterion for suspecting modified bone (Fig. 56). The broken edges of a bone must also be examined. If a bone is broken, the break will generally be rough and angular. Modified bone will have had these breaks smoothed out, sometime so much that no "break" is evident.

Table 5
ATTRIBUTES OF SHELL BEADS AND ORNAMENTS FROM GATECLIFF SHELTER, NEVADA
(adapted from Bennyhoff and Hughes 1983:Table 61)

Types	Cat. No.	Length	Width	Thickness	Diameter	Perforation Diameter
Beads						
small spire-lopped *Olivella*	20.3/535	--	--	--	(5.5)[a]	(2.0)[a]
small spire-lopped *Olivella*	20.3/1388	8.8	--	--	5.2	2.3
barrel *Olivella*	20.3/6401	10.0	--	--	8.5	3.4
small *Olivella* saucer	20.3/2560	5.0	4.7	1.2	5.0	2.0
square *Haliotis*	20.3/3657	8.9	11.6	0.9	--	2.3
square *Haliotis*	20.3/7220	(6.7)[a]	9.0	1.1	--	2.5
Haliotis nacreous disk	20.3/3219	7.0	6.0	0.7	7.0	2.0
thin *Haliotis* disk	20.3/3712	--	--	1.4	(11.5)[a]	(3.5)[a]
stone bead	20.3/2215	7.6	(7.0)[a]	2.0	7.6	3.3
Ornaments						
Haliotis ring	20.3/1540	36.7[b]	7.2	2.3	(70.09)[a]	--
oblong *Haliotis*	20.3/3230	--	17.8	3.0	--	--
mica	20.3/8154	--	(16.0)[a]	0.9	--	3.3

[a] measurement on reworked specimen
[b] measurement based on incomplete specimen

UTILITARIAN ARTIFACTS

A variety of utilitarian bone tools may be encountered. Perhaps the most common tool is the awl or needle (Fig. 57a). Such tools were used extensively in basket manufacturing, in leather working, and in a variety of other tasks. Awls can be made from a variety of bones, large mammal (e.g., deer) metapodials (long foot bones) being quite popular. Broken awl tips may be quite small and may be overlooked if one is not careful.

The shoulder blade bones (scapulas) of large mammals were often made into a variety of tools, including saws, sickles, and sweat removers (Fig. 57b-c). Anytime a scapula, or fragment thereof, is present, it should be examined for modification. Additionally, antler was used as hammers and flakers.

BEADS AND ORNAMENTS

Decorative items of bird, fish, and small mammal bone were commonly used by prehistoric and historical native North American cultures. In addition to those made of bone, aboriginal ornaments also were fashioned from other animal body parts, most notably antler, tooth, claw, and quill. One of the more ambitious early studies of ornamental bone artifacts in western North America was conducted by Gifford (1940), who analyzed over 2,900 specimens recovered from seven distinct archaeological areas in California. This extensive assemblage contained 40 pendants and 1,055 beads/tubes, all of which were further subclassified according to physical attributes.

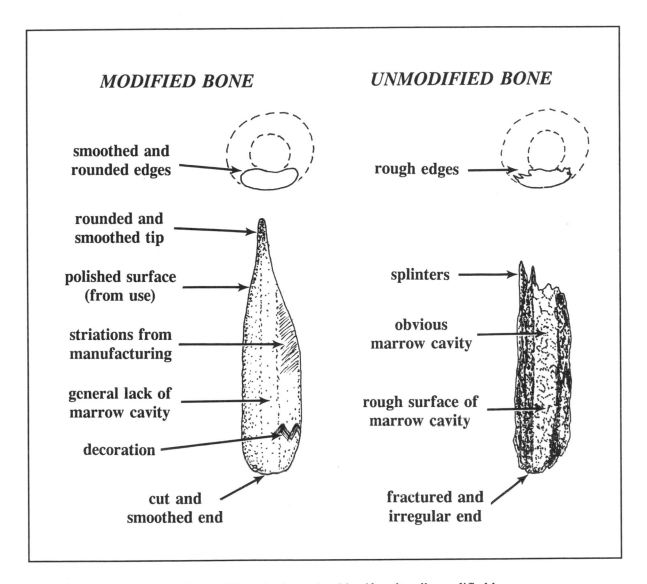

MODIFIED BONE

smoothed and rounded edges

rounded and smoothed tip

polished surface (from use)

striations from manufacturing

general lack of marrow cavity

decoration

cut and smoothed end

UNMODIFIED BONE

rough edges

splinters

obvious marrow cavity

rough surface of marrow cavity

fractured and irregular end

Fig. 56. Some of the criteria used to identify culturally modified bone.

Nearly all bone ornaments fall into one of three groups: pendants, disk beads, and tubes. The first two exhibit characteristics indicating that they functioned primarily as items of personal adornment—either strung together or individually and suspended from the body as a bracelet or necklace, or attached to clothing. Small- and medium-sized (less than about 5 cm. in length) bone tubes most likely functioned as beads, such as those recovered from Hogup Cave, Utah, that were attached to strands of rawhide and *Apocynum* fiber cordage (Aikens 1970). Larger bone tubes may have fulfilled other functions, such as sucking tubes for extracting diseases or poison, as parts of loop snares, as gaming pieces, or as smoking pipes. Various California native groups also used large bird or rabbit bone tubes (often decorated with incised lines filled with dark pigment) as ornaments worn in pierced earlobes or nasal septums.

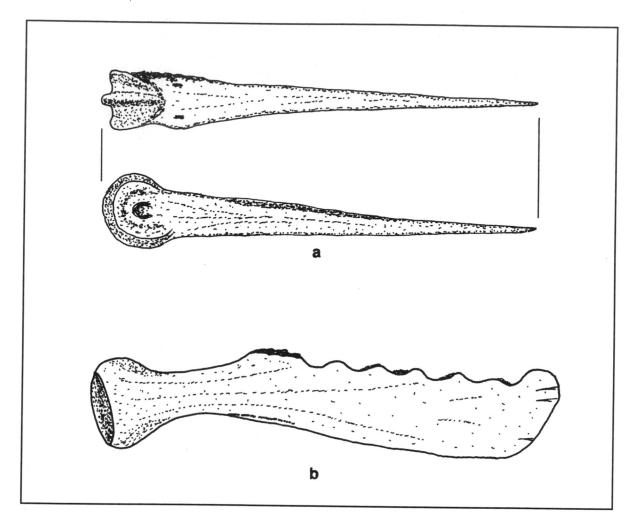

Fig. 57. Some examples of bone tools: (a) awl; (b) scapula saw (no scale).

The manufacturing process associated with bone ornaments is relatively straightforward. Pendants were made by cutting and abrading a piece of bone into the desired shape and then perforating it with some type of drill. Bone tubes commonly were produced by cutting away the distal and proximal ends of bird, rabbit, or hare long bones and smoothing or polishing them. Bone disk beads were made by scoring the long bones of birds or small mammals, cutting the bead blanks from the shaft, and smoothing or polishing them to obliterate rough edges. More than 90 bone beads were recovered from the excavations at Gatecliff Shelter, Nevada, all of which were tubular in form, and fashioned either from jackrabbit or cottontail tibiae or from unidentified bird bones (Thomas 1983:301-302).

CLASSIFICATION AND ANALYSIS

Initial classification of a bone ornament assemblage should emphasize form. Pendant, disk, and tube forms should be examined to determine the genus (and perhaps species as well) of the animal(s) from which the specimens were made. A faunal specialist also will attempt to identify the skeletal elements represented in the assemblage.

Formal laboratory analysis of bone artifacts should include a thorough description of each specimen, recording size (diameter, length, width, thickness [usually in millimeters]), perforation type (conical, biconical, etc.), weight (in grams), and species (if possible). If any of the artifacts are decorated (e.g., with incised lines, punctation, or pigment), provide in-depth discussions of the designs and include line drawings or black-and-white photographs of these specimens. Line drawings or photographs of a representative sample of all other bone artifacts also should appear as figures in the final report.

REFERENCES

Aikens, C. Melvin
    1970   Hogup Cave. University of Utah Anthropological Papers No. 93.

Bennyhoff, James A., and Robert F. Heizer
    1958   Cross-Dating Great Basin Sites by Californian Shell Beads. Berkeley: University of California Archaeological Survey Reports 42:60-92.

Bennyhoff, James A., and Richard E. Hughes
    1983   Material Culture of Gatecliff Shelter: Shell Beads and Ornaments. In: The Archaeology of Monitor Valley 2: Gatecliff Shelter by David H. Thomas, pp. 290-296. Anthropological Papers of the American Museum of Natural History 59(1)

    1987   Shell Bead and Ornament Exchange Networks Between California and the Western Great Basin. Anthropological Papers of the American Museum of Natural History 64(2).

Claassen, Cheryl, and Samuella Sigmann
    1993   Sourcing *Busycon* Artifacts of the Eastern United States. American Antiquity 58(2):333-347.

Fagan, Brian M.
    1991   Ancient North America: The Archaeology of a Continent. London: Thames and Hudson Ltd.

Gifford, E. W.
    1940   Californian Bone Artifacts. University of California Anthropological Records 3(2).

    1947   Californian Shell Artifacts. University of California Anthropological Records 9(1).

Grant, Campbell
    1978   Eastern Coastal Chumash. In: Handbook of North American Indians, Vol. 8, California, Robert F. Heizer, ed., pp. 509-519. Washington: Smithsonian Institution.

Gumerman, George J., and Emil W. Haury
    1979   Prehistory: Hohokam. In: Handbook of North American Indians, Vol. 9, Southwest, Alfonzo Ortiz, ed., pp. 75-90. Washington: Smithsonian Institution.

Hayes, Charles F., III (ed.)
    1989   Proceedings of the 1986 Shell Bead Conference: Selected Papers. Rochester Museum & Science Center, Research Records No. 20.

Heizer, Robert F.
    1951   Preliminary Report on the Leonard Rockshelter Site, Pershing County, Nevada. American Antiquity 17(2):89-98.

Hughes, Richard E., and James A. Bennyhoff
    1986   Early Trade. In: Handbook of North American Indians, Vol. 11, Great Basin, Warren L. d'Azevedo, ed., pp. 238-255. Washington: Smithsonian Institution.

King, Chester
    1978   Protohistoric and Historic Archeology. In: Handbook of North American Indians, Vol. 8, California, Robert F. Heizer, ed., pp. 58-68. Washington: Smithsonian Institution.

Lyman, R. Lee
    1994   Vertebrate Taphonomy. Cambridge: Cambridge University Press.

Morris, Percy A.
    1966   A Field Guide to Pacific Coast Shells, Including Shells of Hawaii and the Gulf of California. (The Peterson Field Guide Series.) Boston: Houghton-Mifflin Co.

    1973   A Field Guide to Shells of the Atlantic and Gulf Coasts. (The Peterson Field Guide Series.) Boston: Houghton-Mifflin Co.

Orchard, William C.
    1929   Beads and Beadwork of the American Indians: A Study Based on Specimens in the Museum of the American Indian, Heye Foundation. Contributions from the Museum of the American Indian, Heye Foundation 11.

Suttles, Wayne
    1990   Environment. In: Handbook of North American Indians, Vol. 7, Northwest Coast, Wayne Suttles, ed., pp. 16-29. Washington: Smithsonian Institution.

Thomas, David H.
    1983   The Archaeology of Monitor Valley 2: Gatecliff Shelter. Anthropological Papers of the American Museum of Natural History 59(1).

Tooker, Elizabeth
    1978   The League of the Iroquois: Its History, Politics, and Ritual. In: Handbook of North American Indians, Vol. 15, Northeast, Bruce G. Trigger, ed., pp. 418-441. Washington: Smithsonian Institution.

Wallace, William J.
    1978   Hupa, Chilula, and Whilkut. In: Handbook of North American Indians, Vol. 8, California, Robert F. Heizer, ed., pp. 164-179. Washington: Smithsonian Institution.

Chapter 8

ANALYSIS OF PERISHABLES

DEFINITION

Perishables are those artifacts made of organic materials that are not ordinarily recovered from the archaeological record (certain ecofacts might also be considered perishables). Most artifacts made from organic materials, such as wood, fiber, and bark, will rapidly decompose when discarded or lost and so are not commonly recovered by archaeologists. Bone, antler, and shell are also organic materials, but are far more dense and will preserve for a relatively long time. Thus, bone, antler, and shell generally are not considered to be perishables.

Decomposition of organics occurs through the actions of microorganisms or chemicals that break down the structure of a given item. For materials to preserve, they must be in unusual environments that stop, or at least slow down, the progress of the microorganisms and/or chemical reactions. Such environments are at the extremes of normal conditions: very dry (e.g., many desert sites, Peru or Egypt), very wet (e.g., the Ozette site in Oregon, some shipwrecks, bog environments [bog chemistry also is important]), or very cold (e.g., Arctic sites). Sometimes, perishable materials were lightly burned so that their forms are preserved; these may be recovered as carbonized and very fragile artifacts. Another possibility for preservation is a cast or impression of the artifact on other, preserved materials (e.g., basketry impressions in clay, see Jennings 1957:208-209). However, dryness is the usual condition encountered by archaeologists, and sites in deserts and/or caves and rockshelters have the greatest potential for containing perishables.

Although artifacts of stone and bone are the most common materials found in sites, much, if not most, of the total artifact inventory of a group was most likely manufactured from perishable materials. The discovery of perishables allows the archaeologist to glimpse a broader range of material culture, gain a better understanding of the range of technological adaptation, and obtain a variety of examples of art and ritual systems.

WHAT TO RECORD: GENERAL GUIDELINES

As with all other artifacts, metric attributes (e.g., length, width, thickness, diameter [all in millimeters], and capacity [in milliliters]) are important to record, not only for comparison to other such materials, but also to discover any patterns of size commonly employed by a particular cultural group. Other attributes to record include any decoration (size, shape, color, etc.) and residues or adhering materials (vessel contents, mastics, ocher, etc.). One should also strive to determine the species of organism used to manufacture the item. Other specific suggestions are provided below in the appropriate sections.

CONSERVATION OF PERISHABLES

The conservation of perishables, or of any other material, involves the removal or neutralization of the agents of decomposition, corrosion, or decay. A variety of conservation methods may be employed, depending on the material and the conditions in which the artifact was found. Perishables should be stored in conditions similar to those of the site where they were found (this requires temperature and humidity controls). A comprehensive review of the conservation of many types of archaeological materials was provided by Cronyn (1990).

Adovasio (1977:11-14) outlined basic procedures for cleaning and conservation of basketry; procedures that apply to a wide variety of perishables. The most important rule is to do as little as possible. Cleaning should be done very gently with a soft nylon brush (do not use water and remember to look for seeds or other items caught within the weave). A dental pick may be used on occasion, but be very careful. Do not attempt to restore, repair, or otherwise alter the material. Be very careful about the use of preservatives; they sometimes can do more harm than good and can contaminate the specimen, making other analyses or dating more difficult, if not impossible. Remember that the perishable item has lasted for hundreds or thousands of years without preservatives; maintaining it in its environment is the best preservative.

Perishables should be stored in a secure place, in a container large enough to accommodate them (rather than forcing them to fit into a smaller container). Make sure that any packing materials will not adhere to the artifacts (cotton tends to stick but polyfelt liner generally will not) or chemically interact with them. Proper environmental control must include regulation of temperature, humidity, and light (incandescent lights can cause fading of designs).

BASKETRY

A basket may be defined as a rigid or semi-rigid item or container of interwoven materials manufactured without a loom, including baskets, matting, and bags (a handwoven bag is considered to be basketry but a cloth bag usually is not; see Adovasio 1977:1). Baskets were widely used in many aboriginal societies, even those with a well-developed ceramic technology. Baskets, or fragments thereof, would have originally been present in the deposits of most archaeological sites; however, due to poor preservation, they are rarely recovered.

Basketry was used for a great number of purposes, including storage, as water containers, in cooking, as ceremonial objects, and even as hats. Some baskets were woven so well as to be watertight—as moisture entered the weave, it would swell and so seal the basket from leakage. Baskets could be used in cooking; not by putting them on a fire, but by placing hot rocks into the material inside the basket. Using this technique, the contents of a basket could be made to boil with no real damage to the basket. Some baskets, such as water bottles, had some material (e.g., pinyon pitch, lac scale insect resin) applied to their surface to make them waterproof.

An excellent review of basketry analysis was presented by Adovasio (1977), who included discussions on methods of analysis, typology, description, cleaning, and conservation. The reader is referred to that work for more detail regarding basketry.

FORM AND FUNCTION

Basketry, as defined above (also see Adovasio 1977:1), may take a variety of forms: actual baskets (three-dimensional containers of various shapes); matting (considered two-dimensional objects even though they do have height), bags (two-dimensional when empty, three-dimensional when full), and assorted forms such as fish traps, clothing, cradles, etc.

Basketry was produced for a variety of functions. The utilitarian functions of basketry include the collection, processing, and storage of resources (food, water, and/or other materials), serving foods or holding items (bowls, plates, and trays), and the transportation of materials (Fig. 58). In addition, some baskets were made for trade or ceremonial purposes, to be given at weddings, to contain sacred items, or for prestige.

CONSTRUCTION

The basic parts of a basket are: (1) the wall; (2) the rim (or "selvage"); (3) the start (located at the bottom of the basket, where the weaving began); (4) the shoulder (if the body of the basket narrows toward the opening); (5) the handle (if any); and (6) the lid (if any; a lid will also have a wall, rim, and start). A basket may also have been damaged and repaired, the repair being a "part" of the basket. The fairly rigid foundation in basketry (not present in all types) is called *warp* and the comparatively flexible stitching is called *weft*.

There are three basic techniques (Fig. 59) used to manufacture basketry: *twined*, *coiled*, and *plaited* (rigid, plaited basketry sometimes is called *wickerware*, see Adovasio 1977:99). Twined basketry has a relatively rigid vertical foundation (warp) and relatively pliable horizontal stitching (weft). The twining may be relatively open or tight. The weft may be angled either to the maker's right ("S-twined") or to the maker's left ("Z-twined") (Fig. 60). Adovasio (1977:20) defined 27 types of twined basketry.

In coiled basketry (Fig. 61), the foundation consists of horizontal elements (called rods, bundles, and/or welts) of relatively rigid materials interwoven vertically by a flexible stitch. Details of construction include spacing of stitches and foundations, type and content of foundation, and type of stitching. There are well over 100 different technological types of coiled basketry possible (Adovasio 1977:62, Figs. 70-76).

Plaited basketry has no real foundation or stitch; the weave is basically the same in both directions (as in many textiles, such as cloth). Plaited basketry is classified on interval of element engagement (Adovasio 1977:99). *Simple plaiting* has one element passing over one other (1/1). *Twill plaiting* has more than one element (i.e., row) passing over more than one other (2/2 or 3/3, etc.), sometimes with specific designs as the result.

MATERIALS

A great number and variety of materials (often in combination) have been used for the construction of baskets. It is necessary to determine the materials available locally in conjunction with

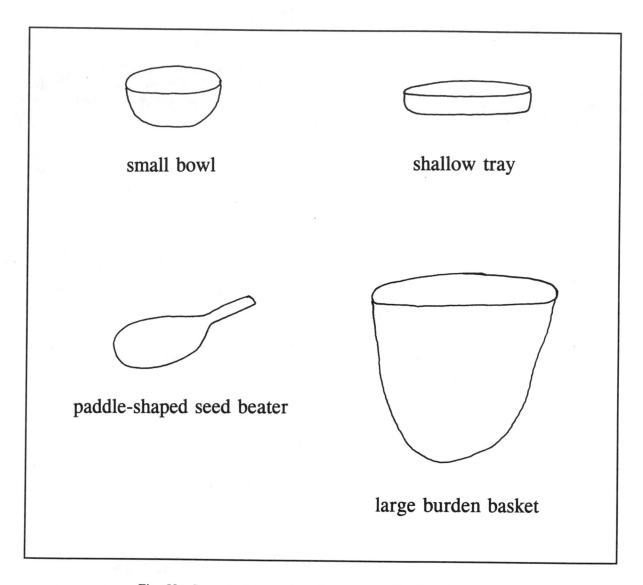

Fig. 58. Several of the various forms/types of baskets (no scale).

the ethnographic data from the area to determine a list of possible plants used in basketry. Identification of plant species requires specialized knowledge and experience.

Occasionally, archaeologists will discover basketry manufacturing materials that were gathered but not yet used. These "raw" materials can be quite informative regarding manufacturing, gathering, location of raw materials, etc.

DECORATION

Two basic forms of basket decoration may be present: (1) designs woven into the basket itself during manufacture; and (2) items attached to the basket. A design woven into a basket requires different

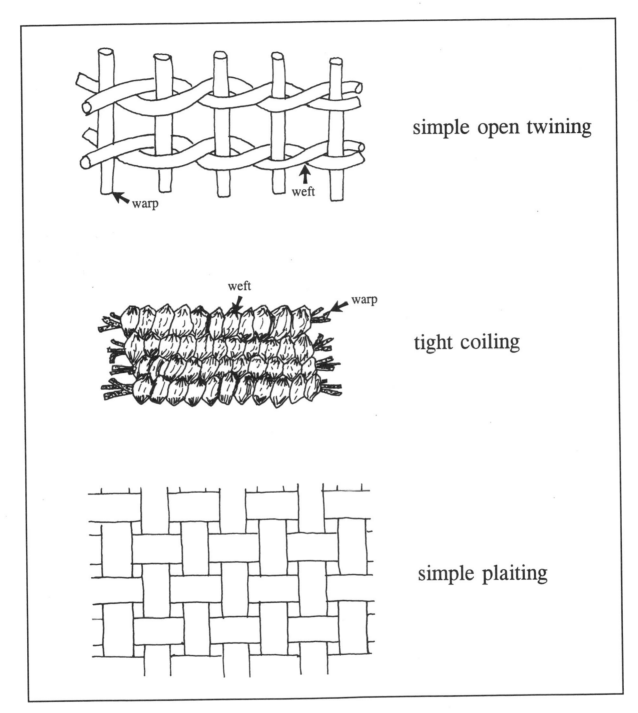

simple open twining

tight coiling

simple plaiting

Fig. 59. The three basic techniques of basketry manufacture (no scale).

colored materials (most often the weft) to be used in a pattern. As the basket was woven, the weaver would change materials at specific places then change back to the original colored material to create the pattern. The different colored materials often were a variety of naturally colored plants, although

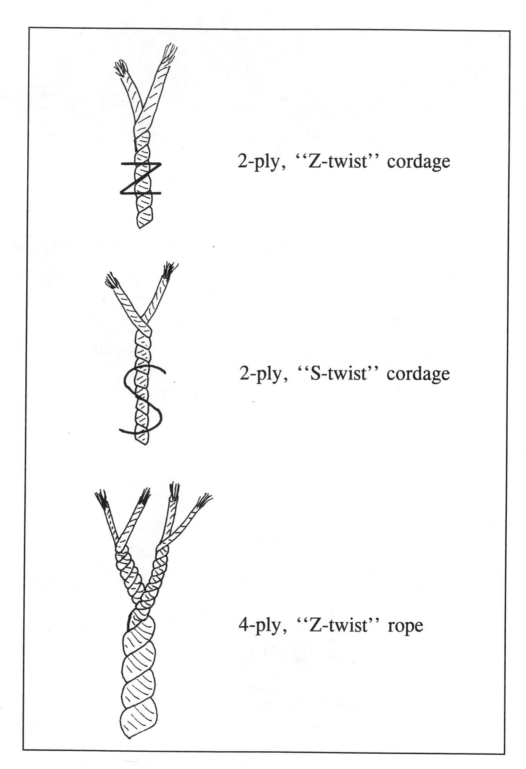

2-ply, ''Z-twist'' cordage

2-ply, ''S-twist'' cordage

4-ply, ''Z-twist'' rope

Fig. 60.   Twist and ply constructions, used in the recordation of cordage and some basketry (no scale).

Fig. 61.   Close coiled basket fragments collected from a dry cave near Promontory Point, Utah. Donated to Weber State University by Floyd Olsen.

sometimes a single material might be dyed. In addition to designs resulting from the use of different colored materials, some designs were created by alternating stitch patterns.

Sometimes, items would be attached to a basket as decoration., Such items included feathers (e.g., the feathers of quail or hummingbirds were used by some California groups), shells, beads, leather, or other materials. Such decorated items likely were not utilitarian in their primary function.

WHAT TO RECORD

In recording the attributes of basketry, follow these general guidelines: (1) record the form (shape) of the specimen (form can sometimes be inferred from fragments if they are large enough); (2) note the construction technique used (twined, coiled, plaited); (3) record the weave (number of elements, type of twist, and whether there is any variation in the weave); (4) record the height, diameter, and volume of whole specimens and the length and width of fragments; (5) note if any splices in the weave are present; (6) note the use of different materials (identify if possible); (7) note any wear (e.g., attrition, polish, charring, stains) on the specimen (location and severity); (8) record any repairs present (including weave and materials used in the repair); (9) note the presence of any resins or sealants (if possible, carefully take a sample and catalog it); (10) note any seeds in the matrix of the weave (such seeds need to be identified); and (11) note any residues (e.g., boiled materials) in the bottom or in the weave (if possible, carefully take a sample and catalog it). Other specific instructions are provided below.

151

Twined Basketry

Adovasio (1977:51) suggested the following measurements be taken on twined basketry: (1) the range of diameter of warps; (2) the mean diameter of warps; (3) the range of diameter of wefts; (4) the mean diameter of wefts; (5) the range in number of warps per centimeter; (6) the mean number of warps per centimeter; (7) the range in number of wefts per centimeter; (8) the mean number of wefts per centimeter; (9) the range in gap between weft rows; and (10) mean gap between weft rows.

Coiled Basketry

For coiled basketry, Adovasio (1977:70-80) recommended recording: (1) the spacing of the foundation (called rods, bundles, and/or welts); (2) the kind, number, and arrangement of foundation elements; and (3) the type of stitch.

Plaited Basketry

Adovasio (1977:107) suggested that the following measurements be taken on plaited basketry: (1) the range of diameter of elements; (2) the mean diameter of elements; (3) the range of angle of crossing of the elements; and (4) the mean of angle of crossing of the elements.

TEXTILES

Textiles (as distinguished from basketry) are relatively flexible, handwoven materials which may or may not form a container. The most commonly recovered material of this type is cordage. Cordage (string, twine, or rope) comes in a variety of forms, thicknesses, and construction (Fig. 62). Cordage was used for such items as netting (see below), bowstrings, nooses, snares, and fasteners. Cordage was made from a variety of materials, mostly plant fibers (see Hoover 1974), and sometimes from hair.

Nets consist of cordage tied together in such a fashion to form a lattice of variably sized mesh. Nets were manufactured for a variety of purposes, such as bags and game traps (e.g., deer nets, rabbit nets, and fish nets). Numerous examples of animal trapping nets have been recovered both ethnographically and archaeologically, one dating to as early as 8,600 B.P. (Frison et al. 1986).

Matting is a flat, woven object made from grass or reeds, often with cordage being used to tie together the bundles of matting material. Matting should be analyzed in the same basic way as basketry.

WHAT TO RECORD

Several attributes are important to note in recording cordage, including *ply* and *twist*. Ply is the strand itself; most cordage was made from more than one ply (otherwise, it would have little strength), usually two, three, or four (Fig. 60). Some large diameter cordage (e.g., ''rope'') may be made from several plies, which themselves are made from several plies (an examination of any modern rope will illustrate this point). Twist is the direction that the cordage was rolled in its manufacture. ''S-twist'' was twisted to the maker's right while ''Z-twist'' was twisted to the maker's left (see Fig. 60). Multiple plies are all twisted in the same direction to prevent unravelling. In addition to ply and twist, record the diameter and length of each specimen.

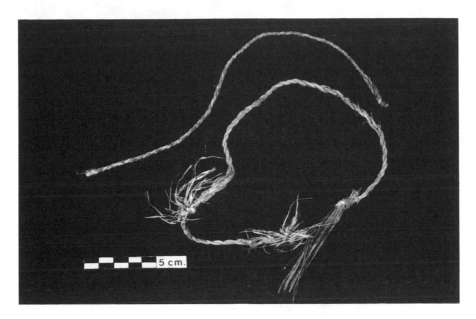

Fig. 62.   Two strands of plant fiber cordage from an unknown level of Hogup Cave, Utah. The thicker specimen is ''Z'' twist and the thinner specimen is ''S'' twist.

ARTIFACTS OF WOOD AND CANE

A large number of artifacts of wood and cane is known to have been used by prehistoric peoples. Wood artifacts include bowls, scoops, digging sticks (often shaped and fire-hardened at the ends), tool handles (Fig. 63), fire hearths (a confusing term; in this case it refers to the flat pieces of wood [the hearth] upon which a stick [drill] is twisted vigorously to start a fire, see Fig. 64), gaming sticks, bows (simple [one piece] or compound [more than one piece]), arrow or dart shafts, wooden projectile points, trap parts (e.g., triggers), art pieces (carvings, masks, figurines, etc.), and many others. In addition to artifacts, wood is also found as parts of structures (e.g., posts, planks, decoration).

Cane artifacts include mainshafts of arrows or darts or containers (e.g., for storage). Cane may also have been used in the construction of structures (e.g., for small walls or light support).

WHAT TO RECORD

With wood and cane artifacts, the basic metric information (length, width, thickness) is fundamental. In addition, note any unusual modification (notches, perforations, etc.), decoration, resins, attached materials (e.g., fletching [feathers] on arrow or dart mainshafts), evidence of wear, and, if possible, material (species of plant).

Many artifacts were made from the skins (or other soft parts) of animals. Such materials include leather, sinew (connective tissue, such as a tendon), fur, and bird skin. Leather items could include clothing (e.g., moccasins [Fig. 65], leggings, thongs [Fig. 66]), shields, bags, quivers, drum coverings,

Fig. 63.   Wooden knife handle with broken haft recovered from an unknown level of Hogup Cave, Utah. At one time, the handle probably held a flaked stone biface secured with sinew (much of which is still present) and perhaps some type of mastic.

Fig. 64.   Wooden fire hearth and drills collected from a dry cave near Promontory Point, Utah. Donated to Weber State University by Floyd Olsen.

structure coverings (tipi covers), and boat coverings. Items of fur include single-piece blankets and robes from large animals, blankets woven from many small animal skins (e.g., rat, rabbit, or bird skin blankets), bags, and quivers.

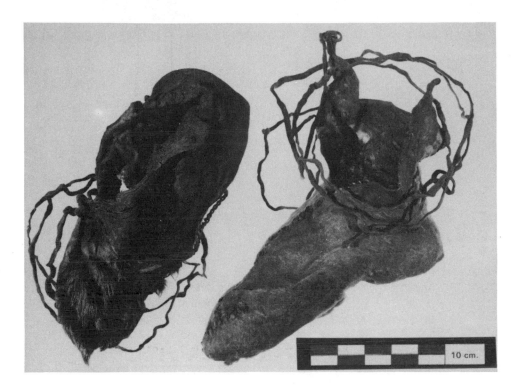

Fig. 65.   Fremont-style hock moccasins, made from a single piece of deer or bison hide, and made by slightly different techniques. One specimen is a tube-type, in which hide from a lower leg was used to form a tube. It was then sewn at one end, and the hock (joint area) formed the heel. The other moccasin was produced by using hide from a lower leg to form a flat piece, then sewn together, with the bend of the hock forming the heel. Both have been stitched with sinew or hide cordage, and a single leather thong was attached to the ankle of each to secure the footwear. Each specimen was worn hair side out, and neither were completely tanned. Both were taken from an unknown dry cave in Utah and donated to Weber State University.

ARTIFACTS OF SKIN OR HIDE

WHAT TO RECORD

When dealing with artifacts of skin or hide, record the following: (1) metric attributes (length, width, thickness, and weight); (2) the species of animal; (3) any surface preparation such as tanning, removal of hair, or other evidence of processing; (4) any decoration present; (5) any details of sewing; and (6) condition, including any repairs. If the item is made from more than one skin (e.g., a rabbitskin blanket), record the number of individual skins used (if possible), what part of the skin was used (e.g., was the skin of the feet and head included?), and if woven, the ply and twist.

155

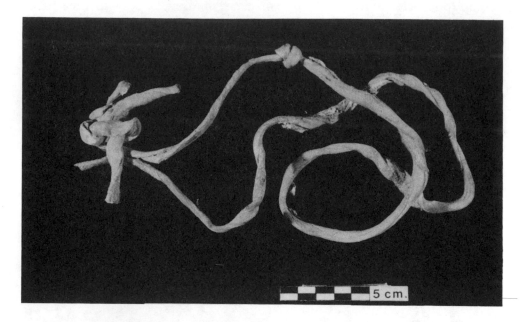

Fig. 66.   Rawhide thong made from large mammal skin and recovered from an unknown level of Hogup Cave, Utah. A simple overhand knot has been made midway along the strand, and another piece of rawhide was attached to one end.

ARTIFACTS OF OTHER PERISHABLE MATERIALS

There is a variety of other artifacts manufactured from perishable materials that might be recovered from an archaeological site, such as small containers made from gourds (plants with melon-like fruits), or objects made from horn (e.g., scoops, parts of bows, scrapers). In cataloging such items, follow the same basic recording guidelines listed above (e.g., metrics, species, modification, condition).

ECOFACTS AS PERISHABLES

Most ecofacts recovered from archaeological sites consist of plant remains or bone. Under normal conditions (open sites), most plant remains will not preserve unless they are carbonized. Where perishable artifacts are preserved, it is likely that ecofacts that would not normally preserve will be present. In such a situation, there may be considerable plant material present, and determining which is cultural and which is noncultural can be a problem (as it is with faunal remains, see Chapter 10).

A variety of possible ecofacts might be present in a site with good preservation. These would include seeds and nuts, corn cobs, and other plant parts (see Chapter 11). Coprolites (desiccated human feces; see Chapter 13) may also be preserved; such materials can be highly informative regarding diet. In addition, quids (discarded chewed plant [e.g., yucca] parts) may provide a great deal of information on dentition (i.e., preserved tooth marks).

REFERENCES

Adovasio, J. M.
  1977 Basketry Technology: A Guide to Identification and Analysis. Chicago: Aldine Publishing.

Cronyn, J. M.
  1990 The Elements of Archaeological Conservation. London: Routledge.

Frison, George C., R. L. Andrews, J. M. Adovasio, R. C. Carlisle, and Robert Edgar
  1986 A Late Paleoindian Animal Trapping Net from Northern Wyoming. American Antiquity 51(2):352-361.

Hoover, Robert L.
  1974 Aboriginal Cordage in Western North America. El Centro, CA: Imperial Valley College Museum Society Occasional Paper No. 1.

Jennings, Jesse D.
  1957 Danger Cave. University of Utah Anthropological Papers No. 27.

Chapter 9

ANALYSIS OF HISTORICAL ARTIFACTS

DEFINITION

In North America, historical materials are associated with Native American and Euroamerican archaeological sites following early European (and later Euroamerican) exploration and colonization. Most historical archaeologists divide their data into four basic categories: (1) *artifacts* (e.g., glass and ceramic fragments, smoking pipes, metal implements, milled lumber, and bone); (2) *ecofacts* (plant and animal remains); (3) *above and below ground features* (e.g., buildings, gravestones, dams, roadways, wall foundations, wells, and graves); and (4) *documents* (e.g., maps, photographs, probate inventories, diaries, and land deeds).

As with all archaeological remains, historical materials are analyzed in terms of their cultural contexts. They oftentimes are associated with very broad cultural contexts because they resulted from the colonial expansion of industrialized nations, such as England, Spain, and France, and therefore represent important early aspects of our modern, global economy. Unlike prehistoric contexts where most objects were made from locally available materials, historical items usually were used by people far from the point of manufacture. Factory records, company catalogs, and period newspaper advertisements provide the researcher with a great deal of information regarding production dates, prices, and manufacturing technology associated with historical materials. This, in turn, allows historical archaeologists to determine which countries and companies supplied goods and materials to frontier, rural, and urban populations.

Attributes of historical artifacts are always recorded and reported using the English system (inches, pounds, and ounces), rather than the metric system (centimeters, grams, and milliliters) used in the recordation of prehistoric materials. This is done since the vast majority of historical artifacts (and features) were manufactured using the English system.

TYPES OF HISTORICAL ARTIFACTS

Numerous types of historical artifacts exhibit readily identifiable attributes directly associated with their method of manufacture. In most instances, changes in manufacturing techniques are well-documented; therefore, many historical artifacts serve as temporal indicators for the archaeologist. Because some types of historical artifacts were produced only for a short period of time, it often is possible to date the use and occupation of a single component historical site to within a 20- or 30-year period. This chapter provides the student with an introduction to historical artifact analysis, and emphasizes the general chronology and function of historical materials. Intensive analyses should be conducted after referring to specialized works for a given region or artifact type, some of which are cited herein.

METAL ARTIFACTS

Metal is a common artifact category in historical archaeology and is represented by a broad range of artifacts such as hardware (wood screws, hinges, bolts), kitchen and table utensils (knives, forks, spoons, ladles), ornaments, and machinery. The tin can is a common metal artifact type that represents food provisioning, and in some cases, wide distribution routes. Barbed wire and wire rope relate to private ownership of land, and mark a shift from the public open range to development of private permanent water sources and settlements. It is critical to remember that metal artifacts often were recycled by both frontier Euroamerican and Native American populations, thereby changing their original form and/or function. For example, nails from old furniture were reused in carpentry; five-gallon kerosene (tagger) cans were cut and flattened for use as house shingles; and empty paint cans were reused as weather-proof storage containers.

Four major categories of metal artifacts most commonly used in establishing historical chronologies are featured in this section: nails, cans, wire (baling and barbed), and cartridge cases. Other metal implements such as tools, hardware, containers, coins, and clasps occur at historical archaeological sites, but are only briefly mentioned here because of space limitations.

Nails

Three basic types of nails occur in archaeological contexts throughout North America: hand-forged, cut, and wire nails (Fig. 67). Hand-forged (or wrought) nails were mostly produced and used before 1800, and therefore are not well-represented in the Far West. Exceptions to this pattern are Spanish sites in Arizona, California, and New Mexico, and perhaps early frontier homestead sites throughout this vast region. For example, in many frontier areas of the Intermountain West, hand-forged nails probably were commonly used up until about 1830 or 1840. Mercer (1924:8) provided the following discussion of wrought nails:

> The crudest kind of wrought nail was simply a piece of soft metal (e.g., iron) hammered into nail form. The earliest nails were likely made this way. By the 18th century wrought nails were fashioned from metal plates rolled in rolling mills to the required thickness and then split by splitting-rollers into nail-rods or split-rods of various sizes, depending on the size and type of nail to be made. These rectangular rods of soft, malleable iron were then taken by nailers and drawn to a point by hammering. Heads were the untapered portion of the shank spread by clamping the shank in a vise and striking it with a hammer.

Cut nails (sometimes referred to as square-cut nails) were made from rectangular strips of iron plate and tapered to a point by a single cut across the plate (Fig. 67). The thickness and height of the plate determined the thickness and length of the nail, while the breadth of the nail at its head and point depended on the amount of taper applied in cutting and the strength of the blow used in forming the head (Fontana and Greenleaf 1962). Square machine-cut nails were first produced in the eastern United States in 1790, and until 1825, were headed by hand with a hammer. Between 1825 and 1830, water-powered machines were developed that headed the cut nails automatically. In the Far West, cut nails dominated from about 1830 to 1890. Regardless of size, hand-forged nails can readily be distinguished from cut nails on the basis of the following features:

160

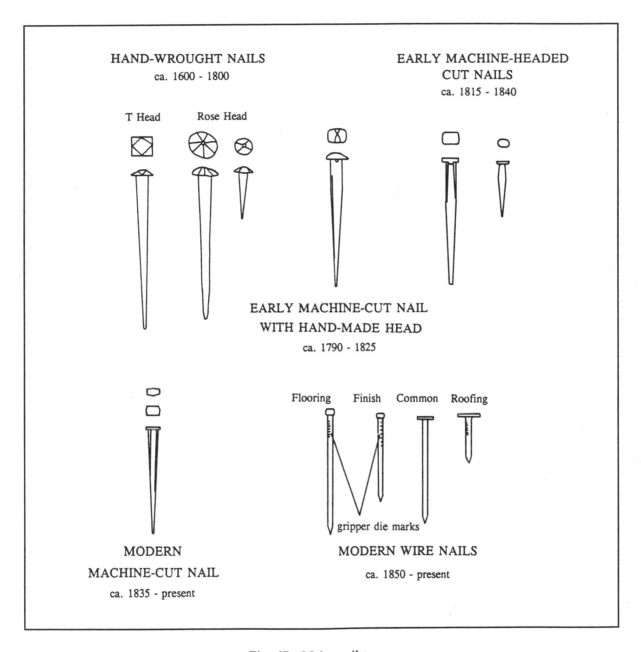

Fig. 67. Major nail types.

1. Hand-forged nails taper on all four sides of the shank toward the point rather than on two opposite sides, as in the case of square-cut nails.

2. Being hand-forged, wrought nails vary in thickness throughout the length of the shank; square-cut nails exhibit uniform thickness, since they were cut from a plate of uniform thickness.

3.   Striations—minute parallel shear marks resulting from the shear of the cutting blade used to make square-cut nails—are absent on shanks of wrought nails (Mercer 1924; Fontana and Greenleaf 1962).

Wire or round nails are the common variety used in North America today (Fig. 67), and were first made in France sometime between 1830 and 1855. During this early period, production of wire nails was semiautomated. Around 1855, French wire nails were produced by a completely automated process. Some of these machines were first exported to the United States in 1873, but large-scale production of wire nails did not occur until the 1880s. It was not until about 1890 that wire nails became more popular than cut nails in the United States. In the Far West, wire nails outnumbered cut nails by about 1900. The following nail chronology was compiled by Fontana and Greenleaf (1962:54-55; also refer to Table 6):

Pre-1800:   Nails were handmade, wrought nails, universally characterized by uneven rectangular shanks that taper on all four sides to a point. For certain purposes, wrought nails continued in use until as late as 1850, and in isolated instances may have been made in the United States when square-cut or wire nails were not available.

1790-1810:   This period was characterized by machine-cut nails, the nail plate being reversed under alternate blows of the cutter. A few stamp-headed nails occurred, but most were headed by a single, hand-driven hammer blow. Angle-headed or L-headed nails made from headless nails also appeared and continued in use until after the 1850s for use in floors and clapboards.

1810-1825:   Machines were invented to make cut nails that obviate the necessity of having to turn the nail plate. Until 1825, such nails continued largely to be headed simply by being struck with a hammer.

1825-1830:   Cutting of nails continued as immediately above, but water-powered machines were developed that headed them automatically. The heads, however, were rather thin and lopsided.

ca. 1830-ca. 1855:   Wire nails were invented in France (hence the term "French nails") that were ground to a point and headed by hand. The first such nails were made in the United States by William Hassall (or Hersel) of New York City. They were rare in the United States during this period.

1830-ca. 1890:   Cut nails were produced in machines that cut and headed them uniformly. Heads were thinner, more uniform, and comparatively square. They were extra heavy on large nails. Cut nails in the United States during this period outnumbered all other kinds in both number and variety.

ca. 1855-present: Machines were invented in France to make complete wire nails automatically. A few were exported to the United States, soon to be replaced by machines of American manufacture. It was about 1890, however, before wire nails outnumbered cut nails.

ca. 1870-present: Cut nails were annealed to prevent them from rupturing when clinched.

ca. 1890-present: Cut nails continued to be manufactured for special purposes (such as securing wood to cement, concrete, or plaster) until about 1950, when they were replaced by cement-coated nails. However, cut nails were still commonly found in subflooring for hardwood floors. It was also probably early in this period that large cut nails were pre-tapered in rolling mills, the nails then cut with parallel rather than diagonally opposing strokes of the knife.

Table 6
NAIL PRODUCTION IN THE UNITED STATES

Year	Nail Type	Amounts
1886	cut nails	8,161,000 kegs
	wire nails	no figures
1894	cut nails	2,425,000 kegs
	wire nails	5,682,000 kegs
1900	cut nails	1,573,000 kegs
	wire nails	7,234,000 kegs

It can be postulated that since nail production averaged 8,000,000 kegs a year for the years cited, the great majority of nails available in 1886 were cut nails. After about 1890, wire nails were the dominant type throughout much of North America, allowing the assignment of the following tentative dates for historical sites based upon the percentages of nail types represented in a given assemblage:

pre-1830	————	wrought nails dominate
1830-1890	————	cut nails dominate
1890-1895	————	50% cut nails, 50% wire nails
1895-1900	————	25% cut nails, 75% wire nails
post-1900	————	greater than 75% wire nails

Classification. Nails have traditionally been classified according to the pennyweight system, a method that is still in use today. This system of measurement is applied to both square-cut and wire nails, and is rendered as "d." Historical archaeologists often subclassify construction nails based upon their lengths and presumed primary functions: small construction nails are defined as 2d-5d and are used in the final stages of carpentry; nails from 6d-16d are called medium construction nails and are used for most purposes; large construction nails are those which are 20d or larger and are used for framing a house, fence construction, or similar activities. Nails from 2d to 10d are based upon 1/4" increments beginning at 1", (i.e., 1" = 2d, 1 1/4" = 3d, etc. up to 3" = 10d), after which pennyweights increase in differential increments, as is illustrated in Table 7.

Table 7
NAIL CLASSIFICATION

1" = 2d	2" = 6d	3" = 10d	4 1/2" = 30d
1 1/4" = 3d	2 1/4" = 7d	3 1/4" = 12d	5" = 40d
1 1/2" = 4d	2 1/2" = 8d	3 1/2" = 16d	5 1/2" = 50d
1 3/4" = 5d	2 3/4" = 9d	4" = 20d	6" = 60d

Caution in the Interpretation of Nails. Caution should always be exercised in assigning occupation dates to sites based solely upon nail typology, because these artifacts often were scavenged from older sites and reused, especially in frontier areas. If possible, it is best to augment temporal information provided by nails with other time-sensitive artifacts (such as bottle sherds, ceramic sherds, or tin cans) recovered from the site under study.

Tin Cans

Tin canisters are among the most common artifacts represented at historical sites in the western United States, but due to preservation factors, are relatively rare in the eastern portion of the country. General familiarity with their evolution allows one to determine approximate occupation dates while recording sites in the field. The tin can would not have been possible without the invention of tinplate. Originally a thin iron sheet coated with tin, early tinplating was replaced by steel coating with a thin sheet of tin around 1875 (Rock 1987:1). Tinplating was first developed in Bohemia between the fourteenth and sixteenth centuries, when artisans discovered the hot dip process for plating tin onto sheets of iron. Germany dominated the industry for three centuries, but in 1620, the Duke of Saxony learned the secret of the process and introduced it to England. By the 1730s, England dominated the tinplate industry and in the eighteenth century began to commercially produce tinplate. Commercial canning of fruit and vegetables in the eastern United States began in 1819 (Busch 1981:103), when all cans were still handmade.

Four primary types of cans have been used to package foodstuffs: *hole-and-cap*; *hole-in-cap*; *vent hole* (match stick filler); and *sanitary* (open-top) cans. The hole-and-cap can is the earliest type of can, and was first produced in western Europe in 1810. Hole-and-cap cans exhibit a filler hole at one end that is closed by a cap. These cans often swelled or burst, and were only used for about ten years before being replaced by the hole-in-cap can (Rock 1984:100).

Hole-in-cap cans date from 1820 to 1930, and contain a filler hole at one end sealed with a tin plate cap that has a pinhole vent in its center (Fig. 68). Introduction of the pinhole vent in the filler cap greatly reduced can failure (Rock 1984:100). Most early (1810-1850) hole-in-cap cans were made completely by hand. To make the body, a piece of tinplate was bent into shape on a roller and the overlapping edges were soldered together. Two round disks were cut for the ends, their edges bent down, or flanged, and soldered to the body.

The hole-in-cap can has a circular hole about an inch in diameter on its top. Food was pushed through the hole, and a cap with a small venthole was soldered over the opening. During processing, when a sufficient amount of steam had escaped, the venthole was closed with a drop of solder. The

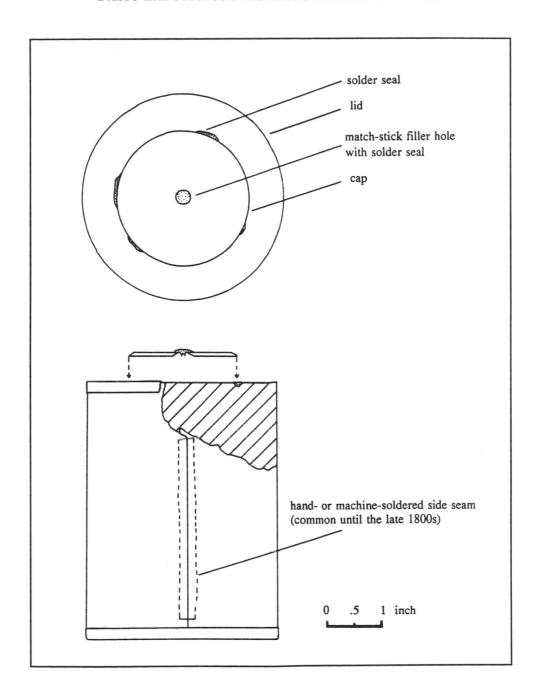

solder seal

lid

match-stick filler hole
with solder seal

cap

hand- or machine-soldered side seam
(common until the late 1800s)

0   .5   1 inch

Fig. 68. Hole-in-cap can.

soldered hole-in-cap can changed little in style through the nineteenth century, but even before the Civil War its manufacture was partially mechanized with the invention of the drop-press in 1847, which flanged the edges of the end disks (Busch 1981:96). Labor problems during the 1870s stimulated improvements in can soldering techniques, and in 1876, the "joker" system was developed. This system featured a machine that automatically attached and soldered can ends by rolling them in a solder bath. Within ten years, the side seam soldering machine was perfected and can manufacturing became entirely automatic (Rock 1987:8).

Vent hole cans were manufactured on a large-scale basis after 1900, and are characterized by stamped ends and a single pinhole or "match stick" filler hole no larger than 1/8-in. in the center of one end. This hole was then closed by a drop of solder (Rock 1984:100). By about 1920, evaporated milk was almost exclusively packaged in vent hole cans.

The most radical change in can history was the switch from the hole-in-cap can to the sanitary can (Fig. 69). The sanitary (or open-top) can was initially developed in Europe, where can ends were attached to the body by hand crimping the edges together, with a rubber gasket in between to make the seam airtight. Max Ams, of the New York-based Max Ams Machine Company, made a major technological breakthrough for the canning industry in 1888 when he invented the double seam method for side-seaming cans (Rock 1984:105). This locking seam held the sides of a can together more effectively, and greatly reduced can failure resulting from build-up of internal pressure (Sacharow and Griffin 1970:9).

In 1896, Charles Ams patented a sealing compound of rubber and gum to replace the rubber gasket, and by 1897 the Ams Machine Company brought out a machine that applied this compound to can ends automatically and crimped the ends to the body in a double seam, which was an improvement over the single seam used in Europe. For a locked side-seam, the edges are crimped together and soldered on the outside only, leaving no external ridge (Fontana and Greenleaf 1962:70). The new can was considered more sanitary because it was soldered on the outside only, and was popularly known as the "Ams can." The first true sanitary cans were produced in 1904, which used double seams, were airtight, and required no solder to fasten the side seam, top, or bottom (Fig. 69). Interiors of sanitary cans were lacquered to prevent chemical reaction of the product with the metal (Rock 1984:101).

Two tin can chronologies are presented below; the first (A) is adapted from Busch (1981), and the second (B) is adapted from Berge (1980).

CHRONOLOGY A

1819 - Beginning of commercial canning in America (fruit and vegetables)
1825 - Thomas Kensett granted U. S. patent for canning food in tin
1856 - Gail Borden granted patent for canned condensed milk
1894 - Ams Machine Company began manufacturing the locked, double-seamed can
1901 - Formation of American Can Company
1935 - Introduction of beer can
1945 - First aerosol cans marketed
1959 - First all aluminum beer can
1962 - Introduction of the beverage can pull-tab
1965 - Introduction of the tin-free steel beverage can

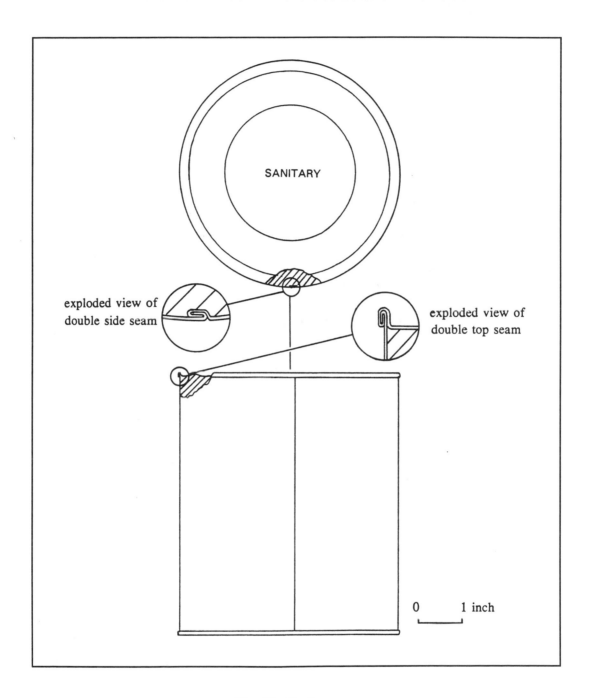

Fig. 69. Sanitary can.

CHRONOLOGY B

1850s - Kerosene patented
1865 - Kerosene canned
1872 - Large-scale meat canning began in Chicago

1875 - Sardines packed in cans
1892 - First tobacco can
1906 - Modern paint can came into use
1909 - Tuna canning began in California
1910 - Flat-sided, hinge-lidded tobacco can came into use
1917 - Ernst Moller, Bayer Company, developed the idea of a pocket-sized aspirin can
1921 - Canned citrus juice first shipped from Florida
1922 - First canned dog food developed by P. H. Chopped
1926 - Canned ham introduced
1933 - Quart can of motor oil first available
1953 - Canned soft drinks became popular

Both can lids and the methods used to open cans reflect, to some extent, what they contained. For example, removable (or slip) lids and pry-out lids typically held dry goods such as tobacco, cocoa, tea, coffee, and baking powder. Key-wind tins usually contained processed meat or sea food (especially sardines). Cans which exhibit puncture holes or spouts, or have been opened with a "church key," all probably contained liquids, thus requiring small openings to remove the contents. Cans cut completely around and X-cut lids are indicative of fruit or vegetables which require larger holes for removal of the product.

The traditional use of can shapes and sizes within the canning industry provides another method for determining the possible contents of cans. Table 8 contains descriptions of some common fruit and vegetable canisters. For a thorough listing of can shapes and sizes, specifications, and standards within the United States canning industry, the interested reader should refer to Rock (1987).

Analysis of Tin Cans. Many can lids and bodies exhibit embossing, which usually indicates the manufacturer, and oftentimes the contents of the can as well. This pattern is especially true of baking powder, lard, and plug cut tobacco canisters. Thorough archival research of embossed label designs can provide manufacturer and product information that is invaluable in determining site age, consumptive patterns, and supply routes/sources. For example, many late nineteenth and early twentieth century sites in eastern California and western Nevada contain can lids that read "GOLDEN GATE/SOLD ON MERIT/16 OZ. NET," and "SCHILLING'S/BEST/12 OZ," both of which contained baking powder and were produced in San Francisco, California, by J. A. Folger and Company and the Sterling Coffee and Spice Mills, respectively. Their presence suggests that many goods and materials used by the occupants of these sites either were made in, or imported to, San Francisco, and then transported eastward along supply routes over the Sierra Nevada into the western Great Basin.

Patterning of can assemblages provides information regarding site function and composition of the population that lived there. Temporary camps tend to contain a limited number and variety of cans, such as those containing condensed milk, vegetables, and tobacco. Base camps usually yield a numerous and diverse array of cans which, in addition to those listed above, might include five-gallon kerosene cans, sardine cans, baking powder cans, tobacco "pails," lard canisters, coffee and tea cans, meat tins, and syrup cans. The presence of certain can types is also useful in determining the dominant economic activity at a site as opposed to simply determining relative length of site occupation. For example, most mining and logging camps contain a relatively high number of 25-pound black blasting powder canisters, and many open-air frontier blacksmith shops contain a high proportion of axle grease canisters (in

168

Table 8
COMMON FRUIT AND VEGETABLE CAN DESCRIPTIONS

Size, Number, or Name	Height	Diameter	Contents
5 oz.	2 7/8"	2 1/8"	not specific
6 oz.	3 1/2"	2 1/8"	not specific
8 oz., regular	3"	2 11/16"	fruits and fruit cocktail
8 oz., tall	3 1/4"	2 11/16"	not specific
No. 300	4 7/16"	3"	tomato and pineapple juice
No. 300X	4 9/16"	3"	tomato juice
No. 1 tall	4 11/16"	3 1/16"	tomato and pineapple juice
No. 303	4 3/8"	3 3/16"	tomato and pineapple juice
No. 2 flat	2 1/4"	3 7/16"	not specific
No. 2 short	4"	3 7/16"	vegetables and fruits
No. 2	4 9/16"	3 7/16"	not specific
No. 2 1/2	4 11/16"	4 1/16"	fruits
No. 3	4 7/8"	4 1/4"	not specific
No. 10	7"	6 3/16"	fruits
gallon	8 3/4"	6 3/16"	olives, fruits and vegetables
No. 1 square	3 1/2"	3 x 3 1/2"	not specific
No. 2 1/2 square	6 1/4"	3 x 3 1/2"	not specific

addition to metal slag, scrap, wagon parts, horseshoes, horseshoe nails, and well-used hearths). The presence of women and children at short-term camps often can be deduced by the presence of lead cold cream jar lids (which often are embossed), and a variety of other metal artifacts such as jewelry, ornate buttons and clasps, and toys (such as small railroad cars).

Wire

A variety of metal wire was used in historical times. In the United States, barbed wire traditionally has been used to contain or repel livestock, enclose fields, or to mark property boundaries, and signifies a radical change in land use from the aboriginal (hunting and gathering) patterns and even from other historical patterns. The innovation of the Bessemer steelmaking process around 1876 had a tremendous effect upon the wire industry because it lowered manufacturing costs and resulted in the mass production of a variety of wire products (Clark 1949, Vol. III:124-125). Barbed wire and bale ties were among the products which experienced a florescence around this time (Washburn 1917:154-157). Washburn was an officer of Washburn and Moen Manufacturing Company, which acquired most of the patents to the new wire technologies. He reported that the first commercially made barbed wire in the United States consisted of a five-ton roll produced in 1874. In 1876, his company acquired several barbed wire patents and began producing it in quantity. A similar florescence in bale ties occurred at the same time, and Washburn and Moen also held many of these patents.

The primary early producer of wire rope and woven wire fencing in the United States also was Washburn and Moen. Wire rope first became popular in the 1880s with a major application being cable railways, which were first constructed in 1889 (Washburn 1917:159). Woven wire fencing also became increasingly common after about 1880 (Washburn 1917:163).

Numerous books have been written on the subject of barbed wire (e.g., McCallum and McCallum 1965; Clifton 1970), and the patents on many variants of barbed wire are well documented, but recycling and reuse of barbed wire presents a dating problem for the archaeologist because early barbed wire types continued to be used long after they were first produced and new types had entered the market. If barbed wire is present on a site it usually indicates a date of post-1875. Patent dates for specific types of barbed wire can be obtained from the works referenced above, as well as from other publications concerning the American wire industry. Most of these works contain illustrations of the different wire types discussed, allowing for direct comparison with the specimens under analysis.

Cartridge Cases

Expended firearm cartridges (metallic cartridge cases) are common components of post-1850s sites and serve as useful temporal markers for the archaeologist. Areas of North America that were colonized during the seventeenth, eighteenth, and early nineteenth centuries contain historical sites that yield ammunition and firearm fragments from smooth-bore flintlock muskets (or fusils) and early rifles, including gunflints, lead shot balls, bullets, and percussion caps.

A Brief History of American Firearms. Flintlock firearms were perfected during the first half of the seventeenth century, and were not substantially modified thereafter. They replaced matchlock firearms in which a burning fuse ignited the gunpowder, which then propelled the shot or bullet. Flintlock arms derive their name from a piece of flint that was held securely in the jaws of a spring-loaded cock. When the trigger was pulled, it released the lock on the spring and the flint struck a steel platform on the frizzen. This produced a spark that ignited the gunpowder in a pan below the frizzen, which then ignited the powder charge within the barrel and propelled the shot or bullet (Lewis 1968).

American rifled flintlocks were first produced in the Lancaster, Pennsylvania region around 1725. This new weapon soon became known as the Kentucky rifle, named for the region where it first saw extensive use. It featured an increased powder charge and barrel length which increased velocity, and a smaller bore which conserved lead. After measuring and emptying a charge of powder into the barrel, lead ball was placed in a patch of lubricated buckskin or cloth and both were rammed down the barrel. This patch method not only reduced loading time and increased accuracy, but helped clear the barrel of the unburned black powder from the previous shot (Williamson 1952). The Kentucky rifle was the first type of firearm with which a skilled marksman could hit a target at 150 to 200 yards, and was used effectively by American sharpshooters during the Revolutionary War, much to the chagrin of the British Army.

As the popularity of the Kentucky rifle spread, ammunition was being improved. Paper cartridges with the ball attached, and containing a measured amount of powder, were first used in military weapons and were widely adopted by outdoorsmen during the late 1700s. Beginning in the early 1800s, percussion locks were developed to ignite powder charges, and after several decades of experimentation and development, the percussion cap replaced the flintlock as a method of igniting gunpowder. Sometime around 1825, experiments were performed with conical lead bullets which, in a rifled barrel, provided greater range and accuracy than the round lead ball.

The next major development in firearms technology was the single-shot, breech-loading rifle, the most famous of which was the one invented by Christian Sharps in 1848 (Williamson 1952:5). The Sharps rifle soon largely replaced muzzle-loading rifles, and until it was superseded by the repeating rifle, was one of the most widely used guns in America. While various individuals were developing early breech-loading weapons during the 1830s and 1840s, other inventors had turned their attention to the development of repeating firearms. The first, most famous, and most successful repeating firearm was the Colt revolver, patented in both England and the United States by Samuel Colt in 1835 and 1836, respectively (Williamson 1952:6).

In 1849, Walter Hunt obtained a patent for a repeating firearm with a tubular magazine under the barrel, which he called the "Volitional Repeater" (Williamson 1952:9). Although a brilliant achievement, the repeating magazine was far too complicated for practical use. Hunt then transferred his patent to George Arrowsmith, whose employee, Lewis Jennings, was assigned the problem of improving Hunt's rifle. Within a few months, he had succeeded in simplifying the lock and repeating mechanism. At this point, Arrowsmith interested a New York capitalist, Courtlandt Palmer, in the possibilities of the new firearm, and Palmer contracted with the firm of Robbins and Lawrence to produce 5,000 Jennings Patent Rifles. It was during the period of this contract that Palmer became associated with the famous duo of Horace Smith and Daniel Wesson. After several encouraging developments, the three individuals formed a limited partnership in 1854 under the name of Smith & Wesson. One year later, a group of eastern capitalists made an offer to buy out Smith & Wesson, and the partners agreed to sell to the new concern.

The newly formed corporation became the Volcanic Repeating Arms Company, and was incorporated in Connecticut in 1855. Meanwhile, Smith and Wesson went on to form their famous pistol company. Volcanic continued to produce the same types of firearms and ammunition begun by the Smith & Wesson partnership. However, due to a lack of working capital and poor performance of their ammunition, Volcanic was declared insolvent early in 1857, and the entire assets of the company eventually were assigned to Oliver F. Winchester. Originally a shirt manufacturer in New Haven, Winchester also was a Volcanic stockholder and had provided a great deal of capital to keep the company afloat. Even before he had acquired the assets of Volcanic, Winchester had organized a new corporation, the New Haven Arms Company, to carry on production of repeating firearms and ammunition under his general management (Williamson 1952:19).

Winchester eventually hired Benjamin T. Henry as plant manager, who was experienced at improving and manufacturing repeating firearms. Between 1858 and 1860, Henry made a major contribution to the New Haven Arms Company and to the firearms world in general in the form of his famous .44-caliber metallic rimfire cartridge and repeating rifle. Immediately after the Civil War, Winchester reorganized his New Haven Arms Company, calling it the Henry Repeating Arms Company, and, in 1866, renamed it again as the Winchester Repeating Arms Company. Since the initial success of the Henry Rifle in 1860, Winchester never again manufactured pistols except for a few experimental models. The first rifle to bear Winchester's name was the Winchester Model 1866 which, like the Henry, was bored for .44-caliber ammunition (Bowman 1958).

Cartridge Case Identification. The self-contained metallic cartridge is a relatively recent development, having been perfected only within the last 125 years or so. Both rimfire and centerfire cartridges were first mass produced between 1856 and 1858 (Barnes 1965). Standard centerfire cartridges with self-contained primers were first widely available after 1868. Several of the better known sources of information on rifle and handgun ammunition were written by Logan (1959), Barnes (1965), and Bearse (1966). Two of the best general sources regarding shotshell bases are Moos (1968) and Vinson (1968). Unidentifiable cartridges usually can be referred to local gunsmiths, who are often quite knowledgeable and eager to help you identify them.

The base of most firearm cartridges is usually stamped with the caliber or gauge, manufacturer's name or initials, and sometimes trade name. American military cartridge case heads usually have the initials of the arsenal or ordnance plant where they were manufactured, plus the last two numbers of the year that the cartridge was made. For example, a head stamp that reads "F 87 R 3" indicates that the case was made at the Frankford Arsenal (F) in March (3), 1887 (87) for a rifle (R) (Berge 1980:223). In addition to the section on cartridges contained in Berge's monograph on the archaeology of Simpson Springs Station, Utah, another excellent archaeological study of ammunition recovered from Fort Bowie, Arizona, was written by Herskovitz (1978).

Manufacturers of headstamps commonly found throughout the western United States are listed in Table 9, as identified by Logan (1959). In the laboratory, cartridge headstamps should be completely described, and a representative sample of the different types present should either be photographed or drawn. Cartridge case dates are determined by the length of time that they were manufactured by a specific company (e.g., Peters Cartridge Co. [1887-1934]), or by the date on the cartridge case. If the observed cartridge cases do not have stamped heads, then general dates can be ascribed from the technique of manufacture. The development of the various cartridge types is outlined in Berge (1980).

The American system measures the cartridge caliber in 100th's or 1000th's of an inch, with the caliber being designated by any one of the following criteria (Bearse 1966:15): (1) bore or diameter of the barrel; (2) barrel-groove diameter; (3) bullet diameter; (4) inside diameter of cartridge case mouth; and (5) arbitrary figure, determined by manufacturer. The caliber may also be designated by the case length or case type. Measurement of a cartridge case with calipers in order to determine specific measurements on the metallic case may be more informative than referring to cartridge type collections. Many books (e.g., Barnes 1965) provide detailed listings of cartridge case measurements which accurately identify a particular cartridge case.

Other Metal Artifacts

Historical sites usually yield other metal artifacts in addition to those mentioned above. Some of these objects, such as coins, are excellent time markers, but many others can only be assigned a very general age. The most important information provided by many metal artifacts concerns site function, rather than age. Many metal objects recovered from subsurface contexts often require treatment baths in the laboratory to remove rust in order for the artifact to be identified. The following categories are meant to provide the student with a more complete inventory of metal artifacts commonly encountered at historical sites.

Apparel Accessories. This category includes such things as buckles and other fastening devices, buttons, buttonhooks, clothing rivets, dress stays, jewelry, shoe parts, and suspender parts.

Table 9
CARTRIDGE CASE HEADSTAMPS AND CORRESPONDING MANUFACTURERS

DM	Des Moines Ordnance Plant
DWM	Deutsche Waffen & Munitions Fabriken [Germany]
F; F.A.	Frankford Arsenal [U.S.]
F. [impressed]	Federal Cartridge Co. [rimfire cartridge cases]
F.V.V. & Co.	Fitch, Van Vechten & Co., New York City
J.G.	Jacob Goldmark, New York [metallic]
H. [impressed]	Winchester Repeating Arms Co. [rimfire cartridge cases]
H. [raised]	Winchester Repeating Arms Co. [early rimfire]
P. [raised]	Phoenix Cartridge Co.
P. [impressed]	Peters Cartridge Co. [absorbed by Remington in 1934]
PC CO.; PETERS	Peters Cartridge Co.
RA: RaUMC; REM-UMC	Remington Union Metallic Cartridge Co. [1902-present]
RW	Winchester Repeating Arms Co. [rifle]
U; UMC	Union Metallic Cartridge Co. [merged with Remington in 1902]
U	Utah Ordnance Plant
U HiSpeed	Remington UMC [on rimfires since WWII]
US; U.S.; USC Co.	United States Cartridge Co.
US [raised]	United States Cartridge Co.
WRA; WRA CO	Winchester Repeating Arms Co.
Super Speed	Winchester Repeating Arms Co.
W; W Co.; WCC	Western Cartridge Co. [1898-present]
WESTERN Super-X	Western Cartridge Co.
1901 NEW RIVAL	Winchester Repeating Arms Co.
1901 LEADER	Winchester Repeating Arms Co.
1901 REPEATER	Winchester Repeating Arms Co.
1901 PIGEON	Winchester Repeating Arms Co.

Coinage. Three broad types of coinage represented in American historical sites include U. S. currency, foreign currency, and tokens.

Hardware and Construction Materials. Hardware and building materials are commonly divided into four areas: construction hardware, builder's hardware, plumbing hardware, and miscellaneous hardware. Besides some of the more obvious elements of construction hardware, such as nails, bolts, and screws, other generalized construction items include brackets, braces, corner irons, drainspouts, spikes, and staples. Builder's hardware refers to a specific group of items limited mostly to various types of door and window hardware. Plumbing hardware includes pipe, pipe fittings, faucets, valve handles, and sink drains. Miscellaneous hardware consists of an incredibly diverse group of artifacts, such as buckets, barrel hoops, chains, grommets, handles, lids and covers, rings and loops, padlocks and keys, rivets, and wire.

173

Tools. Common metal tool types include hammer, axe, and hatchet heads, saw blades, drill bits, screwdriver bits, planes, files, tongs, wrenches, pliers, chisels, hoes, picks, trowels, and shovels. Throughout North America, many native groups acquired and used mass-produced metal tools for traditional activities during the last 100 years (or so) of contact. Examples of such behavior include inserting nails into wooden handles to form awls and rodent/reptile sticks, and using iron rods or crowbars as digging sticks.

Household Items. Household items refer to metal kitchen and table wares (knives, forks, spoons, pots, and pans), interior furnishings (stove parts, casters, lighting devices, and coat hooks), tin cans, and fragments of foodstuff containers.

Personal Items. Examples of personal items are musical instruments, pocket knives, pocket watches, smoking paraphernalia, children's toys, and hygiene items.

Transportation-Related Items. Historical metal artifacts associated with transportation include horse, mule, and ox trappings (horseshoes, muleshoes, oxshoes, toe calks, shoe nails, bits, and buckles), wagon and carriage parts, and automobile parts.

Machinery. Mechanized items associated with mining, railroad, lumber, and agricultural activities usually are represented by various parts of individual machines such as plates, gears, levers, and gauges.

GLASS ARTIFACTS

Fragmented glass containers, windows, and to some extent, beads, usually are well-represented at historical sites. The types and percentages of glass artifacts present at a site are largely determined by the ethnic group who lived there, the length of site occupation, proximity of the site in relation to market sources for glass products, and the types of structures that the site's occupants built.

The art of making glass was first developed in the Old World, where by 1500 B.C., both Egyptian and Mesopotamian artisans produced glass beads and small, crude vessels (Munsey 1970:6). Some of the earliest glass containers were produced in Syria around 100 B.C., when artisans discovered that they could form hollow vessels by blowing air through a tube into a blob of hot glass (Munsey 1970:30). Glass ingredients consist of sand, soda, and lime, with sand (silica) comprising the major ingredient in a batch of glass. The soda is a flux added to promote fusion, which occurs above 2,500 degrees F. Lime is added because soda-silica glass is soluble in water and lime reduces this solubility. After the basic ingredients have fused, the batch is allowed to cool to 1,800 degrees F., whereupon it thickens to the consistency appropriate for blowing.

Bottles

American glassmaking began in 1607 at Jamestown, and the first American glasshouse was established in 1739 by Caspar Wistar in Salem County, New Jersey (Munsey 1970:22). Early American bottles were either free-blown or mold-blown, and soon thereafter, new techniques such as pressing, drawing, and casting were developed. The nineteenth century witnessed a substantial increase in the amount and variety of American glass as glassmakers improved known techniques, which sped up and simplified production. An important stimulus to increased glass production was the development of mass transportation systems which opened new markets.

By the late nineteenth century, a wide variety of goods was packaged in glass containers (bottles). These ranged from foods and beverages, such as pickles and beer, to domestic goods, such as ink and shoe polish. A useful method of analyzing the various types of handmade and machine-made bottles is to focus upon the physical attributes that indicate the mode of manufacture. Classification based on manufacturing methods incorporates numerous attributes of the bottle fragments: finish types, neck types, shoulder types, base types, body types, etc. Glass color, mold type, and inferred function are also important aspects of analysis (Berge 1980:37). The functions of many traditional bottle types (shapes) are well-documented, and with a little practice, most students can become quite proficient at recognizing the basic uses of most bottles.

The following definitions for bottle nomenclature are taken from Berge (1980:37-38), who presented a comprehensive analysis of the bottle assemblage recovered from Simpson Springs Station in western Utah:

The average bottle consists of six basic sections -- finish, neck, shoulder, body, insweep or heel, and base [Fig. 70]. The "finish" is the top section of the bottle attached to the neck from which the bottle contents are obtained and to which a closure is applied to secure the bottle's contents from spoilage or spilling. The upper part of the finish to which a cap would seal itself is the "sealing surface." The diameter of the aperture opening is the "bore." Sometimes a ring of glass is placed around the neck at the base of the finish in order to secure the closure, usually on threaded closures, which are called a "collar." The collar, when present, is the basal portion of the finish. The "neck" is generally an extension of the finish that connects the finish to the shoulder. The neck is usually the same general size and cylindrical shape as the finish. The part of the neck that connects the neck to the shoulder is termed the "root of the neck." The "shoulder" is an extension between the neck and body which connects these sections to form the single unit. Often the body is wider than the neck, and the shoulder serves as a means of reducing the body diameter to the size of the neck and finish. The lower section of the body which attaches to the base is called an "insweep." The "base" is under the section of the bottle on which the bottle rests when not in use. All the weight of the bottle may not rest on the entire surface of the base, if the base is not flat. Curved bases help to withstand internal pressure on the bottle, especially fermented or carbonated contents. If the base is convex, as in some soda pop bottle types, it is called a "round bottom." If the base is slightly concave, it is referred to as a "push-up." On wine bottles, the push-up is much deeper and is termed a "kick-up."

Bottle Chronology. The lengthy bottle chronology below contains important data regarding the evolution of manufacturing techniques (also refer to Table 10).

1700-1800: Typical bottles were the tall or squat bottles with kick-up bases, squat types with long necks, and late types with high kick-ups. Another common bottle type was the Dunmore.

1780-1840: The most common feature of bottles before 1820 was the crude blow-over finish formed by simply cutting the container free from the blow pipe—also called a "sheared lip" (Kendrick 1966:28). Other popular bottles included the Ludlow, Chestnut flasks, and the swirled bottle.

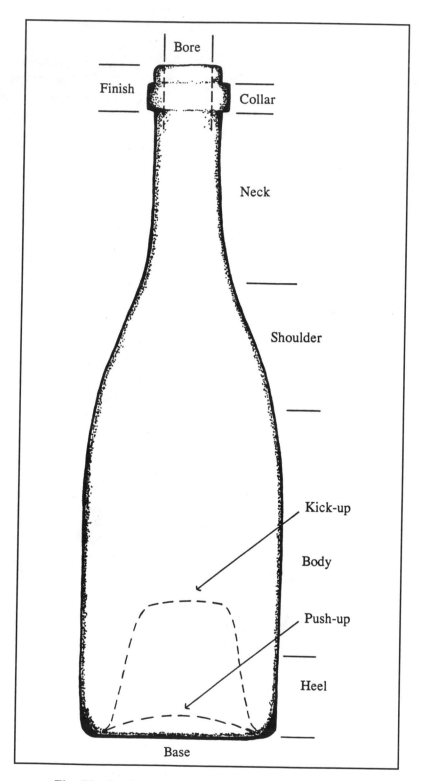

Fig. 70. Bottle nomenclature and corresponding areas.

176

Table 10
GENERALIZED CHRONOLOGY FOR BOTTLE TECHNOLOGY

FREE-BLOWN BOTTLES

to circa 1860

BOTTLE MOLDS

1790-1810	dip molds
1810-1880	iron-hinged bottom mold (2-piece mold)
1870-1910	three-part mold
1870s-1920s	turn molds
1880-1910	closed mouth mold
1904-present	automatic bottle machine

BASE MARKS

pre-1840-ca. 1870	pontil or snap marks
1904-present	cutoff scars
1930s-1940s	valve marks (milk bottles)

LIP FORMS

1810-1840	sheared lips
1840-1860	hand-applied lips
1840-1920	applied lips
1880-early 1900s	fired lips

LIPPING TOOL MARKS

1870s-1920	smooth-lipped

CLOSURES

1870s-1900	inside screw (whiskey bottles)
1879-1915	Hutchinson stopper
1882-1920	lightning stopper
1892-present	crown cap
1892-present	with cork liner
1924-present	roll-on cap
1955-present	with plastic liner

1840-1860: With the glass industry in full bloom, diversification began to take place and new inventions were produced to satisfy the demands of consumers. The bottles of this period and earlier were formed by open molds in which only the body was formed. The neck and finish had to be shaped by hand. This type of mold leaves a seam on the bottle body which terminates on the shoulder or the low neck (Kendrick 1966:47). It was the practice of glassmakers to form finishes by applying a strip of glass around the sheared end of the neck. The manufacture of free-blown bottles died out around 1860, so that the seamless bottles of irregular shapes are seldom encountered after this date.

A common feature up to 1860 on ordinary utility items was pontil marks. This mark, found on the bases of bottles, consisted of an area somewhat circular, rough, and sharp where a glass rod had once been attached to maintain control during the handmaking of the finish.

Between 1850 and 1860, the pontil was gradually replaced by the snap-case (a mechanical device that gripped the base of the bottle body, sometimes leaving a mark on the side of the bottle). The rod was not physically attached to the bottle base, but rather a tong that snapped tight to the bottle heel was used; when removed it left no marks on the base. This left the base free for lettering or decoration (Kendrick 1966:29).

There was little concern over the color of glass until foodstuffs began to be bottled. When consumers wanted to be able to see the contents of bottle, glass had to be made lighter in color. Dark olive-green or black glass, common up to 1860, began to be replaced by clearer and lighter colored types of glass.

1860-1880: The bottles of this period were still produced by somewhat crude manufacturing techniques, but a change was beginning to take place. Colors were becoming more refined and lighter, and clear glass containers began to become popular around 1880. There may have been a refinement in finish because mold seams of this period end just below the finish, an obvious indication that the finish was made separate from the body (Kendrick 1966:47).

An important characteristic of some bottles that first appeared in 1869 was that of embossing them with the names of contents, manufacturers, distributors, slogans, and messages. This practice nearly died out with the advent of automatic bottle machines (1903); paper labels were used extensively on bottles made from such machines (Kendrick 1966:71).

Beer bottles were used only after 1873. Woodward (1958:126-127) noted that pasteurization of beer is a prime requisite for the proper bottling of beer, and since Pasteur's process did not come into active use in the brewing business until 1873, it can be safely assumed that no bottled beer was shipped anywhere in the United States prior to that year.

1880-1900: The common mold of this period was the closed mold in which the entire bottle, except the upper section of the finish or lip, was mold-made. On these bottles, the seam ends at about the middle of the neck. The contours of the finish became more controlled and standardized, resulting in more uniformity of closures (Kendrick 1966:47-48).

In 1892, the semiautomatic "press and blow" process was invented, adaptable only to the production of wide-mouthed containers. In this process, the glass was pressed into the mold to form its mouth and lip first. Then a metal plunger was forced through the mouth and air pressure was applied to blow the body of the vessel. This process was used for the production of fruit jars and early milk bottles. It was not adaptable to narrow-necked bottles due to "bottleneck"; the necks were too small to allow the use of the metal plunger. So the conventional screw-topped bottle did not become common until after 1924, when the glass industry standardized the thread (Kendrick 1966:51).

By 1896, the first of the new semiautomatic machines was in successful operation at the Atlas Glass Works, and in 1898, Ball Brothers installed a similar machine for the manufacture of fruit jars (James 1956:19).

1900-1940:   James (1956:17-18) divided this time period into three phases: (1) 1898 to 1906—semiautomatic machinery for the making of wide-mouthware exclusively; (2) 1905 to 1917—the Owens automatic machine for the making of all kinds of bottles, wide and narrow mouth, and semiautomatic machinery for the narrow-mouth ware; and (3) 1917 to present—semiautomatic machinery made automatic by feed and flow devices.

At the beginning of the twentieth century, a new phase of bottle manufacture commenced. Through the cooperation and financial backing of the Toledo Glass Works, the Owens machine was perfected in 1903. At first, the Owens machine made only heavy bottles, which were in high demand. In 1909, improvements in the machine allowed it to make small prescription bottles. By 1917, other completely automatic bottle-making machines had been invented, and bottles were manufactured automatically throughout the world.

Characteristically, bottles formed by the Owens machine will have heavy bottoms, and thick, even walls, and the seams of the neck molds will not line up with the seams of their bodies. A distinguishing mark left by the Owens machine is a shallow wrinkle in the glass which forms a circle in the base of the bottles. The ring is often off center and may complete its circle by extending up the sidewalls of the bottle. This "Owens ring" formed when the glass, which was sucked up into the lip mold, was cut off from the rest of the glass in the pot (Kendrick 1966:81).

Before 1917, the only fully automatic bottle machine was the Owens, but after that time, the importance of the Owens machine decreased. After 1917, semiautomatic machines greatly decreased in the United States. Between 1916 and 1924, the Hartford-Empire Company was developing the gob feeder machine (James 1956:21-23). Kendrick (1966:83) described this device as follows:

In 1917 an important invention of mechanized bottle production (not used by the Owens machine) was a way of forming a measured amount of molten glass from which a bottle could be blown. It is called a "gob feeder." In this process, a gob of glass is drawn from the tank and cut off by shears. Bottles which have been formed from such a gob, may show a design in the center of its base like a "V" with straight lines radiating out at right angles from the "V".

Bottles produced by an automatic machine have a mold seam that extends to the bore of the finish. By 1920, bottles were refined in that bubbles were eliminated and the thickness of the glass was made more uniform.

Bottle Mold Seams and Accessories. Different types of bottle mold seams date to discrete time periods, and are important aspects of analysis. By 1800, the most widely used method of making bottles and other glassware was by blowing; glass produced by this method is termed free-blown, hand-blown or off-hand-blown (Lorrain 1968:35). Other attributes of free-blown bottles include the presence of a pontil mark, asymmetry, and lack of mold marks.

HISTORICAL ARTIFACTS

Munsey (1970:38-50) provided specific details for recognizing techniques used by manufacturers as various molds changed through time. His methods of identifying the molds used on specific bottles and the time range during which some of the more common manufacturing techniques were used are provided below (refer to Figure 71 for illustrations of some mold types).

1. Non-Shoulder Molds—This type of mold forms the body only and may or may not have mold seams at the shoulder.

    A. Dip mold. The body and base are formed in this one-piece mold. The bottom is slightly smaller than the shoulder, where there may be a mold seam. This type of mold produces a uniform body shape up to the shoulder, and the finish may be handmade.

    B. Pattern mold (mid-1700s through 1800s). Early pattern molds have perpendicular ridges or grooves, and there may be an irregularity in the glass at the shoulder, or a wrinkle at the neck.

    C. Hinged shoulder-height mold (late 1700s through 1800s). This type of mold does not have to be tapered, since the mold apparatus opens at the shoulder. The side seams disappear at the shoulder and the body could be embossed.

2. Full-Height Molds

    A. Bottom-hinged mold (ca. 1810 to ca. 1880). The mold seams on bottles manufactured by this method have seams up the sides and across the base. The seams across the bottom come in two varieties: (1) straight across the bottom; and (2) curved around a slight push-up in the center. The bottom seams may be obliterated to some degree by a pontil scar, except when a snap-case was used, in which case the mold seam would be intact.

    B. Three-part mold with dip mold body (1870 to 1910). This mold produces seams around the shoulder and up to the finish area. It allows versatility in designing the shoulder, such as embossing; however, this was not usually done. It did not provide for embossing on the lower half of the bottle.

    C. Three-part leaf mold (free-blown period of the nineteenth century). This type of mold produces three mold seams equally spaced up the sides of the bottle.

    D. Post-bottom mold. From this type of mold, seams are produced down the sides and to a circle around the bottom.

    E. Cup-bottom mold. The seams from this type of mold run down the sides to the heel and around the outside of the base.

    F. Blow-back mold (mid-1800s). This type of mold leaves a rough and ragged edge around the top of the finish. This rough area is ground down so that the closure can

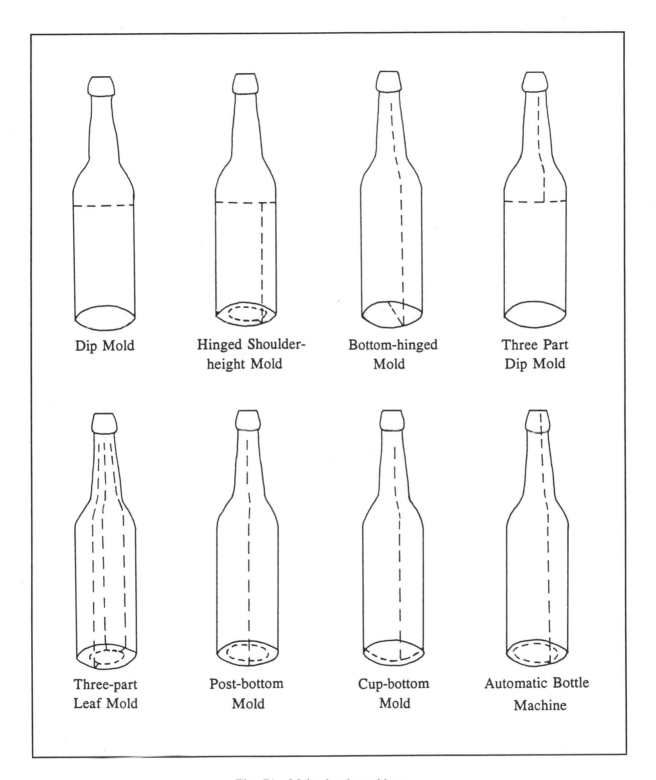

Fig. 71. Major bottle mold types.

seal on the sealing surface. This mold was used in early fruit jars, on which screw threads were molded with the rest of the bottle in one piece.

G. Automatic bottle machine (1904 to present). The advent of the automatic bottle machine produced bottles with new mold seams. These molds produce seams up, over, or around the top of the sealing surface. However, beverage bottles are fire-polished to eliminate the seams so they will not cut the mouth of the drinker of the contents.

In addition to molds, certain processes, accessories, and tools produced distinguishing features on bottles. One such process produced in a full-height mold is called a turn-mold bottle, used between 1880 and 1910. In this process, mold seams were obscured by turning the bottle in the mold. Bottles treated this way are highly polished, cannot be embossed, and show horizontal lines or grooves produced as the bottle is turned in the mold. These turn-mold attributes are commonly found on wine bottles.

During the last half of the nineteenth century, a plate mold was used to emboss lettering or designs on the bodies of bottles. In this process, a plate with the particular desired motif was inserted into the mold. The plate mold, or slug plate, as it was known, helped in the standardization of many bottle shapes, such as milk bottles.

Beginning in about 1904, the Owens automatic bottle machine produced irregular, circular marks, known as cutoff scars (not seams) on the base. Between about 1930 and 1940, some bottle machines produced what is called a "machine-made valve mark." This mark consists of a circle less than an inch in diameter, and is similar to a seam. It is found more commonly on wide-mouth bottles and glass milk containers.

Lipping tools were first developed in England around 1830 and were first used in America about 1850. These tools often erased seams on the finish. In this process, which shaped the top of the bottle, a rod was inserted into the bore while the associated clamp on the outside developed the finish as it was rotated and seams were obliterated by the rotation of the lipping tool. Beginning in the nineteenth century, finishes were made by cutting the bottle from the glassblower's rod and reheating the lip or sealing surface to smooth it. In cases where mold seams came to the top of the finish, the seams were obliterated by the reheating process, producing a flared or fired lip.

A wavy, dimpled, or hammered appearance on a bottle surface is more commonly known as "whittle marks" because they are thought to have been produced by wooden molds. These marks were actually made by blowing hot glass into a cold mold. Free-blown bottles were finished by a method known as empontilling. When the free-blown bottle was at its desired shape and cut from the blowpipe, the finish had to be shaped and fire-smoothed. This was done by attaching a glass rod to the base to turn the bottle while the finish was formed. After the finish was completed, the rod was broken off, leaving a mark known as a pontil scar or "punty."

The snap-case was a mechanical device that gripped the base of the bottle body. Occasionally it left a mark on the side of the bottle where it squeezed the hot glass a little too hard. Machine blowing eventually eliminated the need for empontilling, and the automatic bottle machine did away with the snap cases.

Glass can be produced in practically all colors by adding specific ingredients to the basic glass mixture. Munsey (1970:37) suggested that the color of glass was obtained by adding various compounds (Table 11).

Table 11
COMPOUNDS USED FOR COLORING GLASS

Compound	Color
copper, selenium, or gold	reds
nickel or manganese	purple (amethyst)
chromium or copper	greens
cobalt or copper	blues
carbon or nickel	browns
iron	greens, yellows
selenium	yellows, pinks
tin or zinc	opal or milk white
iron slug	"black glass"

In order to obtain clear glass, the raw materials need to be free of impurities. Very dark greenish-amber glass ("black glass") was popular until the middle of the nineteenth century. Just before the turn of the century, bottles were predominantly green and aqua. Munsey (1970:37) further noted that:

> A number of variables can affect the actual color produced including the amount of the compounds used, the degree to which the basic glass mixture is impure, the temperature and the time-temperature relationship, and the reheating necessary to complete a piece of glass.

In the late 1800s, much of the glass sand, which came from Belgium as ballast for ships, was pale green. This may account for many bottles of this color (i.e., pale green or aqua), though it was not desirable for many products. Manganese was used in bottle glass up to about 1917 in order to give the glass a clearer effect. Precisely when manganese began to be mixed in glass is not definitely known, but it may date back as far as 1810 (Ferraro and Ferraro 1964:79). When exposed to the ultraviolet rays of the sun, the manganese content of glass will cause it to turn "purple"; however, after about 1917, manganese was no longer added to glass. Newman (1970:74) suggested a beginning date of 1880 and a terminal date of 1925 for the use of manganese; thus, purple glass can be dated with some accuracy. Additionally, Kendrick (1966:59-61) noted that:

> With the advent of World War I, our main source of manganese (German suppliers) was cut off. In the U.S. bottle industry, selenium became the predominant chemical used to bleach out the unwanted iron-produced aqua color from the glass. A change-of-color event takes place in this glass which has a high selenium content. With exposure to sunlight its clear appearance changes to an amber hue, or, as I would describe it, the color of ripened wheat. It never gets any darker than a good grade of honey, and there is no need to confuse it with a brown bottle.

Analysis of Bottles. The general objective of bottle analysis is to determine the approximate number of each type of bottle represented in the assemblage, their approximate age, the companies that made them, and their likely source of distribution. It is critical to determine the original contents of the bottles represented in a collection, because this provides insights into the economic patterns and personal habits of the site occupants. In frontier areas far removed from glass manufacturers, bottles (especially wide-mouthed specimens) were commonly reused for storing other foods. This possibility must always be considered when conducting bottle analysis.

Many historical Native American groups used bottle glass to produce traditional tools such as projectile points and scraping tools. Because glass is extremely homogeneous, and is similar to obsidian in its fracture mechanics, it was easily worked with aboriginal flintknapping tools, such as hammerstones and antler tine pressure flakers.

The glass industry traditionally has used distinct bottle shapes to package various products. Figure 72 illustrates several types of alcoholic beverage bottles, Figure 73 depicts two common shapes of patent medicine bottles, and Figures 74 and 75 show various forms of household bottles (as well as a mineral water bottle). Nearly all paneled (flat) bottle fragments represent patent or proprietary medicines, which were popular from about 1860 to 1915. "Patent medicine" is the generic term commonly applied to all remedial agents sold without prescription. Once registered, these brands became known as proprietary medicines. Prior to the Pure Food and Drug Act of 1906, patent medicine manufacturers swindled the public with concoctions claiming extravagant therapeutic results and guarantees. Some products were claimed to cure as many as 30 ailments. Many of these so-called "medicines" consisted of nothing more than alcohol, sugar, and water. Narcotics such as opium were often added to these products in order to increase sales through addiction (Fike 1987:3). Patent medicine bottles typically are rectangular or cylindrical in shape, and usually aqua or light green in color.

Beginning in the late 1800s to early 1900s, many glass manufacturers began to emboss their company's initials or trademark on bottles they produced. These maker's marks usually are located on the base, and an attempt should always be made to identify them during the course of analysis. For example, a bottle base recovered from a site in the Far West embossed with the letters "P.C.G.W." is of a bottle manufactured by the Pacific Coast Glass Works of San Francisco, California, between 1902 and 1924. An excellent source for identification of maker's marks is that by Toulouse (1971).

Conjoinable bottle sherds may be reconstructed (perhaps even glued together), and the number of base, body, shoulder, and finish sherds for each type and color of bottle in the assemblage should be recorded. In collection of highly fragmented specimens, this may be frustrating, but it is important to try to determine the total number of bottles represented in an assemblage.

Window Glass

Flat window glass recovered from historical sites was produced either through the crown, cylinder, or casting method. Crown glass is characterized by small sheets bearing pontil scars, with a great deal of variation in thickness from the center to the edge of the sheet, and curved distortion lines detectable in oblique light (Lorrain 1968:37). The cylinder method produced larger panes of glass of a more uniform thickness with straight distortion lines. The casting method produced plate glass, which was used mostly for small mirrors because of its high cost. However, this type of glass was very clear and lacked distortion (Lorrain 1968:37).

Fig. 72.   Examples of alcoholic beverage bottles: (a) amber beer bottle with
a Crown finish produced in a cup-bottom mold; (b) dark green
bottle (the original contents of which are unknown) exhibiting an
applied, Double Ring finish made in a three-part dip mold; (c)
amber beer or whiskey bottle with an Oil finish produced in a cup-
bottom mold.

Window glass dating from the mid-to-late 1800s to thc early 1900s usually measures between
0.045 and 0.130 inches thick, and is aqua blue or extremely light green in color. In some instances, it
is difficult to distinguish between flat side panel bottle sherds and window glass fragments. Some

Fig. 73.   Examples of patent medicine bottles: (a) specimen with a Blake variant 2 base, Arrow panel body style, and Prescription finish; (b) specimen with an Excelsior base, Arrow panel body style, and a Double Ring finish.

researchers believe that window glass increased in thickness through time (cf. Roenke 1978). Most window glass sherds recovered from subsurface contexts exhibit a surface layer of patina, an opalescent/iridescent film that results from moisture leaching out of the soda and lime in glass and leaving behind a silicate skeleton.

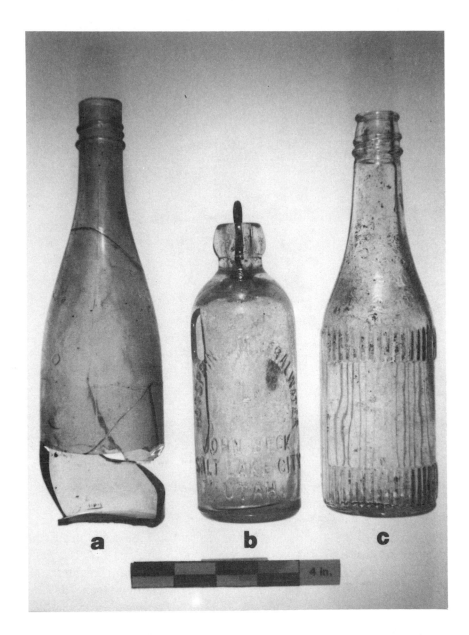

Fig. 74.   Examples of: (a, c) ketchup bottles; (b) mineral water bottle.
The mineral water bottle was produced by John Beck Co. of Salt
Lake City, Utah.

Glass Beads

Glass trade beads and embroidery (seed) beads occur at contact sites all over the world. In the
New World, glass beads arrived with Columbus and were widely used as personal ornamentation and
native trade items throughout colonial times. Christopher Columbus brought green and yellow glass
beads to the New World for use as trade goods (Smith and Good 1982:3-4). They soon became highly

187

Fig. 75.   Examples of preserve bottles: (a) Missouri Style bottle; (b) Dewey Preserve bottle; (c) Oblong
Pickle bottle with an octagonal body.

successful barter items among native groups, and continued to fulfill this role during Spanish exploration
and the conquest of the Caribbean, Florida, and Central and South America (Deagan 1987:156). The
sites of Nueva Cadiz, Venezuela, and Puerto Real, Haiti, have provided the most significant glass bead
assemblage for the early- to mid-sixteenth century Caribbean region (Deagan 1987:162). The Nueva
Cadiz collection has been thoroughly studied and reported (e.g., Fairbanks 1968; Smith and Good 1982),
and provided the basis for the first comprehensive typology of early Spanish beads (Fairbanks 1968).

In North America, beads have received a great deal of scholarly attention for various reasons:
they are important indicators of early historical Native American culture change; they are well-preserved
in the archaeological record; certain types are time sensitive; and they are relatively common in most
parts of the continent. Glass beads also are important behavioral indicators as they oftentimes provide
the only evidence of protohistoric material culture modification and early Anglo contact at native sites
(cf. Arkush 1995:38).

The use of glass trade beads is usually associated with the fur trade in North America, but it also
played an important role in European exploration of the Southeast, Southwest, and Far West. For

example, members of the de Soto expedition of 1539-1543 traded European goods directly in the interior Southeast; members of the Coronado expedition first exchanged beads with various Southwest Indians in 1540; and members of the Escalante expedition were the first to directly distribute glass beads among various Southern Paiute and Ute groups in Utah in 1776. In many parts of western North America, glass trade beads often replaced aboriginal beads of bone, stone, and shell during protohistoric and early historical times.

A large portion of the glass beads traded on the American continent from early contact until the mid-1800s was produced in Venetian glass factories. Venice was the primary bead production center and supplier from the eleventh century onward for beads found throughout Europe and subsequently through the New World (Deagan 1987:158). Early European glass beads also were made by Czechoslovakian (Bohemian) glasshouses, where known production dates back to the tenth century (Kidd 1979:40). The French glass industry was established during medieval times, and first produced glass rosary beads in the fourteenth century (Kidd 1979:40). During the seventeenth century, many Venetian glassmakers defected to other European countries, which then began to produce glass beads. The Dutch bead industry, which was flourishing by the early seventeenth century, benefitted from this process and began to compete with Venetian glasshouses for a share of the New World market. Dutch beads, many of which are imitations of Venetian types, are somewhat common in colonial period sites of the northeastern and southeastern United States (Deagan 1987:158-159).

Glass beads can be divided into four major types, based on the method of manufacture: (1) those made from drawn glass tubing (the most common type in North American native sites); (2) those made by winding molten glass around an iron mandrel (wire wound beads); (3) those made of pressed or molded glass; and (4) those made of blown glass.

It seems likely that the glass factories of Puebla and Guadalajara, Mexico, also produced glass trade beads (C. Sorensen, personal communication 1992). The first glass factory in Puebla was built by Rodrigo de Espinosa in 1542, and represents one of the earliest Old World industries to be established in the New World. The strong possibility that these places produced glass beads apparently has been overlooked by the vast majority of bead researchers. In fact, many of the beads carried by early Spanish explorers and missionaries in the West and Southwest, such as Coronado, Vizcaino, Escalante, Fages, Kino, Junipero Serra, Garces, etc., and that were subsequently distributed among local Indian groups, may very well have been made in Puebla or Guadalajara, and not in Venice or other European factories, as is usually assumed.

Trade beads should not be confused with the later and much smaller glass embroidery beads (sometimes called "seed" beads due to their size) that were popular among various Native American groups around the turn of this century for use in decoration of clothing (e.g., Plains Indians). Seed beads were common in the Plains culture area by about 1840, and were common in the Far West by about 1880. Various groups, such as the Northern Paiute, used seed beads woven in a netted fashion via a bead loom to decorate the exterior surfaces of small coiled baskets after 1900. There are numerous published sources concerning glass beads, and some of the more definitive works include those by Beck (1928); Orchard (1929); Woodward (1967); Sorensen and Le Roy (1968); Kidd and Kidd (1970); Sleen (1973); Karklins (1974, 1983); Kidd (1979); Karklins and Sprague (1980); and Hayes (1983). Important sources regarding Spanish Colonial beads include Fairbanks (1968); Smith and Good (1982); Smith (1983); and Deagan (1987).

HISTORICAL ARTIFACTS

Analysis of Glass Beads. Initial classification of glass beads should be conducted according to manufacturing technique. Most North American bead assemblages were produced by either the drawn (hollow cane) or wound method, but a large collection may also contain some blown and/or pressed specimens. After identifying the production methods represented by a collection, each group can then be subclassified according to color, layering, and shape. To be completely objective with color descriptions, a Munsell color chart should be used. However, this is not absolutely necessary, and standard color descriptions usually are sufficient. It is also important to distinguish between simple beads (those made of one color of glass) and compound beads (those made of two or more colors of glass), and between shapes (e.g., barrel, donut, hexagonal).

For each type of bead in the assemblage, report the ranges for lengths and diameters (in mm.), and compare these with other published sources concerning glass beads within a particular region. Data regarding identity of bead types and their distribution within the site can be presented in tabular form (Table 12). If possible, include a color photograph of the different bead types represented in your assemblage.

Table 12
IDENTITY AND DISTRIBUTION OF GLASS TRADE BEADS FROM LOCUS 24, CA-MNO-2122
(adapted from Arkush 1995:Table 12)

Bead Color and Type	Shape	Surface	Unit 1 0-10 cm.	Unit 1 10-20 cm.	Unit 2 0-10 cm.	Unit 2 10-20 cm.	Totals
white/white opaque, compound	barrel	3	--	--	--	--	3
white/white opaque, compound	donut	4	3	--	--	1	8
white opaque, simple	barrel	3	6	1	--	--	10
red/white, compound, Cornaline d'Allepo	barrel	3	3	--	--	--	6
red/white, compound, Cornaline d'Allepo	donut	3	1	--	--	--	4
red/green, compound, Cornaline d'Allepo	barrel	2	2	--	--	--	4
red/green, compound, Cornaline d'Allepo	donut	2	--	--	--	--	2
red/green, compound	barrel	2	--	--	--	--	2
translucent red, compound	donut	1	--	--	--	--	1
purple, simple	donut	1	--	--	--	--	1
dark blue, simple	donut	--	1	--	--	--	1
sky blue, simple	donut	--	1	--	1	--	2
cobalt blue, simple	hexagonal	--	1	--	--	--	1
sea green, simple	donut	--	1	--	--	--	1
black opaque, simple	barrel	--	1	--	--	--	1
black opaque, simple	donut	--	1	--	--	--	1
TOTALS		24	21	1	1	1	48

Beyond bead manufacturing dates and methods, the ways in which beads were used by different groups is important and, in many cases, culturally specific. Certain groups are known to have had distinct color preferences, and in some cases, used different colored beads for different purposes (e.g., beads used as grave goods versus beads used by the living).

CERAMIC ARTIFACTS

Historical archaeologists generally discriminate between four basic types of ceramic wares, each of which is defined by the relative fusing (vitrification) of the clays during firing: *terra-cotta*, *earthenware*, *stoneware*, and *porcelain*.

Terra-cottas are relatively coarse, porous wares fired at low temperatures, usually under 900 degrees C. The earliest fired pottery throughout the world is classified as terra-cotta, and historical terra-cotta ceramics usually occur in the form of bricks, flower pots, and tiles (Rice 1987:5). Terra-cotta ceramics usually are not covered with a glaze, but may exhibit a slip, and sometimes are subsumed within the broader category of earthenwares.

Earthenwares also include porous, unvitrified clay bodies, but are fired at a wide range of temperatures (800 to 1,200 degrees C.). They may be glazed or unglazed, and although the body itself is not vitrified, the firing temperature may be high enough to allow a glaze to form on the exterior surface (Rice 1987:5). Earthenware artifacts include a wide range of products from coarse items, such as bricks and tiles, to fine items, such as tin-enameled majolicas.

Stonewares are made from fine, dense clays, and are fired at temperatures of about 1,200 to 1,350 degrees C., which usually is high enough to achieve at least partial vitrification of the clay body (Rice 1987:6). They may be unglazed or may exhibit a lead or salt glaze. Stoneware was first produced in England and Germany in the sixteenth and seventeenth centuries (Ramsay 1939), but it was not until the eighteenth century that it was developed into a fine tableware. The potters of Staffordshire, England, were primarily responsible for developing the pure white bodies of stoneware (Berge 1980:190).

Ironstone is a distinct type of stoneware, and is by far the most abundant type of ceramic found in nineteenth century sites in North America. Because of its sturdy character, it was used extensively by the American military during this time (Berge 1980:190). Early ironstone vessels are somewhat thick and have a yellow tint to the paste. Ironstone artifacts made after about 1900 are thinner and lighter, and contain a pure white paste.

The main feature that separates porcelain from earthenware and stoneware is its translucent nature. Porcelain is always vitrified because of the high temperatures at which it is fired (typically ranging from 1,250 to 1,450 degrees C.), and is made of a white-firing, highly refractory kaolin clay. Porcelains were first made in China, and early nontranslucent types mostly date to the T'ang Dynasty of the ninth and tenth centuries (Hobson 1976:148). There are two general types of porcelain: *hard-paste* and *soft-paste*. Hard-paste porcelain is the true "China," a term referring to its place of origin and which has been much misused (Berge 1980:210). Soft-paste porcelain is absorbent and does not appear as fine-grained or dense as hard-paste porcelain.

Composition

The components which make up a historical ceramic artifact are the paste, glaze, decoration, name (if any) of the decorative pattern, and maker's mark. *Paste* refers to the clay fabric which forms the vessel. It is composed of clay and added or natural fluxes which are formed in a wet, malleable state, then fired. The paste is what is commonly referred to as earthenware, stoneware, porcelain, etc. *Glaze* is the glassy, vitreous coating on the outside of a ceramic vessel. It is composed of fused silicate mixtures which are bonded to the ceramic surface. *Decoration* refers to the techniques by which a pattern is applied to the ceramic surface. Patterns can be applied under or over the glaze. Some call for the application of color by a brush or decal, and others, such as molded-relief patterns, alter the paste itself before the firing to produce a desired texture or form.

Pattern name is really an extension or elaboration of the decorative technique. It refers to the manufacturer's name used to list (as in a catalog) a particular pattern (in which case the pattern name might be printed on the base of the vessel). It can also refer to the informal labels archaeologists give to commonly encountered patterns or designs which are awaiting further research to provide official manufacturers' nomenclature. *Maker's marks* or *trademarks* are the printed or impressed marks usually applied to the base of a ceramic vessel and which provide information on the manufacturer, date, and national origin of the ceramic artifact.

History

Most ceramic tablewares encountered in the western United States represent Euroamerican attempts to imitate the expensive Chinese porcelains that strongly influenced the Euroamerican market between the sixteenth and nineteenth centuries. During that period, European Delft (tin-enameled earthenware), salt glaze white stoneware, creamware, pearlware, and other "improved" white earthenwares were developed. By the beginning of the nineteenth century, British ceramic tableware dominated the American tableware market. However, ceramics manufactured in France, Germany, China, Russia, and America also occurred in western North America at this time. By the beginning of the twentieth century, American potters became dominant over the British in the tableware market.

The following sequence is quite general and no doubt varies somewhat from region to region depending on the distance to coastal ports, availability of transportation, and ethnic factors. In late historical sites, the earlier portions of this chronology probably are not represented.

Chinese Export Porcelains. The earliest imported ceramics in western North America were Chinese export porcelains. The end product of 2,000 years of ceramic technology, Chinese export porcelains remained superior to European ceramics until well into the nineteenth century. The porcelain trade proved so profitable to China that the secret of porcelain manufacture was jealously guarded under punishment of death by the Chinese government (Weiss 1971).

Chinese export porcelains were made for the European market and were often modified to meet the tastes and vessel form needs of European and American consumers. These tablewares had fine-textured, vitreous, blue-white, translucent pastes that were covered by a blue-tinted clear glaze. The most popular decorative technique was the blue-and-white, handpainted, underglaze motif, of which Nanking and Canton, forerunners of the Willow pattern, were the most famous historical pattern names. Nanking and Canton decorated porcelains are not uncommon in West Coast sites dating from the first part of the nineteenth century (IMACS User's Guide 1986).

Chinese "Lowestoft" porcelain was quite popular through the beginning of the nineteenth century when entire dinnerware services were made to order in China for American consumers. Often these porcelains were painted with armorial emblems, pictures, or other symbols which included the name of the purchaser or their family crest. Pictures commemorating historical events or western landscape scenes were also popular Lowestoft motifs.

In the 1820s, Rose Medallion style porcelains with gaudy red patterns and pictures of Mandarin figures became popular and continued in popularity for many years. Chinese export porcelains dropped in quality during the first part of the nineteenth century (Tindall 1975) and this, along with the rise in popularity of British white earthenwares and the destruction of the major Chinese potteries at Ching-te-chen, led to a decline in the availability of Chinese porcelains in the western market by the 1850s (Weiss 1971:46).

English White Earthenware. During the eighteenth century, potters in Staffordshire, England, experimented with a series of white paste ceramics in an attempt to emulate the beautiful and expensive Chinese export porcelains of the same time period. These experiments resulted in the invention of white salt glazed stoneware which enjoyed approximately 30 years of popularity in the first part of the eighteenth century (Hume 1969:14), as well as the popular and enduring white earthenwares known as creamware and pearlware.

Introduced by the Wedgwood Company in the 1760s as "Queensware," creamware is characterized by a chalky, soft, porous, cream-colored paste covered with a satiny clear glaze which pools yellow in vessel crevices (Hume 1969). Creamware vessels are usually very thinly potted and plainly decorated with molded-relief or black transfer print designs.

Pearlware was a variation rather than a true improvement on creamware (Hume 1969:23). The pearlware paste is similarly chalky, off-white, and porous, but the glaze has added cobalt bluing agents which cause the glaze to pool blue-green in vessel crevices. Pearlware vessels are usually thicker than creamware vessels and are more often decorated with blue transfer print designs. One common pearlware vessel type is a dinner plate or bowl decorated with a glazed-incised edge design known as shelledge or featheredge.

English-made pearlwares and more refined white earthenwares decorated with transfer printing are by far the most commonly encountered tableware ceramics in western sites dating from the first half of the nineteenth century. Transfer print designs were most often blue in imitation of the Chinese blue on white porcelains, and in fact, the most popular blue transfer print pattern (known as "Willow") is a direct adaptation of a Chinese blue-on-white design. Transfer print decorations commonly depicted idyllic landscape scenes or historic events. Transfer prints also occur in red, black, green, purple, and other color schemes.

Ironstone. By the late 1840s, a dramatic stylistic shift in popular British earthenwares had begun, and this trend is clearly evident in mid-nineteenth century archaeological assemblages throughout North America, and especially the Far West. This change entailed a decline in the popularity of transfer-printed and other colorfully decorated earthenwares which had predominated since the late eighteenth century, and a rapid rise in the availability of "White Ironstone" style vessels. White Ironstone style vessels commonly bear molded relief patterns rather than colored decorations, and have thicker vessel walls than most earlier creamware and pearlware forms. The bodies of some of these pieces are as porous as common earthenwares, while others are more comparable in this regard to stoneware or porcelain. The latter are variously referred to as "semivitreous China," "Hotel China," and "opaque porcelain." White Ironstone apparently dominated the middle-class market in the United States from the 1850s to at least the 1890s.

American Ceramic Tableware. Before 1900, English pottery was considered the finest tableware available in the United States. American-made products which mimicked British vessels were generally thought to be inferior. In 1898, the American Potters Guild was formed to promote American-made ceramic tableware. It apparently succeeded, because by 1909 the Sears catalog carried a full line of fine ceramics, which included goods from several American manufacturers, most notably Homer Laughlin of East Liverpool, Ohio. Although identical products were made by British manufacturers, American potters became famous for their sturdy and simply decorated vitreous earthenwares, commonly known as "Hotel China" (IMACS User's Guide 1986).

Overseas Chinese Ceramics. Chinese ceramics returned in force to the American scene during the 1850s for use by Chinese sojourners in the mining and railroad camps of the Far West. These ceramics were quite different in decoration and vessel form than those made earlier for the Euroamerican export market. Three broad functional categories can be identified: tableware, utility and storage containers, and opium pipe bowls.

Tablewares most commonly included rice bowls and teacups. Serving dishes, soupspoons, and small wine cups were less common. Tablewares were made from a fine, white porcelain or stoneware, with four primary decorative styles: Bamboo (also called Three Circles and Dragonfly, or Swatow), Four Seasons (or Four Flowers), Double Happiness (or Swirl), and Celadon (or Winter Green) (Chace 1976).

Utility wares consisted of stonewares or storage vessels and are distinctively different, but no less common, than tablewares. Generally composed of a coarse, sometimes gritty buff or grey-brown paste with a thick brown or metallic grey-black *jian yu* glaze, utility vessels were generally shipped from China and contained liquor, soy sauce (Fig. 76), ginger, dried vegetables, and other foods (Fig. 77) (Chace 1976).

Although highly variable in form, opium pipe bowls were generally the size and shape of doorknobs. Round styles were most common, followed by eight-sided, then ten-sided styles (Fig. 78). All bowls have a slightly convex smoking surface with a small (1 to 3 mm.) smoking hole in the center, sometimes with an insert, and a larger hole on the bottom with a flange and neck. The clay neck was often removed and replaced with a metal ferrule. Bowls were made of stoneware or earthenware in a variety of colors, the most common being orange or grey. Surfaces may have been plain, burnished, slipped, or glazed. Small Chinese characters or decorations usually were stamped on the bottom or side (Fig. 79). The smoking surface immediately around the small hole may have been burned and worn from preparing and igniting the opium pellet. This part of the bowl is thin and easily broken (Wylie and Fike 1985).

Fig. 76.   Examples of traditional Chinese brown glaze utilitarian stoneware vessels: (a) liquor bottle;
(b, c) spouted jars (e.g., for soy sauce).

The Classification of Historical Ceramics

Historical ceramic classification should emphasize vessel form and function, characterization of paste, ware identification, surface treatment, and manufacturers' hallmarks.

Vessel Form and Function. As with most historical artifacts, the form of a ceramic vessel provides useful information regarding its primary function. However, because many historical ceramic assemblages consist of sherds from highly fragmented vessels, vessel form typically is not used as a classifying criterion. The vast majority of ceramics recovered from historical archaeological sites was used for the preparation, serving, and consumption of food, and generally are classified under the category of kitchen and tablewares. Other functions or activities commonly associated with historical ceramics include storage, personal sanitation, smoking, and recreation.

Forms associated with food include plates, platters, saucers, bowls, covered dishes, pitchers, ladles, mugs, and cups. General household goods, foodstuffs, and beverages, including preserves, ale, ink, and tooth powder, often were stored in ceramic containers such as bottles, jars, and crocks. Ceramic artifacts associated with personal sanitation were parts of toilet sets, which are represented by containers such as ewers (narrow-necked pitchers), wash basins, chamber pots, brush vases, and soap dishes.

195

Fig. 77. Additional examples of traditional Chinese brown glaze utilitarian stoneware containers: (a) straight-sided jar with lid; (b) shouldered jar.

Smoking is commonly reflected by the presence of tobacco and opium pipe fragments (consisting primarily of bowls and stems), as well as ceramic cigar and cigarette holders. Ceramic artifacts commonly associated with toys and games include doll parts, toy cups and saucers, and gaming pieces (e.g., poker chips).

Early ceramic catalogs often are useful in determining vessel forms represented in historical ceramic assemblages, if either large or highly diagnostic portions of individual specimens occur in the collection. An example of an appropriate catalog for identifying late nineteenth and early twentieth century American ceramic vessels is the 1915 edition produced by the Butler Brothers Company of Chicago, Illinois.

Characterization of Paste. Paste attributes are most accurately determined by examining an unglazed, preferably clean or freshly broken ceramic surface. Paste color and texture are perhaps the most readily observable attributes of this analytic area. Paste information, along with surface treatment, vessel form, and maker's mark, can provide enough data to evaluate the function, origin, age, and socioeconomic relevance of a ceramic artifact (IMACS User's Guide 1986). The most common paste colors are variations of white or off-white, yellow-buff, red-brown, and grey. Paste colors often are indicative of certain vessel functions; for example, white paste suggests tableware or personal artifacts, while a yellow-buff paste color suggests crockery or mixing bowls.

Fig. 78.   Examples of Overseas Chinese ceramic opium bowls from Idaho. Upper row—two examples of orange earthenware bowls with circular tops and ten-sided bodies. Lower row—two examples of rust-brown stoneware bowls with circular tops and polished dark gray exteriors.

Paste texture can be described as either coarse or fine. In most cases, a range of texture is probably present, but an adequate descriptive criterion to use in determining whether a paste is coarse- or fine-grained is grain size. If an unglazed edge has visible grains the size of sand or larger, it is said to be coarse. If it has a chalky, powdery, or glassy appearance, it is described as fine (IMACS User's Guide 1986; Rice 1987).

Porosity, Hardness, and Translucence. The attributes of porosity, hardness, and translucence are often used to distinguish between earthenware, stoneware, and porcelain. However, the tests for these attributes can require considerable ceramic expertise to produce consistent results, and can be time-consuming. Although documentation of these attributes is not completely necessary for basic ceramic analysis, a brief discussion of their application to paste identification is included for students with a specific interest in ceramics.

Fig. 79.   Examples of various Chinese stamp marks on bottom of opium
bowl. Virtually every Chinese opium bowl has one or more
"manufacturing" marks in the form of Chinese characters,
symbols, or designs. Complete and accurate translations of such
marks oftentimes are difficult because of alternative meanings and
missing characters. The two circular stamps with four petals
surrounding a central dot in the upper row have been called
"money marks" by translators, and may represent wealth.

Relative porosity or permeability to water can be determined by placing a drop of water on a clean, unglazed ceramic surface. If the water is absorbed, it is porous; if it is not, it is nonporous or vitreous. Stonewares, porcelains, and vitreous earthenwares are nonporous and will not absorb water. Terra-cottas, most white earthenwares (except vitreous varieties), and some yellow wares and red wares are porous. Some Bennington or Rockingham-glazed (see below) yellow earthenwares are nonporous.

In order to determine paste hardness, take a sharp, pointed tool and scrape firmly on the exposed, fresh break of a ceramic sherd. If it is possible to dislodge grains or easily make a scratch, then it is most likely an unimproved earthenware or terra-cotta sherd. If it takes a great deal of pressure to make a scratch, then it is a vitreous or improved earthenware. Good stoneware or porcelain will not scratch.

Only porcelain and some varieties of fine Chinese stoneware exhibit translucence, which is the quality of permitting the passage of light. This can be determined by looking at a light through the thin vessel wall. If the wall transmits light, then the vessel is either porcelain or fine Chinese stoneware.

Ware Identification. In North America, a wide variety of ceramic wares occurs at historical archaeological sites. Some of the more widespread types are as follows: common pottery (terra-cottas and unrefined earthenwares), refined earthenwares (white improved earthenware, vitreous China, yellow ware, and red ware), stoneware (utility stoneware and fine stoneware), and porcelain (Euroamerican porcelain and Chinese porcelain). For complete definitions and descriptions of these wares, consult Rado (1969), Chace (1976), and especially Miller (1980) and Majewski and O'Brien (1987). It is important to note that the standard classification scheme applied to eighteenth century wares is not applicable to nineteenth century ceramics. This is because the range of available wares was greatly reduced by the success of the English ceramic industry during the 1800s, which displaced many fine ware types, such as white, salt-glazed stoneware and tin glazed earthenware (Miller 1980). The major ceramic type available during the nineteenth century was English white earthenware, which included creamware, pearlware, and the stone Chinas. People who made, sold, and used nineteenth century ceramics classified them according to their decorative styles (i.e., painted, edged, dipped, and printed). Therefore, it is best to classify nineteenth century ceramics according to decorative style, which allows one to integrate archaeological and historical data, and to establish a more consistent classification system than one based on ware types.

Surface Treatment. Ceramic surface treatments occur in a variety of combinations, often with two or more decorative techniques in addition to a glaze, as in a molded-relief saucer with transfer print design under a clear glaze. One should always describe the glaze, distinctive decorative techniques, and pattern name (if known). Definitions of common glazes, decorative techniques, and pattern names are described below.

Ceramic Glazes. A ceramic glaze is a glassy, vitreous coating which is usually prepared from silicate mixtures bonded to ceramic surfaces. Maturing temperatures vary according to ingredients (Rado 1969). Glazes vary in color and texture according to their chemical constituents and firing temperatures. Glaze mixtures are fused to the ceramic paste surface during firing to produce a vitreous veneer which can be both protective and decorative. Porous paste ceramics must be glazed in order to be waterproof and sanitary.

Some glazes are used only with certain paste types due to their fusing constituents and required maturing temperatures. Salt glaze, for example, requires the extremely high temperatures characteristic of stoneware firing in order to vaporize sodium chloride for fusing. Glazes also enjoy periods of market popularity as well as revivals. Rockingham flint enamel glaze, which was popular between 1830 and 1870, is occasionally revived for use on decorative vessels today (IMACS User's Guide 1986). Common historical ceramic glaze and slip types include the following:

Bennington - Often used synonymously with Rockingham glaze. Bennington, Vermont, potteries produced all ware types from earthenware to porcelain, but are most famous for their mottled brown glaze, an improvement on the Rockingham glaze patented in 1849 (Norman-Wilcox 1965; Barclay 1976).

Bristol Glaze - A glassy, creamy glaze sometimes colored with iron to make it brown, most commonly found on cylindrical vessels formed by an extruder. Such glazed vessels may be a half brown/half cream color, such as the glazing scheme found on stoneware ale bottles (Barclay 1976). Bristol glaze has been used on commercially made stoneware since the late nineteenth century.

Celadon - A glaze used on Chinese porcelain derived from iron, ranging in color from putty to sea green to blue. Winter green is often considered to be a universal marker for late nineteenth/early twentieth century overseas Chinese sites. In addition to being very common, they were the most expensive type of overseas Chinese tableware (Sando and Fenton 1984). Celadon vessels typically exhibit some of the following distinctive characteristics (Wylie and Geer 1983):

1. Green or blue-green translucent glaze, full of minute bubbles, that exhibits variation in color density depending on thickness.

2. An extremely heavy exterior glaze, especially at the corner of the foot.

3. A very thin, almost transparent interior glaze.

4. A fine, white, vitreous glaze.

5. A scraped rim, sometimes faint yellow, covered with a thin glaze.

6. A slightly flared rim with an expanded lip.

7. A light-colored exterior collar (contrasting thicknesses of glaze).

8. Cobalt blue base marks under the glaze. Rice bowls have a square "reign" mark, and some cups have simple brush strokes with the Chinese characters for sun and moon.

Rockingham - A common lead-based glaze used on earthenware from the late eighteenth century. The glaze is mottled dark brown and yellow (Boger 1971; Barclay 1976).

Salt Glaze - A thin, glassy glaze found exclusively on stoneware fired at a high temperature. Common table salt is thrown into the kiln during firing, and the salt then vaporizes and bonds with the stoneware surface to produce an "orange peel" pitted surface (Norman-Wilcox 1965; Barclay 1976).

Chinese Brown Glaze - A dark brown glaze which may be "semimatte" chocolate brown or almost an iridescent black-brown color (Chace 1976). Also referred to as "jian yu" or "Tiger" glaze.

White Opaque (Tin Enamel) - A lead glaze popular on Mexican earthenware (majolica). It is visibly thick in cross section and often has handpainted designs applied on the glaze.

Albany Slip - A dark brown to greenish-black clay slip which was usually applied to the interior surface of salt glaze stoneware vessels after about 1843. It also occurs on vessel exteriors. The slip derives its name from Albany, New York, where the dark clay for the slip was primarily found.

Decorative Techniques. Decorative techniques commonly found on historical ceramics recovered from archaeological contexts in North America include the following:

Transfer-printing - The process of decorating pottery from paper impressions taken off inked copperplate engravings, first developed in England by the Buttersea Enamel-works (1753-56) (Norman-Wilcox 1965). The design is made of numerous small colored dots that are barely visible to the casual observer. Transfer-printing is *always* underglaze in contrast to decal overglaze (see below).

Decal - A method of multiple color decoration introduced about 1860. Decal colors appear in slight relief when light is reflected from the vessel's surface (Berge 1980). The design is composed of hundreds of raised dots, similar to transfer prints, but placed over the glaze.

Handpainted - Designs applied by hand with a brush or fingers. Irregular, uneven designs are the usual result. Brush marks are clearly visible in most cases. This method of decoration often was applied over a previously fired vessel by relatively unskilled labor. The result is that it was less expensive than other decorated ceramics and the designs were subject to greater deterioration.

Molded Relief - Raised decoration which is an integral part of a vessel mold or form. This style was particularly popular on clear, glazed, white ironstone vessels dating from the second half of the nineteenth century (Wetherbee 1974).

Spatter or Sponge - Mottled, colorful designs applied with a sponge or brush. Popular from 1798 to 1865.

Sprigging - Applied relief design usually in the form of small leaves and flowers (Boger 1971).

Annual/Banded Design - Decorative rings around the exterior rim and base of a vessel, usually in earth tones, applied with a stationary brush and rotating wheel, and often called "engine turned." This type of decoration is often seen on yellow ware and pearlware mugs and bowls.

HISTORICAL ARTIFACTS

Pattern Names. Some of the more common patterns found on historical ceramics include the following:

Flow Blue, Flown Blue, Flowing Blue - A ceramic decoration of transfer print variety, usually blue, made by adding a volatizing mixture during the glaze firing, which resulted in a softened effect. Popular between 1825 and 1862, flow blue also appears in other colors, including green, brown, red, etc.

Gaudy Dutch/Gaudywelch - A pattern style popular between 1810 and 1930. The design generally consists of handpainted stylized flowers in bright colors. Made to appeal to a cheaper market, Gaudy Dutch designs have been observed on ironstone vessels dating from the late nineteenth century (Norman-Wilcox 1965).

Featheredge - A molded border decoration consisting of a swirled feathery band at the edge of a usually scalloped rim on a plate or bowl. The band is usually colored blue or green in contrast to the white vessel. Featheredge, and its variant shelledge, were commonly used on creamware, pearlware, and other white earthenwares between the late eighteenth and mid-nineteenth centuries (Hume 1976).

Willow Pattern - The best known of all transfer print designs. This pattern is a European imitation of a Chinese blue-and-white design which depicts a river with a bridge across it and willow trees on the bank. Two birds are supposed to represent two lovers flying away from an irate father. First produced by English potters in 1780, the Willow pattern is still used today (Barclay 1976).

Mocha - A moss-like decoration obtained by touching the ground color of a white slip with a brush containing pigment. This pattern was popular from 1790 to 1890.

Rebeccah-at-the-Well - A Rockingham-glazed, molded relief design consisting of the raised figure of a woman drawing water from a well. The design was used almost exclusively on teapots and originated in 1852.

Delft - Blue decoration on a opaque white tin glaze, similar in technique to majolica or faience. Delft was an early European attempt at imitating Chinese export porcelain, and was produced in England until the early nineteenth century (Hume 1976).

Canton/Canton Ware - A design common to Chinese export porcelain. Along with the variations called ''Nanking,'' Canton ware was the Chinese forerunner of the Willow pattern. The handpainted design is blue with a white underglaze and a central pictorial theme of a bridge, teahouse, birds, and a willow tree. It reached its height of popularity in the Euroamerican market by 1780, but the quality dropped dramatically after about 1800 (Tindall 1975; Barclay 1976).

Bamboo, Three Circles and Dragonfly, Swatow - A pattern on the outside of rice bowls with four units: three circles, a dragonfly character, a marsh with five big leaves, and a *Prunis* (e.g., cherry) with four wide leaves. These are all arranged counterclockwise (Chace 1976).

Four Seasons, Four Flowers - A pattern composed of the flowering plant of each of the four seasons: cherry, water lily, peony and chrysanthemum. The design was painted crudely in overglaze polychrome enamel in four quadrants in clockwise order (Chace 1976).

Manufacturers' Hallmarks. Manufacturers' hallmarks provide the most practical way of establishing absolute production dates for historical ceramics. Hallmarks usually are applied to the vessel bottom in one of four ways: impressed, printed, hand-painted, or stamped. The maker's full name or initials are typically included in or by the mark. The hallmark may consist of a royal seal or arms, trademark, crest, pattern name, type of body, or initials (Berge 1980:212).

Registry marks are diamond-shaped inscriptions commonly used in England between 1842 and 1883, and provide important information regarding the year, month, and even day of manufacture. Excellent data concerning ceramic hallmarks can be found in Godden (1963) and Wetherbee (1974). In the analysis of historic ceramics, every effort should be made to determine the age and manufacturer of ceramic specimens that exhibit hallmarks.

Analysis of Historical Ceramics

When working with ceramics, it is important to consider availability, need, and preference. Historical ceramics represent goods that were marketed worldwide, and became more common and less expensive with the passage of time. The presence of certain ceramic types within a site may reflect a variety of behaviors, from attempts to imitate fine wares with homemade forms, to the acquisition of high-status, nonutilitarian wares. Ceramic analysis should consider what other locally produced wares may have served the same function as imported wares. Determining the relative proportions of inexpensive, locally produced types to more expensive, imported types will provide information concerning the social and economic status of a site's occupants. Price lists, inventories, and advertisements can provide the researcher with data to create an economic scaling for sites based on their occupants' ceramic expenditures.

If known, the ceramic classifications of the inhabitants of a site also should be considered during analysis. Post-contact, non-European sites often contain European ceramic fragments occurring in contexts suggesting a nonutilitarian function. Such behavior has been documented among various San groups of South Africa, who included exotic ceramic sherds in their medicine pouches along with crystals, ocher, and other charms (P. Jeppson, personal communication 1994). Historical native ceramic vessel forms also can serve as gauges of acculturation, as some native groups produced ceramics with European shapes after colonization of their homeland.

BUTTONS

Buttons recovered from historical North American sites are made from an amazing array of materials, including glass, wood, bone, and shell. Buttons can be roughly dated according to initial dates of industrial innovations and material types. However, the best means of dating buttons corresponds to the presence of maker's marks, quality marks, and registry marks (IMACS User's Guide 1986).

Back Marks

The term "back mark" applies to any stamping found on the back of buttons, including words denoting quality, such as Extra Rich or Superfine, manufacturers' names, uniform makers names, stars, dots, and eagles. The name of a known maker and recorded facts regarding the business can be associated with contemporaneous activities and events to determine with reasonable accuracy just when a specific item was produced, and for what purpose. Even the lack of a back mark will often establish the period of use, since it was not until the early 1800s that button makers began to stamp firm names, trademarks, and designs on button backs (Luscomb 1967:17-18).

Quality Marks

Quality marks refer to certain words found on the backs of buttons made after 1800. It is generally thought that the words functioned to promote sales, as the differences in quality can seldom be noted. Most of the marks appeared between 1800 and 1850, and include terms such as "Rich Gold," "Gilt," and "Rich Orange" (Luscomb 1967:163).

Registry Marks

Registry marks are found on the backs of British-made buttons, and have been documented on ceramic, glass, horn, and metal specimens. A registry mark is diamond-shaped, with letters or numbers at the points of the diamond. At the top point is an extra circle with a letter. The letters and number indicated the material, month, day, and year the button design was registered and bundle inspected (Luscomb 1967:166). A compilation of American button makers and outfitters, including approximate dates of manufacture and button type, can be found in *The Complete Button Book* (Albert and Kent 1949).

Button Materials

A wide variety of materials has been used to produce buttons, including the following:

Agate. Moss agate or chalcedony, cut and polished in various shapes, has long been used to make buttons. Agate disks were available in the 1900 Sears catalog.

Aluminum. In the late nineteenth century, aluminum buttons were more costly than silver or gold. They were produced in one or two pieces and stamped with delicate designs. Aluminum was also used in the 1940s and 1950s, especially for stamped uniform buttons.

Bakelite. Bakelite is a synthetic plastic invented in the United States between 1907 and 1909. Bakelite buttons were produced until about 1930, when other plastics were developed; the buttons were of plain, drab colors, and the word "Bakelite" was molded on the back.

Bone. Disks cut from animal bone have been made in a variety of sizes from prehistoric times. They are usually sew-through types with two to five holes, although some bone buttons have metal rims and shanks. Since 1850, carved and inlaid bone buttons also have been made. Bone buttons dating from the late nineteenth century are somewhat rare, and are most commonly recovered from sites predating the mid-nineteenth century.

Brass. Brass probably is the most common button material, and has been used in the United States since the 1800s for mens' clothing and uniforms. One-piece buttons were most common from about 1800 to 1860, with two-piece buttons predominating after about 1860.

Calico. Calico refers to one type of china button made in the United States between 1848 and 1865. These buttons are decorated with tiny calico transfer designs.

Celluloid. Celluloid is a synthetic, ivory-like material that was developed in 1869. Celluloid is distinguished from ivory by a carbolic or menthol odor produced by heating or rubbing the surface of the button. After 1900, a two-piece button was made by placing a thin piece of celluloid over another type of material.

Glass. Many different types of blown, molded, and fused glass have long been used for buttons. Glass has been used for all types of button construction, and a great range of colors is known. Luscomb (1967:80-89) discussed over 25 different kinds of glass buttons. Prosser buttons (see below) are often confused with glass. Glass should not be confused with ceramic or so-called ''little Chinas'' made by the Prosser process.

Horn. Disk, metal shank, and self-shank buttons cut from horns and antlers of animals were made in the United States and Europe. During the nineteenth century, horn was sometimes processed (or imitation horn was made) and stamped with intricate designs.

Ivory. Elephant, walrus, and hippopotamus tusks and whale teeth were used for ''ivory'' buttons. Ivory can be distinguished from celluloid by the presence of fine-grained striations which are characteristic of the structure of teeth and tusks.

Japanning. This is a lacquering process developed in Europe about 1800. Tin, wood, brass, or other materials were coated with successive layers of high-grade varnish. Black was the most common color for buttons. The term ''lacquered'' refers only to those varnished buttons produced in the Orient.

Pewter. Pewter buttons with wedge and wire shanks were cast in the late eighteenth and early nineteenth centuries for use on men's clothing. After 1800, a pewter button with an iron shank was made. Luscomb (1947:148) listed the names of 21 pewterers whose names appeared on pewter buttons in the early 1800s. After 1810, many pewterers switched to brass but pewter buttons, painted and decorated with other materials, continued to be manufactured through the late nineteenth century.

Plastic. The manufacture of synthetic plastic buttons expanded after 1930. In the 1940s, it was common to trim and inlay other materials into a plastic button body.

Porcelain. Porcelain buttons were manufactured in several styles between 1850 and 1920. Hand-painted floral designs were popular between 1900 and 1920. Porcelain should technically include Prosser (see below) or China buttons, but this has not traditionally been the case.

Prosser. Patented in 1849, the Prosser process combined high fired clays to produce a glassy or vitrified appearance. The most common varieties are black, white, or calico having an appearance of opaque, pressed glass. The backs have a pebbled or orange-peel surface (Sprague 1983:167-172).

Rubber. Between 1849 and 1851, Nelson Goodyear patented and improved the manufacture of hard rubber. Often the name "Goodyear" and the dates "1849-1851" are molded on the backs of hard rubber buttons. These markings refer to the dates of the material patents, not the manufacture date of the buttons. Most buttons were black, or occasionally reddish brown, and ranged from one-quarter inch to two inches in diameter. Geometric designs or concentric rings were molded more often than any other designs. Rubber buttons were also made by the Indian Rubber Company before ca. 1880-1890. Novelty Rubber Co. (indicated as N.R. Co. on the mold) manufactured rubber buttons from 1855 to 1870.

Shell. Because the inner layers of many types of shells are similar, it is difficult to classify buttons according to the types of shells from which they were cut. In the factory, shells are sorted by color regardless of species. Freshwater shells are not as iridescent or brilliant as marine species. In the United States, freshwater shells are used for utilitarian buttons. It is difficult to date shell buttons with certainty because of the long history of shell as a button material. All types of holes, shanks, shapes, decorations, and sizes are used for shell buttons (Luscomb 1967:177-180). Smooth backs generally postdate 1880, and commercially made shell buttons were introduced into the United States from France in 1955 (Fontana and Greenleaf 1962:98).

Classification of Buttons

The book entitled *Antique Buttons: Their History and How to Collect Them* by Peacock (1972) contains valuable information concerning the classification of buttons. Button size is expressed in lines (or linges), with 40 lines being equal to one-inch diameter. Peacock (1972) placed buttons into four groups based on size: diminutive (0 to 15 linges), small (15 to 30 linges), medium (30 to 40 linges), and large (over 40 linges). The following scale was used by Sears Roebuck and Co. in 1908 to correlate lines and inches:

Lines	12	14	16	18	20	22	24
Inches	1/4	5/16	3/8	7/16	1/2	9/16	5/8

For the most part, shirt and dress buttons are smaller than coat and jacket buttons. The 1908 Sears catalog refers to shirt and dress buttons as lines 10 to 20, while vest, coat, and jacket buttons are sized 24 to 36.

Analysis of Buttons

Buttons are good indicators of gender, and in many instances, of the presence of children at a site. These artifacts also provide information concerning the general economic status and activities of a site's occupants, because it is possible to distinguish between fine dress, casual, and work clothing buttons. Buttons from more expensive civilian clothing tend to be ornately decorated and are equipped with metal loop shanks, whereas casual and work clothing had mostly plain, sew-through type buttons with either two or four holes. In frontier areas, homemade buttons of bone, wood, and hard rubber were somewhat more common because of the great distances between many sites and the nearest towns.

In lieu of artifacts and features directly associated with military activities, the presence of military buttons at a site may provide direct evidence that it was occupied by military personnel. However, if buttons were the only definite military items recovered from a site, it may not have been associated with an active militia. Many historical Native American sites yield military buttons from clothing that was scavenged from refuse deposits or battlefields, or were given to native scouts or leaders. Of course, many Euroamerican civilians who at one time had been in the military continued to wear their standard issue clothing after they had been discharged. The same is true of civilians who had access to surplus military clothing, as well as members of private militias. The monograph on material culture from Fort Bowie, Arizona (Herskovitz 1978), contains an excellent section on analysis of mid-to-late nineteenth century military buttons, as well as other military accoutrements and apparel. Examples of military buttons include general service buttons, line eagle device buttons, staff buttons, helmet side buttons, and fly, suspender, and overall buttons (Herskovitz 1978:39).

PLANT AND ANIMAL REMAINS

Unlike prehistoric archaeologists, most historical archaeologists classify plant and animal remains as artifacts and include them in the category of subsistence-related materials. Therefore, the term ecofact (an unmodified natural item used by people) is not commonly used in historical archaeology. Although the identification and analysis of historical and prehistoric faunal and floral remains essentially are the same as prehistoric (e.g., calculating age, sex, MNI [minimum number of individuals], and NISP [number of identified specimens] for fauna, see Chapter 10), certain questions must be asked that pertain to historical contexts (see Jolly 1983; Crabtree 1985). These include the following:

1. What proportions of the faunal and floral assemblages are of introduced domestic versus native wild species?

2. Do faunal materials reflect "barnyard management" (age, sex, and/or size selection for things such as wool production, milking, or breeding)?

3. Were animal bones cut with cleavers or saws?

4. Were animals butchered completely on-site, or were they first partially processed elsewhere and then transported to the study site for final processing?

5. Do bones exhibit charring (suggestive of roasting) or do they lack charring (perhaps suggestive of boiling)?

6. What cuts of meat are present at the site (discriminating between expensive and inexpensive meat cuts aids in determining social and economic status), and does this pattern change through time?

ABOVE AND BELOW GROUND FEATURES

Above and below ground features refer to human-made structures that cannot be removed from the archaeological deposit without adversely impacting their integrity. In other words, they are features have been incorporated into the ground, and require different kinds of documentation and recovery than artifacts. The foundations and walls of buildings are architectural features commonly encountered at historical sites. For the most part, such features are completely exposed, mapped, and photographed in place, and are not removed from the study site, although samples of the building materials may be obtained from the features themselves in order to conduct further documentation and analysis. Building materials that at one time were part of a foundation, wall, floor, or roof often are recovered from within or outside of collapsed/demolished buildings. These include complete or fragmentary ceramic and adobe bricks, wooden planks, mortar, and daub, which are classified as construction materials and are analyzed as such.

Other features commonly associated with historical sites include stone walls, charcoal kilns, interior and exterior hearths, wells, outhouses, graves, roads and trails, irrigation ditches, railroad grades, telegraph poles, and dams. Standing structures such as houses, barns, and churches older than fifty years usually are considered historical cultural resources, and should be recorded. Standing structures should be evaluated and recorded by architectural historians, who are specially trained in recording and assessing the significance of these historical above ground features. Historical archaeologists are interested in the relationships between above and below ground features and standing structures at an individual site, the use of a building's interior space, the content and distribution of artifacts and features within a building, and the orientation of features to the natural and cultural landscape. Many historical archaeologists are especially fond of excavating outhouses (privies), because this is where site occupants often deposited artifacts associated with socially unacceptable behavior or physical conditions, such as liquor bottles and syphilis cures.

HISTORICAL DOCUMENTS

It likely will be necessary to conduct some archival research as part of the analysis of any historical site or materials, as information regarding the function (as indicated in written records) of the site could be critical to its interpretation. Documentary research typically begins with the more obvious, accessible, and recent records (secondary documents), which in turn guide the investigator back to the older, primary documents. Historical documents include a wide variety of materials, such as old photographs, maps, probate inventories taken at death, wills, census data, and diaries. Archival documents provide the archaeologist with extremely detailed information which, when combined with analytic data from artifacts and features, allows for a relatively complete reconstruction of the cultural use and occupation of a site. Although the foregoing certainly is true, it must be kept in mind that most early historical documents are biased in that they tend to concern upper class, white males, and ignore a large segment of the population under study, including middle and lower class men, women, children, and people of "color," such as Native Americans, African slaves and African Americans, and Chinese. Furthermore, historical documents often are extremely ethnocentric, and in many instances, outright racist. This is especially true of written accounts concerning native peoples provided by soldiers, missionaries, and trappers.

There are three general document categories, each of which contains a variety of document types: (1) family records (e.g., bibles, correspondence, diaries, diplomas); (2) institutional records (e.g., church records, educational records, newspapers); and (3) public records (e.g., census records, federal mortality schedules, military records, vital statistic records, court and probate records, tax lists, land records, cemetery records).

Documents are most useful for the direct information that they provide. For example, historical maps, photographs, drawings, or paintings can serve as important aids in relocating sites. Probate inventories and wills help the archaeologist determine what materials were present on-site at the time of an inhabitant's death. Newspaper advertisements are reflective of goods that were available in an area at a given time, and hence allow the archaeologist to anticipate the kinds of artifacts that may be recovered from sites within that area. Historical archaeology also concerns orally documented information about the recent past. This category of documentary resources falls under the rubric of oral history, which includes the stories, myths, songs, and memories people retain from their past and that of their elders. Tape recordings of interviews with long-time residents of study areas can be important components of historical archaeology projects. Interview tapes should be treated as historical documents, and added to a project's archival file, which eventually should be deposited at the appropriate regional curation facility.

CONCLUDING REMARKS

There is a great deal to be learned about human behavior from early historical archaeological and archival materials. Some people question the importance of archaeological studies conducted on historical sites because they assume the vast majority of relevant information about most historical places and events has been thoroughly documented by written records. Although this may be true for major events in literate countries, such as important Revolutionary and Civil War battles, westward emigration, and construction of the Transcontinental Railroad in America, a large percentage of historical phenomena are poorly understood (and in some cases completely misunderstood) because there was nobody there to record them (or they were inaccurately recorded) when they occurred. These latter historical sites and events (as well as those that are "well-documented") can benefit from the skills of archaeologists, who specialize in studying bits and pieces of the past in order to reconstruct extinct lifeways and long-forgotten events. By using modern field and analytic techniques and conducting thorough archival research, we can improve our knowledge of local and regional history and of the individuals who were part of that history. Synthesizing information from different projects dealing with similar historical periods and themes often produces vivid pictures of unique times and places, which in turn increases both our understanding of and appreciation for the people and events that comprise our collective historical past.

REFERENCES

Albert, Lillian S., and Kathryn Kent
    1949   The Complete Button Book. New York: Doubleday and Co., Inc.

Arkush, Brooke S.
    1995   The Archaeology of CA-MNO-2122: A Study of Pre-Contact and Post-Contact Lifeways Among the Mono Basin Paiute. University of California Anthropological Records 31.

Barclay, Paulette
    1976   Ceramic Analysis. In: 1976 Excavations in the Official's Quarters at Fort Ross State Park. Report on file at the California Department of Parks and Recreation, Sacramento.

Barnes, Frank C.
    1965   Cartridges of the World. Chicago: Follet Publishing Company.

HISTORICAL ARTIFACTS

Bearse, Ray
    1966   Centerfire American Rifle Cartridges, 1892-1963. South Brunswick, NJ: A. S. Barnes and Company.

Beck, Horace
    1928   Classification and Nomenclature of Beads and Pendants. Archaeologia 77:1-76.

Berge, Dale L.
    1980   Simpson Springs Station: Historical Archaeology in Western Utah. Salt Lake City: Utah Bureau of Land Management Cultural Resource Series No. 6.

Boger, Louise A.
    1971   The Dictionary of World Pottery and Porcelain. New York: Charles Scribner and Sons.

Bowman, Hank W.
    1958   Famous Guns from the Winchester Collection. Greenwich, CN: Fawcett Publications, Inc.

Busch, Jane
    1981   An Introduction to the Tin Can. Historical Archaeology 15(1):95-104.

Chace, Paul G.
    1976   Overseas Chinese Ceramics. In: The Changing Faces of Main Street, R. S. Greenwood, ed., pp. 509-530. Ventura, CA: City of San Buenaventura Redevelopment Agency.

Clark, Victor S.
    1949   History of Manufactures in the United States. New York: Peter Smith.

Clifton, Robert T.
    1970   Barbs, Prongs, Points, Prickers, & Stickers. Norman: University of Oklahoma Press.

Crabtree, Pam J.
    1985   Historic Zooarchaeology: Some Methodological Considerations. Historical Archaeology 19(1):76-78.

Deagan, Kathleen
    1987   Artifacts of the Spanish Colonies of Florida and the Caribbean, 1500-1800. Volume 1: Ceramics, Glassware, and Beads. Washington: Smithsonian Institution Press.

Fairbanks, Charles
    1968   Early Spanish Colonial Beads. Conference on Historic Sites Archaeology Papers 2(1):3-21.

Ferraro, Pat, and Bob Ferraro
    1964   The Past in Glass. Lovelock, NV: Western Printing and Publishing Company.

Fike, Richard E.
1987   The Bottle Book: A Comprehensive Guide to Historic, Embossed Medicine Bottles. Salt Lake City: Gibbs M. Smith, Inc.

Fontana, Bernard L., and J. Cameron Greenleaf
1962   Johnny Ward's Ranch: A Study in Historic Archaeology. Kiva 28(1-2).

Godden, Geoffrey A.
1963   British Pottery and Porcelain, 1780-1850. London: Arthur Baker, Ltd.

Hayes, Charles F., III (ed.)
1983   Proceedings of the 1982 Glass Trade Bead Conference. Rochester Museum & Science Center, Research Records No. 16.

Herskovitz, Robert M.
1978   Fort Bowie Material Culture. University of Arizona Anthropological Papers No. 31.

Hobson, R. L.
1976   Chinese Pottery and Porcelain: An Account of the Potter's Art in China from Primitive Times to the Present Day. New York: Dover.

Hume, Ivor N.
1969   Pottery and Porcelain in Colonial Williamsburg's Archaeological Collections. Williamsburg: The Colonial Williamsburg Foundation.

1976   A Guide to Artifacts of Colonial America. New York: Borzoi Books.

IMACS (Intermountain Antiquities Computer System) User's Guide
1986   Instructions and Computer Codes for Use with the IMACS Site Form. Prepared by the U. S. Bureau of Land Management, U. S. Forest Service, and University of Utah.

James, Daniel J.
1956   The Evolution of the Glass Container Industry. Fayetteville: University of Arkansas Press.

Jolly, Robert L.
1983   North American Historic Sites Zooarchaeology. Historical Archaeology 17(2):64-79.

Karklins, Karlis
1974   Seventeenth Century Dutch Beads. Historical Archaeology 6:87-101.

1983   Dutch Trade Beads in North America. In: Proceedings of the 1982 Glass Trade Bead Conference, Charles F. Hayes, ed., pp. 111-126. Rochester Museum and Science Center Research Records No. 16.

Karklins, Karlis, and Roderick Sprague
  1980   A Bibliography of Glass Trade Beads in North America. Moscow, ID: South Fork Press.

Kendrick, Grace
  1966   The Antique Bottle Collector. Sparks, NV: Western Printing and Publishing Co.

Kidd, Kenneth
  1979   Glass Bead Making from the Middle Ages to the Early Nineteenth Century. Ottawa: Parks Canada, History and Archaeology 30.

Kidd, Kenneth E., and Martha A. Kidd
  1970   A Classification System for Glass Beads for the Use of Field Archaeologists. Ottawa: Canadian Historic Sites No. 1:45-89.

Lewis, Berkeley R.
  1968   Small Arms and Ammunition in the United States Service: 1776-1865. Washington: Smithsonian Institution Press.

Logan, Herschel C.
  1959   Cartridges. New York: Bonanza Books.

Lorrain, Dessamae
  1968   An Archaeologist's Guide to Nineteenth Century American Glass. Historical Archaeology 2:35-44.

Luscomb, S. C.
  1967   The Collector's Encyclopedia of Buttons. New York: Bonanza Books.

Majewski, Teresita, and Michael J. O'Brien
  1987   The Use and Misuse of Nineteenth Century English and American Ceramics in Archaeological Analysis. In: Advances in Archaeological Method and Theory, Vol. 11, Michael B. Schiffer, ed., pp. 97-209. New York: Academic Press.

McCallum, H. D., and F. T. McCallum
  1965   The Wire That Fenced the West. Norman: University of Oklahoma Press.

Mercer, Henry C.
  1924   The Dating of Old Houses. Old Time New England 14(4).

Miller, George
  1980   Classification and Economic Scaling of 19th Century Ceramics. Historical Archaeology 14:1-40.

Moos, Harry
  1968   U.M.C. Shotshells. Shooting Times Magazine 9(7):38-41.

Munsey, Cecil
    1970   The Illustrated Guide to Collecting Bottles. New York: Hawthorn Books, Inc.

Newman, T. Stell
    1970   A Dating Key for Post-Eighteenth Century Bottles. Historical Archaeology 4(1):70-75.

Norman-Wilcox, Gregor
    1965   Pottery and Porcelain. In: The Concise Encyclopedia of American Antiquities, H. Comstock, ed. New York: Hawthorn Books, Inc.

Orchard, William C.
    1929   Beads and Beadwork of the American Indians: A Study Based on Specimens in the Museum of the American Indian, Heye Foundation. Contributions from the Museum of the American Indian, Heye Foundation 11.

Peacock, Primrose
    1972   Antique Buttons: Their History and How to Collect Them. New York: Drake Publishers, Inc.

Rado, Paul
    1969   An Introduction to the Technology of Pottery. New York: Pergamon Press.

Ramsay, John
    1939   American Potters and Pottery. New York: Hale, Cushman, and Flint.

Rice, Prudence M.
    1987   Pottery Analysis: A Sourcebook. Chicago: University of Chicago Press.

Rock, James T.
    1984   Cans in the Countryside. Historical Archaeology 18(2):97-111.

    1987   A Brief Commentary on Cans. Salinas, CA: Coyote Press.

Roenke, Karl G.
    1978   Flat Glass: Its Use as a Dating Tool for Nineteenth Century Archaeological Sites in the Pacific Northwest and Elsewhere. Northwest Anthropological Research Notes 12(2).

Sacharow, S., and R. G. Griffin
    1970   Food Packaging: A Guide for the Supplier, Processor, and Distributor. Westport, CT: The AVI Publishing Co.

Sando, Ruth Ann, and David L. Fenton
    1984   Inventory Records of Ceramics and Opium from a Nineteenth Century Chinese Store in California. Paper presented at the annual meetings of the Society for California Archaeology, Salinas, California.

HISTORICAL ARTIFACTS

Sleen, W. G. N. van der
    1973   A Handbook on Beads. York, PA: Liberty Cap Books.

Smith, Marvin T.
    1983   Chronology from Glass Beads: The Spanish Period in the Southeast, ca. A.D. 1513-1670. In: Proceedings of the 1982 Glass Trade Bead Conference, C. Hayes, ed., pp. 147-158. Rochester Museum and Science Center Research Records No. 16.

Smith, Marvin T., and Mary E. Good
    1982   Early Sixteenth Century Glass Beads in the Spanish Colonial Trade. Greenwood, MS: Cottonlandia Museum Publications.

Sorensen, Cloyd, Jr., and C. Richard Le Roy
    1968   Trade Beads: The Powerful Companion of the Explorer. San Diego Corral of the Westerners, Brand Book 1:92-129.

Sprague, Roderick
    1983   Tile Bead Manufacturing. In: Proceedings of the 1982 Glass Trade Bead Conference, C. Hayes, ed., pp. 167-172. Rochester Museum and Science Center Research Records No. 16.

Tindall, Hiram
    1975   The Canton Pattern of Chinese Export Porcelain. New York: Main Street/Universe Books.

Toulouse, Julian Harrison
    1971   Bottle Makers and Their Marks. New York: Thomas Nelson, Inc.

Vinson, Carlos
    1968   Collecting Shotshells. In: Gun Digest, 22nd ed., pp. 91-97. Chicago: Follet Publishing Company.

Washburn, Charles G.
    1917   Industrial Worcester. Worcester, MA: The Davis Press.

Weiss, Gustav
    1971   The Book of Porcelain. (Trans. by J. Seligman.) New York: Praeger.

Wetherbee, Jean
    1974   A Handbook on White Ironstone. New York: Privately published.

Williamson, Harold F.
    1952   Winchester: The Gun That Won the West. Washington: Combat Forces Press.

Woodward, Arthur L.
  1958   Appendices to Report on Fort Union, 1851-1891. Report on file at the Arizona State Museum, Tucson.

  1967   Indian Trade Goods. Portland: Oregon Archaeological Society Publication 2:4-15.

Wylie, Henry G., and Richard E. Fike
  1985   Overseas Chinese Opium Smoking Material Culture Survey: Preliminary Results and Request for Assistance. Report on file at the Intermountain Region Office of the U. S. Forest Service, Ogden, Utah.

Wylie, Henry G., and W. Geer
  1983   Opium Pipe Bowls and Celadon Ware from Southern Idaho. Paper presented at the annual meetings of the Society for Historical Archaeology, Denver.

Chapter 10

ANALYSIS OF FAUNAL REMAINS

DEFINITION

The remains of animals in archaeological sites are called *faunal remains*. Faunal remains include those of *all* animals, not just the large ones, and include those from historical contexts (see Chapter 9). (Human remains are technically faunal but are dealt with separately; see Chapter 12.) The two primary goals in the analysis of faunal remains are: (1) the reconstruction of human subsistence (including behavior and technology associated with subsistence and other aspects of culture); and (2) the reconstruction of paleoecology and biogeography (see general reviews of faunal studies by Klein and Cruz-Uribe [1984], Davis [1987], Brewer [1992], and Lyman [1994a]). In addition, information regarding the use of animals for other than strictly subsistence purposes (e.g., entertainment) also is important. Some of the important questions asked include:

> Which taxa [species] were regularly eaten, which were rarely eaten, and which were never eaten [and why]? Which taxa contributed most to the diet? When were particular taxa hunted? How much food did different taxa provide? Were particular age groups or one sex of a taxon preferred over others? Did age, sex, or individual selection vary intertaxonomically? Where were food animals hunted and how were they hunted? [Lyman 1982:335].

Archaeologists also want to understand who was involved in the procurement of food animals (age and/or sexual division of labor), what combinations of foods were preferred (reconstruction of cuisine), and if there was some sort of differential access (due to age and/or gender) to certain foods. It is important to remember that animals were used for purposes other than food (for raw materials, pets, ceremonies, etc.).

Virtually every part of an animal is potentially useable (whether it is actually used is another issue), including hide, hair, meat, blood, marrow, sinew (tendons), bone, and viscera (guts and their contents) (see Lyman 1987a:Table 5.1). Faunal remains may take a variety of forms, including endoskeletons (bone), exoskeletons (e.g., shell, insect parts), soft tissue (e.g., mummified or otherwise preserved remains), and residual proteins. Any or all of these materials may be encountered in an archaeological site; however, bone and shell are the most commonly recovered faunal remains.

The presence of faunal remains within an archaeological site does not, however, automatically indicate that those remains were cultural in origin. Many animals (e.g., rodents, badgers) live their entire lives in sites, die there, and become incorporated into the site deposit. When the site is excavated, their bones are collected by archaeologists, along with the bones of animals used for food by the inhabitants of the site. Sometimes these may be the same species of animal. Nevertheless, even noncultural faunal remains can be informative.

FAUNAL TAXONOMIC CLASSIFICATION

Western societies classify animals based on the taxonomic system (e.g., Kingdom, Phylum, Class, Order, Family, Genus, Species) originally developed by Linnaeus, an eighteenth century Swedish naturalist. The western system (other cultures may use quite different taxonomic systems) is based on morphology and divides the animal kingdom into two basic categories, invertebrates and vertebrates, each of which is divided into phyla. The basic western taxonomic system for animals is briefly discussed below.

INVERTEBRATES

Invertebrates (animals without backbones) vastly outnumber vertebrates in sheer number of both species (97% to 3%) and individuals, but are relatively uncommon in inland archaeological collections. Archaeologists recognize the remains of mollusks in sites and these remains are commonly collected. Other invertebrate remains (e.g., insects) usually are not recognized or are ignored. This section briefly discusses the most common types of invertebrate remains found in archaeological sites.

Mollusks

A mollusk (phylum Mollusca; Fig. 80, commonly called shellfish) is an animal with a soft, unsegmented body often within shells, and includes clams, oysters, snails, slugs, squids, and octopi. Mollusks are divided into five major classes. The *Pelecypoda* (*Bivalvia*) are aquatic (primarily marine) and are encased in a pair of hard, calcareous shells joined by a hinge (e.g., clams, oysters). The *Gastropoda* are generally single-shelled, aquatic (freshwater or marine) animals (e.g., abalone, limpets, snails), but some gastropods are land-dwellers (e.g., land snails). The *Scaphopoda* are elongate mollusks with an elongate conical shell (e.g., tusk shells [*Dentalium*]). The final two classes are the *Polyplacophora* (e.g., chitons) and the *Cephalopoda* (e.g., cuttlefish, squid, octopi). The remains of chitons (shell fragments), cuttlefish (cuttlebones, actually an internal shell), squid, and octopi (beaks) might be found in some archaeological sites. Waselkov (1987) provided a discussion of the study of shellfish from archaeological contexts (also see Bailey 1975).

Insects

Archaeologists rarely deal with the insect remains from a site, usually thinking that they are intrusive and not related to the human occupation of the site. However, virtually all peoples ate and/or used insects (in religious practices, pharmacology, etc.) and their remains should be expected in sites. Even noncultural insect remains may be useful in that they may relate to environmental conditions (e.g., many species are quite sensitive to temperature), site formation processes (ants can displace a great deal of soil and move things around, particularly seeds), and seasonality. Reviews of insect remains in archaeological contexts were presented by Elias (1994) and Sutton (1995).

Several problems exist in the analysis of insect remains (assuming they are collected in the field). The first is the identification of the material. There are few comparative collections and most archaeologists know little about them. Once collected and identified, their quantification is difficult (primarily since they tend to be highly fragmented). Most investigators use number of identified specimens (NISP, discussed below). A generalized insect body is illustrated as Figure 81.

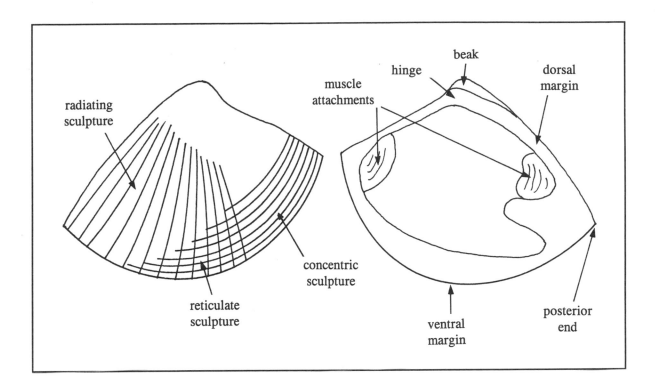

Fig. 80. A generalized mollusk shell (bivalve), no scale.

Other

The remains of other invertebrates also may be found in archaeological sites, including lobsters, crabs, shrimp (marine and freshwater), spiders, scorpions, and worms. These animals must be fully considered in any faunal analysis.

VERTEBRATES

Vertebrates (Phylum Chordata) are animals with backbones (vertebral columns and spinal cords). In most inland sites, the majority of faunal remains will be those of vertebrates. Within the vertebrate group is a number of major categories, as discussed below. Terrestrial (land-dwelling) vertebrates share a common general skeleton and many of the bones have the same names. For example, the two bones of the forearm of a human are called the radius and the ulna. Birds have the same two bones, but in their wings. Most common bones (elements) will share a basic shape; that is, a humerus (upper arm or foreleg) will look similar from species to species. You will begin to recognize elements from their basic shape but then will have to determine the genus and species from their unique attributes. Fish do not share these features.

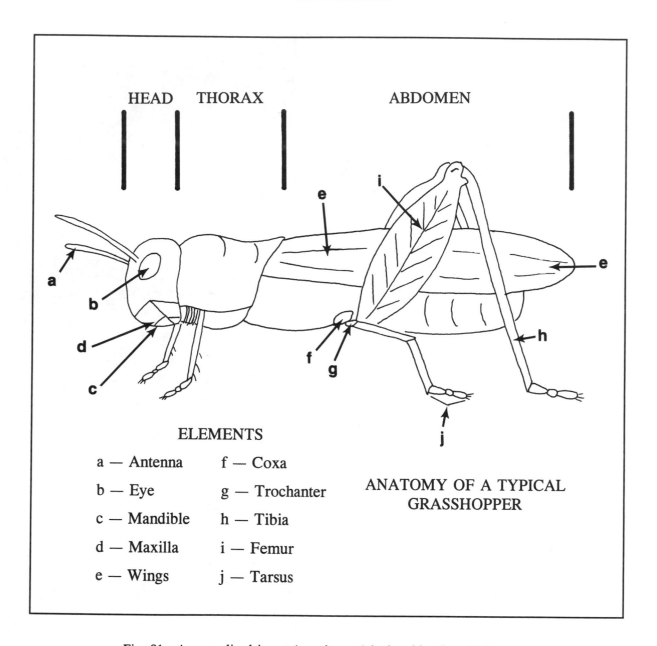

HEAD   THORAX   ABDOMEN

ELEMENTS

a — Antenna   f — Coxa

b — Eye   g — Trochanter

c — Mandible   h — Tibia

d — Maxilla   i — Femur

e — Wings   j — Tarsus

ANATOMY OF A TYPICAL
GRASSHOPPER

Fig. 81. A generalized insect (grasshopper) body with selected elements.

Fish

Fishes are aquatic animals with gills and fins. Fishes lack limbs and so do not have the skeletal elements associated with limbs. In addition, fish have several unique elements that require a specialized knowledge base. There are two major divisions of fishes, cartilaginous and bony fishes. Cartilaginous fishes (e.g., sharks, rays, skates) lack actual bones but have a skeletal system of cartilage that is often reinforced by calcium, particularly in heavy load areas (e.g., vertebrae, jaws). Many of these reinforced elements will preserve in the archaeological record.

Bony fishes have bony skeletons (Fig. 82) and these elements will preserve in the archaeological record in great numbers. The most common fish element usually is the vertebra. Other elements tend to be tabular and thin, fragile, "oddly" shaped (compared to a terrestrial vertebrate skeleton), and have a different hue than bones from other vertebrates. The skull and gill structures may consist of a large number of small bones that are difficult to identify, although some elements bear the same name as other vertebrates (e.g., the mandible [lower jaw]).

Fish vertebrae are often distinctive (Fig. 83) and easy to separate from the vertebrae of other animals. The size of a vertebra will vary depending on its location along the column. Thus, a large vertebra will indicate a large fish, but a small vertebra does not necessarily indicate a small fish. Many fish vertebrae have spines protruding from them, but these are often broken off by the time the vertebrae make it to the screen (the round centrum often being the portion recovered). Sometimes, radiographs (X-rays) may be used to help identify some vertebrae to the species level (e.g., in sharks). Fish vertebrae also may be useful seasonal indicators (Casteel 1972).

Fish scales come in two major forms: hard dermal denticles (called placoid scales, primarily from marine fish), or soft plate-like scales (cycloid scales). All may be present in site soils; in fact, they may be very plentiful in some sites (they sometimes are so abundant that they clog the screens, making the excavation of such sites more difficult). Fish scales can be quite informative regarding species, size, and seasonality (see Casteel 1976:38-71; Wheeler and Jones 1989:145-146; Colley 1990:214). Additionally, all vertebrates (including humans) have small calcium carbonate "ear stones" (called auditory ossicles) within their inner ear to assist in balance or hearing. In fish, these structures are called *otoliths* (Fig. 84) and are relatively large, often preserve well (but are vulnerable to acidic soils), and are identifiable to species (different species of fish have differing numbers of otoliths). In addition, otoliths have growth rings that can be analyzed for information regarding seasonality and water temperature (see Casteel 1976:31; Wheeler and Jones 1989:145, 158; Colley 1990:214). Summaries of fish analyses are available in Olsen (1968), Casteel (1976), Wheeler and Jones (1989), and Colley (1990).

Amphibians

Amphibians are cold-blooded animals requiring a moist environment for egg deposition. Most amphibians lay eggs that hatch into gilled aquatic larvae that then develop into air-breathing adults. A good example of this sequence is the frog tadpoles most schoolchildren have seen. Examples of amphibians include frogs, toads, and salamanders. Many amphibian skeletal elements are the same as mammals. A discussion of amphibian remains from archaeological sites was presented by Olsen (1968).

Reptiles

Reptiles are cold-blooded animals that lay eggs but do not have the larval stage of amphibians, and can lay their eggs in dry environments. Some reptiles are aquatic and some are fully terrestrial. Examples of reptiles include crocodiles, turtles, tortoises, lizards, and snakes. Most reptile skeletal elements are the same as mammals. However, turtles and tortoises have bony shells that, if fragmented, may appear to be large mammal cranial parts. A discussion of reptile remains from archaeological sites was presented by Olsen (1968).

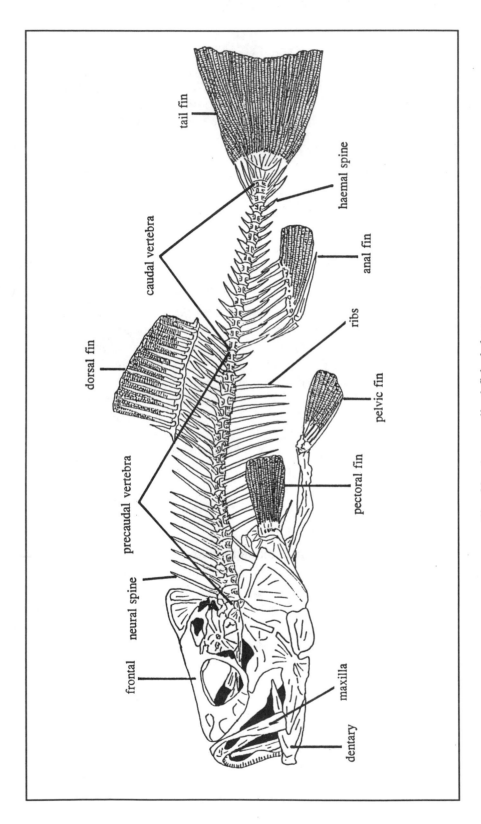

Fig. 82. A generalized fish skeleton.

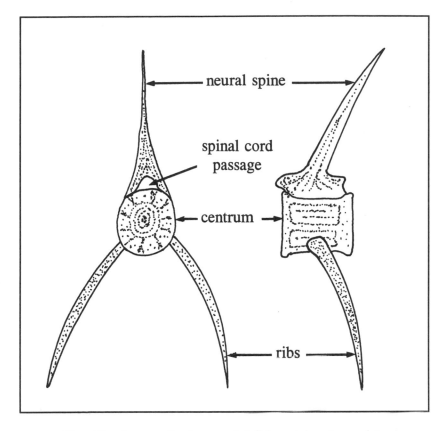

Fig. 83. A generalized precaudal fish vertebra (no scale).

Birds

Birds are feathered, winged animals that fly (although there are some flightless birds). Birds (Class Aves) are divided into at least 21 orders. In addition to their use as food, birds have been widely used for a variety of other purposes. Feathers were (and are still) commonly used for a variety of purposes (decoration, ceremony, arrow fletching), bird skins were used for clothing, containers, and decoys (e.g., skins stretched over tule), bird bones were used as tools, and bird parts (e.g., heads) were used for decoration. It should also be noted that fragments of bird eggshells may be present in a faunal collection. In general, bird bones tend to be rather thin relative to mammal bones and thickness of long bones is a key to the initial identification as bird. While birds share some skeletal elements in common with mammals, many elements are unique (Fig. 85). Several keys to the identification of some of the more common North American species are available (Olsen 1979; Gilbert et al. 1981).

A variety of birds, both large and small, may be expected from archaeological contexts, including those not used as food. Only one North American bird species (the turkey, *Meleagris gallopavo*) was domesticated prior to European contact and may be present in prehistoric sites. Parrots and macaws are known to have been imported into the Southwest from Mesoamerica (Hargrave 1970) and may be present in faunal collections from that region. Several species of European domesticated birds (e.g., the chicken, *Gallus gallus*) may be expected from historical sites.

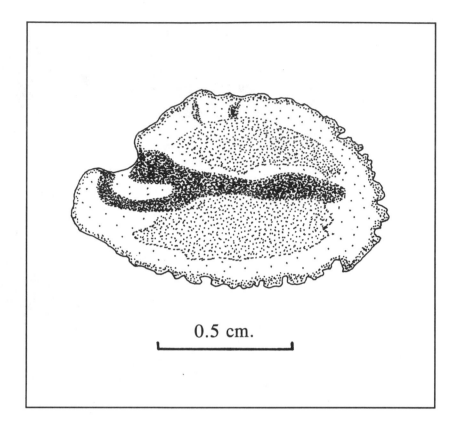

Fig. 84. A generalized fish otolith.

Mammals

Mammals are warm-blooded, hairy animals who bear live young and whose mothers produce milk to feed their young. Mammals are divided into three major types: flying, marine, and terrestrial. Only bats (Chiroptera) fly, and they are not commonly associated with archaeological faunal collections. Mammals share a generally similar limb structure, with common elements (Fig. 86). A general guide to the identification of mammal bone was provided by Gilbert (1980).

Marine mammals include two major groups: Cetacea (whales, dolphins, and porpoises), and Pinnipedia (walruses, sea lions, and seals). Most marine mammals are carnivores, although there are some whales that are not. The Cetacea are fish-like in appearance, with no hair or external ears but with fins and tails. They give live birth at sea and nurse their young. The Pinnipeds ("finfeet") are more mammal-looking, with hair and external ears (interestingly, sea otters are related to weasels and are not Pinnipeds). Pinnipeds feed in the sea but return to land to give birth.

Terrestrial mammals are classified into 10 major orders. The first five consist of relatively small animals. The first order, *Marsupialia*, consists solely of opossums, the only pouched mammal in North America. The second, *Insectivora*, includes shrews and moles. The order *Edentata* consists of sloths (which can be quite large), anteaters, and armadillos. The order *Lagomorpha* contains pikas, rabbits

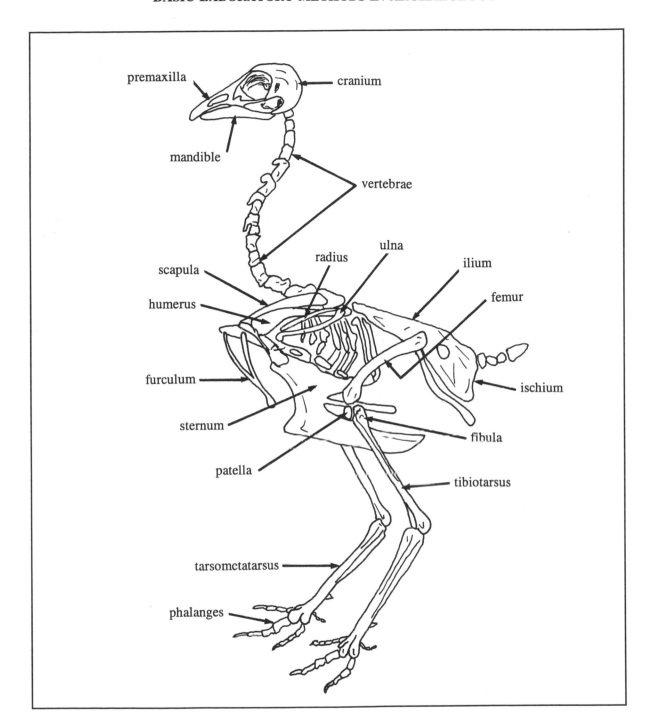

Fig. 85. A generalized bird skeleton.

(Fig. 87), and hares (rabbits and hares are slightly different animals but many people do not make the distinction). The fifth order, *Rodentia*, is quite large and includes chipmunks, marmots, squirrels, prairie dogs, pocket mice, kangaroo mice, kangaroo rats, beaver, mice, rats, voles, and porcupines.

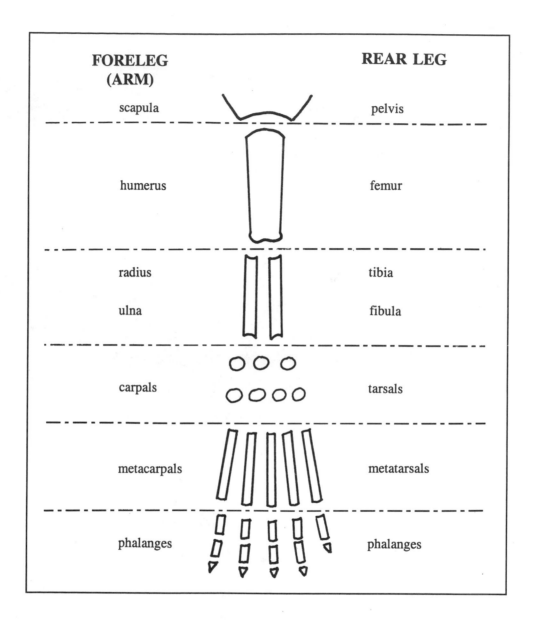

Fig. 86.   The general limb structure of mammals (also applies to amphibians and some reptiles; adapted from Davis 1987:Fig. 2.11).

Lagomorphs and rodents were widely used as food in antiquity and are common constituents in site assemblages.

The last five orders consist of generally larger animals. The order *Carnivora* is comprised of dogs, coyotes, wolves, foxes, bears, raccoons, weasels, skunks, mountain lions (cougars), lynx, and bobcats. The remains of these animals might be found in many faunal subassemblages. The order *Proboscidea* includes mammoths (see Olsen [1979] for a key to mammoth bone) and mastodons, while the order *Sirenia* includes only manatees.

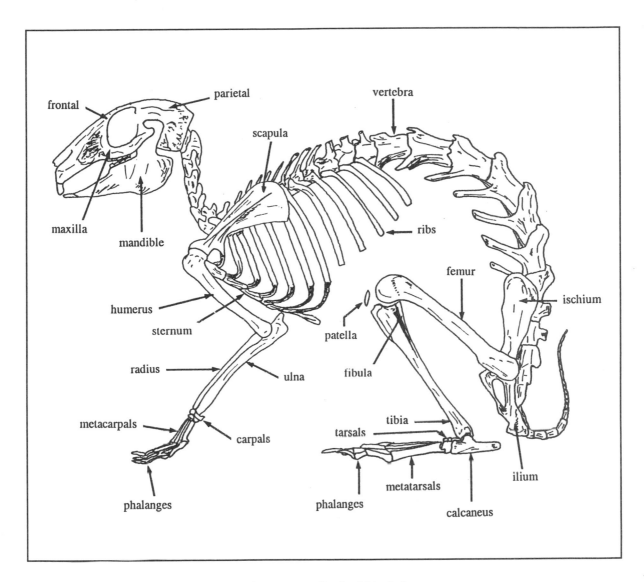

Fig. 87. A generalized rabbit skeleton.

The order *Perissodactyla* (odd-toed, hooved mammals) includes horses and burros, both of which were introduced into North America by Europeans. However, some species of horse were present in North America until the end of the last ice age (at which time they became extinct), and the remains of these animals might be present in very early human sites or in paleontological localities.

Artiodactyla (even-toed, hooved mammals) consists of many large mammals widely used for food. Members of this order include pigs (including domesticated ones), camels (including extinct species of camels), elk, deer, moose, caribou, pronghorn, domesticated cows, bison (Fig. 88), mountain goat (and domesticated goats), and bighorn sheep (and domesticated sheep). Most of the large mammal bone from archaeological sites in North America belong to some species of artiodactyl.

227

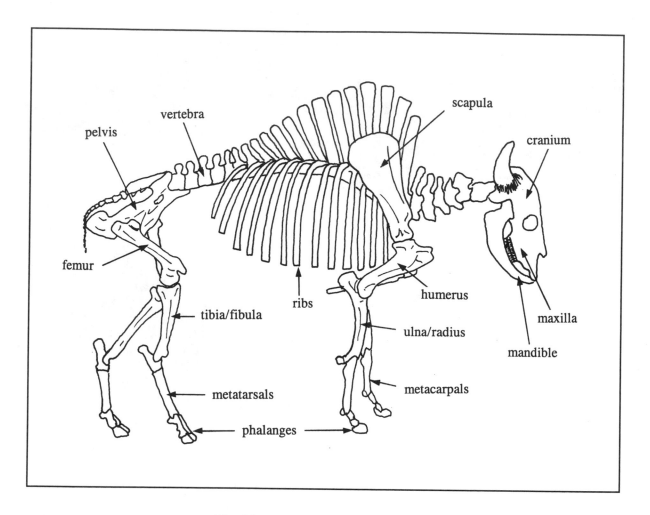

Fig. 88. A generalized bison skeleton.

TERMINOLOGY IN FAUNAL ANALYSIS

The terminology used in the classification and identification of faunal remains is fairly extensive and is generally the same as that used in the analysis of human remains (see Chapter 12). Although there is a great deal of diversity in the definition and use of terms in faunal analysis (see Lyman 1994b), for the purposes of this book, all individual faunal pieces are called *specimens*. Some specimens may be identifiable to the specific part (humerus, femur, rib, etc.) and are called *elements*. Some of the identified elements may then be further identifiable to *taxon* (e.g., family, order, genus, and perhaps even species). All animals will have some elements but some, such as mollusks ("shellfish"), will have only a few, such as a hinge or spire, since most of the material is undifferentiated shell.

In addition to the identification of the element, its orientation (or sidedness) is also important. Since many animals are bilaterally symmetrical, most elements will have counterparts on the other side of the body, so it is important to distinguish which side of the body (*left* or *right*) the element is from (some bones, such as vertebrae, have no such orientation). Most elements will have an orientation relative the length of the body. The *proximal* end is the one closest to the center (or trunk or top) of the body. The *distal* end is the one furthest away from the center. For example, the end of the femur (the upper leg bone) that connects to the hip is the proximal end while the end at the knee is distal. The proximal end of the tibia (the large bone of the lower leg) articulates with the distal end of the femur.

BASIC SKELETAL CLASSIFICATION

The *axial* skeleton is that of the trunk and head, while the remaining elements (the appendages) are grouped into the *appendicular* skeleton. The head comprises the *cranial* skeleton while the remainder of the bones form the *postcranial* skeleton.

The Cranial Skeleton

The cranial skeleton consists of the skull and lower jaw. The skull consists of a number (depending on the species) of interlocked bones. The attached upper jaw is called the *maxilla* and the lower (separate) jaw is called the *mandible*. Skull bones possess a number of distinctive characteristics that make them relatively easy to classify, such as *sutures* (jagged edges where bones join), many unusual bone surfaces (sinuses, foramina [holes], passages, etc.), and dentition (teeth and tooth sockets). Teeth (molars, premolars, canines, and incisors) can often be diagnostic as to taxon (e.g., elephant teeth). The pattern (called the dental formula), spacing, and size of teeth are often characteristic.

The Postcranial Skeleton

The postcranial skeleton includes all bones below the head. Some of these bones are single bones, meaning they have no corresponding bone on the other side of the body (e.g., the vertebral column and the sternum). Others are paired bones (lefts and rights). Limb bones (often called *long bones*) are tubular in cross section and are relatively long. *Short bones* are smaller, tubular bones and include the bones of the feet or paws. *Flat bones* include the pelvis, scapulae (shoulder blades), ribs, and sternum. *Irregular bones* include the vertebrae (including tail bones), carpals (front foot bones), tarsals (rear foot bones), and patellae (kneecaps). Flat and irregular bones are sometimes easy to confuse with some cranial bones.

RECOVERY OF FAUNAL REMAINS

Obviously, faunal remains cannot be classified, identified, quantified, and analyzed unless they are recovered from a given archaeological site. Thus, recovery methods and techniques are critical to understanding the faunal collection from a site.

SCREEN-RECOVERED MATERIAL

Screening is a standard field technique in the excavation of sites and screen size varies from project to project (and even within the same project). Most archaeologists use either 1/4-in. or 1/8-in. mesh screen, but sometimes 1/16-in. is used. *Dry-screening* is the most commonly used technique, leaving the materials in the screen dirty and difficult to recognize. *Wet-screening* results in a greater recognition and thus a greater recovery rate for all materials.

FAUNAL REMAINS

The use of 1/4-in. mesh screen to process site soils is commonplace. However, this practice will result in the loss of many of the very faunal data that archaeologists seek (this screen size is also very poor for recovering floral materials and even some artifacts). This loss increases in percentage as the type of animal gets smaller (Thomas 1969; Grayson 1984:168-172). In fact, some species (e.g., small mammals [Shaffer 1992; Shaffer and Sanchez 1994] and small fish [Gobalet 1989]) may be missed entirely, resulting in a miscalculation of the relative importance of different animals and the development of an incorrect subsistence model (e.g., Gordon 1993). Therefore, we believe that 1/8-in. screen is a minimum requirement in field situations.

FEATURES

Faunal materials discovered in association with features are likely the result of human activities, so the question of cultural versus noncultural origin can often be avoided. For example, if a burned rabbit bone was found in the screen during an excavation, there would always be some question as to whether the bone represented human food residue or a natural death where the bone was burned in a natural fire and then accidentally incorporated into a site. If that same bone was found in the ashes of a firepit, there would be little doubt of its cultural origin. Remains from features are of special importance because of their context.

CHEMICAL RESIDUES

When animals (or plants) are killed and/or processed, parts of the animal will touch the tools used in the procedures. As a result, the tools may retain chemical (protein) residues that can later be detected (refer to discussion in Chapter 13). These nonvisible residues are also faunal remains and should be considered in faunal analyses whenever possible (this is also true for floral remains). Very small quantities of proteins can preserve on stone tools, in coprolites (desiccated human feces), and in soils, and these proteins can be recovered and identified, sometimes to the genus level (e.g., Newman 1990; Newman et al. 1993). (However, there is some evidence to suggest that this type of analysis may not work; see Chapter 13.) This procedure is often erroneously called "blood" residue analysis, but it may be able to identify residual proteins from both animals and plants (DNA analysis may also be possible, see Chapter 13).

The application of this method has very important analytical implications. It now may be possible to identify proteins on specific tools, thus aiding in the functional interpretation of those tools. For example, millingstones (metates) usually are thought to be seed processing tools. However, Yohe et al. (1991) identified the presence of various animal proteins, indicating that certain animals were processed on such milling equipment. Not only did this provide evidence of resource use and associated technology, it also shed light on the processing of bones from those animals whose visibility in the conventional faunal record has always been minimal.

Another important application of protein residue analysis is in expanding the breadth of resources identified at a site, resources that may not be present in the traditional faunal or floral record. The following example illustrates the value of the technique. The macrofaunal analysis of the materials from a 3,000-year-old site (CA-SBR-6580) in southern California resulted in the identification of turtle (*Clemmys marmorata*) and "large mammal" (Sutton et al. 1993). However, pronghorn (*Antilocapra americana*), deer (*Odocoileus* sp.), waterfowl, fish, rodents (rat), lagomorphs, and either porcupine or squirrel were identified in the immunological analysis of both flaked and ground stone artifacts (Newman 1993). The lack of visible faunal remains from similarly aged sites in the region has led researchers to suggest a reliance (specialization) on plant resources (cf. Moratto 1984:153). However, the identification of a wider range of utilized animal resources suggests that the subsistence adaptation of the archaeological culture of this region should be reevaluated (Sutton 1993).

IDENTIFICATION OF FAUNAL REMAINS

Identification begins in the first phase of the cataloging process where the various categories of artifacts and ecofacts are sorted. When looking at all of the materials in the field bag (or in a soil sample, see Chapter 11), it should be relatively easy to separate bone from shell, shell from insect parts, etc. You may not know what animal a bone is from, but determining whether it is bone is relatively easy. Of course, this is not always the case and some items are quite difficult to identify, even to category. If this is the case, ask the instructor or a more experienced student. Sorting errors will be made; do not worry about it too much during the initial cataloging stage.

The first step in the identification of faunal remains is initial sorting into general categories (some elements will be very easy to identify and will not require a step-by-step process). First, separate the elements into cranial, postcranial, and unknown categories. Then separate the postcranial bones into: (1) large tubular bones; (2) small tubular bones; (3) flat bones; (4) irregular bones; and (5) unknown. Make sure to keep all the materials from the same analytical unit together and properly labeled. Follow the same basic procedure for invertebrates.

Identify each element (either whole or fragmentary) by comparing them to the comparative collection (see below). Many of the small fragments can be identified by careful comparison if there are articular surfaces present. Small rib fragments are often easy to identify, as are small cranial fragments. Absolute size of the bone may sometimes be misleading; keep in mind that juvenile bones are smaller than adult bones (also check for epiphysial fusion to get a general idea of age; see below).

Once the element is identified, taxon identification may be possible. Identification proceeds from the initial classification (fish, mammal, insect, etc.) and then becomes more specific. Depending on the setting (geography and age) of the site, certain faunal categories can be considered doubtful. For example, a large bone from a late prehistoric site is unlikely to be mammoth (an extinct species), and so that animal would be at the bottom of the list of potentials (due to the possibility of a fossil being in the site, however, it cannot be eliminated from the list). Identification should begin with the most likely candidates and proceed until the bone is identified. It may be an unexpected taxon for a number of reasons, including the fact the animals were traded in antiquity, that ancient peoples collected odd items (as our fossil mammoth bone in the example above might demonstrate), and that we do not fully understand the prehistoric distributions of animals. Remains unidentified to taxon (even identified elements) should be grouped within general categories (fish, bird, etc.) and then to general size. You should use size categories that correspond to known animals (e.g., deer-sized, coyote-sized, rabbit-sized, and rodent-sized).

The skills, talent, and resources available to the faunal technician will vary, as will the quality of the classification and identification of the faunal sample. The inexperienced analyst should not be afraid to ask for help when needed; remember that those who read your work will assume you knew what you were doing. If you are not certain of an identification, make sure to state that clearly.

COMPARATIVE COLLECTIONS

It is vitally important to have access to skeletal materials of known taxa for comparisons and identification of the archaeological specimens (one cannot learn identification from a book alone). You may be able to glance at a specimen and identify the element, but the elements of many animals look alike and you need known materials to identify the taxon to which an the element belongs. A skilled and experienced person may be able to identify many elements and taxa of common animals, but will still need a comparative collection for less common animals. A good comparative collection will have specimens of different ages and sex for the same species of animal (to account for sexual dimorphism, size due to age, and natural variation within a species).

Some institutions will have comparative collections on hand. If such a collection is not available, or is incomplete, you may wish to begin building your own. If your archaeological work is within your immediate geographic area, most of the animal remains recovered from your site are probably from species that still live in the region and so could be obtained for your collection.

There are several ways to obtain suitable specimens, primarily through picking up road kills (animals accidentally killed by cars). Be aware, however, that some states require permits to collect road kills and to possess skeletal materials. If there is a zoo nearby, it is sometimes possible to get deceased animals from them. Universities have some priority for such animals, but you must make the request. DO NOT PURPOSEFULLY KILL AN ANIMAL JUST FOR ITS BONES.

Most road kills are already partially decomposed, smelly, and/or dried. Also, many of the bones may be broken, perhaps lessening their value as comparative specimens; however, most archaeological specimens also are broken, so bone fragments obtained from road kills can be useful for identification purposes. Whatever the condition of the animal, caution must always be exercised in the collection and transport of such animals. Once collected, there are several methods to prepare a skeleton. The easiest way is to remove as much flesh as possible, bury it for a year or two, then dig it up and recover the bones. The organisms in the soil are very effective at rendering (reducing to bone) the skeleton. One must always be careful to recover the small and fragile bones from the soil (screen the soil).

A second method is to immerse the animal in water for a few weeks or months. Decomposition of the animals will take place fairly rapidly and there is little danger of losing any of the bones. The down side to this method is that it can be messy and smelly. The bones of some large animals contain a great deal of fat and marrow which may result in the bones being ''greasy'' or smelly for many years. Some such fats may be removed by boiling.

For faster results, or for small and/or fragile animals, place the animals in a colony of carrion-eating beetles (dermestid beetles). The beetles will do an excellent job of cleaning the skeleton of flesh, leaving the bones quite intact. The specimen can be removed a bit early so that the connective tissues are still intact, thus leaving the bones articulated. However, for most comparative purposes, a disarticulated skeleton is needed.

After the skeleton is prepared, it should be put into a container (e.g., a small box) for storage. The following information should be recorded on the box for any skeleton processed for comparative purposes: genus and species, general age (infant, juvenile, adult), sex (if possible), collector, collection date, and collection location. More specific information on the preparation and storage of specimens is provided in Wheeler and Jones (1989:177-185) for fish, and Hill (1975) for vertebrates in general.

SEXING

Determining the sex of an animal can provide considerable insight to faunal utilization practices, particularly with domesticated species. For many species, particularly small animals, it often is difficult to determine sex; for some other species it is easier (e.g., the skulls of adult male deer will have antlers). A combination of sex and age data (see below) can be quite informative regarding hunting practices (e.g., in American culture, hunters are only allowed to take mature males of many large game animals), herd composition (e.g., in bison kill sites), and even some subsistence practices (e.g., milk production).

AGING

Age determination of animals can be important in studies of prey selection, seasonality, dietary stress, and domestication. Age at death not only can convey information regarding the demographics of the prey species, but also the season of death (and so contribute to the elucidation of settlement/subsistence patterns). In some cases, age (and size) at death can imply certain technologies (e.g., net sizes with small fish). There are several methods used to determine age, including degree of bone fusion, dental eruption, and annular ring structures (in fish otoliths, scales, and vertebrae, and in mollusk shells, see below).

In mammals, bone growth occurs at the ends of the shafts (*diaphyses*) of the long bones. The ends of the long bones (*epiphyses*) remain unfused (unattached) until the long bone growth is complete. The epiphyses will then fuse to the shaft and the three bones of a juvenile (the two ends and the shaft) will become a single bone in an adult (Fig. 89). The rates of growth and fusion are known for a variety of animals, particularly domesticated ones (Silver 1969; Davis 1987:Table 1.5), and the age of many specimens can be estimated with confidence. In poorly known species, only general age estimates (juvenile or adult) can be made.

Other techniques of aging animals include analyses of the patterns of dental eruption and wear (Hillson 1986:176-230; Davis 1987:39-44), and annular structures (comparable to tree rings), that grow at regular rates or intervals. Many species of mollusks have growth ring structures that some believe can be used for aging (see Waselkov 1987:162-163), while some recent work suggests that they may not (Cerreto 1992). Other annular structures are present in fish otoliths, scales, and vertebrae, which can provide considerable data on age and season of death (see Casteel 1976).

RECORDING THE INFORMATION

Once classification and identification have been completed, all of the data must be recorded. Such recordation is accomplished with the use of a form where the context (site, unit, level, etc.) is listed, then the taxa, element, and condition are detailed. This information should be recorded in a format so that

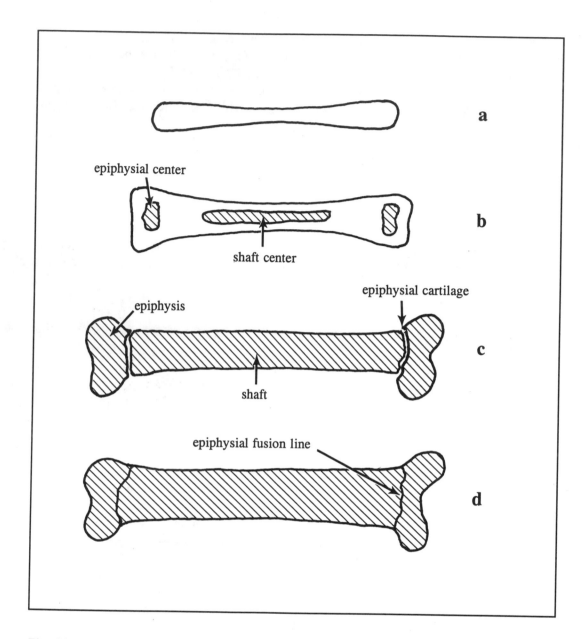

Fig. 89.   General bone (hatched) formation and fusion: (a) initial cartilage; (b) early ossification; (c) adolescent bone; (d) adult bone.

it can be easily computerized and subjected to statistical analyses. Useable examples of such forms (plus the computer codes) are provided at the end of the chapter. Klein and Cruz-Uribe (1984) presented a series of computer programs designed to assist in the analysis of faunal remains (quantification, age and sex profiles, etc., also see Cruz-Uribe and Klein [1986]).

The measurement and recordation of element size also may be important in determining a number of aspects of faunal exploitation or change over time (e.g., domestication). With such data, patterns of prey size may become apparent within or between faunal subassemblages. Such information should be coupled with sex and age data. A guide to bone measurement was provided by von Den Driesch (1976).

In any discussion of faunal remains, the taxa should be listed in proper taxonomic order (see any good reference book for the proper order). This provides consistent organization and removes the bias of "the first listed must be the most important." An example of such a discussion is provided in Appendix 1.

ANALYTICAL CONSIDERATIONS

Faunal remains may occur in one of two basic contexts. If the bones are found in the location where they were processed or eaten, the context is said to be *primary*. Materials in primary context can be used to reconstruct specific behavior patterns, such as butchering, consumption, or processing. Bones discarded as trash and incorporated into the general midden are in *secondary* context. These remains are still very informative but not to the extent of primary materials.

TAPHONOMY

Taphonomy (broadly the study of what happens to materials after death or discard) is a very important consideration in the analysis of any faunal (or any other) collection (see Lyman [1994a] for the definitive work on this subject). Once an animal dies (e.g., is killed for human use), what happens to it? After processing (butchering, grinding, cooking, etc.), it gets discarded. After that, it may be chewed upon by rodents, dragged away and eaten by dogs, washed downstream in a flood, burned in a natural fire, stepped on and broken by people, moved vertically by rodents, etc. (see Fig. 90). In addition, items are damaged during excavation, screening, transport in level bags, washing, sorting, and identification (and then in storage). Quantitative analysis (discussed below), distribution of elements, associations with other materials, and other things are all influenced by taphonomic processes (see Gifford 1981; Lyman 1987b; Wheeler and Jones 1989:61-78).

Bone preservation in nature is an uncommon event. When an animal dies, it falls down and begins to decompose. It may be eaten by other animals, and the bones may be scattered, chewed, digested, and/or fragmented. Bones exposed to the elements will bleach, crack, become brittle, and disintegrate rapidly. To be preserved, bone must be buried rapidly. Bone burial, and so preservation, is common in archaeological sites due to the relatively rapid deposition of soil and the intentional burial of garbage.

PROCESSING ANIMALS

Once animals are procured, they usually are processed (e.g., butchering, cooking) prior to consumption. Some animals (e.g., some insects) may be consumed without any processing.

Butchering

Butchering is the "reduction and modification of an animal carcass into consumable parts" (Lyman 1987a:252, also Lyman 1994a). It consists of a series of actions, usually involving the use of

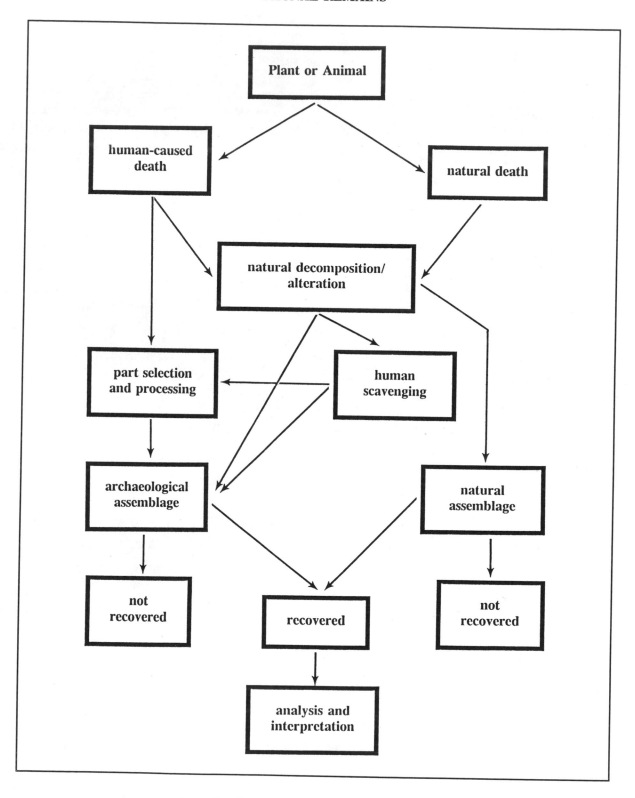

Fig. 90. Generalized Taphonomic Flow Chart.

tools, and results in a pattern of faunal and artifactual remains (see Lyman [1987a] for a comprehensive discussion of butchery studies; also see Lyman [1994a] and Fisher [1995]). The act of butchering involves the disarticulation of the skeleton of the animal and often results in modification to the bone (or shell) in the form of cut marks and certain types of fractures in bone. Such modification often is detectable; however, some natural impacts, such as rodent gnawing or soil action, may mimic cultural modification, so great care is required in interpretation. One type of common butchering mark that can be easily observed is cut marks across joint areas.

Bone Processing

Bones are subject to a variety of processing techniques, including breaking them open to obtain the marrow, and smashing and/or grinding them, either to process the bone itself or as part of the processing of an entire animal. If marrow extraction is the goal, one or two blows with a hammerstone may be sufficient to break it, leaving large bone fragments. If it is to be boiled for marrow and/or grease, the bone may be smashed using a hammer and anvil, resulting in highly fragmented remains. Small animals (e.g., rodents) may be processed (smashed and ground up) whole, including the bone. Again, this would result in already small bones being highly fragmented.

Such processing may be detected in several ways. Careful examination of the bone (perhaps with the assistance of a microscope) might reveal cultural breakage and/or wear patterns. Additionally, testing of processing tools (choppers, hammerstones, milling stones, etc.) might reveal the presence of protein residues indicating such usage.

Cooking

Cooking may be defined as roasting over a fire, baking in an oven, or boiling. Many animals, but certainly not all, are cooked prior to consumption. That an animal was cooked does not necessarily mean that the bones were exposed to fire or heat. Butchering may have resulted in the removal of the flesh, with the bone being discarded, so only the flesh was cooked. However, bone itself contains considerable nutrition (e.g., in grease and marrow) and it may have been boiled to recover such materials.

If bone is exposed to fire or heat, it should be detectable. Exposure to fire is relatively simple to detect; the bone is burned to varying degrees. Lightly burned bone will appear black while badly burned (calcined) bone will be whitish-grey and/or bluish, and perhaps even distorted. Bone exposed to boiling or baking will usually not exhibit obvious evidence of such exposure but it may be detectable microscopically (cellular distortion, etc.). Little work has been conducted in this area. (Remember that not all burned bone is necessarily cultural!)

Certain patterns of burning may be evident on bones and these may tell us a great deal about prehistoric cooking patterns. For example, if a rabbit is butchered, the legs may be removed and cooked over a fire. The meat on the majority of the leg would protect the bone from being burned, but the ends, with little flesh covering them, would be exposed and burned. The resulting bone would be largely unburned, with only the ends being charred.

DISTINGUISHING CULTURAL FROM NONCULTURAL REMAINS

As noted at the beginning of this chapter, the two major goals of faunal analyses are to ascertain human use of animals and to reconstruct paleoenvironments. To approach the latter, it is necessary to distinguish between cultural (animals present in the subassemblage due to human activity) and natural remains at a site. This is sometimes quite difficult (Thomas 1971), particularly for animals that habitually live in the ground (in sites) and around the vicinity of sites. However, a number of approaches may be used to make this determination.

First, it is important to consider the context of the specimen within the site in order to ascertain whether the bone is associated with a feature (e.g., a cooking hearth, a pile of similar bones, or some other obvious cultural feature) or whether it was found within a natural nest or as part of an articulated skeleton. If any of these contexts are clear, the decision may be simple. However, most faunal remains will not have such good field context recorded.

The next criterion to use is the condition of the bone itself. It is often assumed that burned bone is cultural while unburned bone may or may not be. Burning demonstrates exposure to fire but not what caused the fire. Bone that is well burned, however, probably could only get that way through human action. Conversely, unburned bone could still be cultural but demonstrating that it is may be quite difficult. Other things to look for are butchering marks and the physical condition of the bone; for example, fresh bone from a stratum where most of the other bone is mineralized most likely is intrusive and probably not cultural. The geographic context of the specimen also may be important. For example, fish bone found in a desert site away from a major water source was most likely imported (e.g., traded) to the site and so would be cultural. Lastly, the number of specimens of a particular taxon may be useful. If there are many deer bones in a relatively constricted area (a site), they most likely would be cultural since natural bone would not normally accumulate in large quantities in one spot (most natural bone would decompose quickly and not even be found).

Thus, archaeologists tend to view most bone from an archaeological site to be cultural, unless there is some good reason to believe otherwise (e.g., a recent complete skeleton in a nest). This assumption is often based on preservation (natural bone tends not to preserve well since it does not get buried fast enough), and on the aggregate quantity of bone in the site (nonsite soils rarely contain intact bone). An oft-cited exception is rodent bone, animals that may live and die in site soils and get preserved well (they may already be buried when they die). These small animals are the most difficult to interpret.

BONES AS TOOLS

Some of the animal bones from a site have been fashioned into tools, such as awls, scrapers, points, etc. (see Chapter 7). These artifacts are generally analyzed and described in sections devoted to tools rather than to faunal analysis. However, it is important to remember that the bone from which the tool was made came from an animal that was hunted, killed, and likely eaten by people. Such animals must be included in any interpretation of faunal remains.

QUANTIFICATION

Quantifying, or counting, the number of faunal specimens (elements) has always been a major feature in faunal analysis. The purpose of quantification is to measure abundance and to gain an understanding of what animals were being used by humans, how they related to the use of other species, and what they might tell us of paleoenvironmental conditions. Even when quantified, however, it is not really clear what the numbers mean. Does the measured abundance reflect "the relative abundances of taxa that were walking around the landscape, the abundances of taxa that were killed by human hunters, or the abundances of taxa recovered from an excavation?" (Lyman 1994b:47). This is a critical distinction, for as noted above, the recovery techniques used in an excavation are biased, often against small animals, so the quantity of recovered taxa may not accurately represent the abundances of these taxa.

Quantification is undertaken within analytical units; by level, excavation unit, stratum, site, or other division. The choice of analytical unit can have considerable bearing on the results (see below) and caution must be exercised. The two most commonly used measures of abundance are minimum number of individuals (MNI) and number of identified specimens (NISP) (see Lyman 1994b for a discussion of other units of measure). Each has its strengths and weaknesses (see Marshall and Pilgram 1993), but when computerized and used in conjunction may be quite informative (see Cruz-Uribe and Klein 1986).

Quantification methods used in analyses of mollusk remains are slightly different than those used for vertebrate remains. The vast majority of shellfish remains recovered from sites consists of fragmented and undifferentiated pieces of shell. Diagnostic parts (elements) are often present (e.g., hinges) and can be used to generate MNI numbers (remember that bivalves have left and right hinges). Since fragmentation is such a serious problem, NISP numbers are not very useful for shell. Another method of quantification for shellfish is by total weight (by taxon), evaluated against the average weight of an intact specimen. For example, if a complete clamshell weighs 100 grams and there are 450 grams of shell present in the analytical unit (say a 10-cm. level from an excavation unit), a minimum of five clams is represented. This density may then be extrapolated across the site volume for some estimate of overall numbers in the site. However, this method is flawed due to the leaching of carbonates from shell over time, thereby reducing its weight (perhaps by as much as 60%, Waselkov 1987:158). Efforts have been made to overcome this problem (see Waselkov 1987:158).

Number of Identified Specimens (NISP)

The number of identified specimens (NISP) is a summation of the number of specimens (or elements) within an analytical unit that was identified to taxon. This provides a rough idea of the abundance of taxa within the analytical units but often results in an overestimation of the actual abundance. For example, if a single rabbit femur is recovered in a particular level, the NISP is one. If the bone somehow got broken in half (in antiquity, during excavation, in the lab, etc.), both halves would still be identifiable to taxon (having intact ends) so the NISP would be two (known as the fragmentation effect, one of the reasons an understanding of taphonomy is so important). Due to an accident, the NISP doubled—as did the estimation of the importance of rabbit—creating a problem in interpretation. If fragmentation is too great, many of the bones will not be identifiable to taxon and NISP will decrease.

FAUNAL REMAINS

Minimum Number of Individuals (MNI)

The minimum number of individuals (MNI) is a measure of how many different individuals of a particular species are present in a faunal collection (this is somewhat dependent on sample size, see Grayson 1978). This number may be calculated by counting the *most* abundant element. For example, if a collection contains three left deer mandibles, there are at least three deer represented in the collection; the MNI is three. One cannot get three left jaws from one or two deer, and while there may be four or more deer actually in the collection, the *minimum* number is three. If there are three mandibles but five left femora, the MNI is five, the minimum number needed to account for the five left femora. If you have five femora but do not know the orientation (left or right), the MNI would be three; since each animal has two femurs, they must represent at least three deer.

While MNI provides some idea of how many animals are represented in the collection (unlike NISP numbers), it has its problems. Since MNI is calculated from bones recovered from specific analytical units (units, levels, etc.), there is the possibility of overlap and an overestimation of MNI. Suppose you excavate a unit in 10-cm. levels and you find five left rabbit femora in the first level and five right rabbit humeri in the second level. If MNI is calculated by level using these figures, the MNI for the first level is five and the MNI from the second level also is five, a total of 10 for the unit. However, since the element used to calculate the MNI was different from level to level, there is a chance that the humeri are from the same individuals as the femora and that the "actual" MNI is really five. The same problem exists from unit to unit within a site. If MNI is figured from the entire faunal subassemblage, it will invariably result in an underestimation of the animals present. This is one reason many people use NISP rather than MNI.

Estimations of Dietary Contribution

Simple quantification figures on bone do not necessarily reflect economic importance. For example, if a particular faunal collection contains the remains (MNI) of 10 small mammals and one large mammal used as food, which animal was more important to the diet in prehistory? A simple numeric calculation would show a 10:1 ratio in favor of small mammals. However, if the small mammals weighed one pound each (a total of 10 pounds) and the large mammal weighed 100 pounds, the ratio would be 10:1 in favor of the large mammal. Clearly, such calculations can be important to interpretation. There have been some studies done (e.g., for mammals, White 1953; Stewart and Stahl 1977; Lyman 1979; Stahl 1982; for fish, Casteel 1974) to calculate the live weight, available meat (live weight minus bone and hide), and useable meat (what people might actually eat) for a number of species (see Table 13 for a few; many more were calculated by White [1953:Table 14]). Remember, however, that recovery techniques are biased towards large animals and that body weight calculations may serve to increase the bias.

Element Distribution

The distribution of elements (or even of unidentified bone) can have considerable significance in an analysis. Several factors could account for differential element distributions. The first is the fact that not all bones preserve equally; all things being equal, denser and thicker bone (e.g., teeth and long bones) will preserve longer than spongy or thin bone (e.g., vertebrae, skull parts). An understanding of the natural processes affecting the bone (taphonomy) is critical to this issue.

240

Table 13
ESTIMATED EDIBLE MEAT FOR SELECTED SPECIES

Common Name	Scientific Name	Total Edible (g.)	Reference
Canada goose	*Branta canadensis*	2,089	White 1953
mallard duck	*Anas platyrhynchos*	653	White 1953
California quail	*Callipepla californicus*	130	White 1953
Siberian husky (dog)	*Canis familiaris*	10,432 17,000	White 1953 Stewart and Stahl 1977
California sea lion	*Zalophus californianus*	130,550	White 1953
ringed seal	*Phoca hispida*	64,774 27,760	White 1953 Stewart and Stahl 1977
elephant seal	*Mirounga angustirostris*	1,305,500	White 1953
walrus (male)	*Odobenus rosmarus*	522,200	White 1953
prairie dog	*Cynomys* spp.	560	White 1953
ground squirrel	*Spermophilus* spp.	373	White 1953
eastern grey squirrel	*Sciurus carolinensis*	440 162	White 1953 Stewart and Stahl 1977
American beaver	*Castor canadensis*	13,335 6,134	White 1953 Stewart and Stahl 1977
pack rat	*Neotoma* spp.	261	White 1953
jackrabbit	*Lepus* spp.	1,120	White 1953
cottontail rabbit	*Sylvilagus audubonii*	653	White 1953
mule deer	*Odocoileus hemionus*	37,300	White 1953
pronghorn antelope	*Antilocapra americana*	20,515	White 1953
bison (male) bison (female)	*Bison bison*	335,700 147,200	White 1953
armadillo	*Dasypus novemcinctus*	2,798	White 1953

Cultural patterns also affect the distribution of elements, causing them to be nonrandom. One could identify "fish" within a faunal collection and learn that fish was an exploited resource at the site. However, if it could be determined that head elements were in one location while the other elements were in a separate location, it could be possible to distinguish processing locations within the site and perhaps discover artifact associations related to fish processing, etc.

It may also be important to discover which elements are *not* present in the faunal subassemblage. Large animals may be killed at some distance from the camp and butchered in the field, with only certain parts being brought back to camp (the "schlepp" effect; e.g., Daly 1969:149). Thus, it is possible that only limb bones of some large animals would be present in a collection, the axial elements being left at the kill site. An analysis of the kill site faunal subassemblage might reveal cranial and vertebral elements but an absence of limb bones. Such information is necessary to the reconstruction of settlement and subsistence patterns.

THE USES OF FAUNAL DATA IN INTERPRETATION

Once the faunal remains have been classified, identified, and quantified, they need to be interpreted. Identified species may be useful to either studies of human culture (subsistence, settlement, ideology, ethnicity, technology, etc.; see below), to environmental reconstruction, or a number of other questions. To be useful in addressing cultural questions, the bone must be cultural in origin, often a difficult circumstance to demonstrate (as noted above).

SUBSISTENCE PATTERNS

The study of what prehistoric people ate and how they procured their food has long been an intriguing subject for archaeologists. Cultural faunal remains actually form indirect evidence of subsistence since there rarely is an actual demonstration of consumption. While a burned deer bone with butchering marks is unequivocally cultural, it does not unequivocally demonstrate that the deer was eaten; the animal may have been killed and butchered for its skin, with the bone being discarded into the fire. While this scenario seems unlikely, it is important to keep such possibilities in mind.

Faunal remains from coprolites, however, do form direct evidence of consumption. Most faunal remains recovered from coprolites will be those of small animals (see Sobolik 1993), due to the fact that the bones from large animals are too large to ingest (except if highly fragmented). In such cases, the identification of protein residues from the coprolite could add significantly to our understanding of prehistoric diet (see Newman et al. 1993). Direct evidence of ingestion, however, does not necessarily mean the item was eaten as food. People eat things for nondietary reasons and materials present in coprolites may be present as medicine (e.g., Reinhard et al. 1991) or ritual (e.g., the ingestion of ants in ceremonies, see Blackburn 1976).

Archaeologists want to be able to do much more that just compile a list of the animals consumed by group in antiquity. It is important to recover as much detail as possible regarding food preferences, cuisine, differential access to resources (by age and/or gender), or a variety of other factors. A faunal subassemblage may provide some very interesting details. For example, the Olsen-Chubbuck bison kill site in eastern Colorado (Wheat 1972) revealed a great deal of information regarding the hunting and butchering practices of native North Americans ca. 8,500 years ago. In this instance, bison were driven over a cliff into a ravine. They were then butchered in a systematic manner, as revealed in the piles of bones (segregated by element). From this site, archaeologists were able to determine which cuts of meat were taken and when, how much meat (in pounds) was obtained, how many people the meat would feed, and for how long. They also were able to make inferences about which way the wind was blowing that day because bison hunters must approach herds from the downwind direction in order to be successful.

SETTLEMENT PATTERNS

People will usually leave their homes (camps, villages, or towns) to procure animals. They will go out into the landscape to hunt, fish, or gather animals, and will have to live and subsist while they are gone. They may establish hunting or fishing camps, build facilities to trap, process, or store animals, and/or use certain locations to obtain raw materials for use in hunting activities. All of these phenomena result in the creation of archaeological sites associated with animal procurement and processing, part of the total settlement pattern of a people. An understanding of the settlement system of a culture will lead to a greater understanding of their subsistence system (and vice versa). Such data might also be used to reconstruct habitats or catchment zones (e.g., hunting and/or fishing territories [see Casteel 1972]).

SITE INTERPRETATION

Faunal remains may be used to determine spatial patterns within sites and to infer behavior. Archaeologists want to learn and understand how villages were laid out in prehistoric times. This may be determined by ecofacts that reveal where food was stored, the locations of cemeteries in relation to the village proper, "bathroom areas," etc. Faunal remains also provide considerable data on animal domestication, the spread of agriculture, and even some farming practices.

Faunal remains may also be used to infer the function of sites. For example, it is the presence of large quantities of bone in a site, coupled with many differential patterns of elements, that infer butchering and processing. In the absence of evidence for other activities, a site may be interpreted as a kill/butchering site based on the faunal remains.

ENVIRONMENTAL RECONSTRUCTION

Some faunal remains are useful in the reconstruction of past environments. Many species of animals (particularly insects) are confined to specific plant communities, and a delineation of either can illuminate the other. The presence of a particular animal at a site may provide information on the environment of the site at that time, information that may have important consequences for the overall interpretation of the site (and others of that same time range).

IDEOLOGY

As noted above, not all animals were exploited for food or materials (e.g., skins); some were used in ceremonies or may be related to other nonutilitarian practices. Such events or practices represent ideology; the systematic and consistent body of belief (world view) of a culture. While reconstruction of ideology is currently difficult, we must strive to do so, as it is a goal of archaeology.

As part of ideology, practices related to cultural ecology may be reflected in faunal remains. For example, the sudden appearance or disappearance of a particular species may be related to resource conservation practices (taboos) or perhaps changing religious beliefs.

STATUS

All societies have some sort of status hierarchy, based on any number of factors, including age, gender, skill, ascribed authority, or socioeconomic status. With status comes differential access to resources, including animal products (see review by Crabtree 1990:171-177). Such differences may be quite minor or they may be very significant. For example, in highly stratified societies (those with

243

classes or castes), differential access to animal products may be pronounced, with the ''upper'' classes having exclusive access to certain species or the better quality meats. Such patterns can be detected in the archaeological record but should be combined with other data to form a more convincing argument.

ETHNICITY

Cultures (or ethnic units) view the world differently than other cultures and will utilize resources, including animal products, in a distinctive way (see review by Crabtree [1990:177-181]). For example, the faunal remains from contemporary nineteenth century Anglo, Chinese, and Native American sites will be quite dissimilar, even if they are in the same geographic area. Butchery patterns may also be different, including the tools used. Nevertheless, it is difficult to make these distinctions and to determine ''ethnicity'' on the basis of faunal remains alone. Still, this is one goal of any archaeological analysis.

DATING

Faunal remains can sometimes be used as temporal (time) markers to date sites. For example, the presence of fossil species may serve to date a site to the time when such species were extant; thus, a mammoth kill site must date to before ca. 10,000 B.P. The presence of an introduced species (e.g., exotic fish species [Casteel 1972] or cattle) may serve to date that site to the post-contact period. Being organic, bone can also be dated directly by radiocarbon. However, a bone sample submitted for dating should be clearly cultural; otherwise the date will not be very useful.

SEASONALITY

A determination of the season of occupation of a site can help place it in the overall settlement pattern of a culture and provide clues of other activities. The season of death can be determined for some faunal remains. As noted above, epiphyseal fusion and dental eruption sequences can sometimes be used as seasonal indicators for a number of vertebrates (where such sequences are known). In fish, annular structures such as otoliths, scales, and vertebrae can serve the same purpose. In mollusks, annular structures (bands on the shell) may be used (see Waselkov 1987:Table 3.7), but perhaps not (Cerreto 1992).

The distribution of species may also be informative. In some fish (e.g., salmon), their presence in a site implies season of capture since different species occur seasonally. In these cases, however, one must always keep the possibility of storage in mind; season of capture does not necessarily imply season of use.

TECHNOLOGY

Certain technologies can be inferred from faunal remains. As noted above, a great deal could be inferred regarding procurement methods and equipment from the Olsen-Chubbuck site (Wheat 1972). Additionally, the presence of certain small fish in a site may imply specific net sizes (Gobalet 1989). A number of such inferences is possible with careful examination of the bones.

TRADE

Virtually all procured animals were moved about and exchanged, that is traded (an exception might be a small animal discovered and consumed on the spot by a single individual). It may be that the trade was a short-distance exchange between the producer (the hunter or fisher) and the consumer (members of a family in the same camp). It may be that the trade was a long-distance event that involved special preparation of the animal (special butchering, processing, etc.). Long-distance trade of animal products may have involved either parts (e.g., shells for ornaments, hides, wool) or whole animals (e.g., dried fish). Indications of such activities would include the presence of animals outside their natural range, evidence of specialized preparation or transport technology, and perhaps the depiction of "exotic" species in art (rock art or pottery).

DOMESTICATION

Few domesticated animals were present in North America in aboriginal times. Domesticated dogs were widespread and turkeys were domesticated in some regions (e.g., the Southwest). No large animals were domesticated in North America (or in Mesoamerica for that matter; but some camelids [llamas and alpacas] were domesticated in South America). After European contact, however, a wide variety of Old World domesticated species (e.g., horses, cows, pigs, chickens) became widespread.

While not generally applicable to aboriginal contexts in North America, the process of domestication results in a number of patterns in a faunal assemblage that can be detected (see Davis 1987:133-152; Crabtree 1990:162-166). These patterns include: (1) the presence of imported ("exotic") species; (2) a reduction in the number of species exploited and an intensification of those still used; (3) size changes in individual members of the species (individuals tend to get smaller when first domesticated, then larger); (4) a change in sex and age profiles (where females would be kept for breeding and milking while males would be butchered young); and (5) the presence of domesticated pets in human burials.

A NOTE ON FAUNAL REMAINS FROM HISTORICAL SITES

While the basic analytical approaches described above for faunal analysis emphasize prehistoric materials, they also are applicable to historical remains (see discussion in Chapter 9, also see Reitz and Scarry 1985:1-7). There are, however, several major differences between prehistoric and historical faunal materials. The first is that historical faunal remains tend to be less diverse (fewer species) and include domesticated species. This may narrow the species possibilities in the identification process but other factors become more complicated (e.g., sex and age ratios). Another major difference is that documentary information may exist regarding the use, care, technology, prices, etc., of domesticated animals (in official reports, letters, newspapers, advertisements, inventories, tax records, etc.). Such records may be used to determine where and to whom high-priced (quality) materials were sent (as well as low-priced goods), and to demonstrate differential access to certain materials based on gender, ethnicity, and/or social status. Faunal remains also may be used to enhance and/or augment the historical record. A discussion of the role of faunal analyses in historical archaeology was provided by Jolly (1983) and Crabtree (1985, 1990).

REFERENCES

Bailey, G. N.
  1975   The Role of Mollusks in Coastal Economies: The Results of Midden Analysis in Australia. Journal of Archaeological Science 2:45-62.

Blackburn, Thomas
  1976   A Query Regarding the Possible Hallucinogenic Effects of Ant Ingestion in South-Central California. The Journal of California Anthropology 3(2):78-81.

Brewer, Douglas J.
  1992   Zooarchaeology: Method, Theory, and Goals. In: Archaeological Method and Theory, Vol. 4, Michael B. Schiffer, ed., pp. 195-244. Tucson: University of Arizona Press.

Casteel, Richard W.
  1972   Some Archaeological Uses of Fish Remains. American Antiquity 37(3):404-419.

  1974   A Method for Estimation of Live Weight of Fish from the Size of Skeletal Elements. American Antiquity 39(1):94-98.

  1976   Fish Remains in Archaeology and Paleo-Environmental Studies. New York: Academic Press.

Cerreto, Richard
  1992   The Implications of Non-Periodic Growth in Bivalves for Three Seasonality Methods Used by Southern California Archaeologists. Journal of California and Great Basin Anthropology 14(2):216-233.

Colley, Sara M.
  1990   The Analysis and Interpretation of Archaeological Fish Remains. In: Archaeological Method and Theory, Vol. 2, Michael B. Schiffer, ed., pp. 207-253. Tucson: University of Arizona Press.

Crabtree, Pam J.
  1985   Historic Zooarchaeology: Some Methodological Considerations. Historical Archaeology 19(1):76-78.

  1990   Zooarchaeology and Complex Societies: Some Uses of Faunal Analysis for the Study of Trade, Social Statue, and Ethnicity. In: Archaeological Method and Theory, Vol. 2, Michael B. Schiffer, ed., pp. 155-205. Tucson: University of Arizona Press.

Cruz-Uribe, Katheryn, and Richard G. Klein
  1986   Pascal Programs for Computing Taxonomic Abundance in Samples of Fossil Mammals. Journal of Archaeological Science 13:171-187.

Daly, Patricia
  1969   Approaches to Faunal Analysis in Archaeology. American Antiquity 34(2):146-153.

Davis, Simon J. M.
  1987   The Archaeology of Animals. New Haven: Yale University Press.

Elias, Scott A.
  1994   Quaternary Insects and Their Environments. Washington: Smithsonian Institution Press.

Fisher, John W., Jr.
  1995   Bone Surface Modifications in Zooarchaeology. Journal of Archaeological Method and Theory 2(1):7-68.

Gifford, Diane P.
  1981   Taphonomy and Paleoecology: A Critical Review of Archaeology's Sister Disciplines. In: Advances in Archaeological Method and Theory, Vol. 4, Michael B. Schiffer, ed., pp. 365-438. New York: Academic Press.

Gilbert, B. Miles
  1980   Mammalian Osteology. Laramie, WY: Modern Printing Co.

Gilbert, B. Miles, Larry D. Martin, and Howard G. Savage
  1981   Avian Osteology. Laramie, WY: Modern Printing Co.

Gobalet, Kenneth W.
  1989   Remains of Tiny Fish from a Late Prehistoric Pomo Site Near Clear Lake, California. Journal of California and Great Basin Anthropology 11(2):231-239.

Gordon, Elizabeth A.
  1993   Screen Size and Differential Faunal Recovery: A Hawaiian Example. Journal of Field Archaeology 20(4):453-460.

Grayson, Donald K.
  1978   Minimum Numbers and Sample Size in Vertebrate Faunal Analysis. American Antiquity 43(1):53-65.

  1984   Quantitative Zooarchaeology. New York: Academic Press.

Hargrave, Lyndon L.
  1970   Mexican Macaws: Comparative Osteology and Survey of Remains from the Southwest. University of Arizona Anthropological Papers No. 20.

Hill, Frederick C.
  1975   Techniques for Skeletonizing Vertebrates. American Antiquity 40(2):215-219.

FAUNAL REMAINS

Hillson, Simon
    1986   Teeth. Cambridge: Cambridge University Press.

Jolly, Robert L.
    1983   North American Historic Sites Zooarchaeology. Historical Archaeology 17(2):64-79.

Klein, Richard G., and Katheryn Cruz-Uribe
    1984   The Analysis of Animal Bones from Archaeological Sites. Chicago: University of Chicago Press.

Lyman, R. Lee
    1979   Available Meat from Faunal Remains: A Consideration of Techniques. American Antiquity 44(3):536-546.

    1982   Archaeofaunas and Subsistence Systems. In: Advances in Archaeological Method and Theory, Vol. 5, Michael B. Schiffer, ed., pp. 331-393. New York: Academic Press.

    1987a   Archaeofaunas and Butchery Studies: An Archaeological Perspective. In: Advances in Archaeological Method and Theory, Vol. 10, Michael B. Schiffer, ed., pp. 249-337. New York: Academic Press.

    1987b   Zooarchaeology and Taphonomy: A General Consideration. Journal of Ethnobiology 7(1):93-117.

    1994a   Vertebrate Taphonomy. Cambridge: Cambridge University Press.

    1994b   Quantitative Units and Terminology in Zooarchaeology. American Antiquity 59(1):36-71.

Marshall, Fiona, and Tom Pilgram
    1993   NISP vs. MNI in Quantification of Body-Part Representation. American Antiquity 58(2):261-269.

Moratto, Michael J.
    1984   California Archaeology. Orlando: Academic Press.

Newman, Margaret E.
    1990   The Hidden Evidence From Hidden Cave, Nevada. Ph.D. dissertation, University of Toronto.

    1993   Immunological Residue Analysis of Samples from CA-SBR-6580. In: Archaeological Investigations at the Siphon Site (CA-SBR-6580): A Millingstone Horizon Site in Summit Valley, California, by Mark Q. Sutton, Joan S. Schneider, and Robert M. Yohe II, pp. 79-83. San Bernardino County Museum Association Quarterly 40(3).

Newman, Margaret E., Robert M. Yohe II, Howard Ceri, and Mark Q. Sutton
    1993   Immunological Protein Residue Analysis of Non-lithic Archaeological Materials. Journal of Archaeological Science 20(1):93-100.

Olsen, Stanley J.
    1968   Fish, Amphibian and Reptile Remains from Archaeological Sites: Part 1, Southeastern and Southwestern United States. Papers of the Peabody Museum of Archaeology and Ethnology 56(2).

    1979   Osteology for the Archaeologist. Papers of the Peabody Museum of Archaeology and Ethnology 56(3, 4, and 5).

Reinhard, Karl J., Don L. Hamilton, and Richard H. Hevly
    1991   Use of Pollen Concentration in Paleopharmacology: Coprolite Evidence of Medicinal Plants. Journal of Ethnobiology 11(1):117-134.

Reitz, Elizabeth J., and C. Margaret Scarry
    1985   Reconstructing Historic Subsistence with an Example from Sixteenth-Century Spanish Florida. Society for Historical Archaeology, Special Publications Series No. 3.

Shaffer, Brian S.
    1992   Quarter-Inch-Screening: Understanding Biases in Recovery of Vertebrate Faunal Remains. American Antiquity 57(1):129-136.

Shaffer, Brian S., and Julia L. J. Sanchez
    1994   Comparison of 1/8" and 1/4" Mesh Recovery of Controlled Samples of Small-to-Medium-Sized Mammals. American Antiquity 59(3):525-530.

Silver, I. A.
    1969   The Ageing of the Domestic Animals. In: Science in Archaeology, Don Brothwell and Eric Higgs, eds., pp. 250-268. New York: Basic Books.

Sobolik, Kristin D.
    1993   Direct Evidence for the Importance of Small Animals to Prehistoric Diets: A Review of Coprolite Studies. North American Archaeologist 14(3):227-244.

Stahl, Peter W.
    1982   On Small Mammal Remains in Archaeological Contexts. American Antiquity 47(4):822-829.

Stewart, Francis L., and Peter W. Stahl
    1977   Cautionary Note on Edible Meat Poundage Figures. American Antiquity 42(2):267-270.

Sutton, Mark Q.
    1993   On the Subsistence Ecology of the "Late Inland Millingstone Horizon" in Southern California. Journal of California and Great Basin Anthropology 15(1):134-140.

    1995   Archaeological Aspects of Insect Use. Journal of Archaeological Method and Theory 2(3):253-298.

Sutton, Mark Q., Joan S. Schneider, and Robert M. Yohe II
    1993   Archaeological Investigations at the Siphon Site (CA-SBR-6580): A Millingstone Horizon Site in Summit Valley, California. San Bernardino County Museum Association Quarterly 40(3).

Thomas, David H.
    1969   Great Basin Hunting Patterns: A Quantitative Method for Treating Faunal Remains. American Antiquity 34(4):392-401.

    1971   On Distinguishing Natural vs. Cultural Bone in Archaeological Sites. American Antiquity 36(3):366-371.

von Den Driesch, Angela
    1976   A Guide to the Measurement of Animal Bones from Archaeological Sites. Peabody Museum of Archaeology and Ethnology, Peabody Museum Bulletin 1.

Waselkov, Gregory A.
    1987   Shellfish Gathering and Shell Midden Archaeology. In: Advances in Archaeological Method and Theory, Vol. 10, Michael B. Schiffer, ed., pp. 93-210. New York: Academic Press.

Wheat, Joe Ben
    1972   The Olsen-Chubbuck Site: A Paleo-Indian Bison Kill. Society for American Archaeology Memoir No. 26.

Wheeler, Alwyne, and Andrew K. G. Jones
    1989   Fishes. Cambridge: Cambridge University Press.

White, Theodore E.
    1953   A Method of Calculating the Dietary Percentage of Various Food Animals Utilized by Aboriginal Peoples. American Antiquity 18(4):396-398.

Yohe, Robert M. II, Margaret E. Newman, and Joan S. Schneider
    1991   Immunological Identification of Small-Mammal Proteins on Aboriginal Milling Equipment. American Antiquity 56(4):659-666.

FAUNAL ANALYSIS SHEET

Site _____ Date _____ Analyst _____ Page ____ of ____

Acc.	Unit		Level			Taxon Name	Taxon Code			Element Name	Element Code			Side			End			Com.	Age				Condition				No.	Remarks
														Lt	O	Rt	Px	S	Dt		Ad	Sa	Ju	Bu	Ca	Bt	Al		
1	2	3	4	5	6	7	8	9	10	11	12	13	14	15	16	17	18	19	20	21	22	23	24	25	26	27	28	29	30	31	32

FAUNAL ANALYSIS SHEET INSTRUCTIONS AND CODES

Site = enter the site name and number on top of page

Date = enter the date of the analysis (not of the excavation or cataloging) on top of page

Analyst = write your name (and those of your assistants) on top of page

Page = keep track of the pages for the site analysis (e.g., page 6 of 13) on top of page

Acc. = enter the accession number of the site in columns 1 and 2 (you will need to set up a computer code for this)

Unit = enter the unit number in columns 3 and 4 (you will need to set up a computer code for this)

Level = enter the level in columns 5 through 8 (you will need to set up a computer code for this)

Taxon Name = write the common name or the scientific name of the specimen (e.g., deer OR *Odocoileus*) in Column 9

Taxon Code = enter the taxon code in columns 10 through 12 (refer to the provided taxon code sheets)

Element Name = write the name of the element (e.g., femur) in column 13

Element Code = enter the element code in columns 14 through 16 (refer to the provided element code sheet)

Side = enter a yes code (1) as appropriate in one of columns 17 through 19, leave blank if unknown

   Lt = left

   O = none (for bones having no left or right, such as a vertebra)

   Rt = right

End = used for fragmentary specimens; enter a yes code (1) as appropriate in one of columns 20 through 22, leave blank if unknown

   Px = proximal (the end closest to the body)

   S = shaft

   Dis = distal (the end furthest from the body)

Com. = if complete, enter a yes code (1) in Column 23

Age = enter a yes code (1) as appropriate in one of columns 24 through 26, leave blank if unknown

   Ad = adult

   Sa = subadult

   Ju = juvenile

Condition = enter a yes code (1) as appropriate in one of columns 27 through 30, leave blank if unknown (more than one column may have a yes code)

   Bu = burned

   Ca = calcined (very badly burned, e.g., cracked, warped, discolored)

   Bt = butchered (denotes the presence of butchering marks on the element)

   Al = otherwise human-altered (e.g., fractures indicative of breakage for marrow extraction)

No. = enter number of specimens in Column 31 (one if a specific element, may be more than one if a general category such as ''unidentified mammal'')

Remarks = write brief comments as necessary in Column 32

MAMMAL TAXON CODE SHEET

Small/Medium Mammals		Small Mammals		Carnivores		Large Mammals	
001	opossum (*Didelphis marsupialis*)	026	chipmunk (*Tamias* spp.)	051	coyote (*Canis latrans*)	076	horse (*Equus caballus*)
002	shrew (*Sorex* spp.)	027	marmot (*Marmota flaviventris*)	052	wolf (*Canis lupus*)	077	burro (*Equus asinus*)
003	bat (order Chiroptera)	028	Antelope ground squirrel (*Ammospermophilus leucurus*)	053	red fox (*Vulpes vulpes*)	078	unident. perissodactyla
004	pika (*Ochotona princeps*)	029	ground squirrel (*Spermophilus* spp.)	054	kit fox (*Vulpes macrotis*)	079	peccary (*Pecari angulatus*)
005	cottontail rabbit (*Sylvilagus* spp.)	030	prairie dog (*Cynomys* spp.)	055	grey fox (*Urocyon cinereoargenteus*)	080	wild boar (*Sus scrofa*)
006		031	gopher (*Thomomys* spp.)	056	black bear (*Ursus americanus*)	081	elk (*Cervus* spp.)
007		032	pocket mouse (*Perognathus* spp.)	057	grizzly bear (*Ursus arctos*)	082	deer (*Odocoileus* spp.)
008		033	kangaroo rat (*Dipodomys* spp.)	058	ringtail (*Bassariscus astutus*)	083	moose (*Alces alces*)
009		034	beaver (*Castor canadensis*)	059	raccoon (*Procyon lotor*)	084	caribou (*Rangifer* spp.)
010	black-tailed jackrabbit (*Lepus* spp.)	035	mouse (*Reithrodontomys* sp.)	060	marten (*Martes americana*)	085	pronghorn (*Antilocapra americana*)
011		036	mouse (*Peromyscus* spp.)	061	weasel (*Mustela* spp.)	086	bison (*Bison bison*)
012		037	mouse (*Onychomys* spp.)	062	badger (*Taxidea taxus*)	087	mountain goat (*Oreamnos americanus*)
013		038	woodrat (*Neotoma* spp.)	063	skunk (*Spilogale phenax*)	088	musk-ox (*Ovibos moschatus*)
014	unident. rabbit	039	vole (*Microtus* spp.)	064	skunk (*Mephitis mephitis*)	089	bighorn sheep (*Ovis canadensis*)
015	unident. hare	040	porcupine (*Erethizon dorsatum*)	065	otter (*Lutra* spp.)	090	domestic cow (*Bos* sp.)
016	unident. lagomorph	041		066	mountain lion (*Felis concolor*)	091	unident. artiodactyl
017		042		067	lynx (*Lynx rufus*)	092	armadillo (*Dasypus novemcinctus*)
018		043		068		093	manatee (*Trichechus manatus*)
019		044		069	walrus (*Odobenus rosmarus*)	094	
020		045		070	sea lion (*Eumetopias* or *Zalophus*)	095	
021		046		071	seal (*Arctocephalus, Callorhinus, Phoca*, etc.)	096	whale (order Cetacea)
022		047		072		097	
023		048		073	unident. carnivore	098	dolphins and porpoises (order Delphinidae)
024	unident. small/medium mammal	049	unident. rodent	074	unident. medium mammal	099	
025	unident. vertebrate	050	unident. small mammal	075	unident. medium/large mammal	100	unident. large mammal

Note: Blank spaces are intentionally left on the sheet so that other animals may be added.

FAUNAL REMAINS

AMPHIBIAN/REPTILE TAXON CODE SHEET

Frogs, Toads, Turtles, and Tortoise		Lizards		Snakes		Other	
201	toad (*Bufo* spp.)	226	desert iguana (*Diposaurus dorsalis*)	251	racer (*Coluber constrictor*)	276	
202	frog (*Rana* spp.)	227	chuckwalla (*Sauromalus obesus*)	252	corn snake (*Elaphe guttala*)	277	
203	unident. toad or frog	228	zebra-tailed lizard (*Callisaurus draconoides*)	253	gopher snake (*Pituophis melanoleucus*)	278	
204		229	leopard or collard lizard (*Crotophytus* sp.)	254	kingsnake (*Lampropeltis* spp.)	279	
205		232	horned lizard (*Phrynosoma* sp.)	255	garter snake (*Thamnophis* spp.)	280	
206	snapping turtle (*Chelydra serpentina*)	231	whiptail lizard (*Cnemidophorus* spp.)	256	coral snake (*Micruroides* spp.)	281	
207	western pond turtle (*Clemmys marmorata*)	232		257	rattlesnake (*Sistrurus* spp.)	282	
208	western box turtle (*Terrapene ornata*)	233		258	rattlesnake (*Crotalus* spp.)	283	
209	desert tortoise (*Xerobates agassizi*)	234		259		284	
210	green turtle (*Chelonia mydas*)	235		260		285	
211	leatherback (*Dermochelys coriacea*)	236		261		286	
212	softshell turtle (*Trionyx* spp.)	237	unident. lizard	262		287	
213		238	gila monster (*Heloderma suspectum*)	263		288	
214		239		264		289	
215		240		265		290	
216		241		266		291	
217		242		267		292	
218		243		268		293	
219	unident. turtle	244		269		294	
220	unident. tortoise	245		270		295	
221	chelonian (unident. turtle or tortoise)	246		271		296	
222		247		272		297	
223		248		273		298	
224		249		274		299	
225	unident. amphibian	250	unident. lizard	275	unident. snake	300	unident. reptile

Note: Blank spaces are intentionally left on the sheet so that other animals may be added.

AVIAN TAXON CODE SHEET

401	California gull (*Larus californicus*)	426	ptarmigans (*Lagopus* spp.)	451	cormorants (*Phalacrocorax* spp.)	476	redhead (*Aythya americana*)
402		427		452		477	
403	sandhill crane (*Grus canadensis*)	428	scaled quail (*Callipepla squamata*)	453		478	
404	American coot (*Fulica americana*)	429		454		479	mallard (*Anas platyrhynchos*)
405		430	California quail (*Lophortyx californica*)	455	pelicans (*Pelicanus* spp.)	480	
406	roadrunner (*Geococcyx californianus*)	431		456		481	
407	mourning dove (*Zenaidura macroura*)	432		457		482	Canada goose (*Branta canadensis*)
408	pigeons (*Columba* spp.)	433	grebe (*Podiceps* spp.)	458		483	
409		434		459		484	swans (*Olor* spp.)
410	bald eagle (*Haliacetus leucocephalus*)	435	common egret (*Herodias egretta*)	460	Brewer's blackbird (*Euphagus cyanocephalus*)	485	
411	golden eagle (*Aquila chysaetos*)	436		461		486	
412	falcons (*Falco* spp.)	437	great blue heron (*Ardeaherodias hyperonca*)	462	eastern bluebird (*Sialia sialis*)	487	
413	red-railed hawk (*Buteo jamaicensis*)	438		463		488	
414		439		464	common crow (*Corvus brachyrhynchos*)	489	
415	osprey (*Pandion haliaetus*)	440		465		490	
416		441		466		491	
417		442	common loon (*Gavia immer*)	467	blue jay (*Cyanocitta cristata*)	492	
418	prairie chicken (*Tympanuchus* spp.)	443		468		493	
419		444		469		494	
420	sage grouse (*Centrocercus urophasianus*)	445		470	orioles (*Icterus* spp.)	495	willow woodpecker (*Dryobates pubescens*)
421	gray partridge (*Perdix perdix*)	446	barn owl (*Tyto alba*)	471		496	
422		447	great horned owl (*Bubo virginianus*)	472	common raven (*Corvus corax*)	497	
423	ring-necked pheasant (*Phasianus colchicus*)	448	burrowing owl (*Speotyto cunicularia*)	473		498	
424		449		474		499	
425		450		475		500	unident. bird

Note: Blank spaces are intentionally left on the sheet so that other animals may be added.

FAUNAL REMAINS

FISH TAXON CODE SHEET

	Marine Species		Riverine Species		Lake Species		Other
601	leopard shark (*Triakis semifasciata*)	626	catfish (*Ictalurus* spp.)	651	razorback or humpback sucker (*Xyrauchen texanus*)	676	carp (*Cyprinus carpio*)
602		627	Sacramento sucker (*Catostomus occidentalis*)	652		677	hitch (*Lavinia exilicauda*)
603		628	Sacramento squawfish (*Ptychocheilus grandis*)	653		678	thick-tailed chub (*Gila crassicauda*)
604		629		654		679	
605		630	Colorado River squawfish (*Ptychocheilus lucius*)	655		680	
606		631		656		681	hardhead (*Mylopharodon conocephalus*)
607		632	pupfish (*Cyprinodon* spp.)	657		682	Sacramento split-tail (*Pogonichthys macrolepidotus*)
608		633		658		683	bonytail (*Gila elegans*)
609		634		659		684	Sacramento blackfish (*Orthodon microlepidotus*)
610		635		660		685	
611		636		661		686	
612		637		662		687	
613		638		663	unident. sucker	688	
614		639	salmon (*Oncorhynchus* spp.)	664		689	
615		640	trout (*Salmo* spp., *Salvelinus* spp.)	665		690	
616		641	smelt (*Hypomesus* spp.)	666		691	
617		642	striped mullet (*Mugil cephalus*)	667		692	
618		643	bass (*Morone* spp.)	668		693	
619		644	tule perch (*Hysterocarpus traskii*)	669		694	unident. minnow
620		645	bass (*Micropterus* spp.)	670		695	
621	lamprey (*Lampetra* spp.)	646	Sacramento perch (*Archoplites interruptus*)	671		696	
622		647		672		697	
623		648		673		698	
624	sturgeon (*Acipenser* spp.)	649		674		699	
625		650		675		700	

Note: Blank spaces are intentionally left on the sheet so that other animals may be added.

INVERTEBRATE TAXON CODE SHEET

Freshwater Shellfish and Other Freshwater Animals		Marine Shellfish		Insects		Other Terrestrial Invertebrates	
901	mussel (*Anodonta* spp.)	926	bitterswett (*Glycymeris* spp.)	951	stonefly (cf. *Pteronarcys californica*)	976	land snail (cf. *Helminthaglyptha* sp.)
902	mussel (*Margitifera* spp.)	927	mussel (*Mytilus* spp.)	952	termite (Order Isoptera)	977	
903		928	mussel (*Anodonta edentuloides*)	953	Mormon cricket (*Anabrus simplex*)	978	
904		929	mussel (*Anodonta alba*)	954	field cricket (*Gryllus* spp.)	979	
905		930	scallop (*Pectin* spp.)	955	grasshopper (*Melanoplus femur-rubrum*)	980	
906		931		956	grasshopper (*Schistocerca shoshone*)	981	
907		932	oyster (*Ostrea* spp.)	957	grasshopper (*Melanoplus saquinipes*)	982	
908	freshwater gastropod (*Physa* sp.)	933		958	lice (*Pediculus humanus*)	983	scorpion (cf. *Vejovis goreus*)
909		934	clam (*Tivela* spp.)	959	cicada (Family Cicadidae)	984	
910		935	clam (*Saxidomus* spp.)	960	shore fly (*Hydropyrus hians*)	985	
911		936	clam (*Chione* spp.)	961	crane fly (*Tipula infuscata*)	986	
912	crayfish (cf. *Cambarus* spp.)	937	bean clam (*Donax* spp.)	962	fleas (Order Siphonaptera)	987	
913		938		963	moth (*Coloradia pandora*)	988	
914	brine shrimp (cf. *Artemia* sp.)	939	red abalone (*Haliotis rufescens*)	964	sphinx moth (*Hyles lineata*)	989	
915	horseshoe shrimp (cf. *Triops* sp.)	940	green abalone (*Haliotis fulgens*)	965	beetle (*Phyllophaga fusca*)	990	
916		941	black abalone (*Haliotis cracherodii*)	966	ant (cf. *Pogonomyrmex* sp.)	991	
917		942		967	ant (*Formica* sp.)	992	
918		943	limpet (*Megathura* sp.)	968	honey ant (*Myrmecocystus mexicanus*)	993	
919		944	limpet (*Acmaea* spp.)	969	wasps	994	
920		945	cowrie (*Cypraea* sp.)	970	bees (Order Hymenoptera)	995	
921		946	olive shell (*Olivella biplicata*)	971		996	
922		947	olive shell (*Olivella dama*)	972		997	
923		948	chiton (Family Lepidochitonidae)	973		998	
924		949		974		999	
925		950	tusk (*Dentalium* spp.)	975			

Note: Blank spaces are intentionally left on the sheet so that other animals may be added.

FAUNAL REMAINS

COMMON ELEMENT CODE SHEET

Generalized (and Mammal)		Reptile-specific		Bird-specific		Fish-specific	
001	skull (parietal)	041	plastron	081	furcula	121	precaudal vertebra
002	skull (frontal)	042	carapace	082	coracoid	122	caudal (tail) vertebra
003	skull (occipital)	043	precaudal vertebra	083	carpometacarpus	123	parapophysis
004	skull (temporal)	044	caudal (tail) vertebra	084	tibiotarsus	124	haemal spines
005	skull (sphenoid)	045		085	tarsometatarsus	125	scale
006	skull (zygoma)	046		086	premaxilla (beak)	126	otolith
007	unident. skull	047		087		127	pharyngeal
008	maxilla	048		088		128	basioccipital
009	mandible	049		089		129	fin rays
010	molar	050		090		130	brachiostegal
011	premolar	051		091		131	ceratohyal
012	canine	052		092		132	pterygiophores
013	incisor	053		093		133	
014	axis vertebra	054		094		134	pleural ribs
015	atlas vertebra	055		095		135	
016	cervical vertebra	056		096		136	quadrate
017	thoracic vertebra	057		097		137	
018	lumbar vertebra	058		098		138	dentary
019	clavicle	059		099		139	
020	sternum	060		100		140	opercular
021	ribs	061		101		141	
022	scapula	062		102		142	epihyals
023	humerus	063		103		143	
024	radius	064		104		144	
025	ulna	065		105		145	
026	carpals	066		106		146	
027	metacarpals	067		107		147	
028	phalanges	068		108		148	
029	sacrum	069		109		149	
030	pelvis	070		110		150	
031	femur	071		111		151	
032	patella	072		112		152	
033	tibia	073		113		153	
034	fibula	074		114		154	
035	tarsals	075		115		155	
036	metatarsals	076		116		156	
037	metapodial (-carpal or -tarsal)	077		117		157	
038	phalanges	078		118		158	
039	calcaneous	079		119		159	
040	astragalus (talus)	080		120		160	

Note: Blank spaces are intentionally left on the sheet so that other elements may be added.

Chapter 11

ANALYSIS OF FLORAL REMAINS

DEFINITION

The remains of plants (from logs to pollen) found in archaeological sites are called *floral remains*. Floral remains are classified as ecofacts, and like most faunal remains, are not considered to be artifacts. Except in unusual circumstances (see discussion on preservation in Chapter 1), most floral remains preserved and found in archaeological sites are carbonized to some degree. In some sites where preservation has occurred (sites with perishables), uncharred floral remains of cultural origin might be found and should be analyzed and interpreted. However, uncharred floral remains from open sites likely are recent in origin. Nevertheless, even recent floral remains can be useful in learning something about a site, such as determining the extent of bioturbation.

Most of the plant remains recovered from sites (at least those excavated prior to the development of more sophisticated techniques) consist of remains that are visible to the naked eye, such as large, burned seeds and charcoal. Much of this material has been incidentally recovered using methods designed to find artifacts (e.g., while screening). Until recently, the collection and analysis of samples designed specifically for the recovery of floral remains were relatively uncommon. An exception to this is "flotation samples" (discussed below) taken from features or other contexts. However, even in those circumstances, only large floating remains were collected (the material that did not float, called the "heavy fraction," was often discarded). As the discipline has become more sophisticated, the existence and value of microremains is becoming more apparent to researchers.

FLORAL TAXONOMIC CLASSIFICATION

As with animals, western societies classify plants based on the Linnaean taxonomic system of morphology (remember that other cultures may use quite different taxonomic systems). The western taxonomic system divides the plant kingdom into three major categories: ferns (and their allies), conifers, and flowering plants. The widely used, conventional (lay) taxonomic system of terrestrial plants includes ferns, grasses, "flowers," shrubs and bushes, and trees.

TERMINOLOGY IN FLORAL ANALYSIS

Plants possess a number of parts (somewhat equivalent to the term "element" in faunal analysis). Common elements for most plants include roots (and tubers), stems, leaves, flowers, seeds, pollen, phytoliths, and chemical residues. Many plant parts are very fragile (e.g., leaves), some are very small (e.g., pollen), while others are relatively robust (woody parts). People have used all of these plant parts in a variety of ways and for a number of purposes, and one should expect to recover each of these at one time or another in an archaeological site.

FLORAL REMAINS

CATEGORIES OF FLORAL REMAINS

There are three basic categories of floral remains from archaeological contexts: macrofloral, microfloral, and chemical. Each is discussed below. Most such remains are identified using morphological characteristics with the aid of voucher specimens, comparing the structure of the unknown remains with that of known specimens until a match (an identification) is made. However, this method requires that the archaeological specimens be relatively intact and that their morphology be discernible, a condition often not met by archaeological specimens.

Macrofloral Remains

Macrofloral remains are defined as those that are visible to the naked eye (though perhaps not recognizable except to the trained eye), primarily seeds and charcoal. In circumstances of unusual preservation, a much greater diversity of remains may be recovered.

Seeds. Most of the prehistoric seeds recovered from a site will have been charred (otherwise, they would not have preserved) and will be black in color. However, some fresh seeds also are black, so the texture of the seed must be carefully examined to determine if it is burned. Seeds come in varying sizes, from corncob size to very tiny. Some of the most economically important seeds in antiquity are quite small and are very unlikely to be recovered in normal field screening. Once the seeds are cataloged, seek assistance from a qualified biologist or botanist for identification purposes.

As noted above, caution must be exercised in the interpretation of seed remains (see Minnis 1981; Miller and Smart 1984). The context of the specimens is critical: if they were found in a feature, it could be inferred that they were being processed in that feature; if discovered in the general midden, they could be the remains of a rodent nest, of plants growing on the site, of materials used to construct houses, or any number of things. It is imperative, therefore, that investigators consider predepositional, depositional, and postdepositional processes related to plant usage before assigning meaning to macrofloral archaeobotanical assemblages.

Charcoal. Charcoal is the burned, carbonized remains of plants, usually the woody parts (burned seeds usually are considered a separate category). Charcoal can enter a site in a variety of ways, from campfires (ancient and modern) to natural fires. Context is important in making this distinction (see Smart and Hoffman 1988).

Archaeologists tend to assume that most of the charcoal in a site originated from the human activity there. One relative measure of activity from layer to layer is the quantity of charcoal in the midden. However, some archaeologists do not save screen-collected charcoal, so this information must be obtained from soil samples. Quantification of charcoal (by both volume and weight) are important data to collect, as they aid in the interpretation of carbonized materials as they relate to intensity of use, disposal, and cultural significance.

Charcoal (Wood) Identification. It is now possible to identify some wood represented by charcoal to the genus and perhaps even the species level. Again, context is important. The identification of a piece of charcoal from the general midden may not provide any significant information if it cannot be connected with some event in prehistory. On the other hand, charcoal from a hearth feature could demonstrate which plants were being used for firewood, charcoal from a burned structure could indicate what was being used for the construction of houses, etc., thus providing a great deal of information.

Microfloral Remains

Microfloral remains are defined as those plant materials that are visible only with the aid of magnification, primarily pollen and phytoliths.

Pollen. Pollen, in effect, is the sperm cells of plants. Much pollen is airborne and settles onto all ground surfaces. Over time, it will accumulate and be incorporated into midden soils. Pollen preserves quite well and is a common soil constituent. Analysis of the pollen record from level to level can provide a record of the types of plants present in an area over time. Such a record could be very valuable to an archaeologist attempting to discover ecological aspects of site use.

However, pollen analysis should be approached with caution. Pollen records are easy to contaminate (through sampling, bioturbation, etc.) and pollen has a habit of traveling great distances, thus skewing the record for a given area. For example, the pollen record of a lakebed will contain pollen from the entire watershed of the lake, not just the immediate area.

Pollen may also be present on the surface of some artifacts and may be evidence of the processing of particular plants. For example, corn pollen may be present in large quantities on milling implements used to grind corn. The detection of such pollen would indicate the function of the tool.

Phytoliths. Phytoliths are the microscopic silica bodies that form within individual plant cells. They form when the minerals in groundwater accumulate on cell walls (where they may form "shells" in the shape of the cell) or other bodies, the same residue seen as water spots on glasses caused by hard water. When the plant dies and decomposes in the soil, phytoliths enter the soil in large numbers. Archaeologists are just beginning to learn how to properly recover, process, and identify these remains. However, the origin of phytoliths in an archaeological site is always subject to question. The presence of a specific plant does not automatically indicate usage by human populations or that the information is archaeologically significant (see Piperno 1988).

Chemical Residues

When plants are collected and/or processed, parts of the plants will come in contact with tools, (if any) used in the procedures. As a result, the tools may retain chemical (e.g., protein) residues that can later be detected (see Chapter 13) and should be considered in floral analyses whenever possible. Protein residue analysis is often erroneously called "blood" residue analysis; however, it is not limited to blood and may be able to identify residual proteins from plants as well. Analysis of other chemical constituents (e.g., DNA) from plants may also be possible (e.g., Hillman et al. 1993).

RECOVERY OF FLORAL REMAINS

Most floral remains are recovered from either the field screening process or from soil samples taken in the field and processed in the laboratory. Each is discussed below.

FLORAL REMAINS

SCREEN-RECOVERED MATERIAL

Most plant materials (burned seeds and charcoal) recovered from the screen in the field will be relatively large since small specimens will fall through the screen (as most archaeologists use relatively large mesh screen size). If only screen-collected materials were recovered (e.g., no soil samples), the botanical record could be skewed toward large specimens and likely will result in misinterpretation of the site. One must be very cautious about this.

FEATURES

Sometimes plant materials will be recovered within, or in association with, a feature (rather than recovered from the general deposit), either in screening the materials from the feature or from soil samples taken from the feature. Floral materials discovered in association with features are likely the result of human activities, so the question of cultural or noncultural origin can often be avoided. For example, a log used as a roof support in a pueblo is definitely cultural and its identification (and dating) can provide a wealth of information. The same is true of firewood in a cooking hearth.

SOIL SAMPLES

Soil samples are collected for a number of reasons: to obtain charcoal for radiocarbon dating, to recover seeds, to retrieve materials in the soil (e.g., bone and artifacts), to recover pollen or phytoliths, and/or to characterize the soil itself. Flotation and material samples generally are taken from features while column samples generally are taken from the midden in a specific pattern (e.g., levels). In each of these samples, the soils are often screened (e.g., with 1/8-in. mesh) in the laboratory to remove large items and to recover artifacts and ecofacts prior to flotation or washing.

Flotation Samples

The purpose of processing flotation samples is often limited to the recovery of floral remains, based on the principle that such materials are lighter (light fraction) and will "float" in water. The heavy fraction (material that does not float) collects in the bottom of the flotation container. There is a large number of devices available for flotation. The simplest is just a hose, a bucket, and a small screen. A recent review of flotation techniques was presented by Toll (1988).

Most flotation is done using water and most of the floated materials are plant remains. However, some materials (even some plant materials) do not float well (e.g., bone and flakes) and may sink to the bottom of the container. Recovery of organics may be enhanced by the use of chemical additives (such as sodium silicate) that change the specific gravities of various constituents (e.g., bone) so they may be separated by flotation more easily (see Bodner and Rowlett 1980).

Material Samples

Material samples are different from flotation samples in that everything is collected from these samples, not just the floral remains. For example, the interpretation of a hearth may depend as much on lithic remains as on floral materials. It is important to discover all the materials in the soil, not just the floral remains.

BASIC LABORATORY METHODS IN ARCHAEOLOGY

Column Samples

One of the primary purposes of a column sample (generally taken as a column from the wall of an excavation unit) is to discover what was missed in the general field screening, as it is important to recover ALL cultural materials, including, but not limited to, floral remains. Pollen and phytolith analyses (see below) are not undertaken with column samples due to the considerable possibility of contamination.

Processing Soil Samples

The purposes of taking, processing, and analyzing soil samples are multiple. It is important to discover what materials are passing through the screen used in the field. It may be that specific materials are sought, such as charcoal for radiocarbon dating, or materials that are in the soil in or surrounding a feature (an *in situ* soil sample). Special soil samples (e.g., pollen, phytolith, or chemical) would not be processed as described below but sent to a specialist (see below).

Materials. The materials needed to process soil samples include a flotation device (and associated equipment), trays, distilled and tap water, a garden hose, tweezers, sterile vials (to contain material sorted from the samples), vial labels, plastic bags, bag labels, petri dishes, and a dissecting microscope (at least 10X). If no flotation device is available, a bucket or tub and mesh sieves (Nos. 5 and 10 for initial sorting and Nos. 35 or 40 for washing or capture, see Table 14) may be substituted.

Table 14
SCREEN MESH SIZES AND MEASUREMENTS

U.S. Standard	Metric	English
230	63μ = 0.06 mm.	--
120	125μ = 0.12 mm.	--
100	150μ = 0.15 mm.	--
60	250μ = 0.25 mm.	0.0098 in.
40	425μ = 0.42 mm.	0.0165 in.
35	500μ = 0.50 mm.	0.0197 in.
20	850μ = 0.85 mm.	--
18	1.0 mm.	0.0394 in.
10	2.0 mm.	0.0787 in.
6	3.35 mm.	0.25 in.
5	4.0 mm.	0.157 in.

FLORAL REMAINS

Procedures. Prior to processing, measure both the weight (grams) and volume (milliliters) of the sample and make sure this information is recorded in the catalog. Flotation should be used only if organics are sought, or as a first step in separating the light from the heavy fractions (thus making sorting easier).

Flotation. To conduct flotation, place the soil sample in the bottom of the flotation container (e.g., bucket or tub) and fill with water. As the water fills the container, gently agitate the soil so that the organic materials are freed from the surrounding matrix. Most of the organics (the light fraction) will float to the surface of the water where they can be skimmed off and captured using Nos. 35 or 40 mesh screen. As the constant supply of water causes the container to overflow, tip it slightly so that the floating organics will pour into the screen for capture. Once organics cease to come to the surface, carefully drain the water into the screen and save the soils in the container (the heavy fraction) for drying and examination.

Washing Soils. An alternative to flotation is just to wash the soils. If this method is used, simply pour approximately 1/2 cup of the soil sample at a time into Nos. 35 or 40 mesh screen. Run distilled or tap water (depending on which type is required; see below) through the sample, swishing the soil around in the sieve until the soil looks clean. Transfer the cleaned soil to a tray (e.g., a cafeteria tray) and spread evenly to dry (two or three days). Make sure the catalog identification tag is always with the sample. Put the dried soil (with its label) into a bag or other container.

Use distilled water when processing soil samples from which radiocarbon samples will be obtained. Tap water may contain materials that might contaminate radiocarbon samples and result in an erroneous date.

Sorting the Matrix. Decide what magnification is necessary (at least 10X) to examine the material. Place approximately a teaspoon of material in a petri dish and examine it under the microscope or similar instrument. Using tweezers, collect anything from the sample that is not soil. Recent plant parts naturally occur in soil, and while perhaps not directly associated with human occupation of the site, they nonetheless are important. WHEN IN DOUBT, SAVE IT! Place collected materials into properly labeled vials (see below). To avoid mixing samples, do not sort more than one sample at a time. NEVER discard anything; put the matrix (residual soil) back in its bag. Let the project director make the decision to discard the matrix.

Label the collecting vials as follows:

Site Number (Trinomial)
Catalog Number
Test Unit Number
Level
In Situ Designation (if any)
Soil Sample Number (if any, from original bag)
Material Collected (e.g., charcoal)
Name of Processor(s)
Date

BASIC LABORATORY METHODS IN ARCHAEOLOGY

A variety of materials may be found in soil samples (each type of material gets its own labeled bag or vial). These constituents might include the following (more than just floral remains, also note the attributes to record in the catalog):

1. freshwater shell: species (if possible) and weight in grams
2. marine shell: species (if possible) and weight in grams
3. snail shell: species (if possible) and weight in grams
4. fish bone: total number of pieces present and weight in grams
5. fish scales: total number of pieces present and weight in grams
6. otoliths: total number of pieces present and weight in grams
7. insect parts: total number of pieces present and weight in grams
8. recent plant parts: total number of pieces present and weight in grams
9. carbonized plant parts: total number of pieces present and weight in grams
10. seeds: total number of pieces present and weight in grams
11. pigment: total number of pieces present and weight in grams
12. shell artifacts: type, material, length, width, and thickness in millimeters, weight in grams
13. lithic debitage: total number of pieces present (by material) and weight in grams
14. bone artifacts: type, material, length, width, and thickness in millimeters, weight in grams
15. stone artifacts: type, material, length, width, and thickness in millimeters, weight in grams
16. rock (not sand): total number of pieces present and weight in grams
17. miscellaneous: total number of pieces present and weight in grams
18. residual matrix: weight in grams

When the sample is completely examined, put all the vials into the same plastic bag. List all the materials *found or not found* to complete the record.

SPECIAL SAMPLES

At least two types of special samples are taken in the field to recover specific data sets: pollen and phytoliths. Both sample types are subject to strict control in the laboratory. Few institutions have their own pollen or phytolith laboratories, so such samples usually must be sent to a specialist for analysis. This type of analysis is in its infancy and is not yet a standard technique. A great deal of work still must be done on basic identification of species, taphonomy, interpretative frameworks, and sampling tactics.

IDENTIFICATION OF FLORAL REMAINS

The identification of floral remains begins in the first phase of the cataloging process where the various categories of artifacts and ecofacts are sorted. When looking at all of the materials in the field bag (or in a soil sample), it should be relatively easy to initially sort floral remains from other materials. If a question arises, ask the instructor or a more experienced student. Sorting errors will be made; do not worry about it too much at the initial cataloging stage.

Identification proceeds from the initial classification and becomes more specific. Identification should begin with the most likely candidates (as determined by the setting [geography and age] of the site) and proceed until the plant material is identified. It may be an unexpected taxon for a number of reasons, including the fact that plants were traded in antiquity and that we do not fully understand the prehistoric distributions of plants.

The skills, talent, and resources available to the floral technician will vary, as will the quality of the classification and identification of the sample. The inexperienced analyst should not be afraid to ask for help when needed; remember those who read your work will assume you knew what you were doing. If you are not certain of an identification, make sure to state that clearly.

COMPARATIVE COLLECTIONS

As with faunal materials, the best way to identify floral remains is to compare them to an existing and already identified voucher specimen from a comparative collection. A comparative collection can be assembled by obtaining plant specimens (make sure to get representative samples from all parts of the plant), identifying them (the flowers are the best way to identify many plants; it may be necessary to wait for a specific time of year to obtain them), drying them in a plant press, then labeling and storing them. Be sure a sample of the seeds is also obtained.

RECORDING THE INFORMATION

Once classification and identification have been completed, all of the data must be recorded. Such recordation may accomplished with the use of a form, detailing the context (site, unit, level, etc.), taxa, number, and condition of the remains. This information should be recorded in a format so that it can be easily computerized and subjected to statistical analyses. The faunal analysis forms (provided at the end of Chapter 10) could be adapted for use in floral analysis.

In any discussion of floral remains, the taxa should be listed in proper taxonomic order (see an appropriate reference book for the proper order). This provides consistent organization and removes the bias of "the first listed must be the most important."

ANALYTICAL CONSIDERATIONS

As with any archaeological materials, one must consider the context (primary or secondary) of the floral remains in any interpretation. There are numerous ways in which floral remains might enter a site deposit, many of which are unrelated to the human occupation. The mere presence of a plant does not demonstrate that the plant was used by humans in antiquity. In addition, it is important to consider taphonomy, how floral remains may have been altered or moved about in the deposit since their original deposition (refer to Figure 90).

DISTINGUISHING CULTURAL FROM NONCULTURAL REMAINS

The same basic criteria used in distinguishing cultural from noncultural remains at a site that were detailed in Chapter 10 for faunal remains also apply to floral remains. In review, one must consider both the context of the specimen within the site and its condition. For example, floral remains found in rodent nests are usually natural, as are those that are unburned.

QUANTIFICATION

There are at least five methods used to quantify plant remains: (1) absolute counts, (2) ubiquity, (3) ranking, (4) diversity, and (5) ratio. Absolute count is literally the "raw number of each taxon in each sample" (Popper 1988:60) and assumes that the count represents how much the plant was used in antiquity. Ubiquity ignores the count per sample and records the number of samples in which a taxon is present (Popper 1988:60-61). Ranking (Popper 1988:64-66) uses absolute counts, then translates those numbers into ranks (for example, a count of 0-10 is given a rank of 1, a count of 11-20 is given a rank of 2, etc.), which are then compared. A diversity measurement "summarizes data to describe the composition of a plant assemblage" (Popper 1988:66). For example, diversity can be an index of the total number of taxa and the relative abundance (clustering) of each taxon in the samples. Ratios (Miller 1988) are used to compare unequal data sets, either different sized samples or ratios of different taxa.

No one measure of quantification is always best. One must consider the nature of the samples and the conditions they require. Popper (1988:69) noted that:

> as the measurements move away from absolute frequencies, we lose information on abundance. But more specific measurements, such as absolute counts and ranking, require greater control over preservation and context than ubiquity. Ratios . . . also treat the data with greater specificity than ubiquity analysis. . . . Ubiquity is less reliable (especially for measuring the frequencies of rare taxa) when there are few samples in a group. Ranking requires high counts of data. All paleoethnobotanical analyses require careful grouping of samples for accurate results.

THE USES OF FLORAL DATA IN INTERPRETATION

Once the floral remains have been classified, identified, and quantified, they need to be interpreted. Identified species may be useful to studies of human culture (subsistence, settlement, ideology, ethnicity, technology, etc.; see below), environmental reconstruction, among others. To be useful in addressing cultural questions, the plants in question must be cultural in origin, often a difficult circumstance to demonstrate (as noted above).

SUBSISTENCE PATTERNS

The study of what plants prehistoric people ate, how plants were procured, and how they were processed and prepared for consumption is most interesting. Most floral remains form *indirect* evidence of diet; finding the remains of economic plants in a site does not demonstrate that the plants were eaten. Such consumption is assumed based on ethnographic analogy; we know that corn is eaten by current Pueblo Indians, so if we find corn in an ancient Pueblo site, the assumption is that it was used for food. While this may be a well-justified assumption, remember that it is only an assumption. Direct evidence of consumption (although not necessarily as food) are present only in coprolites or gut contents (e.g., from a mummy), and may also be inferred from bone chemistry.

SETTLEMENT PATTERNS

People will often procure plant resources at some distance away from their homes (camps, villages, or towns). They will go out into the landscape to gather plants and will have to live and subsist while they are gone. Additionally, they may establish small camps, build storage and/or processing facilities, and/or use certain locations to obtain raw materials for use in plant gathering activities. All of these phenomena result in the creation of archaeological sites associated with plant procurement and processing, part of the total settlement pattern of a culture. An understanding of the settlement system of a culture will lead to a greater understanding of their subsistence system (and vice versa). Such data might also be used to reconstruct habitats or catchment zones (e.g., gathering territories).

SITE INTERPRETATION

Floral remains can be used to determine spatial patterns within a site, to infer behavior, and to learn and understand how villages were laid out in prehistoric times. This may be determined by ecofacts that reveal where food was processed, stored, and discarded. Floral remains also provide considerable data on domestication, the spread of agriculture, farming practices, crop processing and preparation, and disposal (Reddy 1994).

Plant remains may also be used to infer the function, or even the presence, of a site. For example, some sites in Mesoamerica have been discovered by noting the presence of Ramón trees, a plant used by the ancient Maya and that still grows in and around those sites. This is similar to the standard archaeological survey technique of looking for vegetation changes that might reflect soil differences (e.g., the presence of midden soils) to locate sites. In the case of the Ramón tree, it could be considered a cultural marker (as it was purposefully planted) in addition to being a vegetative marker of sites.

The discovery of the remains of plants known to be "weeds" in ancient agricultural fields may be used to imply the presence of such fields in the area. Such remains would take the form of seeds, pollen, and/or phytoliths.

ENVIRONMENTAL RECONSTRUCTION

It is possible to determine past environments by studying floral remains. At Star Carr, a Mesolithic site in England (Clark 1954), pollen remains and deer antlers recovered from the site (coupled with correlating data of known seasonal cycles of deer antler growth), provided the investigators with information regarding the variety and geographic range of the resources exploited. The pollen inferred a forest of birch and pine, the antlers indicated the presence of red deer, roe deer, and elk, and the time of year was determined by knowledge of cycles of antler growth and shedding. Floral remains in a site can also indicate a wet or arid, or hot or cold, environment.

IDEOLOGY

Floral remains can be used to infer ancient behavior, especially the symbolic interpretation of burial practices and mortuary goods. A good example of this is a Neanderthal burial (Shanidar Cave IV) in Iraq (Trinkhaus 1983). From the pollen samples taken, we know that a man buried 60,000 years ago had daisies, cornflowers, and hollyhocks associated with his grave. If that association were purposeful (there is disagreement on this point), it would provide insight into burial and social interaction. In any case, because we know when these particular flowers bloom, the season of death can be determined.

Another interesting example of interpreting grave goods is the practice of placing food in graves. Archaeologists and ethnologists know from modern Native Americans that this practice was intended to help the deceased person reach her/his destination in the afterlife. Tobacco was used the same way.

STATUS

All societies have some sort of status hierarchy, based on any number of factors, including age, gender, skill, ascribed authority, or socioeconomic status. With status comes differential access to resources, including plant products. Such differences may be quite minor or they may be very significant. For example, in highly stratified societies (those with classes or castes), differential access to plant products may be pronounced, with the "upper" classes having exclusive access to certain species. Such patterns can be detected in the archaeological record but should be combined with other data to form a more convincing argument.

ETHNICITY

Cultures (or ethnic units) view the world differently than other cultures and will utilize resources, including plant products, in a distinctive way. For example, the floral remains from nineteenth century Anglo, Chinese, and Native American sites will be quite dissimilar, even if they are contemporary and in the same geographic area. Nevertheless, it is difficult to make these distinctions and to determine "ethnicity" on the basis of floral remains alone. Still, this is one goal of any archaeological analysis.

DATING

As they are organic, floral remains can be dated by the radiocarbon technique (see Chapter 13). If certain types of wood are recovered, it also is possible to use dendrochronology, commonly called tree-ring dating (see Chapter 13). This method originated in the Southwest where wood used in the construction of pueblos provided a basis of comparison.

SEASONALITY

A determination of the season of availability for some plants may help to infer the season of occupation of a site, thereby furnishing evidence of the overall settlement pattern of a culture and providing clues of other activities. The distribution of species may also be informative, as some plants were traded.

TECHNOLOGY

Floral remains can sometimes be used to infer some technologies. Some plants require specific technologies for procurement (e.g., pinyon hooks for pulling down pine cones) and processing (e.g., the tannic acid must be leached out of acorns and yucca must be baked). The presence of such plants can be used to infer certain activities and tools.

FLORAL REMAINS

TRADE

Virtually all procured plant materials were traded in prehistory. Perhaps the trade was a short-distance exchange between the producer (the gatherer) and the consumer (members of a family in the same camp). It may be that the trade was a long-distance event that involved special preparation of the plant (parching to preserve the seed, etc.). Indications of such trading activities would include the presence of certain plant species outside their natural range, evidence of specialized preparation or transport technology, and perhaps the depiction of "exotic" species in art (rock art or pottery).

DOMESTICATION

A number of domesticated plants were present in North America in aboriginal times. The majority of domesticated plants (corn, beans, squash) originated in Mesoamerica, but some were later modified by North American groups (e.g., Hopi corn). The presence of domesticated species may indicate farming and/or trade with farmers.

Domestication results in several patterns in a floral assemblage that can be detected. These patterns include: (1) the presence of imported ("exotic") plant species; (2) a reduction in the number of wild plant species exploited and an intensification of the domesticated species; and (3) size changes in seeds and other parts (corn cobs became larger over time).

REFERENCES

Bodner, Connie Cox, and Ralph M. Rowlett
    1980   Separation of Bone, Charcoal, and Seeds by Chemical Flotation. American Antiquity 45(1):110-116.

Clarke, J. G. D.
    1954   Excavations at Star Carr. Cambridge: Cambridge University Press.

Hillman, Gordon, Sue Wales, Francis McLaren, John Evans, and Ann Butler
    1993   Identifying Problematic Remains of Ancient Plant Foods: A Comparison of the Role of Chemical, Histological and Morphological Criteria. World Archaeology 25(1):94-121.

Miller, Naomi F.
    1988   Ratios in Paleoethnobotanical Analysis. In: Current Paleoethnobotany, Christine A. Hastorf and Virginia S. Popper, eds., pp. 72-85. Chicago: University of Chicago Press.

Miller, Naomi F., and Tristine Lee Smart
    1984   Intentional Burning of Dung as Fuel: A Mechanism for the Incorporation of Charred Seeds into the Archaeological Record. Journal of Ethnobiology 4(1):15-28.

Minnis, Paul E.
    1981   Seeds in Archaeological Sites: Sources and Some Interpretive Problems. American Antiquity 46(1):143-152.

Piperno, Doloris R.
    1988   Phytolith Analysis: An Archaeological and Geological Perspective.   San Diego: Academic Press.

Popper, Virginia S.
    1988   Selecting Quantitative Measures in Paleoethnobotany. In: Current Paleoethnobotany, Christine A. Hastorf and Virginia S. Popper, eds., pp. 53-71. Chicago: University of Chicago Press.

Reddy, Seetha N.
    1994   Plant Usage and Subsistence Modeling: An Ethnoarchaeological Approach to the Late Harappan of Northwest India. Ph.D. dissertation, University of Wisconsin, Madison.

Smart, Tristine Lee, and Ellen S. Hoffman
    1988   Environmental Interpretation of Archaeological Charcoal. In: Current Paleoethnobotany, Christine A. Hastorf and Virginia S. Popper, eds., pp. 167-205. Chicago: University of Chicago Press.

Toll, Mollie S.
    1988   Flotation Sampling: Problems and Some Solutions, with Examples from the American Southwest. In: Current Paleoethnobotany, Christine A. Hastorf and Virginia S. Popper, eds., pp. 36-52. Chicago: University of Chicago Press.

Trinkhaus, Eric
    1983   The Shanidar Neanderthals. New York: Academic Press.

GENERAL ETHNOBOTANY REFERENCES

Hastorf, Christine A., and Virginia S. Popper (eds.)
    1988   Current Paleoethnobotany. Chicago: University of Chicago Press.

Miksicek, Charles H.
    1987   Formation Processes of the Archaeobotanical Record. In: Advances in Archaeological Method and Theory, Vol. 10, Michael B. Schiffer, ed., pp. 211-247. New York: Academic Press.

Chapter 12

ANALYSIS OF HUMAN REMAINS

DEFINITION

Human remains are defined as the biological remains of humans, primarily bones, but including preserved tissues as well (e.g., mummies). Human remains provide an important source of information regarding a wide variety of anthropological questions, including diet and nutrition, social status, cultural practices, and paleodemography. In addition, the study of human remains has important medical and legal applications, including the understanding and tracking of disease through time, forensics (e.g., the identification of murder victims; Dailey 1983), understanding past population dynamics, and many others. It is important to study human remains from all groups at all time periods.

When talking about human remains, most archaeologists think first of burials and cremations. However, human remains may be discovered in a variety of geologic and archaeological contexts that do not necessarily reflect intentional interment of the dead. A good example of such a find is the "Iceman" recently discovered in the Alps in central Europe. That person died *in situ* and was not buried or otherwise disposed of by his cultural unit after his death. Some cultures (e.g., the Ashaninca of eastern Peru) dispose of their dead in rivers where the bodies wash downstream, decompose, and the bones ultimately are scattered and deposited in alluvium somewhere in the Amazon River system.

Inhumations are bodies that are interred (buried or entombed) unburned. A *primary inhumation* is a burial located in the place in which it was originally interred. A *secondary inhumation* is a burial that has been interred and left to decompose, then disinterred with the bones buried in another place, sometimes in groups (i.e., in a large pit or ceramic vessel, etc.). An intact secondary inhumation is usually easy to distinguish from a primary inhumation, as none of the bones should be articulated.

Cremations are bodies that have been burned. The efficiency of such burning is variable and there may be significant quantities of bone that remain. Like inhumations, a cremation may be primary (buried in the pit in which it was burned) or secondary (interred away from the cremation pit, as in western cultures).

Individuals may be interred (either as inhumations or cremations) singly (*isolated interments*) or in groups (*multiple interments*). Cemeteries usually consist of a number of individual and/or multiple interments within a specific area. Over time, interments may infringe upon one another, creating confusion regarding which remains and offerings belong to which body. With careful excavation and recordation, however, this problem can often be avoided.

Body orientation is another important factor in the analysis of cultural practices in the treatment of the dead. For example, if burials are habitually placed facing in a particular direction, some aspect of religious belief may be involved. There is a number of terms used to describe the position of the body itself. When the body is positioned with the knees drawn loosely toward the chest, it is called *flexed*.

Tightly flexed is when the knees are touching the chest with the arms folded close to the body. A *supine* position is on the back, with the face upward, and a *prone* position is lying flat on the stomach, or with the face down. There are combinations of these terms (e.g., prone and flexed) and there may be other terms applied for other positions.

Individuals may also be secondarily interred in common depositories called *ossuaries*. In such cases, the deceased would be placed in locations where the flesh would decompose, after which the bones would be reinterred in the ossuary. The catacombs in Paris and Rome, where the bones of untold thousands of individuals are interred, are two good examples of such a facility. One of the problems with ossuary remains is that the bones of specific individuals become mixed with those of others, reducing the value of the remains for anthropological study. In spite of these problems, considerable information regarding past populations can be gained by the study of ossuary remains (Ubelaker 1974).

LEGAL AND ETHICAL ISSUES IN THE ACQUISITION AND ANALYSIS OF HUMAN REMAINS

In addition to the archaeological and medical values of human remains are other values that limit or preclude their study. Such remains may represent the ancestors of people currently inhabiting an area and those people may object to the removal and study of their ancestors. In the United States, there are numerous laws regarding the removal of human remains. California, for example, requires a specific course of action (under Section 7050.5[b] of the Health and Safety Code) if human remains are discovered on private or state-owned lands. First, the work that resulted in the discovery (for example, an archaeological excavation) must cease and the county coroner must be notified immediately. The coroner then must notify the state Native American Heritage Commission who, in turn, designates a "most likely descendant" to deal with the matter. This person (or persons) then instructs the archaeologist as to what is acceptable treatment (ranging from closing the excavation, to removal and immediate reburial, to removal, study, and then reburial). Failure to comply with this law constitutes a felony. Many other states have recently developed similar laws (e.g., Oregon and Idaho).

In addition, the Federal Government operates under a variety of federal laws and regulations. Under the Native American Graves Protection and Repatriation Act (NAGPRA), the Federal Government requires an inventory of all Native American remains and sacred objects within federal depositories (plus all institutions that receive federal funds). If requested by local Native American representatives, those materials must be returned (repatriated).

One problem that archaeologists face is the vague legal definition (at least in California) of human remains. The law talks about "burials" and "associated" artifacts. Does this mean that isolated human teeth or other small bones are not covered under the law? What about human protein detected on an artifact? What about fossilized human remains that do not actually contain any biological constituents (fossils are actually stone casts of the original)? These issues have not been addressed legally.

CONSERVATION OF HUMAN REMAINS

Great care should be exercised when dealing with human remains in order not to damage or alter the bone, mix elements of one group with those of other groups, or misplace them. Of equal importance is the respectful treatment of the remains; they represent actual people and should be treated as such.

CLEANING

Human bone (or any bone) is fragile and should be cleaned only if necessary. The natural decomposition process results in the loss of bone strength and mass that may have been replaced by soil. The removal of that soil may weaken the bone such that it could break. Remove only the soil necessary to identify, measure (including weight), and examine the bone. Do not wash the bone if it can be avoided. Use only soft materials to clean the bone, such as soft brushes and wooden probes. Do not use trowels, dental picks, wire brushes, etc. These items may damage the bone and might even leave marks that someone could mistake for natural alterations or cut marks.

It may be that careful examination of the surface of the bone would require washing. If so, the following procedure should be employed (adapted from White 1991:280). Wash the material in lukewarm water without detergent. Wash over a screen so that small bones or fragments do not get lost. Use soft tools as described above. Check the sediment at the bottom of the screen and sink for small bones and fragments. Make sure to keep all the materials from the same individual (or analytical unit) together and properly labeled. Dry in a protected area for 24 to 48 hours, depending on the conditions. FRAGILE REMAINS SHOULD NOT BE WASHED!

LABELING

In many archaeological laboratories, it has been standard practice to write catalog numbers directly onto the bone surface using waterproof ink. In porous bone, a subcoating of preservative is applied, the number is then written on the bone, and a second layer of preservative is then placed over the number. The purpose of such a procedure is to insure that elements from different individuals are not mixed. While this is an excellent procedure to prevent mixing, it may well contaminate the bone (for dating, chemical analyses, etc.) and it may not be acceptable from the point of view of the descendants. Archaeologists must include humanistic values in the decision-making process. If numbering individual specimens is not acceptable, place the specimens in plastic bags and label the bags (as is done with other materials).

PRESERVATION AND RECONSTRUCTION

If bone is very fragile and weak, it is possible to reinforce it with the addition of a preservative (e.g., Glyptol or Duco diluted in acetone). However, this will contaminate the bone and make future chemical analyses or dating difficult, if not impossible. In addition, the use of preservatives may not be culturally acceptable. In general, chemical methods for preservation are not recommended.

Several fragments of bone may fit together, so it may be possible to reconstruct a larger fragment of an element, or even a complete one. To do this usually requires the use of a chemical mastic (with all the pitfalls for future analysis and dating) and should be done only if the reconstructed portion would be informative. For example, there is no need to glue together a femur broken into two pieces since the metric data from that element could be obtained without reconstructing the pieces. However, the reconstruction of a cranium could provide data not obtainable from the fragments alone.

Reconstruction is accomplished by first identifying those fragments that can be refitted with each other and then determining whether they should be glued. If gluing is necessary and permissible, glue is applied to the broken edges and the edges joined, after which the bone is allowed to dry in a sandbox where the sand supports the pieces without stress (make sure to use clean sand). Wooden toothpicks (or other similar devices) can be used for structural support and as bridging devices.

It may sometimes be necessary to make plaster or rubber casts of certain specimens. It is vital to ensure that reconstruction efforts do not alter the specimen such that casting would be impossible or inaccurate. Refer to White (1991:286) for instructions regarding molding and casting.

IDENTIFICATION

TERMINOLOGY

The terminology used in the identification and classification of human remains is fairly extensive (see White 1991:28-35; Buikstra and Ubelaker 1994:177-182) and is generally the same as that used in faunal analysis (see Chapter 10). The basic terms include the name of the bone (*element*), the side of the body (*left* or *right*; but some bones, such as vertebra, have no such orientation), which end of the bone (*proximal* or *distal*), the ends of the long bones (*epiphyses*), the joints (*articular surfaces*), and the minimum number of individuals (*MNI*) in the collection. The number of identified specimens (*NISP*) is used in faunal analysis (see Chapter 10) but is generally not used in reference to human materials.

Antemortem (or *premortem*) is the term used to refer to events or processes that occurred to an individuals body prior to death. For example, if a broken bone shows evidence of healing or infection (which can only occur during life), the fracture was antemortem. Changes to the skeleton that occurred after death are *postmortem*. *Perimortem* means that it is not clear whether the event took place before or after death. For example, if the skull is fractured, does not show healing, and is clearly not a recent break, then it is possible that the break occurred during life but the person died soon thereafter, perhaps as a result of the fracture.

BONE CLASSIFICATION

The Skull

The skull consists of some 29 bones (13 major bones; Fig. 91). The skull minus the mandible (lower jaw) comprises the *cranium* and the skull minus the facial bones comprises the *calvarium*. Skull bones are relatively thin, and often curved. They also contain several distinctive characteristics that make them relatively easy to identify, such as *sutures*, sinuses, *foramina*, passages, and dentition.

Dentition. Humans normally possess 32 teeth; 12 molars, 8 premolars, 4 canines, and 8 incisors, a dental formula of 2-1-2-3. Many people in the United States are having their third molars (the "wisdom teeth") removed due to overcrowding. As a result, the jaw is becoming shorter and our dental formula is in the process of changing to 2-1-2-2. Infants are generally born with no teeth but they erupt within their first few years. These teeth are *deciduous* (we call them "baby teeth") and are lost as they are pushed out by the eruption of the permanent teeth. The timing and sequence of tooth eruption is relatively well-known and can serve as an important method to determine age.

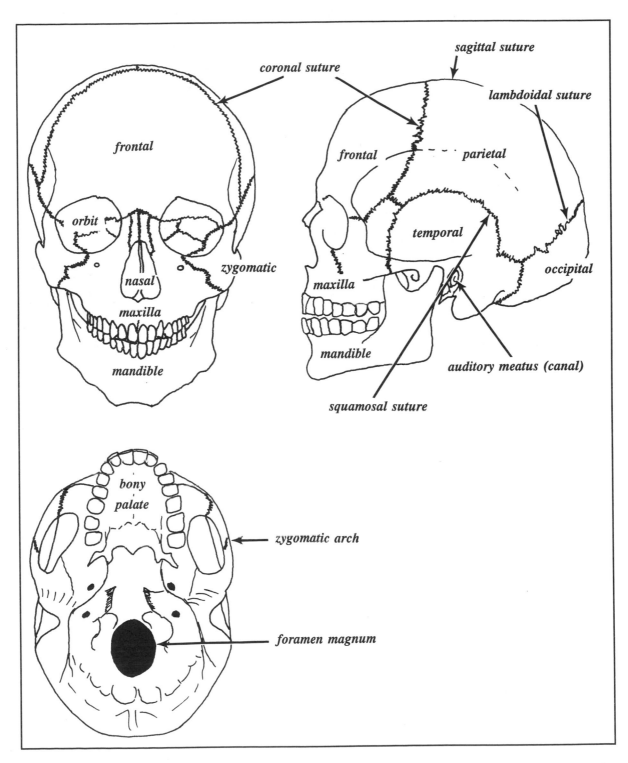

Fig. 91.   Front, side, and basal aspects of the human skull with major bones and features identified (after Bass 1987:Figs. 13 and 14; and Brothwell 1981:Fig. 2.2), no scale.

Deciduous teeth can be fairly easily distinguished from permanent teeth, since they are smaller, often lack roots (or, if roots are present, they are smaller), and have thinner enamel (and so may be more yellow in color) (see Bass 1987:263; White 1991:112). The presence of deciduous teeth is not necessarily indicative of an interment (since everyone loses a set during life) but the possibility cannot be excluded. Permanent teeth may be lost antemortem as a result of a pathology, but their presence in a collection should be a red flag for an interment.

Teeth wear down as they are used during life and patterns of wear can be informative as to diet, health, and age of a population. These aspects are discussed below under pathologies.

The Postcranial Skeleton

In an adult, the postcranial skeleton consists of 177 bones (see Fig. 92 for a listing of the major bones). Twenty-seven of these are single bones (e.g., the vertebral column and the sternum). The remainder (150) are paired bones (lefts and rights). In humans (after Bass 1987:7), the limb bones (often called *long bones*) are tubular in cross section and are relatively long (>20 cm.). *Short bones* are small (<10 cm.), tubular bones; these include the bones of the hands and feet, as well as the clavicles (collar bones). *Flat bones* include the pelvis, scapulae (shoulder blades), ribs, and sternum (breastbone). Such flat bones might be confused with cranial bones. *Irregular bones* (again, easy to confuse with some cranial bones) include the vertebrae, carpals (wrist bones), tarsals (ankle bones), and patellae (kneecaps).

INITIAL SORTING

The first step in the identification of bones is initial sorting into general categories (some bones will be very easy to identify and will not require a step-by-step process). First, separate the bones into cranial, postcranial, and unknown categories. Then separate the postcranial bones into: (1) large tubular bones; (2) small tubular bones; (3) flat bones; (4) irregular bones; and (5) unknown. Follow the labeling procedure discussed above.

Identify each element (either whole or fragmentary) by comparing them to actual (and identified) human materials. Many of the small fragments can be identified by careful comparison if there are articular surfaces present. Small rib fragments are often easy to identify, as are small cranial fragments. Absolute size of the bone could be misleading; remember that juvenile bones are smaller than adult bones (also check for epiphysial fusion to get a general idea of age, see below). Both Bass (1987) and White (1991) provide extensive discussions and descriptions (drawings and photographs) of human bone and their identification.

METHODS OF ANALYSIS

METRIC ANALYSIS

Metric analysis is literally the measurement of the various bones. Absolute measurements are useful for some purposes (e.g., estimation of stature), while indices (various combinations of absolute measurements) are used for other purposes. When measuring or handling bones, always use great care. Place the bones on soft surfaces, such as a bean bag, to avoid fractures or other damage. Styrofoam donut rings are effective for holding skulls.

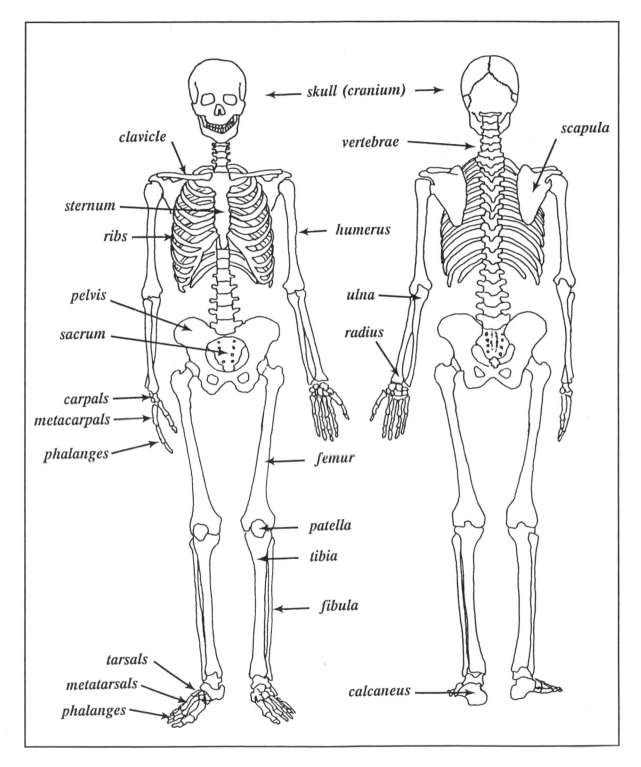

Fig. 92. Front and back views of the human skeleton with major bones identified.

A number of basic tools are used to take the measurements, always in the metric system (centimeters, millimeters). Both sliding (see Fig. 8) and bow calipers are important basic tools. In addition, an osteometric board is necessary to measure tubular bones. Other osteometric tools used for more specialized purposes include a coordinate caliper and a head spanner (see Bass 1987:11). Each measurement should be taken three times, with the results being averaged.

A large number of potential measurements can be made on the skeleton and, as noted above, many of these measurements can be combined to produce indices which themselves serve to describe the bones. Below are presented some of the very basic skeletal measurements; the interested reader should refer to more technical treatments of anthropometric methods to conduct any detailed analyses.

Only complete portions of the bone should be measured. If the bone is broken, but all the pieces are present, it may require reconstruction prior to measurement. If the broken bone can be temporarily reassembled (e.g., just by holding it with your hands) and measured, or if the pieces can be measured and the measurements combined (but be careful to get accurate measurements), this would be preferable to gluing the bone together.

Measurement of the Skull

The basic measurements of the skull are shown in Figure 93 (also see Bass [1987:62-92], Brothwell [1981:79-84], and Buikstra and Ubelaker [1994] for more detailed treatments). These should be taken with a bow caliper, pushing the caliper back and forth across the area being measured until the maximum reading is attained. Keep track of the measurements and which specimen is being measured.

Some indices are useful in describing the skull (and ultimately of populations). For example, the Cranial Index (CI; in living people it is called the Cephalic Index) is a measure of the shape of the skull and is calculated as:

$$\text{Cranial Index} = \frac{\text{maximum cranial breadth X 100}}{\text{maximum cranial length}}$$

An average skull (mesocrany, or mesocephalic) has a CI of about 75 to 80, meaning that the skull is longer than it is wide. A CI of under 75 is classified as long-headed (dolichocrany) and a score over 80 is classified as broad- or round-headed (brachycrany) (see Bass 1987:69). A complete discussion of the various measurements of the skull was provided by Bass (1987:62-92).

Measurement of the Postcranial Skeleton

Like the skull, a large number of measurements can be made and indices computed on the postcranial skeleton. One should consult Brothwell (1981), Bass (1987), White (1991), and Buikstra and Ubelaker (1994) for more detailed discussions and instructions on these measurements. In any initial analysis, a number of basic measurements should be taken. These include: the maximum length of the bone (usually a tubular bone) using an osteometric board; the diameter of the midpoint of the tubular bone (this is determined by measuring the length of the bone using a bow or sliding caliper); and the maximum width of the ends of the bones (again using a bow or sliding caliper) (see Fig. 94). Make sure to accurately record the measurements.

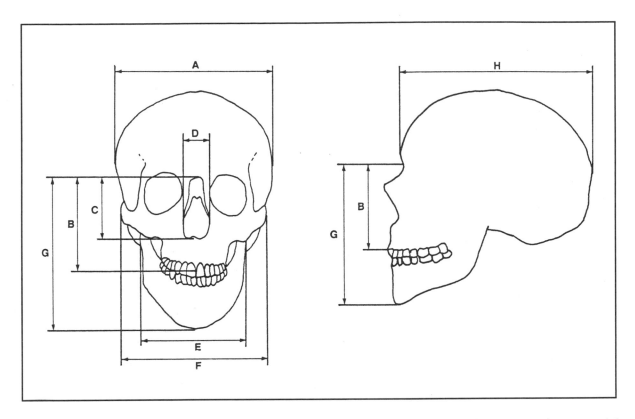

Fig. 93.   Basic measurements of the skull (adapted from Bass 1987:Figs 38 and 39): (a) maximum cranial breadth; (b) upper facial height; (c) nasal height; (d) nasal breadth; (e) bicondylar breadth; (f) facial width; (g) total facial height; (h) maximum cranial length.

OTHER ANALYSES

A variety of other techniques may be employed in the analysis of human remains. One of the more useful is radiography (X-rays). Radiographs can show features not visible to the naked eye, such as some healed traumas, bone density (as related to osteoporosis), and unerupted teeth not otherwise visible in the jaws. Since there is no danger of overexposure to the bone, multiple radiographs may be taken.

An examination of bone through a microscope may reveal important information. Such a technique would be used to investigate surface alterations and to distinguish natural from human-caused marks. Microscopic examination also may be useful in the identification of disease, other pathologies, and age (e.g., osteon densities, see Buikstra and Ubelaker 1994:165).

The analysis of the chemistry of the bone may reveal a variety of data. For example, isotope ratios can reveal the kinds of foods that made up the primary diet of an individual, an aid in determining whether that individual was an agriculturalist or a hunter/gatherer (through the analysis of carbon isotopes). Price (1989) provided a comprehensive discussion of some of the potentials for the chemical analysis of human bone (also see Klepinger 1994; Pate 1994).

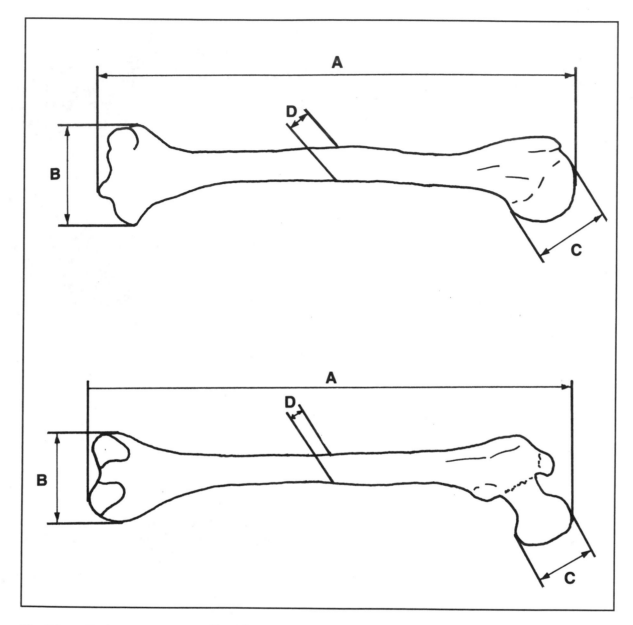

Fig. 94.   Basic measurements of long bones (upper is a humerus, lower is a femur [not to scale]; adapted from Bass 1987:Figs 90 and 142): (a) length; (b) width of distal end; (c) diameter of proximal end; (d) midshaft diameter.

The study of the DNA in human bones is just beginning and will undoubtedly prove to be an invaluable aid in answering a number of questions. These include racial and/or ethnic affiliation, reconstruction of kinship patterns, sex, and medical status. This avenue of research will expand greatly in the near future.

NONMETRIC VARIATIONS

Nonmetric variations are those that cannot be discovered by the metric measurements of the bones. These include variations in the number of teeth (e.g., extra molars), crowding or impaction of teeth (that may result in a pathology, see below), the natural variation in the shape of the bones (they are never *exactly* alike), variation in the number and placement of various foramina (nerve and blood vessel holes in the bone), degree of ossification, variation in the interior structure of the bone, presence or absence of some features, etc.; the list can be very long. Many nonmetric traits may be related to environmental influences or to circumstances relating to the life of the specific individual (e.g., very robust muscle attachments in the bones of a weightlifter, certain changes in the leg bones of someone who sat cross-legged for long periods).

ESTIMATIONS OF AGE, SEX, STATURE, AND RACE

Age

Ages of humans may be grossly divided into four categories: *infant* (up to 2 years); *juvenile* (2 to 10 years); *subadult* (10 to 21 years); and *adult* (21 and older). Often, age classification for an individual is limited to one of these broad categories; the precise age being indeterminate due to the variation of indicators by sex and population. A variety of methods to estimate age in an individual (chronological age at death, not time elapsed since death) is used. Three common methods are discussed below (see White [1991:308-320] and Buikstra and Ubelaker [1994:21-38] for more detailed discussions). It is best to use several techniques together to gain more accuracy.

The first method of age estimation is the analysis of the closure of the epiphyses; the fusing of the ends with the shaft of a long bone (although several of the pelvic bones also may be used). This is measured as being unfused, 1/4 fused, 1/2 fused, 3/4 fused, and fully fused (see White 1991:313). Unfused epiphyses undoubtedly indicate an infant or early juvenile, while fully fused bones likely are those of adults.

The second method of analysis is the closure of cranial sutures. This method of aging skeletons was once commonly used, fell into disfavor (Brothwell 1981), and has since been resurrected (Meindl and Lovejoy 1985; also see White 1991:313). Suture closure and obliteration schedules seem to vary considerably with race and sex (Rogers 1984) and largely have been unreliable as an accurate age indicator. However, if suture obliteration is evident, it is probably indicative of a mature adult. For example, Rogers (1984:Table IV) showed lambdoidal suture closure taking place between ages 26 and 40. This method should be used only as a very general estimate of age.

The third common method of age estimation is the analysis of dental eruption. Different deciduous teeth erupt at different ages, generally between one and three. These teeth are replaced by permanent teeth between about five and 12 years of age. The sequence and timing of tooth eruption and replacement are reasonably well-known and can help (coupled with other indicators) to estimate age of juveniles and subadults.

ANALYSIS OF HUMAN REMAINS

Although tooth wear has been utilized as a method of determining age, it is dependent on many variables, age being only one. Thus, while it is fair to suggest that a significantly worn tooth belongs to an adult, aging skeletons based solely on tooth wear is not advisable. However, when dealing with a large group of individuals from a fairly homogeneous population (sharing the same general rate of tooth wear), relative tooth wear (hopefully coupled with other aging data) could serve as an indicator of age. Osteon (bone cell) densities may also be a useful indicator of age.

Sex

Many animals display *sexual dimorphism* (physical differences between males and females) in size and shape of skeletal materials. While this also is true of humans, sexual differences in size and shape are less significant, and show more (and considerable) overlap, than in some other primates. Nevertheless, skeletal differences between the sexes do exist. Sexual dimorphism in humans is most observable in adults; younger individuals are not developed to the degree necessary for identification. In general, the skeletal elements of females are smaller and less robust than those of males. Along with the skeletal differences, associated artifacts may be useful in determining sex.

A few very basic techniques may be used to estimate sex from an examination of the pelvis. Three of the simplest methods (see Fig. 95) are: (1) the size of the "passage" through the complete pelvis (including the sacrum); (2) the width of the sciatic notch; and (3) the measurement of the subpubic angle. These techniques are just general estimates and are not the best indicators; however, they are easy to do in the laboratory. Perhaps the best way to sex a specimen is the examination of the pubis for evidence of such characteristics such as a ventral arc and dorsal pits (not a simple technique, see Fig. 95 for location). For more detail on sexing techniques, refer to the discussion of sexing in Bass (1987:200-206), White (1991:320-327), and/or Buikstra and Ubelaker (1994:16-21). In any such analysis, the more concordant techniques employed, the better.

Stature

Stature (height) is estimated by the measurements of long bones applied to a formula or table. Unfortunately, populations vary widely and there is no single, valid measure. Stature tables for American whites (male and female), American blacks (male and female), and Mesoamericans (males and females) are provided in Bass (1987:22-29).

Race

Based on current knowledge, race can only be estimated from the skull; the rest of the skeleton shows no (demonstrable) differences (Bass 1987:83). In general, skulls of Caucasoids, Negroids, and Mongoloids (including American Indians) exhibit a number of characteristics that can be used to distinguish between these three groups (see Bass 1987:83-92). One of the initial indicators (but not conclusive) of Mongoloids (including American Indians) is the presence of *shovel-shaped incisors*, a depression present in the lingual (the side closest to the tongue) aspect of the maxillary (upper jaw) incisors (front teeth). In historical archaeology, such distinctions are critical since cemeteries may contain individuals of diverse ancestry (Europeans, Africans, Chinese, etc.). In addition to the cranial characteristics, associated artifacts may be useful in determining race and/or ethnicity.

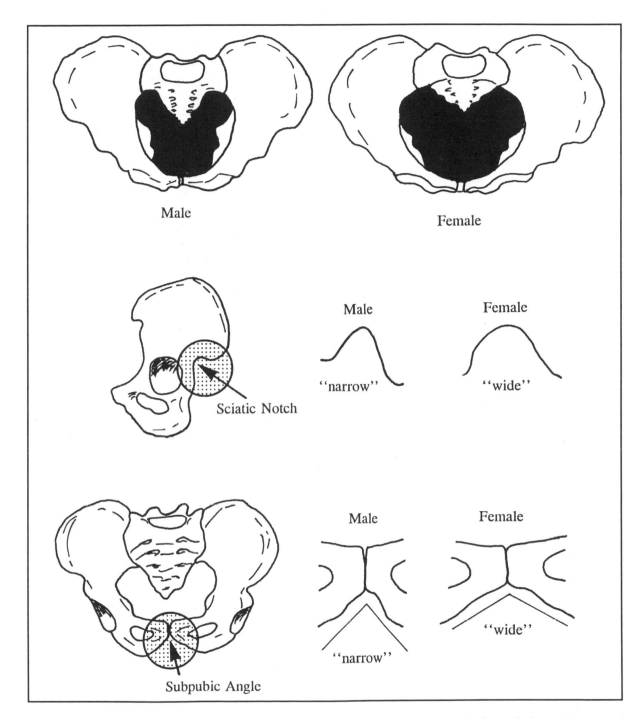

Fig. 95.   Three methods for sexing a pelvis. Upper: the size of the ''passage'' through the pelvis (viewed from above), note that the passage size of the female pelvis is much larger (e.g., the shaded area) to accommodate birth. Middle: the width of the sciatic notch, note that the female notch is wider. Lower: the measurement of the subpubic angle, note that the female angle is wider. Adapted from Bass (1987:Figs. 120, 131, 134, 135, and 136) (no scale).

PATHOLOGIES

Pathologies in skeletal remains are the result of disease, degeneration, and trauma visible in the skeleton. The most common skeletal pathologies are related to degeneration, with trauma being the second most common form (White 1991:335). The most common categories of pathologies are noted below, but no detailed discussion is included as the subject matter is too extensive and specialized. An excellent and comprehensive review of human skeletal pathologies was presented by Ortner and Putschar (1981; also see White 1991; Buikstra and Ubelaker 1994:107-158).

Degeneration

Changes to bone occur as an individual ages. Perhaps the most common affliction is osteoporosis, a condition of bone loss (deossification) caused by a number of disorders. This condition affects both men and women, but affects women earlier in life. This results in a variety of problems, including frequent fractures that are difficult to heal.

Arthritis, the inflammation of the joints, is another condition associated with aging, but it is not limited to the aged. Osteoarthritis is the destruction of the cartilage in a joint and by the formation of adjacent bone. The visible pathologies are often manifested as polished bone surfaces (from direct bone-on-bone wear), the formation of bone along the edges of the joint (lipping), and/or bone spurs (exostosis) in and around the joint. This disorder is commonly visible in vertebrae.

Trauma

Trauma may be defined as a disruption to the bone (White 1991:335), and includes fractures (including violent weapons damage; e.g., arrow perforations), *trephination* (cutting holes into a living skull), amputation, and artificial skull deformation. Trauma may result in the death of the individual, or the person may survive the event. If they survive, there will be evidence of bone regeneration (healing), possible infection, and perhaps other related pathologies.

People have intentionally altered (traumatized) bones for a variety of reasons. Artificial skull deformation was practiced by a number of cultures (and still is by some cultures). An excellent example is the Maya, who wrapped the cranium of young noble people so that the skull would grow into a particular shape (see Fig. 96a) that was considered aesthetically pleasing. Another form of artificial skull deformation results from a child being strapped to a cradleboard for its first few years. This results in the flattening of the occipital bone (Fig. 96b), a characteristic feature carried throughout life (see discussion in Buikstra and Ubelaker 1994:160-163).

Trephination is the surgical cutting of holes into the cranial vault (Fig. 96c) and is known worldwide. The purpose of such a procedure is varied and includes medical treatment of chronic headaches, magic, and prestige. Survivors of the procedure would show healing around the wound, perhaps even complete closure of the hole. Trephination has not been documented in North America (see discussions in Ortner and Putschar [1981:95-100] and Buikstra and Ubelaker [1994:159-160]).

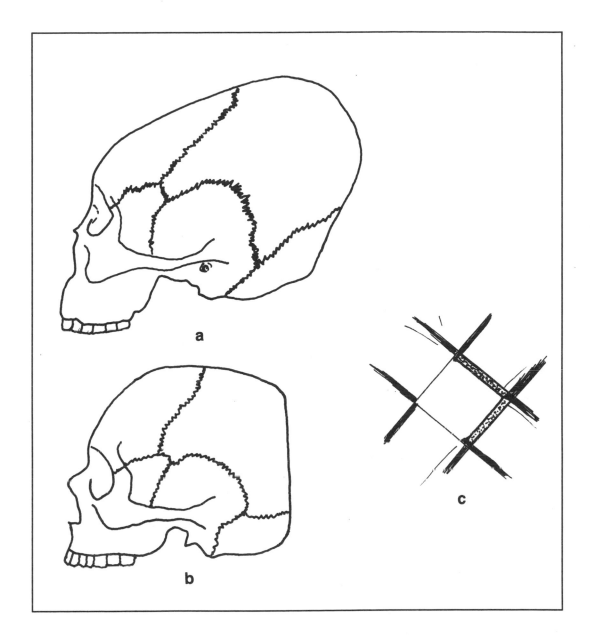

Fig. 96.   Examples of skull alterations: (a) artificial deformation (e.g., Mayan, note the flattening of the forehead and the elongation of the skull); (b) occipital flattening (slightly exaggerated) from the use of a cradleboard; and (c) an unhealed trephination hole (no scale).

Bone alteration has not been limited to the skull.   For example, the Chinese practiced the purposeful deformation of the feet of some young females (foot-binding), which resulted in the malformation of the foot bones (see Ortner and Putschar 1981:Fig. 105). This practice was intended to enhance prestige (women unable to work due to their status) and resulted in the limiting of mobility.

Infectious Disease and Nutrition

Poor health may manifest itself in the skeleton, either visibly or chemically. A variety of conditions results in alterations of the bones, including disease and nutritional deficiencies. Lesions or growths on bone can result from a number of conditions, including tuberculosis, tumors, or infections. Nutritional deficiencies may result in skeletal abnormalities. For example, scurvy (Vitamin C deficiency) results in bone thinning and pathological fractures in fast-growing portions of bones (e.g., ends of long bones, most notable in children). Rickets (Vitamin D deficiency) results in bent and distorted (e.g., bowed) limbs.

Stress (e.g., times of poor diet or disease) may also manifest itself in the bone. During times of stress to an individual, normal bone growth may be interrupted, resulting in layers of denser bone, called *Harris lines*. Harris lines may be visible by radiograph (a medical X-ray) or in cross section. Their presence can be used to estimate the age at which the individual was stressed.

Other

A variety of other skeletal pathologies is known, but these are uncommon. They include malformation of entire skeletons due to genetic error (e.g., a two-headed baby), and abnormal endocrine secretions (e.g., from the pituitary and thyroid glands) resulting in gross abnormalities in the skeleton, such as gigantism or dwarfism.

Dental Pathologies

Dental pathologies (see Buikstra and Ubelaker 1994:47-68) take several forms, most notably tooth wear, caries (cavities), and periodontal disease, but may include the purposeful modification (engraving, coloring, or removal) of teeth for cosmetic reasons. Tooth wear occurs throughout life as the teeth grind the various foods consumed. If that food contains grit (perhaps as a result of grinding the foods on stone milling tools), considerable tooth wear will rapidly occur.

Caries (what we commonly call cavities) are the result of the decalcification of tooth enamel and/or dentin as a result of bacterial action on the teeth. Left unchecked, caries can evolve into abscesses, resulting in tooth loss, bone loss, general infection, and even death. Many caries and abscesses are easily visible in dentition, and evidence of healing (e.g., bone resorption) may be present. Periodontal disease is the infection of the tissues surrounding a tooth. If untreated, this can result in the loss of gum tissue, bone resorption, and ultimately the tooth. Further infection (e.g., an abscess) also is possible as a result of periodontal disease.

Teeth as Tools. Humans have used their teeth as tools, resulting in their modification (see Molnar 1972). Larsen (1985) identified a pattern of dental modification as related to tool use in a series of 171 skeletons from the western Great Basin. Sixteen of the 1,931 teeth examined exhibited narrow, transverse grooves on the midocclusal surfaces of anterior teeth (Larsen 1985:393). All of the examples belonged to five older adult males and were related to the use of the teeth as part of the production of other cultural items (e.g., grasping cordage with the teeth). Other such grooves are known interproximally (between the teeth). Other examples have been documented in California (Schulz 1977; Sutton 1988).

CREMATIONS

Most human remains from archaeological contexts are unburned bones from inhumations. However, bone often survives the process of cremation and can be analyzed. Such bone often is highly fragmented, calcined (very badly burned), and distorted, and the teeth tend to explode, making it difficult to identify parts as specific elements, to discover pathologies, or to obtain complete metric and/or nonmetric data. Additionally, aboriginal cremation practices often included procedures (e.g., the stirring of the fire) which resulted in the further fragmentation and scattering of the bone.

On the positive side, burned or calcined bone resists weathering and will remain preserved longer than unburned bone. Also, some artifacts (or portions thereof) might be preserved in cremations that would not usually be present in inhumations (such as basketry). The usual presence of large quantities of charcoal in cremations makes radiocarbon dating of the features easier, without having to date the remains themselves.

A number of studies have dealt specifically with cremations, although few have been conducted on remains from North American sites. Only within the last thirty years have anthropologists anywhere considered cremated human remains to be of enough scientific value to merit their collection and evaluation (Gejvall 1969). Many of these analyses, as well as discussions related to the study of cremated bone, have taken place in Europe (Wells 1960; Brothwell 1981), but several important contributions have been made by Americans (Merbs 1967).

POSTMORTEM ALTERATION

Bone is modified by the body in various ways while an individual is living (antemortem), through genetic control, pathologies, and stress (e.g., robust muscle attachments in an individual who was used to heavy work). Postmortem (after death) modifications also occur. Many of these modifications will occur as natural processes (e.g., decomposition of the tissues, soil conditions, roots, animal gnawing, etc.). Understanding these taphonomic processes is important for the interpretation of the remains.

Cultural postmortem modifications (those changes caused by other humans) also may occur and manifest themselves on the skeleton. A dramatic example of such modification is cremation, which has profound effects on the condition of the bone (natural fires can burn bone but not to the extent that purposeful cremation will). A number of other cultural modifications may also be present. For example, cut marks on a skull (not to be confused with root marks) may indicate scalping. Cannibalism may be indicated by other types of cut marks and/or smashed long bones (to extract marrow) (see White 1991:393-406).

INTERPRETIVE APPROACHES

The general study of diet, nutrition, health, demography, etc., in and between populations, both synchronically (at one time) or diachronically (over time), requires the accumulation and analysis of numerous skeletal samples, so that averages and trends become apparent. The more (and better) data obtained, the more that can be accomplished. This is not to say that an individual skeleton cannot be interesting or informative.

ANALYSIS OF HUMAN REMAINS

Archaeologists have traditionally relied on ecofactual data to demonstrate diet and on some skeletal pathologies to discuss nutrition (actually the effects of malnutrition). It has only been with the fairly recent development of sophisticated chemical analyses that archaeologists have become aware of the vast potential that human bone holds for the delineation of prehistoric human diet, health, biology, and economy.

DIET AND NUTRITION

Larsen (1987; also see Huss-Ashmore et al. 1982) provided a review of the use of skeletal data in prehistoric contexts. Larsen (1987) discussed growth and development (growth rates, stature, dentition, sexual dimorphism, etc.) of the skeleton as it may reflect diet and nutrition (aspects of an economy). Many of the methods involved the measurement of pathological conditions (as were discussed above) and how they might relate to diet and nutrition. Some of the more interesting aspects of these analyses are those of the differences between hunter-gatherers and agriculturalists. Among other things, these involve differential nutrition as a partial measure of the subsistence economy, and pathologies as related to nutritional stress. For example, Larsen (1983) suggested that the increase in dental pathologies in a prehistoric population on the Georgia coast was the result of the shift to agriculture (and so to foods that result in more caries). Walker and Erlandson (1986) saw a decrease in dental pathologies in a coastal California population and suggested that this reflected a shift from plant foods to fish.

The recent use of stable carbon isotope data (see Chisholm 1989) to infer the contribution of different food groups (e.g., marine foods versus agricultural plants) to the diet is of great interest to many archaeologists. Some plants utilize a photosynthesis chemistry wherein they will contain more of the isotope C_4 than C_3 and vice versa. As animals (including people) eat those plants, the chemistry of their tissue will reflect their diet. For example, corn is a C_4 plant, thus human bone with a high content of C_4 likely came from a person who ate corn (e.g., an agriculturalist). A person with a greater C_3 content probably subsisted more on wild resources. Such measures can be of immense value when attempting to delineate the role of domesticated plants in the diet, such as researching the role of agriculture in the Anasazi diet. Similar efforts have been made in the analysis of trace elements (see Armelagos et al. 1989; Buikstra et al. 1989; Price 1989).

HEALTH

The same basic methods used in the study of diet and nutrition in skeletal remains are used in the study of health. Bone condition and pathologies can communicate a detailed portrait of the health of an individual. Coupled with data from other individuals, a picture of the health of a population will emerge.

DEMOGRAPHY

Paleodemography, the study of the numbers and distribution of people in ancient populations, has been attempted from human remains. Such studies include efforts to determine life span, gender ratios, and population stress (e.g., from disease). One such study comparing a Native American population with that of ancient Egypt and Bronze Age Austria showed that there was greater infant mortality in the Native American population. However, once past infancy, that same Native American group had a much greater chance of surviving to a much greater age than the other two. Interestingly, all three groups had a peak death age between 25 and 35 years old.

Skeletal remains can be used to determine age at time of death and sex, data critical to demographic analysis. However, this is somewhat limited; for example, sex may be determined by the sciatic notch in the pelvis. This marker does not appear until puberty; therefore, in the skeletal remains of children, sex cannot be determined (DNA analysis holds some promise in this area). A physical anthropologist can, however, determine the approximate age of a child by observing the stage of dental eruption (discussed above).

SOCIAL INFERENCES

Social status can sometimes be inferred by the actual size of individuals. One anthropologist made a case (rightly or not) that in a society in which taller males were found in richer tomb burials than males found in ordinary burials, that the taller males had much more substantial and protein-rich diets than the shorter males.

In some human remains, cultural practices such as cranial deformations address what some believe to be a culture's concept of beauty or aesthetics. For example, as noted earlier, the Maya shaped the skull, evidently in infancy, so that it elongated or eliminated the forehead and put a bump on the top of the head. The custom of foot-binding infant females in ancient China (as noted earlier) is another example of a cultural practice that deformed bones.

MISUSE OF HUMAN DATA

People vary widely in physical appearance but are remarkably similar genetically. Physical variation is sometimes quite obvious (e.g., the stature of the Inuit of Alaska compared to that of the San of South Africa) and reflects environmental conditions (in this example, temperature). Cranial capacity (supposedly reflecting brain size) also varies; "normal" ranges between about 900 and 1,600 cc. (cubic centimeters), and while it is true that males tend to have larger brains than females (although there is considerable overlap), we all know that "bigger is not necessarily better."

Many attempts have been made to equate brain size with intelligence and to tie those figures to sex and ethnic (or racial) divisions. Traditionally, white males have conducted such studies, with the result that they have always rated higher than other groups. There is no real evidence that there are differences in intelligence based on sex or race, but such attempts continue. An excellent review of the misuse of human metric data was presented by Gould (1981).

REFERENCES

Armelagos, George J., Barrett Brenton, Michael Alcorn, Debra Martin, and Dennis P. Vangerven
    1989   Factors Affecting Elemental and Isotopic Variation in Prehistoric Human Skeletons. In: The Chemistry of Prehistoric Human Bone, T. Douglas Price, ed., pp. 230-244. Cambridge: Cambridge University Press.

Bass, William M.
    1987   Human Osteology: A Laboratory and Field Manual (third edition). Missouri Archaeological Society Special Publication No. 2.

ANALYSIS OF HUMAN REMAINS

Brothwell, D. R.
1981   Digging Up Bones (third edition). Oxford: Oxford University Press.

Buikstra, Jane E., and Douglas H. Ubelaker (eds.)
1994   Standards for Data Collection from Human Skeletal Materials. Arkansas Archaeological Survey Research Series No. 44.

Buikstra, Jane E., Susan Frankenberg, Joseph B. Lambert, and Liang Xue
1989   Multiple Elements: Multiple Expectations. In: The Chemistry of Prehistoric Human Bone, T. Douglas Price, ed., pp. 155-210. Cambridge: Cambridge University Press.

Chisholm, Brian S.
1989   Variation in Diet Reconstructions Based on Stable Carbon Isotope Evidence. In: The Chemistry of Prehistoric Human Bone, T. Douglas Price, ed., pp. 10-37. Cambridge: Cambridge University Press.

Dailey, R. C.
1983   Osteology for the Investigator. In: Handbook of Forensic Archaeology and Anthropology, D. Morse, J. Duncan, and J. Stoutamire, eds., pp. 76-85. Tallahassee: Florida State University Foundation, Inc.

Gejvall, N.
1969   Cremations. In: Science in Archaeology, Don Brothwell and E. Higgs, eds., pp. 468-479. New York: Basic Books.

Gould, Stephen Jay
1981   The Mismeasure of Man. New York: W. W. Norton & Company.

Huss-Ashmore, Rebecca, Alan Goodman, and George J. Armelagos
1982   Nutritional Inference from Paleopathology. In: Advances in Archaeological Method and Theory, Vol. 5, Michael B. Schiffer, ed., pp. 395-474. New York: Academic Press.

Klepinger, Linda L.
1994   Can Elemental Analysis of Archaeological Skeletons Determine Past Diet and Health? In: Ancient Technologies and Archaeological Materials, Sarah U. Wisseman, ed., pp. 87-97. Amsterdam: Gordon and Breach.

Larsen, Clark Spenser
1983   Behavioral Implications of Temporal Changes in Cariogenesis. Journal of Archaeological Science 10:1-8.

1985   Dental Modifications and Tool Use in the Western Great Basin. American Journal of Physical Anthropology 67:393-402.

1987   Bioarchaeological Interpretations of Subsistence Economy and Behavior from Human Skeletal Remains. In: Advances in Archaeological Method and Theory, Vol. 10, Michael B. Schiffer, ed., pp. 339-445. New York: Academic Press.

Merbs, C. F.
1967   Cremated Human Remains from Point of Pines, Arizona: A New Approach. American Antiquity 32(4):498-506.

Meindl, Richard S., and C. Owen Lovejoy
1985   Ectocranial Suture Closure: A Revised Method for the Determination of Skeletal Age at Death Based on the Lateral-anterior Sutures. American Journal of Physical Anthropology 68(1):57-66.

Molnar, S.
1972   Tooth Wear and Culture: A Survey of Tooth Function Among Some Prehistoric Populations. Current Anthropology 13:511-526.

Ortner, Donald J., and Walter G. J. Putschar
1981   Identification of Pathological Conditions In Human Skeletal Remains. Smithsonian Contributions to Anthropology No. 28.

Pate, F. Donald
1994   Bone Chemistry and Paleodiet. Journal of Archaeological Method and Theory 1(2):161-207.

Price, T. Douglas
1989   Multi-Element Studies of Diagenesis in Prehistoric Bone. In: The Chemistry of Prehistoric Human Bone, T. Douglas Price, ed., pp. 126-154. Cambridge: Cambridge University Press.

Rogers, S. L.
1984   The Human Skull: Its Mechanics, Measurements, and Variations. Springfield: Charles C. Thomas.

Schulz, Peter D.
1977   Task Activity and Anterior Tooth Grooving in Prehistoric California Indians. American Journal of Physical Anthropology 46:87-91.

Sutton, Mark Q.
1988   Dental Modification in a Burial from the Southern San Joaquin Valley, California. In: Human Skeletal Biology: Contributions to the Understanding of California's Prehistoric Populations, Gary D. Richards, ed., pp. 91-96. Coyote Press Archives of California Prehistory No. 24.

ANALYSIS OF HUMAN REMAINS

Ubelaker, Douglas H.
    1974   Reconstruction of Demographic Profiles from Ossuary Skeletal Samples: A Case Study from the Tidewater Potomac. Smithsonian Contributions to Anthropology No. 18.

Walker, Phillip L., and Jon M. Erlandson
    1986   Dental Evidence for Prehistoric Dietary Change on the Northern Channel Islands, California. American Antiquity 51(2):375-383.

Wells, C.
    1960   A Study of Cremations. Antiquity 34:29-37.

White, Tim D.
    1991   Human Osteology. San Diego: Academic Press.

Chapter 13

ARCHAEOMETRY AND SPECIAL ANALYSES

DEFINITION

Archaeometry (or Archaeological Science) is a large field of work that entails the physical and/or chemical analyses ("measurement") of archaeological substances, their constituents, age, residues, etc. In addition, there are other distinctive studies on archaeological materials that are undertaken by archaeologists and other specialists. The basics for some of these techniques are described below.

ARCHAEOMETRY

DATING

Dating is one of the most important aspects of archaeological analysis. Archaeologists cannot do much interpretation or grand synthesis of the history or prehistory of an area unless we can control time. There are three major divisions of dating: *relative*, *chronometric (or absolute)*, and *experimental*. It is important to remember that even though objects and events can sometimes be dated, this does not automatically mean that the interpretations given to those objects or events are correct. Interpretation relies greatly on common sense, logic, and an understanding of what dating methods (including their assumptions) are really all about.

Relative Dating

Relative dating can only indicate if something is older or younger than something else, not its actual age. Nonetheless, relative dating techniques can be extremely useful and was the only dating system available to archaeologists for many years. Four of the most commonly used relative dating techniques are briefly discussed below.

Superposition. The most common method of relative dating used in the field is *superposition*. The Law of Superposition states that something located above something else is younger, since the lower item had to have existed first for the upper one to have been deposited upon it. For example, if you have a stack of dinner plates, the top one is the last one placed on the stack (the youngest). One plate cannot be inserted into the center of the stack without great difficulty (and danger to the plates). Applying the Law of Superposition, archaeologists generally assume that what is above is younger than what is below.

There are exceptions to this general rule. Disturbance is a factor that must always be considered when dealing with superposition. Rodents sometimes wreak havoc on sites, moving material up and down through the deposit. If this is the case, superposition of small objects (artifacts and ecofacts) may not correspond to relative age. Human and natural disturbance can also affect superposition (e.g., burial pits or trash pits excavated into lower strata, wind and water erosion). Sometimes geological activity will reverse strata, but this is uncommon in most sites (very old sites in Africa have these problems) and such an occurrence is fairly easy to recognize.

SPECIAL ANALYSES

Cross-Dating. *Cross-dating* is using what is known about one site (or location) to date another site. If we know that squares are always younger than triangles and that triangles are younger than circles, we can deduce the relative age of an isolated triangle (found at another site) by comparing it with the known sequence from the other site(s). This obviously entails some assumptions, e.g., that the ages of triangles and squares are always different, and that our original superposition information was correct.

Fluorine. *Fluorine* dating measures differences in the fluorine content of materials. Fluorine is a substance that is present in groundwater, but in differing quantities depending upon the location. Bone absorbs fluorine and the quantity of fluorine in a bone can be measured. If two bones are deposited in the same place at the same time, their fluorine content should be the same (or nearly so). If Bone A has less fluorine than Bone B, an archaeologist would assume that the difference means that Bone A had been in the ground (i.e., exposed to the fluorine in the groundwater) for a shorter period of time than Bone B, and is therefore younger. No measurement of actual time is involved, only that A is younger than B. Because fluorine concentrations differ from place to place (and the process of absorption is also affected by other factors, like temperature), fluorine dating is only useful within limited contexts. A good example of the usefulness of fluorine dating is related to the exposure of the Piltdown fraud (see Feder [1990:40-56] for a discussion of the Piltdown hoax).

Seriation. *Seriation* is a technique used to place sites in time relative to each other. With this technique, the idea of popularity is used; that a new item (or style) will begin to be used, will gain in popularity, peak, decline in popularity, and eventually disappear. The resulting distributional curve over time will resemble the plan view of a ship, commonly called a "battleship curve" (a bar graph can also be used). To use this technique, one must plot the distributions (in percentage) of at least several related constituents over space (sites) and time. As the popularity of pottery style "A" increases, the popularity of style "B" decreases (one cannot increase in percentage without a decrease in the other, there can only be 100% in the total). Once these relative frequencies are known, newly considered sites can be placed in time relative to the others (see Table 15, Fig. 97).

Chronometric (Absolute) Dating

A chronometric date is a measurement of age in actual years (often with an error factor attached), rather than an assessment of whether something is older or younger than something else. There are numerous techniques that are used, each with different advantages and disadvantages. The two chronometric techniques most often used by archaeologists are dendrochronology and radiocarbon. Other techniques include archaeomagnetism, thermoluminescence (see below), fission track, paleomagnetism, and potassium-argon dating (see Michels 1973).

Dendrochronology. *Dendrochronology* (tree ring dating), is the only method yet developed that can be truly absolute. It can result in a date accurate to the exact year, perhaps even the season. The growth ring patterns (ring width varies with climatic conditions) of woody plant remains from an archaeological site can be matched with an existing ring sequence (a skeleton plot) from that area and a date, or range of dates, may be obtained. The process is dependent on several factors. First, a skeleton plot must exist for your specific area (a plot from another area cannot be used since climatic conditions differ). Second, the wood from a particular site must be from a *sensitive* species, one that adds one ring a year (Douglas Fir, yellow pine, etc.). *Complacent* species (e.g., juniper) are those that will not consistently add one ring a year and cannot be used.

296

Table 15
RELATIVE DATING OF SEVERAL SITES USING SERIATION

Site	Style A	Style B	Style C	Style D	Total %
No. 1	0	40	60	0	100
No. 2	10	60	30	0	100
No. 3	30	50	20	0	100
No. 4	50	30	20	0	100
No. 5	70	10	10	10	100
No. 6	80	0	0	20	100
No. 7	70	0	0	30	100
No. 8	60	0	0	40	100

Once the percentages are plotted on the table, they can be graphically illustrated (see Fig. 97 below). An undated site can be fit into the sequence by measuring its percentages of styles. For example, if site No. 9 had percentages of "20, 55, 25, and 0" for styles A through D respectively, it would date between sites No. 2 and 3.

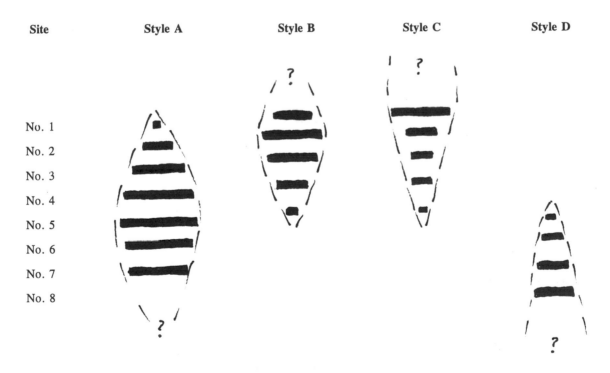

Fig. 97. Battleship curves based on the data in Table 15.

Like any technique, one must use caution in the interpretation of a dendrochronology "date." It may be correct, but it may not relate to the *use* of the wood. For example, one could date the cutting of a tree used as a beam in the construction of a structure (if you had the *outer* ring), but if the beam had been reused later in time, the date would still be of the initial cutting, not its reuse in a later structure.

Radiocarbon. *Radiocarbon dating* is the most commonly used chronometric technique in North America and will work on just about any organic material. Perishable materials, residues in ceramic vessels, organics surviving within pottery, charcoal from fires, animal bone or shell, carbonized plant materials, and even some soils can be dated with radiocarbon.

The basic idea behind the technique is rather straightforward, but the practical application is more difficult. Carbon is a very common constituent in the atmosphere, mainly in the form of carbon dioxide. The usual form of carbon is ^{12}C and is quite stable. Another form of carbon, ^{14}C, is an unstable radioactive isotope produced in the upper atmosphere and mixes with the ^{12}C. All living things incorporate ^{14}C into their tissues while they are alive and the concentration of ^{14}C within living tissue remains the same during life. When something dies, however, no new ^{14}C is taken in and the amount within the tissue begins to decrease at a known rate through radioactive decay.

Because the half-life (the amount of time required for 50% of a radioactive material to decay) of ^{14}C is known to be 5,700 years, it is possible to measure the amount of ^{14}C in an organic sample and deduce how long ago it died, when it ceased to take in new radioactive carbon. For example, if an organism contained 100 "units" of ^{14}C when it died and it now contains 50 units, it must have died 5,700 years ago (half of its original 100). In another 5,700 years, the sample will contain half of the 50, or 25 "units" of ^{14}C, then 12.5 units, then 6.25 units, etc. Eventually, so little ^{14}C remains that it cannot be measured. Thus, radiocarbon dating currently has a maximum range of about 50,000 years.

It seems simple enough; however, there are several issues that complicate things. First, radiocarbon production in the atmosphere has varied through time and, as a result, the concentration of ^{14}C has varied. These variations result in radiocarbon dates not directly corresponding to calendar dates. Thus, we get dates in "radiocarbon years" before present. Fortunately, these variations have been mapped for the last 8,000 years by obtaining ^{14}C dates directly on tree rings dated by dendrochronology, so radiocarbon dates younger than about 8,000 years can be corrected to calendar years.

Second, we measure the decay of ^{14}C atoms on the *average*, a statistical measurement. If an organic specimen has 100 ^{14}C atoms, an average of 50 of them would be expected to decay in 5,700 years. Perhaps only 47 of them actually decay, or maybe 54. A radiocarbon assay number (date) includes an error factor (usually expressed as one standard deviation) to account for the statistical estimate of the behavior of the population of atoms. A radiocarbon "date" is an estimate of the ^{14}C remaining in the sample, and thus an estimate of how long ago the organism died. A radiocarbon date of 1,250 $\pm$ 100 means that the death of the specimen occurred 1,250, plus or minus 100 years ago, or between 1,150 and 1,350 radiocarbon years ago. But there is only a 67% chance (statistically) that the organism actually died within that 200-year period (within the error factor, or one standard deviation of the date). To increase the chances of being correct, the standard deviation must be increased to two, or a 400-year span. At two standard deviations, there is a 95% chance that the specimen died between 1,050 and 1,450 radiocarbon years ago. While this range seems wide, it does provide a pretty good control of time. If there were multiple radiocarbon assays from the same sample, much tighter control would be possible.

Conventional radiocarbon dating costs between $200 and $250 (in 1995), and results may be obtained in as little as a few days (for an extra fee). The process requires a relatively large sample size. For example, approximately 5 grams of charcoal, 60 grams of bone, 30 grams of shell, and/or 10 grams of wood are generally required to get a date. Smaller samples could be used, perhaps even as small as 0.5 grams of suitable carbon, but such samples require extra counting time (and an extra fee from the radiocarbon lab).

Smaller samples can be dated using the accelerator mass spectrometry (AMS) method. This technique directly counts ^{14}C atoms in a nuclear accelerator and a date can be obtained from a very small sample. The cost is about three times that of a conventional date (and it takes longer to get the results).

Chronometric Dating of Ceramics. In addition to the use of radiocarbon to date ceramics (see De Atley 1980), several specialized techniques are available to date ceramics or other fired clays, such as archaeomagnetism and thermoluminescence.

Archaeomagnetism. Archaeomagnetic dating is based on thermoremnant magnetism of ferromagnetic minerals that typically occur in clays or clayey soils. In unfired clays, the direction of these minerals is random, but when heated to a dull red heat, some of the mineral grains become aligned with the earth's magnetic field, and upon cooling, retain this orientation. Features associated with ceramic production (such as kilns, pits, and surface firing areas) can be dated by this magnetic direction method, which compares the thermoremnant magnetism of archaeological specimens with independently dated secular variation curves that document the long-term changes in declination and inclination of magnetic north for different regions (Michels 1973:130-131).

The magnetic intensity method can also be used to date portable ceramic objects (e.g., vessels) recovered from regions where independent secular variation curves have been established. This is a destructive method in which several cubic centimeters of sample material are heated to successively higher temperatures, and is best applied to ceramics that have been fired in an oxidizing atmosphere well beyond 600 degrees C. (Rice 1987:440). Tite (1972) claimed that this method provides accurate dates with a standard deviation of between 5% and 15%.

Thermoluminescence. Thermoluminescence (TL) dating is based on the fact that the materials from which ceramic fabrics are made contain certain amounts of radioactive impurities that emit alpha, beta, and gamma radiation. Part of the energy from this radioactive decay is accumulated and stored as trapped electrons and electron "holes" in the crystal lattice of ceramic materials. When the mixture of clay and filler is fired to temperatures of 500 degrees C. or higher, the heat acts as a "zeroing" event and frees the trapped electrons and holes, returning the clay and filler to a zero level of stored electrons and holes (Rice 1987:440-441). The accumulation of new trapped electrons and holes then starts again, in effect acting as a clock that enables scientists to determine the time of the last major heating event for the ceramic artifact.

The age of a ceramic object is determined by quickly heating a sample in a controlled setting up to a temperature of about 500 degrees C., at which point thermoluminescence (light) is emitted and recorded by means of a photomultiplier tube. The glow recorded by the photomultiplier tube is measured with an electrometer, which in turn is attached to a recorder that plots a graph (glow curve) of light

299

intensity versus temperature (Michels 1973:193). The amount of light emitted in this reheating is proportional to the age of the specimen since its last intensive heating episode, which presumably represents its original firing. TL ages on ceramics reportedly have an average standard deviation of 15% from the "true" age of specimens determined independently by more reliable chronometric dating techniques. However, ceramics are highly susceptible to external sources of radiation in the form of cosmic and gamma rays, and because each sample must be independently calibrated for its own TL sensitivity and radiation dose rate, the method has not enjoyed widespread use. Thermoluminescence has proven to be especially effective in authentication studies of ceramic objects in museum collections.

Relative Dating Used in Conjunction with Chronometric Dating. Relative and chronometric dating techniques can be used in conjunction. If the upper portion of a site is dated at 1,000 years old, then the material in the lower portion must be older than 1,000 years. How much older may not be known. Conversely, if the bottom of a site is dated, the material above it must be younger. It is important to take into account all of the cautions noted in the section on superposition and disturbance.

Experimental Techniques

Experimental techniques are those that are not yet proven; they may be relative or chronometric methods, they may only work under special circumstances, or they may ultimately not work at all. For example, the amino acid racemization chronometric dating technique (measuring the conversion of "L" to "D" forms of amino acids as a factor of time) apparently does not work in North America, but may in parts of Africa.

Another example is the cation-ratio dating technique, used to date organic materials on rock surfaces, and thus the rock art on them (radiocarbon dating of these materials also is conducted). While there have been claims of success, many archaeologists are skeptical and the technique is not widely accepted.

Obsidian Hydration. One method that may be on the verge of common usage as a chronometric dating technique is *obsidian hydration*. Obsidian is natural, volcanic glass, predominately black in color. Most archaeologists already accept the use of this technique as a relative method, and the "bugs" in making it useful for chronometric dating are being worked out. While the general theory of obsidian hydration is fairly simple, there is a number of important factors to consider in the use of the technique.

On a freshly broken obsidian surface, water (actually a substance chemically very similar to water) diffuses into the matrix of the glass; the longer the surface is exposed, the deeper the penetration of water into the matrix. This penetration is visible under a microscope as a different-colored layer and can be measured (in microns). Thus, we can cut a piece of obsidian, prepare the sample, and measure the hydration layer (rind or band). If we know how long it takes to create one micron, we can extrapolate the age of a 7.6-micron band. Or so goes the theory.

In reality, the diffusion of water into the glass is a chemical reaction, regulated by the internal chemistry of the glass, temperature, and humidity (the source of the water). Since obsidians from different places have different microchemistries, we must know the source so that the chemistry can be determined. We need to have some idea of temperature history (often inferred from average air temperature taken from weather records and translated into "Effective Hydration Temperature"), and the role of humidity must be understood (which it is not).

The biggest problem is that it is not known if hydration occurs at a steady linear rate or if the rate of hydration slows as the band becomes thicker (an exponential rate). For example, if the rate is linear, one micron would equal 100 years, two microns would equal 200 years, three microns would equal 300 years, etc. If the rate is exponential, one micron would equal 100 years, two microns would equal 150 years, three microns would equal 190 years, etc. Calendar dates cannot be assigned if the rate of hydration is not known.

Some researchers are trying to deduce the rate by tying measurements with radiocarbon dates. If an obsidian sample was 10.0 microns and was associated with a radiocarbon date of 2,000 years, one could argue that the obsidian hydrated at an average rate of 200 years per micron. If we had enough of these data points, we might be able to learn the rate and then apply it to samples not associated with radiocarbon dates. Although some would not agree, for the time being it is probably best not to use obsidian hydration as a chronometric technique.

MATERIALS SOURCING

The geographic place of origin of many materials can be determined through geochemical sourcing (comparing the chemical "fingerprint" of a material of unknown origin with fingerprints of known sources until a match is made). This technique is commonly conducted on obsidian but also works with some other materials (steatite, shell, turquoise, etc.). Such analyses are often conducted with a high-powered X-ray machine (the XRF technique) or in a nuclear reactor (the neutron activation technique). Both methods identify and measure the chemical constituents of the glass, producing a "fingerprint." Sourcing is important for several reasons, including matching with hydration data for rate determination, and to gain an understanding of prehistoric trade patterns (and how they may have varied over time if the material could be dated).

PROTEIN RESIDUE ANALYSIS

All organisms (plants and animals) contain proteins within each of their cells. Prehistoric peoples processed plants and animals with various tools and, as a consequence, proteins of those organisms came into contact with the tools. It is believed that at least some such proteins are very sturdy and can preserve for long periods of time. If such preserved proteins could be extracted from a tool and identified, the identity of the plant or animal (sometimes even the genus) on that tool could be discovered (see Loy 1983; Newman and Julig 1989; Hyland et al. 1990; Newman 1990; Yohe et al. 1991; Kooyman et al. 1992; Loy and Hardy 1992; Loy 1993; Tuross and Dillehay 1995). This type of analysis also can work on soils and coprolites (see Newman et al. 1993). Many archaeologists erroneously call this "blood residue analysis," but many different proteins, not just hemoglobin, are tested for.

There is a number of researchers who dispute the merit of protein analysis. The problems appear to center on whether proteins can actually preserve on archaeological materials (Cattaneo et al. 1993; Downs and Lowenstein 1995; Eisele et al. 1995). These problems remain unresolved and great caution must be exercised in the interpretation of protein residue results.

SPECIAL ANALYSES

There are several techniques used in protein residue analysis, perhaps the most common being *cross-over immunoelectrophoresis (CIEP)*, described briefly here. In CIEP, the samples are washed with a 5% solution of ammonium hydroxide, causing any surviving proteins on the surface of the sample to go into solution. The solution is then tested against a suite of antisera from known plants and animals. If there is a reaction between the unknown and one (or more) of the knowns, the unknown can then be identified. This is, in effect, an allergy test. Usually a blind test of the site soils is conducted to insure that the proteins discovered on tools are the results of cultural activity rather than natural contamination (e.g., ground squirrel urine deposited long after the site was occupied).

There is a number of analytical problems and limitations with the technique. The first is preservation. It may be that a negative result means that nothing preserved, or that the correct protein was not tested for, or that the tool was never used; it is currently impossible to determine the difference. For this reason, only the *positive* results can be used in interpretation. The second problem is that we can only test for a few (several dozen) species. As more antisera are developed, this will improve. The third problem is the possibility of contamination. Loose proteins in soils might contaminate artifacts (if a mouse urinated on a metate, one might get a positive for mouse but that would have nothing to do with the archaeology of the site). This possibility is tested by processing soils for proteins (so one needs soil samples from the site as well). Proteins might also get on artifacts from handling, SO DO NOT WASH ARTIFACTS OR UNNECESSARILY HANDLE THEM.

DNA STUDIES

The genetic code for all organisms is in the form of *deoxyribonucleic acid (DNA)*. In humans, several billion base pairs are present, and together they contain all of the instructions for the construction and functioning of the person. DNA is present in all cells and can preserve over fairly long periods of time. For example, DNA has been extracted from insects preserved in amber that are over 100 million years old. It may be that DNA also may be preserved in older materials, including fossil bone. In archaeological contexts, DNA is present in human remains (e.g., bone and mummified tissue) and can be recovered (see Loy 1993; Richards et al. 1993; Hagelberg 1994). Such information could be used to determine genetic relationships between populations or even between individuals (as in the case of some Egyptian mummies). In recent DNA work, Sutton et al. (1995) identified the sex of coprolite depositors. Such work, coupled with dietary analysis (see below), may detail sex-specific diet. The potential is quite exciting.

DNA analyses are usually conducted by biochemists; few archaeologists have the training or equipment for such tasks. If one has materials from a site for which DNA analysis may be useful, a biochemist who specializes in that work should be contacted.

RESIDUE ANALYSIS

Sometimes archaeological materials retain residues (not to be confused with protein residue analysis) that may represent a variety of materials, including those used as food (e.g., dried food residues in a pot) and for technological purposes (e.g., resin on a basket or pot, the mastic on a hopper mortar) (see Heron and Evershed [1993] for a recent review). Such residues may be either visible surface residues or those absorbed into a porous surface (e.g., the wall of a ceramic vessel). In addition to visual identification of some samples (e.g., with a conventional or scanning electron microscope), others may be identified using various chemical techniques (see Heron and Evershed 1993:260-270), including infrared spectroscopy, chemical analysis (e.g., carbon, hydrogen, and nitrogen or CHN), gas chromatography (GC), and gas chromatography/mass spectrometry (GC/MS). Each of these techniques require that a "fingerprint" of a known substance be obtained and compared to that of the unknown archaeological material. This involves building a data base of known materials of comparison.

Perhaps the two most useful and practical of these techniques are GC and GC/MS. GC involves putting the substance to be identified in solution (often using chloroform). That solution is placed into a GC machine where it travels up a "column." As the solution passes through the column, the various compounds will change to gas at different points along the column, where they are measured. The lighter compounds will change to gas early, with the heavier compounds making it further up the column before changing to gas. The resulting graph (see Fig. 98) charts the relative abundance of each compound and the place on the column where it changed to gas. However, while "fingerprints" can be compared, none of the compounds are identified. The addition of mass spectrometry to the GC technique (GC/MS) allows for each compound to be identified and thus for greater precision in the matching of "fingerprints."

OTHER ANALYSES

USE-WEAR ANALYSIS

Use-wear analysis is an attempt to determine the function of a tool by examining (microscopically) the wear patterns present on its edges. In theory, this would seem logical and easy to conduct. However, there have been numerous attempts to do this and each has had problems. While it is known that using a tool will result in wear observable on the tool, it is usually difficult, if not impossible, to identify the material that caused the wear; that is, whether it was wood, hide, bone, etc. Work on this type of analysis continues (also see Chapter 5).

COPROLITE STUDIES

Coprolites (preserved human fecal matter) constitute a source of considerable information regarding prehistoric diet, nutrition, health, and pharmacology (see Fry [1985], Sobolik [1990], and Reinhard and Bryant [1992] for recent reviews of coprolite studies). Unfortunately, coprolites are very fragile and susceptible to decomposition, and so are rarely recovered archaeologically.

Coprolites form direct evidence of substances consumed (as opposed to standard faunal and floral remains that form indirect dietary evidence), although not always as food. Archaeologists studying coprolites make a number of assumptions (often with great merit) regarding the nature and origin of such specimens. First, it is assumed that the materials present in coprolites were ingested by the person from whom the coprolite came and that such materials can be readily identified. Second, coprolites usually are viewed as largely representing the subsistence aspect of diet, as the identification and interpretation of substances ingested for ceremonial and/or medicinal purposes (Shafer et al. 1989) are more difficult. Third, it is assumed that each specimen represents a unique elimination event (one individual at one time) and is not mixed or combined with other events. (In spite of this, obvious fragments, possibly representing separate events, frequently are grouped together as one specimen for analysis.) Further, it generally is assumed that materials present in a coprolite represent the materials consumed within the 24-

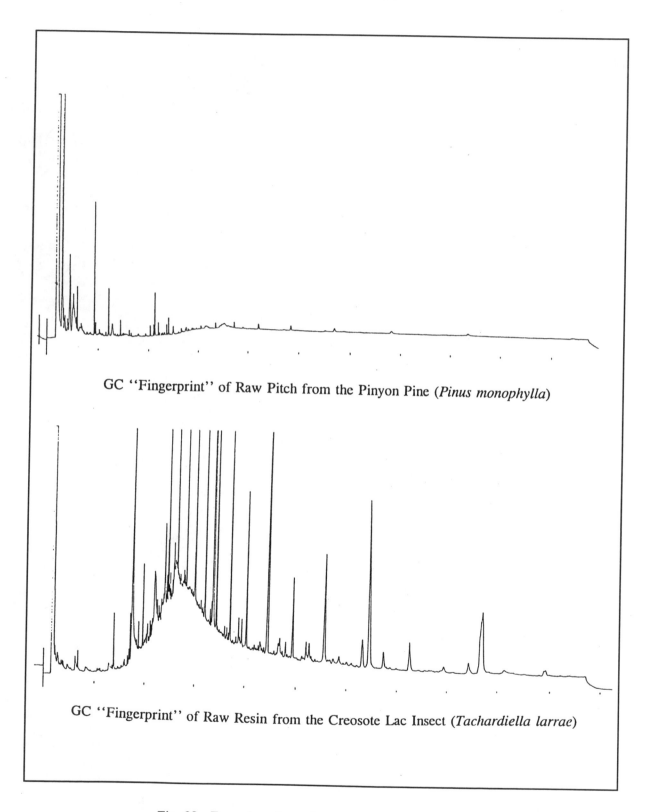

GC "Fingerprint" of Raw Pitch from the Pinyon Pine (*Pinus monophylla*)

GC "Fingerprint" of Raw Resin from the Creosote Lac Insect (*Tachardiella larrae*)

Fig. 98. Examples of gas chromatography "fingerprints."

hour period preceding its deposition (e.g., Fry 1985:128), although this may not be the case (e.g., Sobolik 1988a:207). As such, they likely are a combination of several meals (e.g., Watson 1974:240).

Other factors are of note in coprolite analysis (see Sobolik 1988b:114). As the surviving (e.g., visible) materials are those that were not digested, only the indigestible part of the diet is visually represented and the taphonomic problems associated with coprolites (e.g., digestion, processing, preservation) are not currently understood. However, this is changing with the addition of the protein residue technique that can identify nonvisible constituents (Newman et al. 1993). Coprolites may be discovered singly or in concentrations that probably represent latrines. While the population responsible for a latrine coprolite deposit generally is assumed to be homogeneous, this may not be the case. If a particular segment of the population (e.g., with perhaps particular culinary customs) used a specific latrine, the sample would be skewed and the interpretations incorrect (latrine reuse over time may be an additional concern). However, since these factors cannot currently be controlled, most researchers appear to assume sample homogeneity. (Cumming's [1989] study of coprolites from Nubian mummies is a rare example of these factors being known.) Recent advances in DNA analysis of coprolites (Sutton et al. 1995) may also help to alleviate this problem.

Analysis of Coprolites

The analysis of coprolites involves their proper identification (as human rather than nonhuman), separation of dietary materials from the matrix (usually by rehydration and wet-screening), sorting identifiable materials, identifying the sorted components, and interpreting the results. Identification is based on morphology, context, and/or smell when rehydrated (they will often regain their rather unique smell). One method of rehydration is accomplished using a 0.05% solution of trisodium phosphate for several days to a week. Water is not recommended since it tends to damage floral and other remains by causing them to swell unevenly and fracture. The resulting specimen is then washed through fine mesh screen. The constituents in the screen are then dried, separated, and identified (some of the material may have to be identified by specialists). This then forms the data for reconstruction of the aboriginal diet.

While this is wonderful stuff, not all things that are eaten pass through the digestive tract in recognizable form (e.g., meat). Until the advent of protein residue analysis (see above), this dietary component was essentially lost. Coprolites also contain DNA, pollen, and phytoliths, and some effort should be made to test for these remains as well. Recovered DNA could assist in the reconstruction of social status and diet, sharing behavior, and many things not even considered by researchers yet. Several good examples of coprolite studies include Wilke (1978) for the western United States, Sobolik (1991) for Texas, and Cummings (1989) for Nubia.

Interpretation of Coprolites

Most researchers focus on an analysis of constituents present in a coprolite. The constituents recovered are listed and their relative abundance within the sample (often consisting of numerous individual coprolites) is discussed. Relative abundance often is assumed to represent relative importance in the diet. This results in a very generalized view of the diet represented by the specimens, since they are grouped into one analytical unit. Little attention is given to patterns of resource combination and utilization evident within the overall sample. The resulting interpretations must be very broad.

Another way to deal with such an analysis is to compare the contents of each specimen with every other specimen; in other words, to conduct a statistical analysis (such as a cluster analysis) of the constituents. This may result in the delineation of specific patterns of resource use that may vary within the larger sample. One may be able to reconstruct specific "meals," dietary preferences, use of seasonings, etc.; in short, to reconstruct "cuisine." If such information is coupled with floral and faunal data from the site in general, even more interesting interpretations could result. Several examples of such an approach are Sutton (1993) and Sutton and Reinhard (1995).

SOILS ANALYSIS

Many interesting things can be learned from archaeological soils (separate from cultural materials contained within soils). Cultural soils (middens) contain a variety of information regarding site formation and cultural activities (see Stein 1985). For example, if clays were imported onto the site for use in house construction, the site soil may contain a higher proportion of clays than ordinarily expected (especially around houses). The same might be true of sand or other soils.

Natural soils also can be very informative. If the site (presumably on a fairly stable geologic surface) was formed on top of an older unstable geologic surface (such as an alluvial fan), an argument regarding hydrologic and/or climatic change (i.e., less rainfall and thus a less active fan surface) might be made. Additionally, there may be culturally sterile soil layers separating midden strata. If so, knowing the geologic origin of those soils, whether alluvial (water) or eolian (wind), could be quite useful. There is a number of properties to look for in soils analysis that fall into two basic categories: morphological and chemical.

Morphological Attributes of Soils

Soils are comprised of varying proportions of sand, silt, and clay (derived from decomposing rock), plus mixed-in organic materials. Morphological characteristics include soil type and color. Soil type can be roughly determined by the percentage of its constituents (sand, silt, and clay; see Fig. 99). The percentage of the constituents can be determined by several mechanical techniques, including screening the soil through different size screens or placing the soil in a water solution and measuring the percentage of the constituents as they settle out. Particles defined as coarse sand measure between 2.00 and 0.20 mm.; fine sand measures between 0.20 and 0.02 mm.; silt measures between 0.02 and 0.002 mm.; and clay particles measure under 0.002 mm. in diameter.

Color is also an important aspect of soils. Color often is used by archaeologists in the identification of culturally altered soils (many middens tend to be darker than the surrounding natural soils due to the increased content of charcoal, ash, and other organic materials). Soil color is measured using a Munsell color chart. This system quantifies color in a standardized way and allows for accurate comparisons of soils.

Chemical Attributes of Soils

Soil chemistry is of great interest to archaeologists (e.g., Cook and Heizer 1965). Among the chemical attributes interesting to archaeologists are soil pH and phosphate content. Soil pH is the measure of the acidity and alkalinity of the soil on a scale of 1 to 14 (Fig. 100). There are various

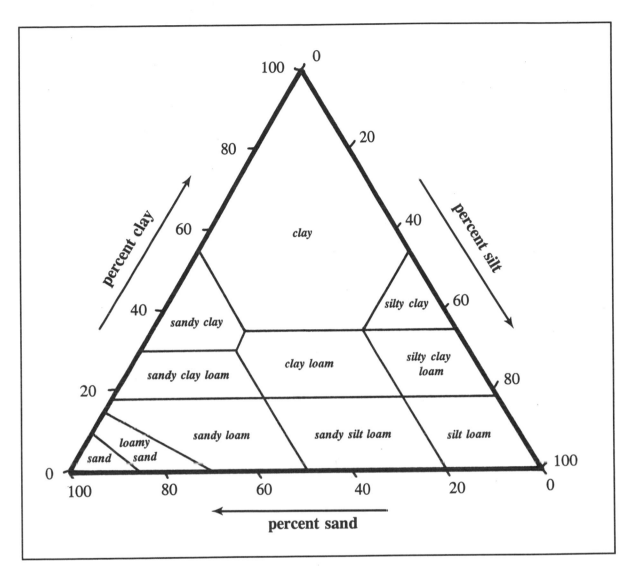

Fig. 99. Particle classification and soil types (from White 1979:Fig. 2.3).

reasons why soils have a particular pH, some of which may be related to cultural alteration of the soil. The pH of midden can influence preservation of a variety of materials. For example, both extreme soil acidity (Gordon and Buikstra 1981) and alkalinity greater than pH 7.9 (Linse and Burton 1990) have been found to contribute to bone decomposition. If there are few faunal remains from a site, it may be prudent to determine the pH of the soil to determine the possibility that it is the result of a preservation bias rather than a cultural practice. Most metals also will preserve poorly under acidic conditions.

Phosphates (any of a number of chemical compounds containing phosphorus) are contained within a variety of organic materials, including fats, bone, and dung. If such materials are concentrated in the soil of an archaeological site, the determination of phosphate concentrations could be used in any number of informative ways, including the determination of site boundaries (or at least midden boundaries), areas

pH	Condition
1	extremely acidic
2	extremely acidic
3	very acidic
4	strongly acidic
5	moderately acidic
6	slightly acidic
7	neutral
8	slightly alkaline
9	moderately alkaline
10	strongly alkaline
11	very alkaline
12	extremely alkaline
13	extremely alkaline
14	extremely alkaline

Fig. 100. The pH scale.

used for livestock, and the presence of decomposed bone. The measurement of phosphates over an area requires the collection and analysis of a fairly large number of soil samples, usually taken across a site in a grid (e.g., a site measuring 100 by 100 meters would require the collection of 10,000 samples using a one-meter grid).

REFERENCES

Cattaneo, C., K. Gelsthorpe, P. Phillips, and R. J. Sokol
    1993   Blood Residues on Stone Tools: Indoor and Outdoor Experiments. World Archaeology 25(1):29-43.

Cook, S. F., and Robert F. Heizer
    1965   Studies on the Chemical Analysis of Archaeological Sites. Berkeley: University of California Publications in Anthropology Vol. 2.

Cummings, Linda Scott
    1989   Coprolites from Medieval Christian Nubia: An Interpretation of Diet and Nutritional Stress. Ph.D. dissertation, University of Colorado, Boulder.

De Atley, Suzanne P.
    1980   Radiocarbon Dating of Ceramic Materials: Progress and Prospects. Radiocarbon 22:987-993.

Downs, Elinor F., and Jerold M. Lowenstein
    1995   Identification of Archaeological Blood Proteins: A Cautionary Note.   Journal of Archaeological Science 22:11-16.

Eisele, J. A., D. D. Fowler, G. Haynes, and R. A. Lewis
    1995   Survival and Detection of Blood Residues on Stone Tools.   Antiquity 69:36-46.

Feder, Kenneth L.
    1990   Frauds, Myths, and Mysteries: Science and Pseudoscience in Archaeology.   Mountain View, CA: Mayfield Press.

Fry, Gary F.
    1985   Analysis of Fecal Material.   In: The Analysis of Prehistoric Diets, Robert I. Gilbert, Jr. and James H. Mielke, eds., pp. 127-154.   Orlando: Academic Press.

Gordon, Claire C., and Jane E. Buikstra
    1981   Soil pH, Bone Preservation, and Sampling Bias at Mortuary Sites.   American Antiquity 46(3):566-571.

Hagelberg, Erika
    1994   Ancient DNA Studies.   Evolutionary Anthropology 2(6):199-207.

Heron, Carl, and Richard P. Evershed
    1993   The Analysis of Organic Residues and the Study of Pottery Use.   In: Archaeological Method and Theory, Vol. 5, Michael B. Schiffer, ed., pp. 247-286. Tucson: University of Arizona Press.

Hyland, D. C., J. M. Tersak, J. M. Adovasio, and M. I. Siegel
    1990   Identification of the Species of Origin of Residual Blood on Lithic Material.   American Antiquity 55(1):104-113.

Kooyman, B., Margaret E. Newman, and Howard Ceri
    1992   Verifying the Reliability of Blood Residue Analysis of Archaeological Tools.   Journal of Archaeological Science 19:261-264.

Linse, A., and J. H. Burton
    1990   Bone Solubility and Preservation in Alkaline Depositional Conditions.   Paper presented at the annual meetings of the Society for American Archaeology, Las Vegas.

Loy, Thomas H.
    1983   Prehistoric Blood Residues: Detection on Tool Surfaces and Identification of Species of Origin.   Science 220:1269-1271.

    1993   The Artifact as Site: An Example of the Biomolecular Analysis of Organic Residues on Prehistoric Tools.   World Archaeology 25(1):44-63.

SPECIAL ANALYSES

Loy, Thomas H., and B. L. Hardy
1992   Blood Residue Analysis of 90,000-year-old Stone Tools from Tabun Cave, Israel. Antiquity 66:24-35.

Michels, Joseph W.
1973   Dating Methods in Archaeology. New York: Seminar Press, Inc.

Newman, Margaret E.
1990   The Hidden Evidence From Hidden Cave, Nevada. Ph.D dissertation, University of Toronto.

Newman, Margaret E., and P. Julig
1989   The Identification of Protein Residues on Lithic Artifacts from a Stratified Boreal Forest Site. Canadian Journal of Archaeology 13:119-132.

Newman, Margaret E., Robert M. Yohe II, Howard Ceri, and Mark Q. Sutton
1993   Immunological Protein Residue Analysis of Non-lithic Archaeological Materials. Journal of Archaeological Science 20(1):93-100.

Reinhard, Karl J., and Vaughn M. Bryant, Jr.
1992   Coprolite Analysis: A Biological Perspective on Archaeology. In: Archaeological Method and Theory, Vol. 4, Michael B. Schiffer, ed., pp. 245-288. Tucson: University of Arizona Press.

Rice, Prudence M.
1987   Pottery Analysis: A Sourcebook. Chicago: The University of Chicago Press.

Richards, Martin, Kate Smalley, Bryan Sykes, and Robert Hedges
1993   Archaeology and Genetics: Analyzing DNA from Skeletal Remains. World Archaeology 25(1):18-28.

Shafer, Harry J., Marianne Marek, and Karl J. Reinhard
1989   A Mimbres Burial with Associated Colon Remains from the NAN Ranch Ruin, New Mexico. Journal of Field Archaeology 16:17-30.

Sobolik, Kristin D.
1988a   The Importance of Pollen Concentration Values from Coprolites: An Analysis of Southwest Texas Samples. Palynology 12:201-214.

1988b   Diet Change in the Lower Pecos: Analysis of Baker Cave Coprolites. Bulletin of the Texas Archaeological Society 59:111-127.

1990   A Nutritional Analysis of Diet as Revealed in Prehistoric Human Coprolites. The Texas Journal of Science 42(1):23-36.

1991   Prehistoric Diet and Subsistence in the Lower Pecos as Reflected in Coprolites from Baker Cave, Val Verde County, Texas. University of Texas at Austin, Texas Archeological Research Laboratory, Studies in Archeology 7.

Stein, Julie K.
     1985   Interpreting Sediments in Cultural Settings. In: Archaeological Sediments in Context, Julie K. Stein and William R. Farrand, eds., pp. 5-20. Orono: Center for the Study of Early Man, Peopling of the Americas, Edited Volume Series, Vol. 1.

Sutton, Mark Q.
     1993   Midden and Coprolite Derived Subsistence Evidence: An Analysis of Data from the La Quinta Site, Salton Basin, California. Journal of Ethnobiology 13(1):1-15.

Sutton, Mark Q., and Karl J. Reinhard
     1995   Cluster Analysis of the Coprolites from Antelope House: Implications for Anasazi Diet and Cuisine. Journal of Archaeological Science 22 (in press).

Sutton, Mark Q., Minnie Malik, and Andrew Ogram
     1995   Determination of Gender from Coprolites by DNA Analysis. Journal of Archaeological Science 22 (in press).

Tite, M. S.
     1972   Methods of Physical Examination in Archaeology. London: Seminar Press, Inc.

Tuross, Noreen, and Tom D. Dillchay
     1995   The Mechanism of Organic Preservation at Monte Verde, Chile, and One Use of Biomolecules in Archaeological Interpretation. Journal of Field Archaeology 22(1):97-110.

Watson, P. J.
     1974   Theoretical and Methodological Difficulties in Dealing with Paleofecal Material. In: Archaeology of the Mammoth Cave Area, P. J. Watson, ed., pp. 239-241. New York: Academic Press.

White, R. E.
     1979   Introduction to the Principles and Practice of Soil Science. New York: John Wiley & Sons.

Wilke, Philip J.
     1978   Late Prehistoric Human Ecology at Lake Cahuilla, Coachella Valley, California. Berkeley: Contributions of the University of California Archaeological Research Facility No. 38.

SPECIAL ANALYSES

Yohe, Robert M. II, Margaret E. Newman, and Joan S. Schneider
    1991   Immunological Identification of Small-Mammal Proteins on Aboriginal Milling Equipment. American Antiquity 56(4):659-666.

Chapter 14

ARCHAEOLOGICAL ILLUSTRATION

DEFINITION

Illustrations are an important component of any archaeological report. Such illustrations include drawings and/or photographs of the site, maps, soil profiles, and artifacts. The production of these illustrations can be therapeutic (but frustrating to some) in that it provides a break from the demands of technical report writing and presents an opportunity to channel one's artistic energies. In some ways, however, it is one of the more challenging aspects of archaeological analysis and documentation. There is no easy way to make high-quality illustrations, especially those done with pen and ink. The best way to learn is to examine various well-illustrated archaeological reports and illustrating guides (e.g., Dillon 1985) and practice several different styles of drawing.

Technical drawings found in high cost publications usually are made by professional scientific illustrators; but with practice and perseverance, most people can master the basic techniques of technical drawing and eliminate the need to hire professional illustrators. The vast majority of figures contained in academic journals, monographs, and texts consists of pen-and-ink drawings and black-and-white photographs. Color illustrations are expensive to reproduce, and are therefore somewhat rare in scholarly publications. Many of the high-quality color photographs contained in magazines such as *National Geographic* are produced from Kodachrome slides (P. J. Wilke, personal communication 1991).

Archaeological illustrations should always be planned out before they are made. Most illustrations intended for publication cannot be larger than about 8 by 6 inches, whether it is portrait style (where the figure is longer than it is wide) or landscape style (on its side, where the figure is wider than it is high). Several steps need to be taken in the production of illustrations, including, but not limited to, deciding what is to be illustrated, determining how many artifacts can fit into one figure, making drafts of the drawings, and determining how large and in what orientation they need to be.

PEN-AND-INK DRAWINGS

Pen-and-ink drawings usually are made with technical pens (Staedtler is a common type) and sometimes fine details are completed with crow feather quills. Always use waterproof drawing ink, such as that made by Staedtler or Pelikan. Paper should be drafting velum or acetate sheet. It is preferable to use paper gridded with nonphoto blue lines (these are lines that will not normally reproduce during the photocopying process) in order to keep things square. It is important to note, however, that the side of the paper with the grid printed on it will not always take ink properly and the grid lines may sometimes show on a reproduction of the drawing. To avoid these problems, always draw on the side *not* gridded with the blue ink (as the paper is thin, you can still see the lines).

Line widths are critical and must allow reproduction at the appropriate scales while still rendering lines of adequate definition. Remember, always make your drawings with the intention that they will be reduced in size, as this allows small mistakes and incongruities to "disappear" and will result in a more aesthetic figure. Many final figures appear as 70% or 80% reductions of their original size. Also, remember to always wash your hands before doing any artwork. There is nothing more frustrating than to have completed half of a well-executed drawing and then deface it with hand oils, grease, and/or dirt. Of course, you can always use correction fluid (white-out) to repair errors (both of ink and dirt), but this should be viewed as a last resort.

ARTIFACT DRAWINGS

Line drawings of artifacts often are more desirable than black-and-white photographs because they typically show more detailed surface topography of archaeological specimens than do photographs. Several strategies can be used to produce direct 1:1 scale artifact drawings, such as photocopying or photographing the artifact, making a tracing of it from the photocopy or photograph, and then filling in the detail using an ink pen.

Technical illustrators use different techniques in making line drawings. Some of the more common types of illustrations include stipple, underscore, scratchboard, hatch, and coquille, examples of which are shown in Figure 101. Many artists use the stipple technique when illustrating objects with smooth surfaces, such as ground stone, ceramics, or shell and bone artifacts (refer to examples of such illustrations in the appropriate chapters). The stipple effect can be produced either by hand-produced dots, or by actually cutting out and laying down dry transfer stipple patterns from acetate matte sheets produced by companies such as *Zip-a-Tone* and *Chartpak*. Flaked stone artifacts often are drawn using the scratchboard technique (or variations thereof), which is excellent for replicating the flake scar patterns on bifaces, dart and arrow points, etc. As noted above, when first learning to create technical illustrations, the student should consult one of several published sources on archaeological illustration (e.g., Dillon 1985).

Pen-and-ink drawings also allow you to draw individual objects separately and create a composite figure with the various drawings. Individual drawings should be mounted on a larger sheet with either scotch tape (preferable) or a thin veneer of roll-on printer's wax (wax will sometimes stain velum paper). A popular waxer is made by the Lectro-Stik Corporation, and can be purchased for about $50.00. It also is a good idea to include a bar scale in a corner of your figure. Avoid using scale information such as "1 cm. = 5 cm.," because the reproduction process changes the scale, and therefore the stated size ratio. If you do not want to use a bar scale, simply state the actual size of a given specimen in the figure caption. For example, "Actual size of upper left specimen is 8.5 cm. long, all other specimens same scale." However, we strongly recommend the use of a bar scale in all cases.

If possible, have the printing services section of your institution make a Photometric Transfer (PMT) of all figures in the proper proportion (90% of original size, 80% of original size, etc.). A PMT is a high-quality, glossy photo reproduction, and usually must be provided by the author(s) for professional publications. This is a camera-ready figure, and results in an exceptionally clear and smudge-free figure.

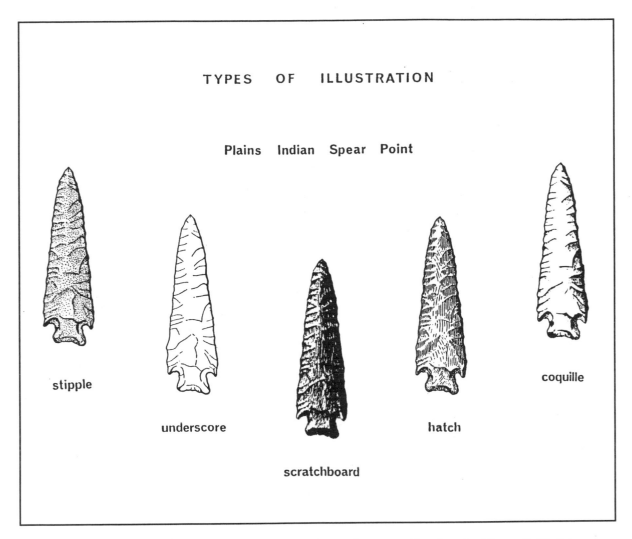

TYPES OF ILLUSTRATION

Plains Indian Spear Point

stipple

underscore

scratchboard

hatch

coquille

Fig. 101. Examples of different pen-and-ink illustration types (drawings by Henry J. Wylie).

MAPS

Virtually all archaeological reports will contain maps; of the site location(s), of the site itself, of features in the site, of soil profiles, etc. There are two basic types of maps that are made, *plan-view* (the view from overhead looking down) and *profile-view* (view from the side). Sometimes, the same thing will be depicted from different angles using both plan- and profile-views in the same map (Fig. 102).

In both types of maps, you must identify the subject of the map (site map, feature map, etc.), provide a legend to identify the various items shown on the map, and supply a scale. When making maps with ink, follow the same protocol as with artifact drawings. When drawing maps, make a rough draft in pencil, correcting everything as you go. Once the draft is complete, ink the final. Try to make the original maps fairly large so that small details can be drawn without difficulty. Have them reduced to their finished size with a PMT.

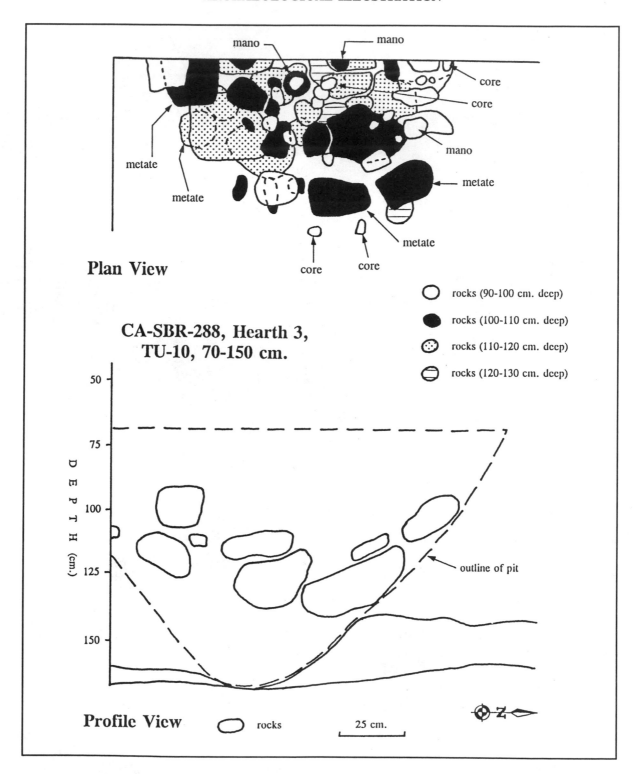

Fig. 102. Example of a plan- and profile-view map of the same feature on a map. Note the scale, orientation, legend, etc.

Plan-View Maps

Plan-view maps are overhead views of something (e.g., like most road maps). An example of a plan-view map is provided as Figure 103. Most archaeological site reports will have at least two plan-view maps; one of the site location, and one of the site itself. Other plan-view maps might include feature maps, artifact distribution maps, or topographic maps (or combinations therein). *Topography* is a depiction of elevation using contour lines. Most site maps will include the topography (elevation and slope of the ground surface), so contour lines likely will be present (refer to USGS topographic maps to see how they are done). Plan-view maps must have an orientation, usually in the form of a north arrow (denoting true or magnetic north). Maps are traditionally oriented on the paper with north at the top. This is sometimes not possible due to the shape of the site, but follow this custom whenever possible.

Profile-View Maps

Profile-view maps are used to show a cross section of something or a depiction of something that is oriented vertically, like a wall or streamcut (Fig. 104). Since the map shows something vertical, no north arrow is used; instead a statement of the orientation is made. For example, if a map of a soil profile is made, the legend will state what the orientation of the profile is, such as north, south, southeast, etc.

If a series of separately identified units (e.g., soil horizons) are shown, some shading (such as *Zip-a-Tone* screen) likely will be needed. Many screen designs are available and some have standard meanings (see Fig. 105). Make sure you try to adhere to these meanings to avoid confusion; however, it is not essential as long as the legend identifies everything properly. Remember that white (unscreened, blank) can be an identified unit; try to make the largest unit the blank one, as it will save time, effort, and screen material.

PHOTOGRAPHY

BLACK-AND-WHITE PHOTOGRAPHY

Most of the photographs taken for archaeological reports will be black and white. These typically include those of environmental settings, site overviews, unit sidewalls/stratigraphy, *in situ* features, and artifacts. All photographs should be glossy and printed either at 5 x 7" or 8 x 10". They should be equal to or larger than the size at which they will be published, because photographs invariably will be reduced in the publication process.

Modern 35 mm. cameras can produce high-quality, black-and-white or color photographs both outdoors and in the studio. A good camera to start with is the fully manual Pentax K-1000 equipped with a 50 mm. lens. This model is a great field camera because it is relatively inexpensive, sturdy, and has virtually no automated or electronic components that can be harmed or broken by adverse field conditions.

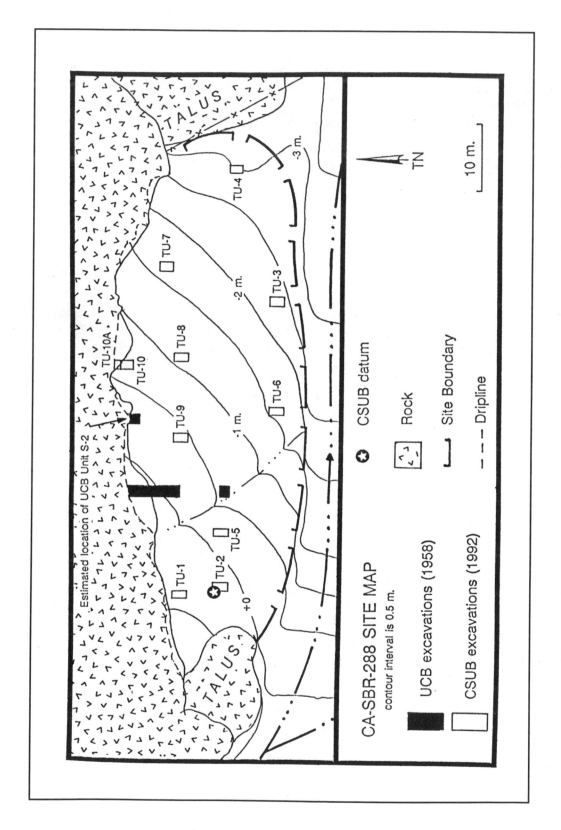

Fig. 103. Example of a plan-view map of a site. Note the scale, orientation, and legend.

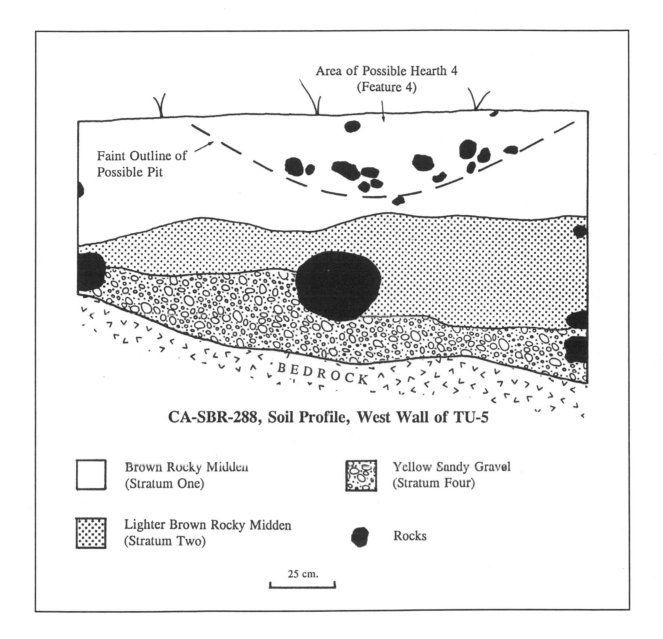

Fig. 104. Example of a profile-view map of a unit sidewall. Note the scale, orientation, and legend.

Good detail can be ensured by the lack of camera movement. In the field, try to use a tripod with a cable release, and a shutter speed and lens aperture commensurate with local conditions. In the studio, use a copy stand with polarized tungsten lights to achieve high-quality artifact photographs. A copy stand holds the camera directly over the specimens, and tungsten lights set up on each side of the stand will eliminate reflections. The lights can be arranged in such a way as to highlight certain artifact attributes, such as parallel transverse flaking on flaked stone tools. In some cases, you may wish to use only one light at a certain angle. When using tungsten lights, you also must use a tungsten film (which is made

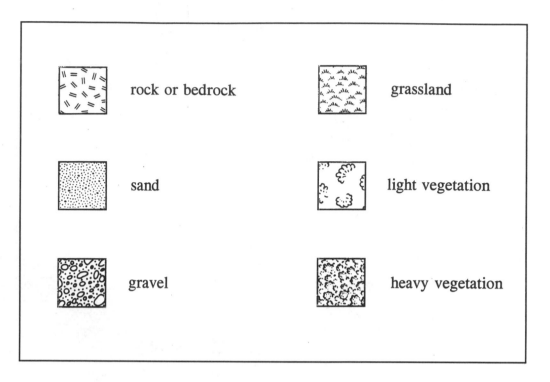

Fig. 105. Examples of some screen patterns with standard meanings.

by most major companies, e.g., Kodak, Fugi, Ilford). The most popular tungsten film speeds for studio photography consist of ASA 80 and 160.

Several different backgrounds can be used to maximize contrast and enhance artifact detail of black-and-white studio photographs. Some people prefer to lay their artifacts on a light box equipped with fluorescent lights mounted below a sheet of white, translucent plastic. Light boxes reduce shadows created by overhead lights, and create a balanced lighting environment. In some cases, you may wish to use art matte board (or velvet-like cloth) as a background. If the artifacts are dark in color, use a light-colored background; if they are light-colored, use a dark-colored background. This ensures good contrast between the specimens and background, and prevents the edges of the artifacts from becoming obscured and appearing to merge with the background.

Some general rules of thumb regarding archaeological photography include bracketing the lens aperture of your camera and making several exposures of the same object(s). Once you obtain a reading from a hand-held or self-contained light meter, make an exposure at that f-stop, and one each below and above the original f-stop. This ensures that you will obtain a negative with maximum contrast, and hence a high-quality print. Use a fine-grained film with a good range of gray tones such as Ilford FP4 (ASA 125) or Kodak T-MAX 100. Lens filters can bring out detail not readily apparent to the naked eye, and screen out glare and haze; a variety of filters can be used for both indoor and outdoor photography.

Include a bar scale in your studio photographs that is of a proper size. For example, a photograph of small objects such as beads and arrow points should include a bar scale that is 5 cm. long.

Larger artifacts, such as ground stone objects and historical bottles, should be photographed with a scale that is about 10 or 20 cm. long.

Use a good quality lens. The focal length of the lens can distort the shape of the image, either to your advantage or disadvantage (see Mang [1965] for a discussion of lens focal length in archaeological photography). It is always a good idea to either take a photography course or to read a comprehensive book on photography before attempting major photographic projects. Some texts, such as the one by Howell and Blanc (1992), concern only archaeological photography. Numerous others, such as those by Blaker (1976, 1977) and Keppler (1974), deal with field and scientific photography and general photography, respectively.

Enhancement of Black-and-White Artifact Photographs

Various powders and liquids have been used to enhance the topographic relief of artifacts, especially those of flaked stone. Spray deodorants, condensed milk, metallic (aluminum or bronze) powders (Callahan 1987), and ammonium chloride powder (Weide and Webster 1967) all have been used to enhance surface detail and make contrasting color densities uniform. Liquids tend to muddle detail, and aluminum is now believed to be associated with Alzheimer's disease; therefore neither of these methods is recommended. Other disadvantages associated with using aluminum powder is that you will never be able to completely remove all of it from the specimen(s), and the results oftentimes are overly dramatic. Of all the different substances used to coat and enhance the details of artifacts, ammonium chloride powder seems to be the best. It is easy to apply and remove, does not appear to be toxic, and provides good results. When using ammonium chloride powder, also use harsh, low-angle lighting to eliminate shadows and highlight details.

COLOR PHOTOGRAPHY

While color photographs are rarely used for technical publications, color slides are often needed for paper presentations, class lectures, etc. You should take color slides of your site or project in the field and of some of your artifacts in the laboratory. For color slides, use the same rules of thumb as when taking black-and-white photographs.

COMPUTER-ASSISTED ILLUSTRATION

Modern computer graphics programs are now easily capable of producing acceptable maps and illustrations. Many such maps are not as high a quality as well-drawn pen and ink maps, but the quality is improving. Some map-making programs are able to produce a contour map just from a data set (e.g., a series of transit shots), making the work much easier. Charts and graphs can be produced using other software (see Figure 26 for an example of such a graph).

Graphics programs usually require some specific computer hardware, including some minimum of memory, a graphics card, and a laser printer (needed for camera-ready materials). In addition, it takes time to learn how to use the programs (probably important in the long run).

ARCHAEOLOGICAL ILLUSTRATION

CONCLUDING REMARKS

The above sections provide a general overview of archaeological illustration. Most students can become proficient at pen-and-ink drawings with practice, but good archaeological photography requires a great deal more experience—both in the field and in the laboratory. Consult the photographic supervisor in the technical services section of your institution before attempting indoor photography of archaeological specimens. He or she probably will be glad to assist with your task if you schedule an appointment. They already have the proper kinds of equipment and facilities to produce publishable black-and-white photographs. You can save yourself a great deal of time, energy, and perhaps money by working with a staff photographer at your institution.

REFERENCES

Blaker, Alfred A.
    1976   Field Photography: Beginning and Advanced Techniques. San Francisco: W. H. Freeman and Company.

    1977   Handbook for Scientific Photography. San Francisco: W. H. Freeman and Company.

Callahan, Errett
    1987   Metallic Powder as an Aid to Stone Tool Photography. American Antiquity 52(4):768-772.

Dillon, Brian D. (ed.)
    1985   Student's Guide to Archaeological Illustrating. University of California, Los Angeles, Institute of Archaeology Publications.

Howell, Carol L., and Warren Blanc
    1992   A Practical Guide to Archaeological Photography. University of California, Los Angeles, Institute of Archaeology Publications.

Keppler, Herbert
    1974   The Honeywell Pentax Way (eighth edition). Garden City, NJ: Amphoto.

Mang, Fred E.
    1965   The View Camera in Archaeological Photography. In: Contributions of the Wetherill Mesa Project, D. S. Osborne, assem., and B. S. Katz, ed., pp. 227-230. Memoirs of the Society for American Archaeology No. 19.

Weide, David L., and Gary D. Webster
    1967   Ammonium Chloride Powder Used in Photography of Artifacts. American Antiquity 32(1):104-105.

SAMPLE EXCAVATION REPORT

An outline example of an excavation report is provided below. The purpose of each section is discussed, and some sample text is provided in bold type. While specific report requirements vary from region to region, this example will at least serve as a guide.

Title: **ARCHAEOLOGICAL INVESTIGATIONS AT THE EXAMPLE SITE**

List the author(s) of the report
Provide their affiliation (e.g., University, Museum, Agency, Company)

INTRODUCTION

Briefly tell the reader the nature of the project, where the site is, what was done, etc. Do this in two or three paragraphs. Include one or two maps of the location of the site.

NATURAL ENVIRONMENT

Discuss the geographic location (elevation, etc.) of the site. Next, discuss the plants and animals present in the area.

CULTURAL SETTING

Outline the relevant information known on the archaeology of the area (e.g., culture history, major research questions, previous work, etc.). Then provide a brief overview of the ethnographic setting, including the known indigenous groups of the area.

RESEARCH DESIGN

Explain (as best you can) why the project was conducted. What were the researchers looking for? Why was this site chosen rather than some other? What kinds of data were being sought (and what kinds were not) and why?

RESEARCH METHODS

SITE DESCRIPTION

Describe the site in some detail, including dimensions (horizontal size and depth), elevation, vegetation community, midden and/or surface scatter, general artifact content, and initial interpretation (village, camp, etc.). Include a map, plus some photographs if possible, of the site.

FIELD METHODS

Describe the field techniques employed at the site (as best you can). Include unit size, level size, screen size, equipment used, etc.

LABORATORY METHODS

Describe the general laboratory cataloging methods. Include a description of any special methods or handling.

RESULTS

STRATIGRAPHY AND SOILS

Describe the stratigraphy (the strata). It may be as simple as "midden" and "sterile" but may be more complex. Describe the soils (sand, loam, clay, etc.) and include color (e.g., Munsell values). Discuss, if you can, how the soils and stratigraphy relate to site formation processes, disturbance, and interpretation of the assemblage. Include a map of the stratigraphy.

FEATURES

Describe any features found at the site. Begin with surface features (e.g., bedrock milling features) and proceed to subsurface features (structures, burials, hearths, pits, rock scatters, etc.). Include a map of each.

MATERIAL CULTURE

Briefly summarize the recovered materials and include a summary table. A general description example is provided below for manos and metates; use the same format for each artifact category. A table providing the provenience and attributes for each artifact category should be provided. If there are fewer than three (3) specimens in a category, describe them in the text rather than in a table.

SAMPLE TEXT:

Ground Stone

Manos. Thirteen manos were recovered, nine of which are complete. Of the nine, two are Type I, five Type II, one Type III, and one unclassified. The provenience and attributes of each are provided in Table XX. Each of the Type I specimens was discovered in the upper 50 cm. of the deposit while the Type II examples were all found below that depth. This may suggest a temporal difference between the two types. Immunological analysis was undertaken on each of the manos with rat being identified on one.

SAMPLE TABLE:

Table XX
PROVENIENCE AND ATTRIBUTES[a] OF COMPLETE MANOS, THE EXAMPLE SITE

Cat. No.	Provenience	Material	Type[b]	Burned	L	W	T	Weight	Fig.
T-001	Trench 1	quartzite	IIa	no	126	106	73	1,454.2	
11-013	Unit 11, 100-110	granite	IIb	no	140	112	49	1,170.0	XXa
11-016	Unit 11, 90-100	granite	IIa	no	121	97	50	1,003.0	XXb
49-021	Unit 49, 80-90	granite	--	yes	65	58	49	290.3	
52-018	Unit 52, 30-40	granite	Ib	no	119	89	47	754.4	
54-017	Unit 54, 40-50	granite	Ic	no	121	87	48	831.5	
58-019	Unit 58, 30-40	granite	III	yes	139	110	72	1,682.2	
101-065	Unit 101, 130-140	quartzite	IIc	yes	102	82	60	227.6	XXc
102-018	Unit 102, 110-120	granite	IIa	no	109	76	57	719.5	XXd

[a] metric attributes are in millimeters and grams
[b] types described in text; -- = unclassified

Describe the remainder of the artifacts in the same general fashion (the following categories are common). Note the heading orders.

Ground Stone
  Metates.
  Mortars
  Pestles.
  Unidentified Ground Stone.
Flaked Stone
  Projectile Points.
  Bifaces.
  Cores.
  Hammerstones.
  Debitage.
Shell Beads
Historical Artifacts
Fire-Affected Rock

FAUNAL REMAINS

All of the faunal remains from the site must be described. First, of course, they must have been identified (see Chapter 10). Describe the methods used for the faunal analysis and then describe all of the material. There may be a separate special report on the faunal study; summarize the findings here and include the full report as an appendix.

SAMPLE TEXT:

In the laboratory, all faunal materials were counted and weighed prior to taxonomic assessment. Diagnostic elements were separated and identified to the species level whenever possible using the comparative vertebrate skeletal collection at CSU, Bakersfield. Materials not identifiable to at least the genus level were assigned to the next appropriate taxonomic level (Family, Class, Order). Highly fragmented mammalian bones not identifiable beyond class level were separated into size range groupings: rodent-sized, rabbit-sized, coyote-sized, and large mammal-sized.

Invertebrates

Invertebrates are animals too. Describe any insects (bugs and/or casings), arachnids, shells, etc., that may have been found.

Vertebrates

Provide a brief summary of what vertebrate remains were found. Describe them in detail as shown below.

Species Accounts

This is the section in which a detailed description of each species is provided, including a listing of the elements recovered. Make sure that you include birds and amphibians (if any) and list in proper taxonomic order.

SAMPLE TEXT:

Class Reptilia

Order Squamata
Suborder Sauria (Lizards)

Material: 2 skull fragments; 3 vertebrae; 1 humerus; 1 femur.

Comments: These remains likely represent at least several lizards, including the desert iguana (*Dipsosaurus dorsalis*). The desert iguana is known to have been eaten by the Kawaiisu (Zigmond 1986).

Class Mammalia

Mammalian remains comprise the bulk of the faunal remains from the sites. Hares, rabbits, and rodents seem to have had the greatest economic significance.

Order Lagomorpha--rabbits, hares, and pikas
Family Leporidae--rabbits and hares
Lepus californicus (black-tailed hare)

Material: 11 skull fragments, 9 maxilla fragments, 15 mandible fragments, 15 vertebra fragments, 5 scapulae, 5 humeri, 3 ulnae, 4 radii, 35 metapodials, 43 phalanges, 1 femur, 6 tibiae, 6 calcanea, 1 tarsal.

Comments: In antiquity, hares seem to have been an important food source in the deserts of southern California and the Great Basin (Basgall 1982; Reynolds and Shaw 1982; Langenwalter et al. 1983; Yohe 1984; Kent 1985; Yohe et al. 1986). This information is mirrored in the ethnographic record (Gifford 1931; Steward 1938; Bean 1972). Gifford (1931) noted that jackrabbits were driven along dry waterways by setting fire to vegetation, and then killed with throwing sticks. Driving into nets also was a common method of capture used extensively in southern California and the Great Basin (Kroeber 1925; Steward 1938). The Kawaiisu may also have used brush fire surrounds to facilitate the capture of these animals (Zigmond 1986).

Order Rodentia
Suborder Sciuromorpha
Family Sciuridae--squirrels and chipmunks
Spermophilus **sp. (ground squirrel)**

Material: 1 mandible

Comments: These remains were found together in a rodent burrow and likely represent a natural death.

Faunal Exploitation Activities at the Example Site

Discuss any patterns of the use of animals that you can see in the recovered materials. Perhaps they always ate rabbits in the spring. Maybe there were no fish, even though the site was located on a river. There are many interesting things that can be said.

FLORAL REMAINS

Describe any floral remains recovered from the site (see Chapter 11). Begin with seeds, then discuss charcoal and any other remains. If there is information on pollen and/or phytoliths from the site, include that information here. There likely would be separate special reports on each of these studies; summarize the findings here and include the full reports as appendices.

OBSIDIAN STUDIES

If obsidian was recovered from your site, discuss the results of both the obsidian sourcing and hydration studies you have conducted on your material. Do these data relate to trade patterns? What are the temporal implications of the hydration data?

SAMPLE EXCAVATION REPORT

DATING

Describe the methods used to date the site. Perhaps you have a radiocarbon date or two, some obsidian hydration data, time-sensitive artifacts, or geomorphological data. It is possible you have nothing and cannot tell how old the site is. In that case, simply say so.

CONCLUSIONS

What was learned from this site? Describe all of the various findings made, from trade, to dating, to social organization, to whatever. Discuss how your site relates to other archaeological work done in the region, what old ideas appear wrong, what new ideas you have (and why), and what remains unanswered. What should we do in the future to answer such questions or to test your ideas?

ACKNOWLEDGEMENTS

Thank the people who helped with the field and laboratory work, the persons at the institution from whom the material was borrowed, the people who identified the floral or faunal remains or whatever, and the people who helped write or edit the text.

REFERENCES

All of the references cited in the text must be included in the references section. There is a number of different styles that may be used, follow the format assigned to you. The references listed below are in the style of the *Journal of California and Great Basin Anthropology*.

Basgall, Mark E.
   1982   Faunal Analysis of an Open Air Site in the El Paso Mountains. In: Archaeological Investigations in the El Paso Mountains of the Mojave Desert: The Bickel and Last Chance Sites, Kelly R. McGuire, Alan P. Garfinkel, and Mark E. Basgall, eds., pp. 123-140. Report on file at the Southern San Joaquin Valley Archaeological Information Center, California State University, Bakersfield.

Bean, Lowell J.
   1972   Mukat's People: The Cahuilla Indians of Southern California. Berkeley: University of California Press.

Bennyhoff, James A., and Richard E. Hughes
   1987   Shell Bead and Ornament Exchange Networks Between California and the Western Great Basin. Anthropological Papers of the American Museum of Natural History 64(2).

Bezy, R. L. (ed.)
   1981   Reptiles. In: Complete Field Guide to North American Wildlife (Western Edition), pp. 391-462. New York: Harper and Row.

Bonner, Wayne H., and E. Jane Rosenthal
   1988   Column Sample Analysis: Composition Control. Appendix A In: The Bulrush Canyon Project: Excavations at Bulrush Canyon Site (SCAI-137) and Camp Cactus Road Site, Santa Catalina Island, by E. Jane Rosenthal, pp. 105-107. Pacific Coast Archaeological Society Quarterly 24(2&3).

Heizer, Robert F., and Thomas R. Hester
   1978   Great Basin Projectile Points: Forms and Chronology. Ballena Press Publications in Archaeology, Ethnology and History No. 10.

Kroeber, Alfred L.
   1925   Handbook of the Indians of California. Bureau of American Ethnology Bulletin 78.

Langenwalter, P. E., III, R. E. Langenwalter, and J. G. Strand
   1983   Analysis of Vertebrate Animal Remains and Implications for Aboriginal Subsistence. In: Archaeological Studies at Oro Grande, Mojave Desert, California, Carol H. Rector, James D. Swenson, and Philip J. Wilke, eds., pp. 109-138. Redlands: San Bernardino County Museum Association.

Meighan, Clement W., D. M. Pendergast, B. K. Schwartz, Jr., and M. D. Wissler
   1959   Ecological Interpretation in Archaeology: Part I. American Antiquity 24(1):1-23.

Steward, Julian
   1938   Basin Plateau Aboriginal Socio-Political Groups. Bureau of American Ethnology Bulletin 120.

Twisselmann, Ernest C.
   1967   A Flora of Kern County. The Wasmann Journal of Biology 25(1 and 2).

Yohe, Robert M., II
   1984   A Report on Faunal Remains from a Special Purpose Site in the Western Mojave Desert. Pacific Coast Archaeological Society Quarterly 20(4):56-72.

Zigmond, Maurice
   1981   Kawaiisu Ethnobotany. Salt Lake City: University of Utah Press.

   1986   Kawaiisu. In: Handbook of North American Indians, Vol. 11, Great Basin, Warren L. d'Azevedo, ed., pp. 398-411. Washington: Smithsonian Institution.

GLOSSARY OF ARCHAEOLOGICAL TERMS

This glossary is not intended to be comprehensive, but to briefly define some of the terms used in the text. Not all terms in the text are included, but some terms not in the text are included.

AMS radiocarbon dating: A technique of radiocarbon dating where the atoms are directly counted using an accelerator mass spectrometer.

aboriginal: The indigenous or native group of a particular region and their respective culture.

absolute (chronometric) dating techniques: Dating methods that assign an age in years to an event or object. Examples of chronometric dating techniques are dendrochronology and radiocarbon.

accession number: The number assigned to an archaeological collection that identifies its origin; part of the catalog number.

activity area: A discrete area within a site containing a grouping of artifacts and/or features indicating that a specific activity occurred there.

adult: An age category for humans (21 and older).

aggregate (or mass) analysis: The analysis of debitage using size as the prime criterion.

antemortem (or premortem): The term used to refer to events or processes that occurred to an individual's body prior to death.

appendicular skeleton: The bones of the appendages (arms, legs, tail).

apron: The lip or exposed portion of a prehistoric cave or rockshelter, the soil of which typically contains durable cultural materials such as flaked stone and ceramic artifacts.

archaeological assessment: An aspect of cultural resource management in which the surface of a project area is systematically covered by pedestrian survey in order to locate, document, and evaluate archaeological materials therein (also see **survey**).

archaeology: The study of prehistoric and early historical cultures and processes of cultural adaptation and change, relying mostly upon the material remains associated with those societies. The major goals of archaeology include reconstructing long sequences of human culture (culture history), reconstructing past lifeways, studying cultural process (documenting/understanding cultural change and stability), and understanding how the archaeological record is formed.

archaeomagnetism: A dating technique used to determine the last firing event of clays or clayey soils based on thermoremanent magnetism of ferromagnetic minerals in the materials.

archaeometry (or Archaeological Science): The large field of work that entails the physical and/or chemical analyses ("measurement") of archaeological substances, their constituents, age, residues, etc.

archaic tradition: In the New World, a cultural stage denoting a lifestyle generally lacking horticulture, domesticated animals, and permanent villages. In western North America, archaic groups consisted mostly of small, mobile, hunter-gatherer groups.

arrowshaft straightener: A tool used to straighten and smooth wood and/or reed arrowshafts.

articular surface: The portion of a bone connecting with other bones.

artifact: Any object manufactured or modified by humans that can be picked up or removed from the ground without affecting its integrity (as opposed to an archaeological feature).

assemblage: All of the artifacts documented at or recovered from a site.

atlatl: An Aztec term for spear thrower, a wooden shaft or board used to propel a long, composite spear/dart equipped with a relatively large flaked stone dart point. Atlatls increased the range and force of the spear, and in western North America comprised the main hunting weapon from about 6,500 B.C. to A.D. 500.

attribute: A well-defined feature of an artifact that cannot be further subdivided. Archaeologists identify different types of attributes based mostly upon form, style, and technology in order to classify and interpret artifacts.

axial skeleton: The bones of the trunk and head.

B.P.: A term denoting "years before present" in which one counts backward from the present. This designation is often associated with uncalibrated radiocarbon dates in which the "present" is A.D. 1950 (due to subsequent radiocarbon contamination of the atmosphere).

bag wear: The damage that can occur to artifacts and ecofacts during excavation, transportation, and cataloging.

bead: A small circular, tubular, or oblong ornament with a perforated center; usually made from shell, stone, bone, or glass.

biface: A stone tool that has been flaked on both sides (faces).

biface thinning flake: A flake that has been removed from a biface through percussion as part of the reduction process. These flakes typically were removed from an unfinished biface (or blank) in order to make it thinner; hence the term. There are different types of biface thinning flakes reflecting early- to late-stage reduction.

bifacial blank: A biface in the early stages of production displaying only percussion flaking and no evidence of pressure flaking. In many cases, blanks were traded and/or transported from their area of origin and subsequently used as bifacial cores from which flake blanks were detached for production of dart or arrow points.

bifacial core: A core that has had flakes removed from multiple faces, may be mistaken for a large biface blank.

bioturbation: The alteration of the site by nonhuman biological agents (e.g., burrowing rodents).

bipolar percussion: A type of percussion that involves the placement of raw material (usually small rounded or oval cobbles) on an anvil stone and striking it from the top.

blade: A specialized type of flake that is long and narrow with nearly parallel margins (very small blades are called microblades).

blank: A roughly shaped flake or piece of raw material.

bulb of percussion: The convex surface of a flake near the platform; the portion of the cone of force present in the flake.

calvarium: The skull minus the facial bones.

catalog: The list of numbers assigned to items in an archaeological collection, along with the detailed information about each of the items.

catalog number: The unique number assigned to each individual item (or group of items) in an archaeological collection.

cephalic index: A measure of the shape of the skull.

ceramics: Clay (often fired) artifacts, usually vessels.

chalcedony: A semitranslucent, silica-rich, fine-grained quartz or chemical sedimentary rock that is commonly pale blue, off-white, or light gray in color, and is a popular toolstone material of prehistoric peoples. It often was heat treated to control/reduce bending fractures during reduction. Heat treated chalcedony appears waxy and somewhat lustrous to the naked eye.

chert: An opaque, chemical, sedimentary rock with a high silica content and consisting essentially of cryptocrystalline quartz or fibrous chalcedony. In the eastern U. S., chert is often called "flint," and also was a popular toolstone material for prehistoric native North Americans.

chopper: An axe-like flaked stone implement chipped at one end to create a sharp edge, usually hand-held along the blunt margin or edge, and used for heavy duty chopping/cutting tasks.

chronometric (absolute) dating techniques: Dating methods that assign an age in years to an event or object. Examples of chronometric dating techniques are dendrochronology and radiocarbon.

classification: The process of placing materials into categories.

coiled basketry: Basketry whose the foundation consists of horizontal elements of relatively rigid materials interwoven vertically by a flexible stitch.

coiling: A ceramic vessel construction technique where a ceramic vessel formed from the base up with long coils or wedges of clay that were shaped and joined together (also a construction technique used in basketry).

component: An association of all of the artifacts from one occupation level at a site. A component typically is associated with a distinct prehistoric phase, most of which span several hundred years. Archaeological sites are either single component (representing one phase of prehistoric use/habitation), or multicomponent (representing several or many phases of prehistoric occupation).

composite tool: An artifact made of multiple parts (e.g., a modern knife with a metal blade and a wooden handle).

compression rings: The faint lines on the dorsal side of a flake, indicating the direction of force.

conchoidal fracture: The fracturing of stone along the force lines of the Hertzian cone, as a BB fractures glass.

context: The provenience of an item; its relationship with other items.

coprolite: Desiccated human feces often found preserved in prehistoric cave sites or low desert open-air sites. Coprolite analysis provides excellent information concerning prehistoric subsistence systems.

copy cat: A tool that, pressed against an irregular surface, will duplicate the form so that the shape of the object can be drawn.

core: A piece of stone from which flake blanks were removed and subsequently fashioned into tools. Cores can be classified as bifacial, unidirectional, or multidirectional.

core tool: Tools made from discarded cores that often appear to have been used as hammers, choppers, or scraping tools.

cortex: The outer rind of cobbles or other raw material.

cortical (or primary) flake: A flake with its dorsal aspect completely covered by cortex.

cranial skeleton: The bones of the head (including the mandible).

cranium: The bones of the skull, not including the mandible.

crazing: In lithics, a cross-hatched pattern of fractures, observable on the surface of a stone, as the result of excessive temperature exposure; in ceramic analysis, a situation in which differential shrinkage causes the surface of the vessel to crack while the remainder of the vessel wall remains undamaged.

cremation: The practice of disposing of the dead by burning the body.

cross-dating: A dating technique using what is known about one site (or location) to date another site.

cross-over immunoelectrophoresis (CIEP): One of the several techniques used in protein residue analysis.

culture: The system of shared meanings and behaviors used by humans in adapting to and interacting with both the physical and cultural environment. "A culture" is a group of people that share a specific set of behaviors and beliefs. An archaeological culture consists of a uniform set of artifacts and features confined to a particular region and time span; it may or may not represent an actual group of people.

DNA (deoxyribonucleic acid): The genetic code for all organisms, present in all cells.

debitage: Waste flakes resulting from flaked stone tool production. Debitage literally means "waste" in French, and results from both percussion and pressure flaking.

deciduous teeth: The "baby teeth" of an individual, lost during life.

dendrochronology (tree ring dating): A chronometric dating method that can yield an age by counting the rings in certain species of wood to determine when that wood grew.

diaphyses: The shafts of the long bones.

direct (free-hand) percussion: The use of a hammer directly on a stone.

distal: In lithic analysis, the upper portion or tip of an artifact (furthest from the haft); in faunal analysis, the end of the element furthest away from the center of the body.

early-stage biface: A biface in the initial step of manufacture, usually with sinuous edges and simple surface topography.

earthenware: Ceramics fired at temperatures high enough for vitrification to begin.

ecofacts: Natural biological objects recovered from archaeological sites, usually modified by human behavior, such as the remains of plant and animal foods.

edge-modified flake: A flake with evidence of modification along one or more edges, whether by natural forces, human use, or bag wear.

element: In faunal analysis, the specific part (humerus, femur, rib, etc.) of the animal.

epiphyses: The ends of the long bones.

eraillure scar: The small flake scar on the dorsal side of a flake next to the platform. It is the result of rebounding force during percussion flaking.

ethnocentrism: The belief of a group (usually an ethnic group or culture) that they are superior to other groups.

excavation: The systematic and controlled digging into a site (see large-scale excavations and test excavations).

experimental dating techniques: Dating techniques that are not yet fully developed or reliable, such as obsidian hydration.

fabric: The body of processed clay and temper additives in ceramics.

faunal remains: The remains of animals from archaeological sites.

feature: Any object or structure made or modified by humans that is typically incorporated into the ground, and which cannot be removed from its location without affecting its integrity, such as a hearth, a storage pit, a burial, or rock art panel.

fire hearth: A flat piece of wood upon which a stick (drill) is twisted vigorously to start a fire.

flake: A piece of stone removed from a core as the result of percussion or pressure flaking.

flake scar: One of many small surface concavities on cores, flakes, bifaces, unifaces, and projectile points marking an area of previous flake detachment.

flaked stone artifacts: Tools produced by the removal of flakes (or chips, commonly referred to as debitage) from the stone to create a sharp surface. Projectile points, bifaces, unifaces, and cores are common flaked stone artifact types.

flake tools: Casual cutting implements typically consisting of large pieces of debitage detached from a core; not formed tools. Flake tools also are referred to as utilized flakes and sometimes exhibit pressure flaking along one or two edges.

flat bones: Generally flat, nontubular bones, including the pelvis, scapulae, ribs, and sternum.

fletching: The pieces of feather attached to the end of an arrow or dart; used to stabilize its flight.

flexed: A term used to describe the position of a burial, where the body is positioned with the knees drawn loosely toward the chest.

flexible rule: A tool used to draw curved lines or to outline the shape of an object so that its form can be drawn.

floral remains: The remains of plants from archaeological sites.

fluorine dating: A dating technique that uses differences in the fluorine content of materials to place them in time relative to each other.

foramina: Any of a wide variety of holes in bones for nerves, blood vessels, etc.

geofact: A naturally shaped stone that resembles an artifact.

glaze: The glassy, vitreous coating on the outside of a ceramic vessel.

ground stone artifacts: Tools that have been modified or produced by grinding or pounding stone on stone, as in the processing of seeds or other materials. Manos, metates, mortars, and pestles are common ground stone artifacts. Ground stone tools used to crush, pound, grind, or otherwise process materials are also commonly referred to as "milling implements." Many other types of tools and ornaments were made by grinding stone to a smooth surface: axes, pipes, beads, shaft straighteners, etc.

haft: A handle of a compound tool, usually of wood or bone.

hammerstone: A cobble used for percussion flaking of cores, bifacial blanks, and preforms. Most hammerstones were "softer" than the toolstone material they were used upon to avoid breaking the artifact during production.

handstone (or mano): A hand-held milling stone used to process materials on a metate. Manos usually are described as either one- or two-handed (depending upon their size), and exhibit milling facets on one or two faces.

hard hammer technique: The use of a hammer that is harder that the material being hammered or struck.

Harris lines: Alternating patterns of arrested (abnormal) and normal bone growth resulting from stress, such as starvation and disease.

hearth: The remains of a prehistoric fireplace often represented by one or more of the following: ash, charcoal, fire-cracked rock, burnt floral and faunal remains, and soil discoloration.

Hertzian Cone of Force: The cone shape in which the energy of a projectile impact in high silica content stone radiates through the structure of the stone.

historical archaeology: The archaeology of materials dating after the presence of written records in an area.

hole-and-cap can: A type of metal can that was sealed with a cap soldered over the filler hole.

GLOSSARY

hole-in-cap can: A type of metal can with a circular hole about an inch in diameter on its top; a cap with a small venthole is then soldered over the hole, and the vent is sealed with a drop of solder.

Holocene (or Present): The current geological epoch that began at the end of the Pleistocene epoch (ca. 10,000 B.P.) and which is generally characterized by a warmer climate than that of the Pleistocene.

hopper mortar: A mortar whose sides are formed by a bottomless basket attached to the stone.

indirect percussion: The use of a stone, bone, wood, or antler hammer (or billet) to strike a stone, wood, or antler punch, which in turn, applies force on a stone to break it.

infant: An age category for humans (up to 2 years).

inhumation: The disposal of the dead by burial.

in situ: A Latin phrase meaning "found in place," used to refer to an item that has a precise provenience; the exact measurements of its location in the unit.

interior (tertiary or noncortical) flake: A flake having no cortex.

irregular bones: Irregularly shaped bones, including vertebrae, carpals, tarsals, and patellae.

isolate: One or two artifacts occurring by themselves and not associated with an archaeological site; generally thought to represent items lost or discarded by people as they moved through an area.

jasper: An opaque cryptocrystalline quartz or chemical sedimentary rock that essentially is a chert, and in the western U. S. is reddish brown, dark yellow, orange, or purple in color. Jasper was a popular toolstone material for native peoples of North America.

juvenile: An age category for humans (2 to 10 years).

large-scale excavations: An excavation where a large number of units is dug (sometimes called data recovery or mitigation); a strategy designed to recover a large quantity of information useful to answer specific questions generated in the research design.

late-stage biface: A biface in the final step of manufacture, usually with relatively straight edges and complex surface topography.

levels: Specific layers of soil removed during excavation and processed for cultural materials.

lithic: Of, or pertaining to, stone.

lithic scatter: A common class of sites where tools were made or repaired, resulting in a large number of flakes (and typically few other artifacts) at a site.

locus: A distinct portion of an archaeological site, typically separated from other parts of the site by space devoid of cultural materials. Many open air sites consist of various loci spread over a relatively large area.

long bones: The large bones of the limb (often tubular in cross section).

lot number: The number assigned to an archaeological collection that identifies an aspect of context within a collection; part of the catalog number.

MNI (minimum number of individuals): In faunal analysis, the minimum number of individuals represented in a collection.

macrofloral remains: Those plant remains from archaeological sites that are visible to the naked eye, primarily seeds and charcoal.

mano (or handstone): A hand-held milling stone used to process materials on a metate. Manos usually are described as either one- or two-handed (depending upon their size), and exhibit milling facets on one or two faces.

manuport: An unmodified item imported to an archaeological site in antiquity.

margin: The edge of a stone tool or flake.

medial: The middle portion of an artifact or faunal element.

metate (or milling stone): A slab or block shaped stone upon which materials are processed with a mano. Most metates are first roughly formed through percussion flaking, and then finished by abrading and pecking with another rock.

microfloral remains: Those plant remains from archaeological sites that are visible only with the aid of magnification, primarily pollen and phytoliths.

midden: Soils that have been chemically altered by the deposition of grease, debris, and organic refuse as the result of human use and habitation. Midden soils typically are darker in color and contain more nitrogen than natural surrounding soils.

milling stone (or metate): A slab- or block-shaped stone upon which materials are processed with a mano. Most metates are first roughly formed through percussion flaking, and then finished by abrading and pecking with another rock.

modeling: A ceramic vessel construction technique where a mass of clay is handworked into a rough approximation of the vessel through punching, pinching, and/or drawing.

Mohs scale: A scale from 1 to 10 used to determine hardness of materials, talc being 1 and diamond being 10.

molding: A ceramic vessel construction technique where a flat, circular mass of clay is pressed into a concave mold, or placed over the top of a convex mold.

mortar: A rock (but sometimes wood) with a manufactured concavity of varying depth and diameter within which materials are pounded, crushed, or ground.

multidirectional core: A core that has had flakes removed from two or more directions.

multifaceted platform: A platform with more than one plane of detachment, such as on the margins of some bifaces or multidirectional cores.

Munsell color chart: A standard, objective chart used to describe color.

NISP (number of identified specimens): In faunal analysis, the number of identified specimens in a collection.

noncortical (interior or tertiary) flake: A flake having no cortex.

obsidian: Volcanic glass, typically black or dark-colored, derived from rapid cooling of rhyolitic magma. When struck with another hard object, such as a hammerstone, obsidian nodules break through conchoidal fracture and yield flakes that are extremely sharp. Wherever available, obsidian was the preferred toolstone material of prehistoric peoples, and was traded over hundreds, and in some cases, thousands, of miles.

obsidian hydration: A dating technique that measures the water absorbed into the obsidian matrix and assigns a date based on the depth of water penetration.

obsidian sourcing: A method to fingerprint unknown obsidian samples and compare them to known sources, in order to determine the source of the unknown sample.

olla: A globular-shaped, narrow-mouthed, aboriginal ceramic vessel, often used to store water or seeds. Olla is a Spanish term applied to ceramic vessels used to store and cool water.

ossuary: A depository where the bones of a number of individuals is secondarily interred.

otolith: In fish, the small calcium carbonate "ear stones" (called auditory ossicles in other animals) within the inner ear used for assistance in balance or hearing.

oxidizing atmosphere: Ceramic firing atmosphere characterized by an abundance of free oxygen which combines with elements in the paste and yields clear colors of the ceramic body.

PMT (Photometric Transfer): A high-quality, glossy photo reproduction of a figure.

paddle-and-anvil: A technique used in the construction of ceramics in which a flat object such as a wood paddle was used to strike the exterior surface of the vessel as a convex stone or clay anvil was held against the corresponding interior surface.

paleomagnetism: A dating technique that measures the magnetic direction of natural clay particles (e.g., lake clays), matching the direction with dates of pole movement.

paleoanthropologists: Anthropologists specializing in the study of the "first" humans.

palette: Small, flat, shaped, and polished utensils (usually of stone) probably used to grind pigments.

partially cortical (or secondary) flake: A flake possessing some cortex on its dorsal aspect.

paste: The clay substance of pottery excluding temper/filler additives.

paste texture: In ceramic analysis, the appearance of the ceramic paste as determined by clay particle size.

pathology: In skeletal remains, changes in the bone due to disease, degeneration, or trauma.

percussion flaking: The method of flake removal where the flake is detached from the stone by striking it with a hammer.

perimortem: The term used to refer to events or processes that occurred to an individual's body when it cannot be determined whether it was before or after death.

perishables: Artifacts made from organic materials that ordinarily would decay but for some reason were preserved. Such artifacts include basketry, cordage, and leather.

pestle: A cylindrical or subcylindrical stone generally used within a mortar to crush, pound, or grind materials.

petroglyph: A type of rock art where the design is pecked into the rock surface.

pictograph: A type of rock art where the design is painted on the rock surface.

plaited basketry: Basketry with no real foundation or stitch; the weave is basically the same in both directions.

plan-view: The view from overhead looking down, commonly used in maps.

platform: The place on a core or flake where it was struck by a hammer (see **single** and **multifaceted platforms**).

Pleistocene: The geological epoch prior to the present (Holocene) and lasting from approximately 1.8 million to 10,000 years ago. This time was characterized by cooler temperatures and lower sea levels than today, and by the advance and retreat of extensive glaciers.

ply: The strand(s) of material used in the construction of cordage.

porcelain: Ceramics made of a white-firing, highly refractory kaolin clay fired at temperatures high enough (typically ranging from 1,250 to 1,450 degrees C.) to vitrify the clay body.

postcranial skeleton: All bones other than those of the cranial skeleton.

postmortem: The term used to refer to events or processes that occurred to an individual's body after death.

pot lid: A small portion (flake) of stone that may ''pop off'' a core during heat treatment due to rapid heating or excessive temperature, creating many small flake (pot lid) scars on the surface.

preform: A bifacially flaked piece of stone that exhibits both percussion and pressure flaking, and which usually is triangular in shape, indicating that it was being fashioned into a projectile point or knife.

prehistoric archaeology: Archaeology that deals with materials that date prior to written history within the region under consideration.

premortem (or antemortem): The term used to refer to events or processes that occurred to an individuals body prior to death.

pressure flaking: The method of flake removal where the flake is detached from the stone by the application of pressure rather than being struck.

primary context: The original location of an item.

primary (or cortical) flake: A flake with its dorsal aspect completely covered by cortex.

profile-view: The view from the side, commonly used in maps.

prone: A term used to describe the position of a burial, where the body is lying flat on the stomach, or with the face down.

prospect: A site where stone was tested for suitability, whether the stone was used or not.

protein residue analysis: The recovery and identification of proteins preserved in or on archaeological materials.

provenience: The location of an item (artifact, feature, or ecofact) in a site.

proximal: In lithic analysis, the basal portion of an artifact (closest to the haft); in faunal analysis, the end of the element closest to the center of the body.

quarry: A place where stone was removed from a larger source (e.g., a mine) to subsequently manufacture tools.

radiocarbon dating: A chronometric dating technique that measures the amount of radioactive carbon present in an organic sample to determine the data at which the organism died.

reducing atmosphere: Ceramic firing atmosphere characterized by insufficient oxygen for complete combustion of the fuel and insufficient draft, resulting in the presence of reducing gases.

reduction: The removal of mass from a stone.

relative dating techniques: Dating techniques that provide the correct order of events and relative age of archaeological materials compared to other such materials. Examples of relative dating techniques used by archaeologists include stratigraphic superposition, seriation dating, and cross-dating.

rockshelter: A shallow overhang against the face of a cliff or large rock outcrop that served as the temporary residence of a prehistoric group.

S-twist: Cordage ply twisted to the maker's right.

sanitary can: A type of metal can whose edges are machine crimped together, with a rubber gasket between the edges to make the seams airtight.

schlepp effect: A term used in faunal analysis to recognize a differential distribution of faunal elements due to some elements being left at the butchering or kill site.

secondary context: The location of an item after it has been moved away from its primary context.

secondary (or partially cortical) flake: A flake possessing some cortex on its dorsal aspect.

seriation: A technique used to place sites in time relative to each other based on the rising and declining popularity of items or styles.

settlement pattern: The way in which (and why) sites are distributed across the landscape.

sexual dimorphism: The physical differences (e.g., the size and shape of the skeleton) between the males and females of a species.

shatter: All angular waste resulting from stone toolmaking activities that are not otherwise diagnostic.

sherds (or shards): Pieces of broken pottery.

short bones: The smaller bones of the limbs (primarily those tubular bones of the feet or paws).

shovel-shaped incisor: A depression present in the lingual aspect of the maxillary incisors, indicative of Mongoloids (including American Indians).

simple tool: An artifact consisting of a single part (e.g., a modern nail file).

single-facet platform: A platform on a biface or core with a single plane of detachment.

sintering: A process in which the edges of the clay particles soften and adhere to one another; this process begins at about 350 degrees C. and is completed by 700 degrees C.

site: A geographic place where there is evidence of past human activity.

soft hammer technique: The use of a hammer that is softer that the material being hammered or struck.

specimens: In faunal analysis, all individual faunal pieces.

stoneware: Ceramics made from fine, dense clays, and fired at temperatures of about 1,200 to 1,350 degrees C. (usually high enough to achieve at least partial vitrification).

stratigraphy: Layers in soils or site deposits.

subadult: An age category for humans (10 to 21 years).

superposition: A common method of relative dating based on the fact that something located above something else is younger, since the lower item had to have existed first for the upper one to have been deposited upon it.

supine: A term used to describe the position of a burial, where the body is lying on the back, with the face upward.

survey: In archaeology, a systematic examination of land to document the archaeological resources located therein (also see **archaeological assessment**).

sutures: The jagged edges where the bones of the skull join.

taphonomy: The study of what happens to materials after death or discard.

taxon: The scientific classification of an organism.

temper: Either organic or nonorganic agents added to ceramics to reduce shrinkage and/or cracking during firing.

terra-cotta: Ceramics fired to a range sufficient for sintering of clay particles to begin.

tertiary (interior or noncortical) flake: A flake having no cortex.

test excavation: Small-scale excavation conducted to determine the presence, nature, extent, content, age, structure, and research potential of a site.

textiles: Relatively flexible, handwoven materials which may or may not form a container (e.g., rugs, cordage).

thermoluminescence dating: A dating technique based on the measurement of remanent radioactive impurities in clay.

thrusting spear: A hand-held spear used for stabbing rather than throwing.

tightly flexed: A term used to describe the position of a burial, where the body is positioned with the knees touching the chest and the arms folded close to the body.

tool kit: A distinct combination of artifacts, usually task-oriented.

transect: A linear survey route covered by archaeologists to locate cultural resources.

trauma: A disruption to bone (e.g., a fracture).

tree ring dating (dendrochronology): A chronometric dating method that can yield an age by counting the rings in certain species of wood to determine when that wood grew.

trephination: The procedure of cutting holes into a living skull.

trinomial: The Smithsonian (national) system of archaeological site numbering. The trinomial ("three number") consists of the state number (or alpha designation), the county alpha designation, and the site number.

twined basketry: Basketry with a relatively rigid warp and relatively pliable weft.

twist: The direction that cordage was rolled in its manufacture; either "S-twist" or "Z-twist."

typology: The classification of a group of things based on a series of criteria.

unidirectional core: A core that has had flakes removed from only one direction.

use-life continuum: The sequence a tool goes through from production to discard.

vent hole can: A type of metal can characterized by stamped ends and a single pinhole or "match stick" filler hole no larger than 1/8-in. in the center of one end. This hole was then closed by a drop of solder.

vitrification: When clay particles fuse together as glass; this process starts between 800 and 900 degrees C. and is completed at about 1,200 degrees C.

ware: A class of pottery whose members share similar technology, paste, and surface treatment.

warp: The fairly rigid foundation in basketry.

weft: The comparatively flexible stitching in basketry.

GLOSSARY

Z-twist: Cordage ply twisted to the maker's left.